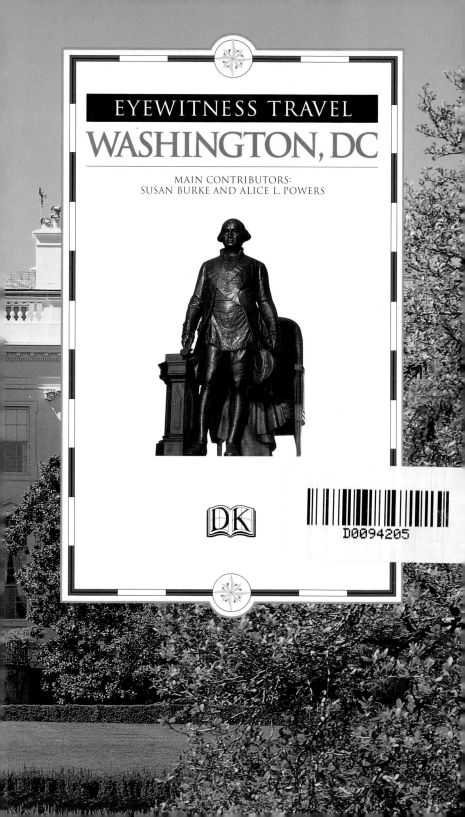

EYEWITNESS TRAVEL
WASHINGTON, DC

MAIN CONTRIBUTORS:
SUSAN BURKE AND ALICE L. POWERS

DK

D0094205

LONDON, NEW YORK,
MELBOURNE, MUNICH AND DELHI
www.dk.com

PROJECT EDITOR Claire Folkard
ART EDITORS Tim Mann, Simon J.M. Oon
SENIOR EDITOR Helen Townsend
EDITORS Emily Anderson, Felicity Crowe
US EDITOR Mary Sutherland
DESIGNERS Gillian Andrews, Eli Estaugh,
Elly King, Rebecca Milner
DTP Sam Borland, Maite Lantaron
PICTURE RESEARCHERS Brigitte Arora, Katherine Mesquita
PRODUCTION Mel Allsop

CONTRIBUTORS
Susan Burke, Alice L. Powers, Jennifer Quasha, Kem Sawyer

PHOTOGRAPHERS
Philippe Dewet, Kim Sayer, Giles Stokoe, Scott Suchman

ILLUSTRATORS
Stephen Conlin, Gary Cross, Richard Draper, Chris Orr &
Associates, Mel Pickering, Robbie Polley, John Woodcock

Reproduced by Colourscan, Singapore
Printed and bound by South China Printing Co. Ltd., China

First American Edition, 2000
06 07 08 09 10 9 8 7 6 5 4 3 2

Published in the United States by Dorling Kindersley Publishing, Inc.,
375 Hudson Street, New York 10014

Reprinted with revisions 2002, 2003, 2004, 2005, 2006

Copyright © 2000, 2006 Dorling Kindersley Limited, London

Published in Great Britain by Dorling Kindersley Limited.

A CATALOGING IN PUBLICATION RECORD IS AVAILABLE
FROM THE LIBRARY OF CONGRESS.

ISSN 1542-1554
ISBN 0-7566-1552-6
ISBN 978-0-75661-552-9

Front cover main image: Jefferson Memorial

◁ The White House

CONTENTS

HOW TO USE THIS GUIDE 6

Fountain in Dumbarton Oaks

INTRODUCING WASHINGTON, DC

FOUR GREAT DAYS IN WASHINGTON, DC 10

PUTTING WASHINGTON, DC ON THE MAP 12

THE HISTORY OF WASHINGTON, DC 16

WASHINGTON, DC AT A GLANCE 30

WASHINGTON, DC THROUGH THE YEAR 36

View toward the Lincoln Memorial
from Arlington National Cemetery

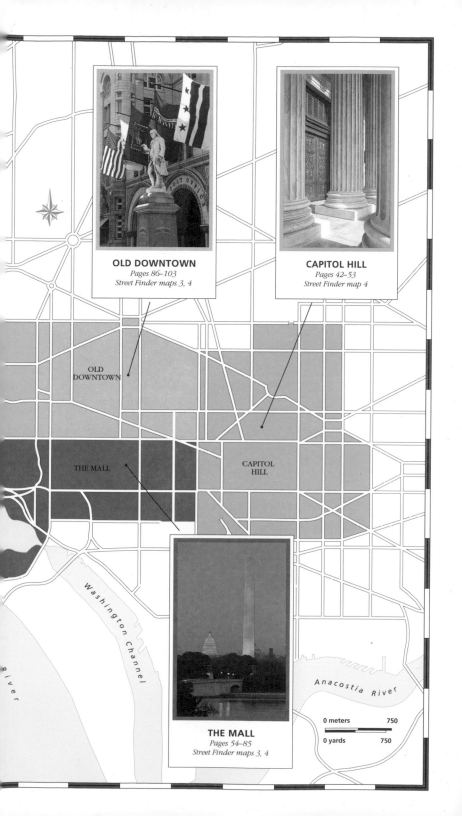

OLD DOWNTOWN
Pages 86–103
Street Finder maps 3, 4

CAPITOL HILL
Pages 42–53
Street Finder map 4

OLD
DOWNTOWN

CAPITOL
HILL

THE MALL

Washington Channel

Anacostia River

iver

THE MALL
Pages 54–85
Street Finder maps 3, 4

0 meters	750
0 yards	750

EYEWITNESS TRAVEL
WASHINGTON, DC

Columns from the US Capitol building, now in the National Arboretum

WASHINGTON, DC AREA BY AREA

CAPITOL HILL
42

THE MALL
54

Map seller outside the National Gallery of Art on the Mall

OLD DOWNTOWN
86

THE WHITE HOUSE
AND FOGGY BOTTOM
104

GEORGETOWN
120

FARTHER AFIELD
128

THREE GUIDED
WALKS 146

BEYOND
WASHINGTON, DC
152

TRAVELERS' NEEDS

WHERE TO STAY
172

RESTAURANTS, CAFES,
AND BARS
182

SHOPPING IN
WASHINGTON, DC
196

ENTERTAINMENT IN
WASHINGTON, DC
200

SURVIVAL GUIDE

PRACTICAL
INFORMATION 210

TRAVEL INFORMATION
218

Senate Bean Soup

WASHINGTON, DC
STREET FINDER 224

GENERAL INDEX 230

ACKNOWLEDGMENTS
239

Monticello, home of Thomas Jefferson in Charlottesville, Virginia

HOW TO USE THIS GUIDE

This guide helps you to get the most from your stay in Washington, DC. It provides detailed practical information and expert recommendations. *Introducing Washington, DC* maps the city and the region, sets it in its historical and cultural context, and gives an overview of the main attractions. *Washington, DC Area By Area* is the main sightseeing section, giving detailed information on all the major sights,

with photographs, illustrations and maps. *Farther Afield* looks at sights outside the city center, and *Beyond Washington, DC* explores other places within easy reach of the city. Carefully researched suggestions for restaurants, hotels, entertainment, and shopping are found in the *Travelers' Needs* section, while the *Survival Guide* contains useful advice on everything from changing money to traveling on Washington's Metrorail system.

FINDING YOUR WAY AROUND WASHINGTON, DC

The center of Washington has been divided into five sightseeing areas, each with its own chapter, color-coded for easy reference. All sights are numbered and plotted on an area map for each chapter.

The area shaded pink is shown in greater detail on the Street-by-Street map on the following pages.

2 **Street-by-Street map** *This gives a bird's-eye view of the heart of each sightseeing area. Interesting features are labeled. There is also a list of "star sights" that no visitor should miss.*

The Visitors' Checklist provides detailed practical information.

1 **Area Introduction** *This describes the history and character of the area and has a map on which the sights have been plotted. Other key information is also given.*

Each area has color-coded thumb tabs

Locator Map

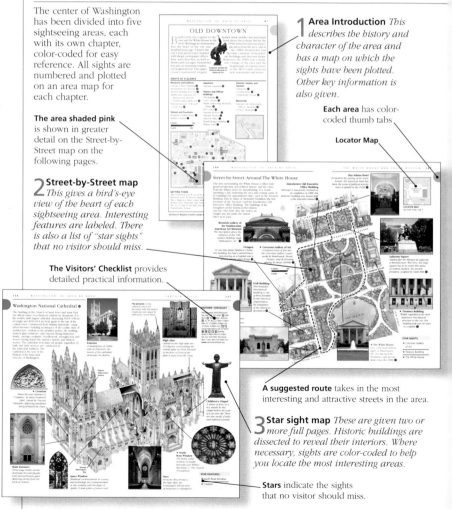

A suggested route takes in the most interesting and attractive streets in the area.

3 **Star sight map** *These are given two or more full pages. Historic buildings are dissected to reveal their interiors. Where necessary, sights are color-coded to help you locate the most interesting areas.*

Stars indicate the sights that no visitor should miss.

WASHINGTON, DC AREA MAP

The colored areas shown on this map (inside the front cover) are the five main sight-seeing areas used in this guide. Each is covered in a full chapter in *Washington, DC Area by Area (pp40–127)*. They are highlighted on other maps throughout the book. In *Washington, DC at a Glance (see pp30–35)*, they help you to locate the top sights. The *Street Finder (see pp224–229)* shows you the sights from these five areas on a detailed street map of Washington.

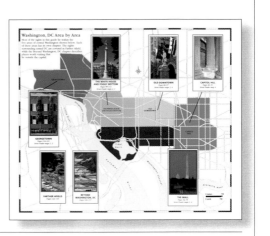

4 Detailed information *All the important sights are described individually. They are listed in order, following the numbering on the area map.*

Practical information is provided in an information block. The key to the symbols used is on the back flap.

The Introduction outlines the areas covered in this section and their historical context.

A map of the city shows the location of the Farther Afield sights in relation to the city center.

5 Farther Afield *This section covers those sights that lie just outside central Washington and are easily accessible from the city center.*

6 Beyond Washington *Places worth visiting that are situated within a day's travel of Washington are described here. They include interesting cities, historic towns, and national parks.*

Special sights, such as this national park, are highlighted with maps or detailed illustrations.

INTRODUCING WASHINGTON, DC

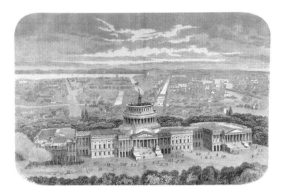

FOUR GREAT DAYS
IN WASHINGTON, DC 10–11

PUTTING WASHINGTON, DC
ON THE MAP 12–15

THE HISTORY OF WASHINGTON, DC 16–27

WASHINGTON, DC AT A GLANCE 30–35

WASHINGTON, DC
THROUGH THE YEAR 36–39

FOUR GREAT DAYS IN WASHINGTON, DC

Lincoln Memorial

Although many of the capital's highlights are easily recognized, these great days in Washington, DC will introduce visitors to its unexpected treasures. The city boasts not only world-renowned works of art and majestic monuments, but picturesque neigh- borhoods and beautiful gardens. All the sights can be reached on foot or by public transportation. Feel free to dip into the itineraries as you wish. Price guides show the daily cost for two adults or for a family of two adults and two children including lunch.

The White House, the Presidential residence

MONUMENTAL CITY

- Lincoln Memorial
- World War II Memorial
- Corcoran Gallery of Art
- The White House

TWO ADULTS allow at least $35

Morning
Start your day at the **Lincoln Memorial** *(see pp84–5)*, six blocks south of the Foggy Bottom Metro stop. Inside, on the north and south walls, you will find inscriptions of President Lincoln's **Gettysburg Address** *(see p163)*. In front of the memorial, to the left of the Reflecting Pool is the moving **Vietnam Veterans Memorial** *(see pp82–3)*. Engraved on the black granite are the names of Americans who died in the the war. Then make your way through the shady Constitution Gardens back to the Reflecting Pool. To the east of this stands the **World War II Memorial** *(see pp82–3)*. Here you can see the Freedom Wall, its inscriptions, and the bas reliefs showing the US at war. After this memorial,

move on to 17th Street where there are several historic buildings including the **Organization of American States** and the **Daughters of the American Revolution** *(see p114)*. Drop into the **Corcoran Gallery of Art**, one of the country's first art galleries *(see p113)*. Have lunch here, or head to a café near Pennsylvania Avenue.

Afternoon
Stroll down Pennsylvania Avenue, passing the red brick Renwick Gallery, Blair House (where presidential guests stay), and **The White House** *(see pp108–9)*. Walk around the White House to the Visitor Center at 1450 Pennsylvania Avenue. Afterwards, visit the **US National Archives** *(see p90)* to see historic documents including the *Declaration of Independence* and the *Bill of Rights*. End your day with a tour of **Ford's Theater** *(see p96)* where Lincoln was shot, followed by a

meal in **Chinatown** *(see pp96–7)* or **Old Downtown** *(see pp86–103)*.

BLACK HISTORY

- Frederick Douglass House
- Mary McLeod Bethune Site
- U Street landmarks
- A night of jazz at Blues Alley

TWO ADULTS allow at least $20

Morning
Spend the morning at the **Frederick Douglass House**, a 15-acre estate in Anacostia *(see p145)*. Frederick Douglass, a fugitive slave who became a famous abolitionist, named his house Cedar Hill. Almost all of the furnishings are original (look out for the walking stick collection). Cross the river to **The Shaw Neighborhood** *(see p141)* with its lovely Victorian houses. This is where prominent African Americans lived in the 1940s. Visit the **Mary McLeod Bethune Council House** *(see p140)*, home of the civil rights leader and founder of the National Council of Negro Women.

Lincoln Theatre, the venue for many of Duke Ellington's performances

Georgetown's pretty gardens and houses, a delightful neighborhood to stroll through

Lunch at **Ben's Chili Bowl** on U Street, a delightful place that was once the Minnehaha silent movie theater.

Afternoon

Stroll along U Street, once known as Black Broadway. Audiences went wild when Duke Ellington performed at the **Lincoln Theatre** *(see p140)*. He lived nearby at numbers 1805 and 1816 13th Street. Visit the **African American Civil War Museum and Memorial** honoring black soldiers *(see p133)*. End the day in style in Georgetown with dinner and jazz at **Blues Alley** *(see pp202–3)*.

ART AND SHOPPING

- **National Gallery of Art**
- **Lunch on the Mall**
- **Georgetown Shopping**
- **Washington Harbor**

TWO ADULTS allow at least $34

Morning

To experience the full scope of art covered at the **National Gallery of Art** *(see pp58–61)*, you'll want to visit both the West Building (13th–19th century European and American art) and the East Building (modern and contemporary art). Don't miss the Matisse Cut-Outs in the tower of the East Building. Have a coffee break at the Espresso Bar on the Concourse level. Outside, in

the Garden Court (north side of East Building), find the Andy Goldsworthy installation entitled *Roof*, a study of domes. Wander through the enchanting Sculpture Garden to the Pavilion Café, overlooking the ice rink, a charming spot for lunch.

Afternoon

Now head to **Georgetown** *(see pp120–7)*. You could take the 90-minute walk *(see p148–9)*. But if shopping is your ultimate goal, go to M Street or Wisconsin Avenue for an impressive number of galleries and shops and a range of stylish goods – Italian ceramics, lamps, antiques, and prints, as well as cutting edge fashion. To finish, you could have tea at the **Four Seasons Hotel** *(see p176)*, or have a drink at **Washington Harbor** while watching the boats *(see p122)*.

A FAMILY DAY

- **Visit the National Zoo**
- **National Air and Space Museum**
- **Washington Monument**

FAMILY OF FOUR allow at least $45

Morning

Start early at the **National Zoo** *(see pp138–9)*, checking at its Visitor Center for feeding times, talks, and training sessions (entry is free). If you follow the

Olmstead Walk, you should spot giant pandas, giraffes, Kandula the baby elephant, and gorillas at the Great Ape House. Have lunch at the eaterie on Lion/Tiger Hill, or at one of the snack bars.

Afternoon

Go by metro to the **National Air and Space Museum** *(see pp64–5)*. Discover facts such as the cruising speed of the *Spirit of St. Louis*, or the reason Skylab was covered with a coating of gold. Catch a film at the IMAX theatre, where you can experience flying without leaving the ground. Then head for the **Washington Monument** *(see p78)* and take the elevator to the top for the spectacular view. Finish off at the **Kennedy Center** *(see pp118–19)* in Foggy Bottom, for free entertainment (theater, dance, or music) on the Millennium Stage at 6pm.

Washington Monument, for a fabulous view of the city

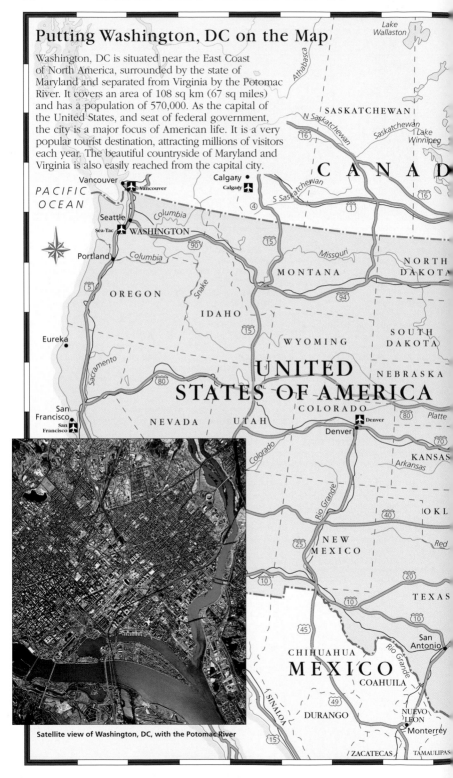

Putting Washington, DC on the Map

Washington, DC is situated near the East Coast of North America, surrounded by the state of Maryland and separated from Virginia by the Potomac River. It covers an area of 108 sq km (67 sq miles) and has a population of 570,000. As the capital of the United States, and seat of federal government, the city is a major focus of American life. It is a very popular tourist destination, attracting millions of visitors each year. The beautiful countryside of Maryland and Virginia is also easily reached from the capital city.

Lake Wallaston

PACIFIC OCEAN

Vancouver

Calgary

CANAD

SASKATCHEWAN

N Saskatchewan

Saskatchewan

Lake Winnipeg

S Saskatchewan

Seattle

Sea-Tac WASHINGTON

Columbia

Portland

Columbia

Missouri

MONTANA

NORTH DAKOTA

OREGON

Snake

Eureka

IDAHO

WYOMING

SOUTH DAKOTA

Sacramento

UNITED

NEBRASKA

STATES OF AMERICA

San Francisco

NEVADA   UTAH

COLORADO

Denver

Denver

Colorado

KANSAS

Arkansas

Platte

Rio Grande

OKL

NEW MEXICO

Red

TEXAS

San Antonio

Rio Grande

CHIHUAHUA

MEXICO

COAHUILA

SINALOA

DURANGO

NUEVO LEON

Monterrey

ZACATECAS   TAMAULIPAS

Satellite view of Washington, DC, with the Potomac River

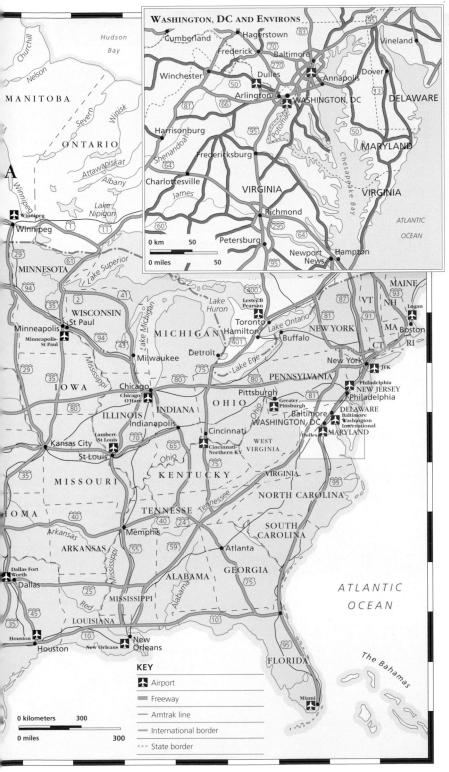

WASHINGTON, DC AND ENVIRONS

Cumberland
Hagerstown
Frederick
Baltimore
Vineland
Winchester
Dulles
Annapolis
Dover
Arlington
WASHINGTON, DC
DELAWARE
Harrisonburg
MARYLAND
Shenandoah
Fredericksburg
VIRGINIA
VIRGINIA
Charlottesville
James
Chesapeake Bay
ATLANTIC
OCEAN
Richmond
Petersburg
Newport News
Hampton

0 km   50
0 miles   50

MANITOBA
Hudson Bay
Churchill
Nelson
Seven
Winisk
ONTARIO
Attawapiskat
Albany
Winnipeg
Lake Nipigon
A
Winnipeg
MINNESOTA
Lake Superior
Lake Huron
Lester B Pearson
MAINE
Logan
St Paul
WISCONSIN
Toronto
Hamilton
Buffalo
NEW YORK
VT
NH
MA
Boston
RI
Minneapolis
Minneapolis-St Paul
MICHIGAN
Lake Ontario
CT
Milwaukee
Detroit
Lake Erie
New York
JFK
IOWA
Chicago
Chicago O'Hare
PENNSYLVANIA
Philadelphia
NEW JERSEY
Philadelphia
Mississippi
INDIANA
OHIO
Pittsburgh
Greater Pittsburgh
DELAWARE
Baltimore Washington International
ILLINOIS
Indianapolis
Cincinnati
WASHINGTON, DC
Baltimore
Kansas City
Lambert-St Louis
Cincinnati-Northern KY
WEST VIRGINIA
Dulles
MARYLAND
St Louis
Ohio
KENTUCKY
VIRGINIA
MISSOURI
Tennessee
NORTH CAROLINA
IOMA
TENNESSEE
Arkansas
Memphis
SOUTH CAROLINA
ARKANSAS
Mississippi
Atlanta
GEORGIA
ATLANTIC
OCEAN
Dallas Fort Worth
Dallas
ALABAMA
Red
MISSISSIPPI
LOUISIANA
Houston
Houston
New Orleans
New Orleans
FLORIDA
The Bahamas
Miami

KEY

✈ Airport
━ Freeway
─ Amtrak line
─ International border
┄ State border

0 kilometers   300
0 miles   300

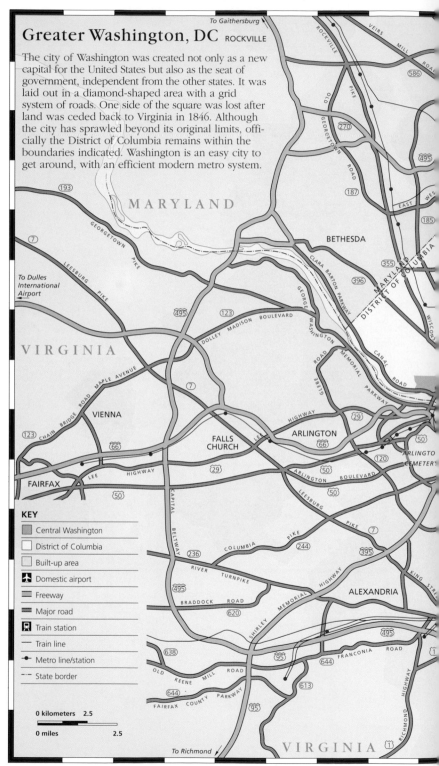

Greater Washington, DC

The city of Washington was created not only as a new capital for the United States but also as the seat of government, independent from the other states. It was laid out in a diamond-shaped area with a grid system of roads. One side of the square was lost after land was ceded back to Virginia in 1846. Although the city has sprawled beyond its original limits, officially the District of Columbia remains within the boundaries indicated. Washington is an easy city to get around, with an efficient modern metro system.

To Gaithersburg

ROCKVILLE

MARYLAND

BETHESDA

To Dulles International Airport

VIRGINIA

VIENNA

FALLS CHURCH

ARLINGTON

FAIRFAX

ARLINGTON CEMETERY

ALEXANDRIA

MARYLAND

DISTRICT OF COLUMBIA

KEY

Central Washington

District of Columbia

Built-up area

Domestic airport

Freeway

Major road

Train station

Train line

Metro line/station

State border

0 kilometers   2.5

0 miles   2.5

To Richmond

VIRGINIA

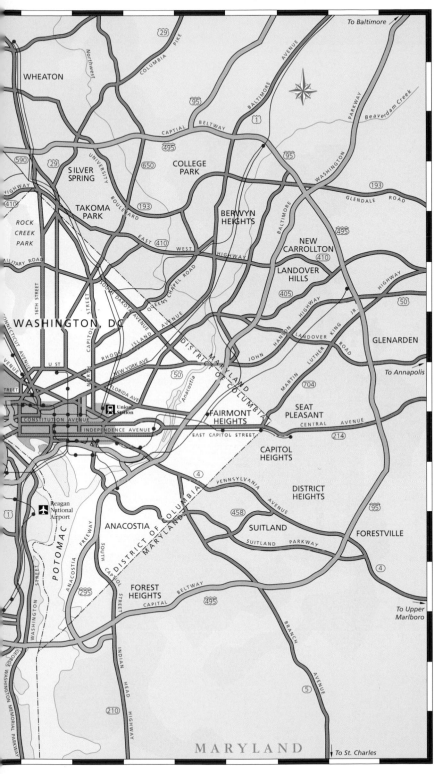

THE HISTORY OF WASHINGTON, DC

Native Americans settled in what is now the District of Columbia as long as 6,000 years ago. Archeologists have discovered traces of three villages in the area; the largest was called Nacotchtanke. Its people, the Anacostines, settled along the Potomac River and a smaller tributary now named the Anacostia River.

ENGLISH SETTLEMENT

In December 1606 Captain John Smith of the Virginia Company, under the charge of King James I of England, set sail from England for the New World. Five months later he arrived in the Chesapeake Bay and founded the Jamestown colony. A skilled cartographer, Smith was soon sailing up the Potomac River. In 1608 he came to the area that would later become Washington.

The English settlers who followed supported themselves through the fur trade, and later cultivated tobacco and corn (maize). The marriage in 1614 between John Rolfe, one of the settlers, and Pocahontas, daughter of the Indian chief Powhatan, kept the peace between the English and the Indians for eight years. Struggles over land ownership led to massacres in 1622. The English finally defeated the Indians in 1644, and a formal peace agreement was made in 1646.

The settlement of Jamestown, Virginia, in 1607

The first Africans arrived in the region in 1619 and worked as indentured servants on plantations. They were given food and lodging as payment for serving for a fixed number of years. However, within the next 40 years the practice changed so that blacks were purchased for life, and their children became the property of their master. As the number of plantations grew, so did the number of slaves.

In the late 1600s another group of settlers, this time Irish-Scottish, led by Captain Robert Troop, established themselves here. Along the Potomac River two ports, George Town (later Georgetown) and Alexandria, soon became profitable centers of commerce. Here planters had their crops inspected, stored, and shipped. In both towns streets were laid out in rectangular patterns. With rich soil, plentiful land, abundant labor, and good transportation, the region rapidly grew in prosperity.

TIMELINE

1607 Captain John Smith founds Jamestown settlement in Virginia

1619 The first Africans arrive in American colonies

Captain John Smith (1580–1631)

1751 George Town is established

1600	1650	1700	1750

1646 The Indians and the English reach a peace agreement in the Tidewater and Potomac region

1748 Tobacco merchants granted land for the town of Alexandria

1634 Lord Baltimore founds Catholic colony in Maryland

◁ **George Washington by Rembrandt Peale, painted 1824–5**

REVOLUTIONARY YEARS

Some 100 years after the first settlers arrived, frustration over British rule began to grow, both in the Potomac region and elsewhere in the 13 American colonies. In 1775, the colonies began their struggle for independence. On April 19, shots were fired at Lexington, Massachusetts by American colonists who wanted "no taxation without representation," thus beginning the War of Independence.

On July 4, 1776, the Declaration of Independence was issued as colonists attempted to sever ties with Britain. Revolt led to revolution, and the newly formed United States won an important victory at Saratoga, New York in 1777. The French came to the aid of the Americans and finally, on October 19, 1781, the British, led by Lord Cornwallis, surrendered at Yorktown, Virginia. This ended the war and assured the independence of the United States. The peace treaty was signed in Paris on September 3, 1783. Britain agreed to boundaries giving the US all territory to the south of what is now Canada, north of Florida, and west to the Mississippi River.

Meeting in New York of first delegates of Congress to discuss location for a new capital city

The Continental Congress, a legislative body of representatives from the newly formed states, appointed a committee to draft the country's first constitution. The result was the Articles of Confederation, which established a union of the newly created states but provided the central government with little power. This later gave way to a stronger form of government, created by the delegates of the Federal Constitutional Convention in Philadelphia in May, 1787. George Washington was unanimously chosen to be president. He took office on April 30, 1789.

Lord Cornwallis

A NEW CITY

The Constitution of the United States, ratified in 1788, allowed for the creation of a seat of government, not to exceed 10 square miles, which would be ruled by the United States Congress. This area was to be independent and not part of any state. At the first meeting of Congress in New York City in 1789, a dispute arose between northern and southern delegates over where the capital should be located. Secretary of the Treasury Alexander Hamilton and Secretary of State Thomas Jefferson worked out an agreement whereby the debts incurred by northern states

TIMELINE

1775	1780		1785	1790	1795

1781 The British surrender at Yorktown

1783 The US and Britain sign the Treaty of Paris

1787 The Federal Constitutional Convention meets in Philadelphia

1793 President Washington lays the Capitol's cornerstone

1775 The first battles of the American Revolution are fought at Lexington and Concord

Articles of Confederation

1789 Delegates gather in New York City to discuss a location for the capital

1791 President Washington obtains land for the capital city

1792 Construction begins on the President's House (later the White House)

during the Revolution would be taken over by the government, and in return the capital would be located in the south. George Washington chose an area that incorporated land from both Maryland and Virginia, and included the towns of Alexandria and Georgetown. It was to be known as the city of Washington. At Suter's Tavern in Georgetown, Washington convinced local residents to sell their land for £25 an acre. He chose a surveyor, Andrew Ellicott, and his assistant Benjamin Banneker, a free African-American, to lay out the streets and lots. Washington also accepted the offer of Major Pierre Charles L'Enfant to create a grand design for the new capital city *(see p67)*.

In 1800 the government was moved to Washington. President John Adams and his wife Abigail took up residence in the new President's House, designed by James Hoban, which was later renamed the White House by Theodore Roosevelt. The city remained empty of residents for many years while the building works took place.

Ellicott's engraved map of 1792, based on L'Enfant's plan

WAR OF 1812

Tension with Britain over restrictions on trade and freedom of the seas began to escalate during James Madison's administration. On June 18, 1812, the US declared war on Britain. In August 1814, British troops reached Washington and officers at the Capitol fled, taking the Declaration of Independence and the Constitution with them. First Lady Dolley Madison escaped from the White House with Gilbert Stuart's portrait of George Washington.

On August 24, the British defeated the Americans at Bladensburg, a suburb of Washington. They set fire to the War Department, the Treasury, the Capitol, and the White House. Only a night of heavy rain prevented the city's destruction. The Treaty of Ghent, which finally ended the war, was signed on February 17, 1815 in the Octagon.

The British attack on Washington, DC in August 1814

1814 The British set fire to Washington

1815 President Madison signs the Treaty of Ghent with Britain

1802 Robert Brent appointed first mayor of Washington

1812 US declares war on Britain

1800	1805	1810	1815

1800 The seat of government is transferred from Philadelphia to Washington

1804 President Jefferson initiates the Lewis and Clark expedition which resulted in the discovery of America's West Coast

The signing of the Treaty of Ghent

The Baltimore and Ohio Railroad's "Tom Thumb" locomotive racing a horse-drawn car

REBIRTH

With the end of the War of 1812 came a period of renewed optimism and economic prosperity in Washington. Washingtonians wanted to make their city a bustling commercial capital. They planned to build the Chesapeake and Ohio Canal to connect Washington to the Ohio River Valley and thus open trade with the west. Construction on the Baltimore and Ohio Railroad line also got under way. As the population grew, new hotels and boarding-houses, home to many of the nation's congress-men, opened up. Newspapers, such as the *National Intelligencer,* flourished.

In 1829 an Englishman called James Smithson bequeathed a collection of minerals, books, and $500,000 in gold to the United States, and the Smithsonian Institution was born.

Construction began on three important government buildings, each designed by Robert Mills (1781–1855): the Treasury Building, the Patent Office, and the General Post Office building. Also at this time, the Washington National Monument

Chained slaves walking past the unfinished Capitol building

Society, led by George Watterston, chose a 600-ft obelisk to become the Washington Monument, again designed by the architect Robert Mills.

SLAVERY DIVIDES THE CITY

Racial tension was beginning to increase around this time, and in 1835 it erupted into what was later known as the Snow Riot. After the attempted murder of the widow of architect William Thornton, a botany teacher from the North was arrested for inciting blacks because plant specimens had been found wrapped in the pages of an abolitionist newspaper. A riot ensued, and in the course of the fighting a school for black children was destroyed as well as the interior of a restaurant owned by Beverly Snow, a free black. As a result, and to the anger of many people, black and white, laws were passed denying free blacks licenses to run saloons or eating places.

Nothing has been more divisive in Washington's history than the issue of slavery. Many Washingtonians were slaveholders; others became ardent abolitionists. The homes of several

TIMELINE

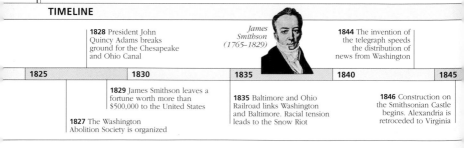

1828 President John Quincy Adams breaks ground for the Chesapeake and Ohio Canal

James Smithson (1765–1829)

1844 The invention of the telegraph speeds the distribution of news from Washington

| 1825 | 1830 | 1835 | 1840 | 1845 |

1829 James Smithson leaves a fortune worth more than $500,000 to the United States

1827 The Washington Abolition Society is organized

1835 Baltimore and Ohio Railroad links Washington and Baltimore. Racial tension leads to the Snow Riot

1846 Construction on the Smithsonian Castle begins. Alexandria is retroceded to Virginia

abolitionists and free blacks, as well as black churches, were used as hiding places for fugitive slaves. On an April night in 1848, 77 slaves attempted to escape the city, and boarded a small schooner on the Potomac River. But the following night they were captured and brought back to Washington, where they were sold at auction. The incident served only to heighten the tension between pro-slavery and anti-slavery groups. Slavery was abolished in Washington in 1862.

THE CIVIL WAR

In 1860, following the election of President Abraham Lincoln, several southern states seceded from the Union in objection to Lincoln's stand against slavery. Shots were fired on Fort Sumter in Charleston, South Carolina on April 12, 1861, and the Civil War began. By the summer, 50,000 volunteers arrived in Washington to join the Army of the Potomac under General George B. McClellan. Washington suddenly found itself in the business of housing, feeding, and clothing the troops, as well as caring for the wounded. Buildings and churches became makeshift hospitals.

Black residents of Washington celebrating the abolition of slavery in the District of Columbia

Victory parade through Washington, DC to celebrate the end of the Civil War in April 1865

Many people came to nurse the wounded, including author Louisa May Alcott and poet Walt Whitman.

Thousands of northerners came to help the war effort. They were joined by hordes of black people heading north to escape slavery, so that by 1864 the population of Washington had doubled that of 1860, reaching 140,000.

After skirmishes on July 12, 1864, witnessed by Lincoln himself at Fort Stevens, the Confederates retreated. By March 1865 the end of the war appeared to be close at hand. Parades, speeches, and band concerts followed Confederate General Robert E. Lee's surrender on April 9, 1865. Yet the celebratory mood was short-lived. Disturbed by the Union Army's victory, John Wilkes Booth assassinated President Lincoln at Ford's Theatre during the third act of *Our American Cousin* on April 14, 1865. Lincoln was taken to the house of tailor William Petersen, across the street from the theater, where he died the next morning (see p96).

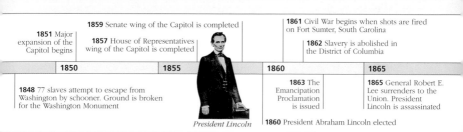

1851 Major expansion of the Capitol begins

1859 Senate wing of the Capitol is completed

1857 House of Representatives wing of the Capitol is completed

1861 Civil War begins when shots are fired on Fort Sumter, South Carolina

1862 Slavery is abolished in the District of Columbia

1850	1855	1860	1865

1848 77 slaves attempt to escape from Washington by schooner. Ground is broken for the Washington Monument

President Lincoln

1863 The Emancipation Proclamation is issued

1860 President Abraham Lincoln elected

1865 General Robert E. Lee surrenders to the Union. President Lincoln is assassinated

POST CIVIL WAR

The Freedmen's Bureau was created to help provide African Americans with housing, food, education, and employment. In 1867 General Oliver Otis Howard, commissioner of the bureau, used $500,000 of the bureau's funds to purchase land to establish a university for African Americans. He was president of this institution, later named Howard University, from 1869 to 1873.

On February 21, 1871, a new "territorial government" was formed to unite Georgetown, the city of Washington, and the County of Washington into the District of Columbia. A governor and a board of public works were appointed by President Ulysses S. Grant. Alexander "Boss" Shepherd, a member of the board of public works, paved streets, installed streetlights, laid sidewalks, planned parks, and designed an advanced sewerage system. But the District's debts rose uncontrollably. As a result, Congress quickly tightened its reins and established home rule. It took over some of the District's debts, and appointed three commissioners to work within a set budget.

Frederick Douglass

Washington became a city of contrasts, attracting both rich and poor. One of the most distinguished literati in the city was Henry Adams, best known for his autobiographical work, *The Education of Henry Adams.* He lived on Lafayette Square next door to John Hay, Secretary of State and also a man of letters. One of Washington's most prominent African Americans, Frederick Douglass, lived at Cedar Hill, across the river in Anacostia. Born a slave in Maryland, he escaped north to freedom where he started an abolitionist newspaper. During the Civil War he became an adviser to President Lincoln.

Many lived well, including the growing middle class, which moved to the new suburbs of Mount Pleasant and LeDroit Park, yet a large number of the poor made their home in Washington's hidden alleys.

A NEW CENTURY

In 1901 Senator James McMillan of Michigan spearheaded a plan to improve the design of Washington by partaking in the "city beautiful" movement, in vogue at the time. L'Enfant's plan was finally completed, and the Mall between the Washington Monument and the US Capitol was laid out. Architects Daniel Burnham,

The Library of Congress under construction

TIMELINE

1867 Howard University is established

1877 Frederick Douglass moves to Cedar Hill. First issue of the *Washington Post*

1884 Washington Monument is completed

1901 Senator James McMillan spearheads "city beautiful" movement

1889 Construction on the Library of Congress begins

1870   1880   1890   1900

1871 Territorial government is formed

Oliver Otis Howard (1830–1909)

1878 First telephone service in Washington becomes a municipal corporation

1897 First automobile in the District of Columbia

1899 The Height of Buildings Act puts vertical limitations on all construction in DC

Suffragettes demanding a hearing for imprisoned leader, Alice Paul

attracted small businesses, theaters, nightclubs, and restaurants. It became home to many successful musicians and writers; Duke Ellington and the opera star Madame Evanti lived here, as did poets Langston Hughes and Paul Dunbar. Alain Locke, a professor of philosophy at Howard, and Jean Toomer, author of *Cane*, were also residents.

Charles F. McKim, and others planned the building of a memorial to honor President Abraham Lincoln.

When the US entered World War I in 1917, growing numbers of women came to Washington to fill the posts vacated by men. Suffragists took to the streets to campaign for the right to vote. The National Women's Party, led by Alice Paul, picketed the White House to urge President Wilson to endorse a constitutional amendment to give women the vote.

African Americans in Washington were not only banned from voting but also faced discrimination in housing and education. After a local black battalion was excluded from a World War I victory parade, tension mounted. On July 20, 1919, riots erupted on the streets and did not stop for four days. Although discrimination continued, the 1920s were a period of commercial, artistic, and literary success for the black community. The area around U Street and Howard University

ROOSEVELT USHERS IN A NEW DEAL

Following the stock market crash of 1929, federal workers received salary cuts, and many other Washingtonians lost their jobs. As a result, President Roosevelt created the "New Deal," an ambitious public works program to reduce unemployment. People were paid to do a range of tasks, from planting trees on the Mall to completing some of the city's edifices, such as the Supreme Court, the government office buildings of the Federal Triangle, and the National Gallery of Art.

Roosevelt's wife, Eleanor, was a champion of the poor and a tireless reformer. In 1939, when Marian Anderson, the African American singer, was denied permission by the Daughters of the American Revolution to perform at Constitution Hall, Eleanor Roosevelt arranged for her to sing at the Lincoln Memorial instead, to a crowd of 75,000.

President Franklin D. Roosevelt with First Lady Eleanor

1906 Teddy Roosevelt's daughter, Alice, is married in the White House

1908 Opening of Union Station, designed by Daniel Burnham

1918 Washington celebrates Armistice Day

1919 Race riots continue for four days

Marian Anderson (1897–1993)

1910	1920	1930	1940

1917 US enters World War I

1920 The 19th amendment, granting suffrage to women, is ratified

1929 The Great Depression begins

1933 New Negro Alliance is formed to improve the status of blacks

1939 Marian Anderson performs at the Lincoln Memorial

After the US entered World War II in December 1941, Washington's population soared. Women from all across the country arrived in the capital, eager to take on government jobs while the men were overseas. They faced housing shortages, and long lines as they waited to use rationing coupons for food and services. The city also offered a respite for soldiers on leave. Actress Helen Hayes, a native Washingtonian, opened the Stage Door Canteen where celebrities provided food and entertainment.

Soldiers on patrol after the death of Martin Luther King, Jr.

THE CIVIL RIGHTS MOVEMENT

In 1953 the Supreme Court's ruling in the Thompson Restaurant case made it illegal for public places to discriminate against blacks. With the passage of other anti-discrimination laws, life in Washington began to change. In 1954, the recreation department ended its public segregation. In the same year, on May 17, the Supreme Court ruled that "separate educational facilities are inherently unequal."

On August 28, 1963, more than 200,000 people arrived in the capital for the "March on Washington" to support civil rights. From the steps of the Lincoln Memorial, Marian Anderson

John F. Kennedy, Jr. salutes his father's casket at Arlington Cemetery in 1963

sang again and Reverend Martin Luther King, Jr. shared his dream in words that would echo for generations (see p91).

In November 1963, the nation was stunned by the assassination of President John F. Kennedy in Dallas, Texas. An eternal flame was lit at his funeral in Arlington Cemetery by his widow, Jaqueline. Five years later, on April 4, 1968, Martin Luther King was shot. Killed at the age of 39, he is revered as a hero and a martyr.

Anti-Vietna
protesters in
Washington in 1969

The opening of the Kennedy Center for Performing Arts in 1971 indicated the growing international character of the city. Several art museums with impressive collections (the East Wing of the National Gallery of Art, the Hirshhorn, the National Museum of American Art, and the National Portrait Gallery) also opened to enrich the city's cultural life. The construction of the Metro helped alleviate traffic problems. The embassies, the foreign banking community (the World Bank,

TIMELINE

1940 First plane lands at National Airport

1945 The first atomic bomb is dropped on Hiroshima, ending World War II

1973 Washingtonians gain the right to elect a mayor

1963 Martin Luther King gives "I Have a Dream" speech

1969 250,000 anti-Vietnam War protesters march

1950

1960

1970

1941 The National Gallery of Art opens. After Japan attacks Pearl Harbor, the US enters World War II

Dr. Martin Luther King, Jr. (1929–68)

1964 Washington residents vote in a presidential election for the first time

1974 President Richard Nixon resigns following criminal investigation

the International Monetary Fund, and the Inter-American Development Bank), and the increasing number of immigrants, provided a cosmopolitan flavor.

HOME RULE

Residents of the District of Columbia have never been given full representation in American politics, as they have no congressman. (Until the 23rd Amendment of 1961 they could not even vote for president – the 1964 election was the first in which they took part.) In 1967, with people clamoring for a greater say in local government, President Lyndon Johnson replaced the system of three commissioners, set up by Congress in 1871, with an appointed mayor and a city council with greater responsibility in policy and budget issues. The result was the city's first elected mayor in over 100 years, Walter E. Washington. Residents were permitted to elect a non-voting delegate to Congress in 1971, and the Home Rule Act of 1973 allowed the people to elect both mayor and city council.

In 1978 Marion Barry succeeded as mayor. Born in Mississippi and raised in Tennessee, he came to Washington in 1965 to work for civil rights. He was the city's mayor for 16 of the next 20 years, but toward the end of his tenure, a large deficit and dissatisfaction with city politics developed. Middle-class families, both white and black, were beginning to flee the increasingly crime-ridden city for the safety of the suburbs.

Walter E. Washington campaigning for re-election

In 1995 Congress stripped the mayor of much of his power and appointed a five-person "financial control board" to oversee the city's affairs. The election in 1998 was won by Anthony Williams, an outsider who offered a fresh outlook and financial stability. Congress returned to the mayor much of the authority it had taken away. Within months of taking his new office it appeared that Mayor Williams was turning the city around. The budget was operating with a surplus, the population had stabilized, and unemployment was down.

The new millennium augurs a smoothly run government and a capital city renowned for an efficient transportation system, a rich cultural life, and a community that is proud of its diversity. The new administration under Mayor Williams has transformed the city's image. No longer dubbed the crime capital of the United States, Washington, DC has once again become a mecca for tourists and a safer, cleaner place for its residents.

Fireworks lighting the Washington Monument during the 2000 celebrations

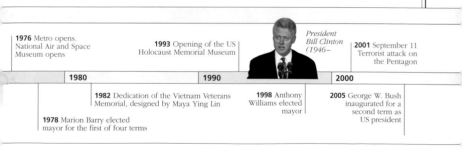

1976 Metro opens. National Air and Space Museum opens

1993 Opening of the US Holocaust Memorial Museum

President Bill Clinton (1946–

2001 September 11 Terrorist attack on the Pentagon

1980

1990

2000

1982 Dedication of the Vietnam Veterans Memorial, designed by Maya Ying Lin

1998 Anthony Williams elected mayor

2005 George W. Bush inaugurated for a second term as US president

1978 Marion Barry elected mayor for the first of four terms

The American Presidents

The presidents of the United States have come from all walks of life; at least two were born in a log cabin – Abraham Lincoln and Andrew Jackson. Others, such as Franklin D. Roosevelt and John F. Kennedy, came from privileged backgrounds. Millard Fillmore attended a one-room schoolroom and Jimmy Carter raised peanuts. Many, including Ulysses S. Grant and Dwight D. Eisenhower, were military men, who won public popularity for their great achievements in battle.

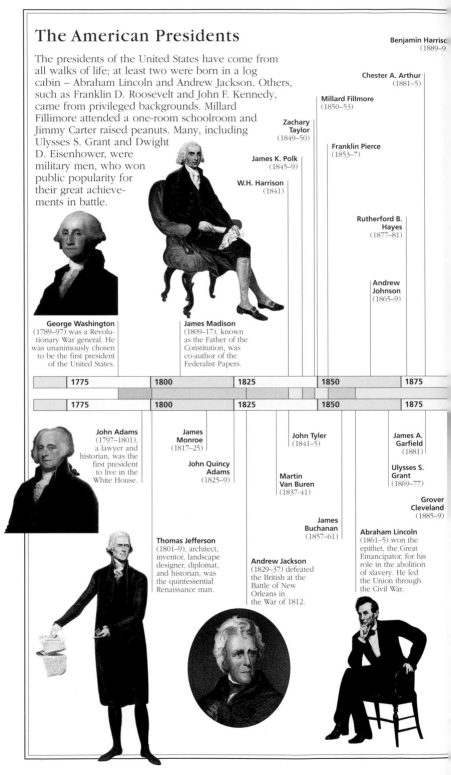

Benjamin Harrison
(1889–9[...])

Chester A. Arthur
(1881–5)

Millard Fillmore
(1850–53)

Zachary Taylor
(1849–50)

James K. Polk
(1845–9)

W.H. Harrison
(1841)

Franklin Pierce
(1853–7)

Rutherford B. Hayes
(1877–81)

Andrew Johnson
(1865–9)

George Washington
(1789–97) was a Revolutionary War general. He was unanimously chosen to be the first president of the United States.

James Madison
(1809–17), known as the Father of the Constitution, was co-author of the Federalist Papers.

1775	1800	1825	1850	1875

1775	1800	1825	1850	1875

John Adams
(1797–1801), a lawyer and historian, was the first president to live in the White House.

James Monroe
(1817–25)

John Quincy Adams
(1825–9)

John Tyler
(1841–5)

Martin Van Buren
(1837–41)

James Buchanan
(1857–61)

James A. Garfield
(1881)

Ulysses S. Grant
(1869–77)

Grover Cleveland
(1885–9)

Thomas Jefferson
(1801–9), architect, inventor, landscape designer, diplomat, and historian, was the quintessential Renaissance man.

Andrew Jackson
(1829–37) defeated the British at the Battle of New Orleans in the War of 1812.

Abraham Lincoln
(1861–5) won the epithet, the Great Emancipator, for his role in the abolition of slavery. He led the Union through the Civil War.

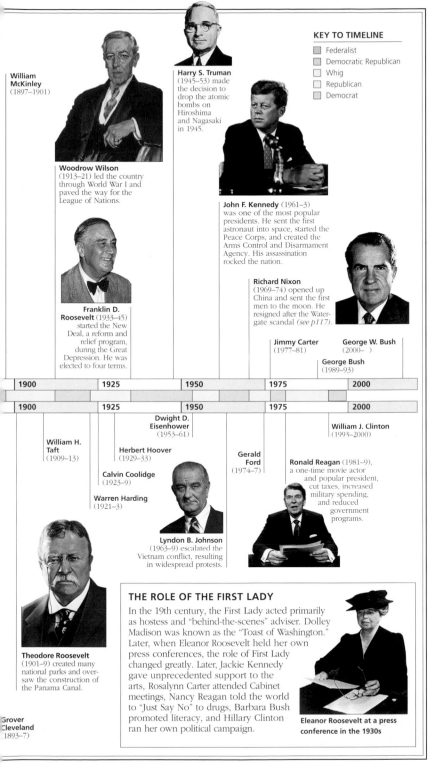

William McKinley (1897–1901)

KEY TO TIMELINE
- Federalist
- Democratic Republican
- Whig
- Republican
- Democrat

Harry S. Truman (1945–53) made the decision to drop the atomic bombs on Hiroshima and Nagasaki in 1945.

Woodrow Wilson (1913–21) led the country through World War I and paved the way for the League of Nations.

John F. Kennedy (1961–3) was one of the most popular presidents. He sent the first astronaut into space, started the Peace Corps, and created the Arms Control and Disarmament Agency. His assassination rocked the nation.

Richard Nixon (1969–74) opened up China and sent the first men to the moon. He resigned after the Watergate scandal (see p117).

Franklin D. Roosevelt (1933–45) started the New Deal, a reform and relief program, during the Great Depression. He was elected to four terms.

Jimmy Carter (1977–81)

George W. Bush (2000–)

George Bush (1989–93)

| 1900 | 1925 | 1950 | 1975 | 2000 |

| 1900 | 1925 | 1950 | 1975 | 2000 |

Dwight D. Eisenhower (1953–61)

William J. Clinton (1993–2000)

William H. Taft (1909–13)

Herbert Hoover (1929–33)

Gerald Ford (1974–7)

Ronald Reagan (1981–9), a one-time movie actor and popular president, cut taxes, increased military spending, and reduced government programs.

Calvin Coolidge (1923–9)

Warren Harding (1921–3)

Lyndon B. Johnson (1963–9) escalated the Vietnam conflict, resulting in widespread protests.

Theodore Roosevelt (1901–9) created many national parks and oversaw the construction of the Panama Canal.

THE ROLE OF THE FIRST LADY

In the 19th century, the First Lady acted primarily as hostess and "behind-the-scenes" adviser. Dolley Madison was known as the "Toast of Washington." Later, when Eleanor Roosevelt held her own press conferences, the role of First Lady changed greatly. Later, Jackie Kennedy gave unprecedented support to the arts, Rosalynn Carter attended Cabinet meetings, Nancy Reagan told the world to "Just Say No" to drugs, Barbara Bush promoted literacy, and Hillary Clinton ran her own political campaign.

Eleanor Roosevelt at a press conference in the 1930s

Grover Cleveland (1893–7)

How the Federal Government Works

Great Seal of the United States

In September 1787, the Constitution of the United States of America was signed *(see p91)*. It was created as "the supreme Law of the Land," to ensure that it would take precedence over state laws. The powers of the federal government were separated into three distinct areas: the legislative branch to enact the laws, the executive branch to enforce them, and the judicial branch to interpret them. No one branch, however, was to exert too much authority, and the system of checks and balances was instituted. Provisions were made for amending the Constitution, and by December 1791 the first ten amendments, called the Bill of Rights, were ratified.

CHECKS AND BALANCES

The system of checks and balances means that no one branch of government can abuse its power.

The Executive Branch: The President can recommend and veto legislation and call a special session of Congress. The President appoints judges to the courts and can grant pardons for federal offenses.

The Judicial Branch: The Supreme Court interprets laws and treaties and can declare an act unconstitutional. The Chief Justice presides at an impeachment trial of the President.

The Legislative Branch: Congress can override a presidential veto of a bill with a two-thirds majority. Presidential appointments and treaties must be approved by the Senate. Congress also oversees the jurisdiction of the courts and can impeach and try the President and federal judges.

The Senate, *sitting in session in the US Capitol.*

THE EXECUTIVE BRANCH

The President, together with the Vice President, is elected for a four-year term. The President suggests, approves, and vetoes legislation. The Executive also develops foreign policy and directs relations with other countries, serves as Commander-in-Chief of the armed forces, and appoints ambassadors. Secretaries to the Cabinet, composed of various heads of departments, meet regularly to advise the President on policy issues. Several agencies and councils, such as the National Security Council and the Office of Management and Budget, help determine the executive agenda.

Seal of the President

EXECUTIVE BRANCH

|

PRESIDENT

|

VICE PRESIDENT

|

CABINET

Ulysses S. Grant *served as the US President from 1869 to 1877.*

Henry A. Wallace *served as Vice President under Franklin D. Roosevelt, from 1941 to 1945.*

The White House *is the official residence of the US President.*

Madeleine Albright, *the first woman to serve as Secretary of State, was appointed in 1997.*

THE JUDICIAL BRANCH

The Supreme Court and other federal courts determine the constitutionality of federal, state, and local laws. They hear cases relating to controversies between states and those affecting ambassadors or citizens of different states. They also try cases on appeal. The Supreme Court consists of nine justices appointed for life by the President.

JUDICIAL BRANCH

9 SUPREME COURT JUSTICES

OF WHOM ONE IS CHIEF SUPREME COURT JUSTICE

The Supreme Court *is the highest court in the United States and is the last stop in issues of constitutionality.*

Thurgood Marshall *was the first African American to be a Supreme Court Justice. He held the position from 1967 to 1991.*

Oliver Wendell Holmes, *Supreme Court Justice from 1902 to 1932, was a strong advocate of free speech.*

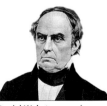

Earl Warren *was Supreme Court Justice from 1953 to 1969. He wrote the unanimous opinion in Brown v. Board of Education (1954). (See p48).*

THE LEGISLATIVE BRANCH

The Congress of the United States consists of two bodies, the House of Representatives and the Senate. Representatives to the House are elected by the voters in each state for a two-year term. The number of Representatives for each state is determined by the state's population. The Senate is composed of two Senators from each state, elected for six-year terms. Congress regulates commerce and is empowered to levy taxes and declare war. This branch also makes the laws: bills discussed, written, and revised in legislative committees must be passed first by the House and by the Senate before being approved by the President.

Daniel Webster *served both in the House of Representatives (1813–17) and in the Senate (1822–41).*

LEGISLATIVE BRANCH

HOUSE OF REPRESENTATIVES

SENATE

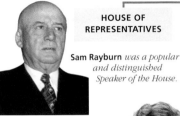

Sam Rayburn *was a popular and distinguished Speaker of the House.*

Edward Kennedy, *leader of the United States' most famous political family, has served in the Senate since 1962.*

The US Capitol *is home to both the House of Representatives and the Senate.*

WASHINGTON, DC AT A GLANCE

Washington is more than just the political capital of the United States. It is also the home of the Smithsonian Institution, and as such is the cultural focus of America. Its many superb museums and galleries have something to offer everyone. Always one of the most popular sights, the president's official residence, the White House, attracts millions of visitors each year. Equally popular is the National Air and Space Museum, which draws vast numbers of visitors to its awe-inspiring displays of air and spacecraft. Also unique to Washington are its many monuments and memorials. The huge Washington Monument, honoring the first US president, dominates the city skyline. In contrast, the war memorials, dedicated to the thousands of soldiers who died in battle, are quietly poignant.

WASHINGTON'S TOP TEN ATTRACTIONS

The White House *See pp102–111*

Vietnam Veterans Memorial
See p83

National Air and Space Museum
See pp62–5

National Gallery of Art
See pp58–61

Kennedy Center
See pp118–19

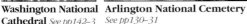

Washington Monument
See p78

Washington National Cathedral *See pp142–3*   **Arlington National Cemetery**
See pp130–31

Lincoln Memorial
See p84

US Capitol
See pp50–51

◁ **View from the US Capitol looking down Pennsylvania Avenue**

Museums and Galleries in Washington, DC

Few cities can claim to have as many museums and galleries in such a concentrated area as Washington. The Mall forms the main focus because it is lined with museums, most of which are owned by the Smithsonian Institution *(see p72)*. They cover a wide range of exhibits, from great works of art to space shuttles to mementos of major events in American history. Admission to most of the museums and galleries is free.

National Museum of American History
This statue of a toga-clad George Washington is one of millions of artifacts in this museum of American history (see pp74–7).

GEORGETOWN

THE WHITE HOUSE AND FOGGY BOTTOM

Tidal Basin

Potomac River

Corcoran Gallery of Art
This Beaux Arts building houses a collection of American and European art and sculpture, including some of the best works by US artists of the 19th and 20th centuries (see p113).

US Holocaust Memorial Museum
Photographs, videos, and re-created concentration camp barracks bring to life the brutality of the Holocaust and movingly illustrate the terrible fate of Jews in World War II Nazi Germany (see pp80–81).

National Museum of Natural History
A huge African elephant is the focal point of the building's main foyer. The museum's fascinating exhibits trace the evolution of animals and explain the creation of gems and minerals (see pp70–71).

0 meters   500
0 yards   500

Smithsonian American Art Museum and National Portrait Gallery
This Neoclassical building houses the world's largest collection of American paintings, sculpture, photographs, and crafts (see pp98–101).

OLD DOWNTOWN

CAPITOL HILL

THE MALL

National Gallery of Art
The futuristic East Building houses the 20th-century art in this collection, while the 1930s West Building is home to older works (see pp54–61).

National Air and Space Museum
Washington's most popular museum has exhibits from aviation and space history, including the Wright Brothers' first airborne plane and the Apollo 14 space module (see pp62–5).

Monuments and Memorials in Washington, DC

As the political center of the United States, and home of its president, Washington has a great number of monuments and memorials honoring America's key figures and historic events. The most well-known among these are the Washington Monument and the Lincoln Memorial – sights of great interest to all who visit the city. For those who wish to remember the countless men and women who lost their lives fighting for their nation, there are poignant monuments, set in tranquil parks, where visitors can reflect in peace.

Korean War Veterans Memorial
Created in 1995, the 19 stainless steel, larger than life-size statues of this memorial recall the thousands who died in the Korean War (see p83).

GEORGETOWN

Lincoln Memorial
This emotive and inspirational marble figure has often been the focus of civil rights protests (see p85).

Iwo Jima Statue (US Marine Corps Memorial)
This iconic memorial depicts US Marines capturing the Japanese island of Iwo Jima at the end of World War II (see p132).

Potomac River

Vietnam Veterans Memorial
Visitors to this dramatic memorial are confronted by a sobering list of names on the V-shaped granite walls (see p83).

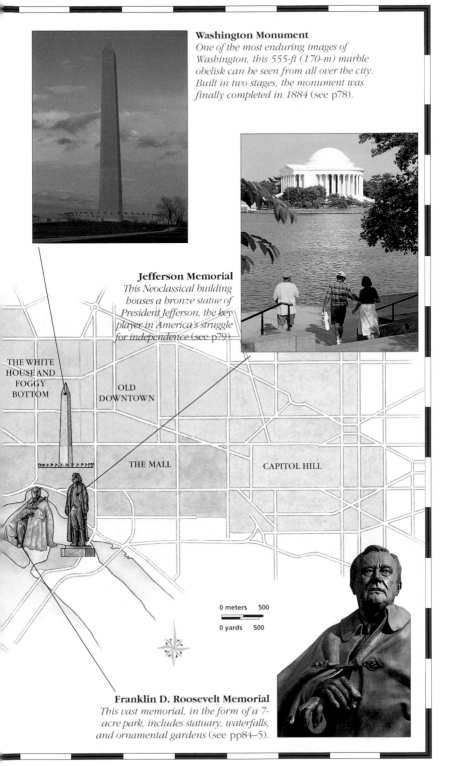

Washington Monument
One of the most enduring images of Washington, this 555-ft (170-m) marble obelisk can be seen from all over the city. Built in two stages, the monument was finally completed in 1884 (see p78).

Jefferson Memorial
This Neoclassical building houses a bronze statue of President Jefferson, the key player in America's struggle for independence (see p79).

THE WHITE HOUSE AND FOGGY BOTTOM

OLD DOWNTOWN

THE MALL

CAPITOL HILL

0 meters   500

0 yards   500

Franklin D. Roosevelt Memorial
This vast memorial, in the form of a 7-acre park, includes statuary, waterfalls, and ornamental gardens (see pp84–5).

WASHINGTON, DC THROUGH THE YEAR

A wide variety of events takes place in Washington, DC all through the year. In early April, when the famous cherry blossoms bloom, the city really comes to life. Parades and outdoor festivals begin, and continue through the summer as more and more people come to explore the DC area in June, July, and August.

Patriotic member of the public celebrating Independence Day

The White House is the main focus for visitors, and it plays host to many annual events during all seasons – the Easter Egg Roll in the spring, and a Candlelight tour at Christmas. Some of the more popular events are listed below; for further details contact the Washington, DC Convention and Visitors Association *(see p211)*.

SPRING

The air is clear in springtime in Washington, DC, with crisp mornings and warm, balmy days. The cherry tree blossoms surrounding the Tidal Basin are world famous and should not be missed, although the area does get very busy. Memorial Day is a big event in DC; it marks the official beginning of summer, and is celebrated in many ways.

MARCH

Washington Home and Garden Show, DC Convention Center, 801 Mount Vernon Place, NW (7th St and New York Ave, NW). *Tel 249-3000.* A vast array of garden items.
St. Patrick's Day *(Mar 17)*, Constitution Ave, NW. Parade celebrating Irish culture, with food, music, and dancing. There are also celebrations in Old Town Alexandria.

Smithsonian Kite Festival *(last Saturday)*, Washington Monument. *Tel 357-2700.* Kite designers fly their best models and compete for prizes.

APRIL

National Cherry Blossom Festival *(early Apr)*, Constitution Ave, NW. *Tel 619-7222.* Parade, concerts, and dancing to celebrate the blooming of Washington's famous trees.
White House Egg Roll *(Easter Mon)*, White House Lawn. *Tel 456-2200.* Children from three to six, aided by an adult, roll eggs in a race across the lawn.
Imagination Celebration *(Sept–May)*, Kennedy Center. *Tel 467-4600.* A series of plays aimed at young children.
Thomas Jefferson's Birthday *(Apr 13)*, Jefferson Memorial. *Tel 619-7222.* Military drills, speeches, and wreath-laying.
Shakespeare's Birthday Celebration *(end of Apr)*, Folger Shakespeare Library,

Mother-and-daughter team in the Easter Egg Roll at the White House

201 E Capitol St, SE. *Tel 544-4600.* A day of music, plays, food, and children's events.

MAY

Flower Mart *(first Fri & Sat)*, Washington Cathedral. *Tel 537-6200.* Flower booths, music, and crafts.
Memorial Day Weekend Concert *(last Sun)*, West Lawn of Capitol. *Tel 619-7222.* National Symphony Orchestra performs. **Memorial Day** *(last Mon)*, Arlington National Cemetery. *Tel (703) 607-8000.* US Navy Memorial. *Tel 737-2300.* Vietnam Veterans Memorial. *Tel 619-7222.* Wreath-laying, speeches, and music to honor war veterans. **Memorial Day Jazz Festival** *(last Mon)*, Old Town Alexandria. *Tel (703) 883-4686.* Live, big-band jazz music.
Twilight Tattoo Military Pageant *(7pm every Wed, May–Aug)*, Ellipse south of the White House. *Tel 703-696-3718.* Military parade presenting the history of the US Army.

Cherry tree blossoms surrounding Jefferson Memorial at the Tidal Basin

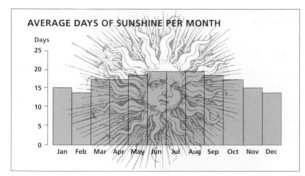

AVERAGE DAYS OF SUNSHINE PER MONTH

Days: 25, 20, 15, 10, 5, 0

Jan Feb Mar Apr May Jun Jul Aug Sep Oct Nov Dec

Sunshine Chart
The amount of sunshine per month in Washington does not vary greatly – even in winter months half the days will enjoy blue skies. In summer the sunshine is at its most persistent, although it is best to be prepared for the occasional rainstorm. The chart gives the number of days per month with little or no cloud.

SUMMER

In June, July, and August, visitors come to Washington, DC from far and wide. The streets and parks are packed with people enjoying the sunshine. Many attractions become overcrowded, so it is important to call ahead and make reservations at this time of year.

The summer months can also be extremely hot and humid; even so, parades and outdoor fairs are usually very popular. Independence Day on July 4 is particularly exciting, with a parade during the day and fireworks at night.

JUNE

Shakespeare Free for All
(throughout Jun), Carter Barron Amphitheater, Rock Creek Park. **Tel** 547-895-6000. Nightly performances by the Shakespeare Theater Company, free of charge.
Alexandria Waterfront Festival
(first or second weekend), Oronoco Bay Park, Alexandria. **Tel** *(703) 549-8300.* Tall ships, games, and music celebrating maritime history. **Smithsonian Festival of American Folklife**
(late Jun–early Jul), The Mall. **Tel** 633-1000. A huge celebration of folk culture, including music, dance, games, and food. **Washington National Cathedral Summer Festival of Music** *(mid-Jun–mid-Jul)*, Washington National Cathedral. **Tel** 537-6200. A varied program of modern and classical concerts. **Dance Africa** *(mid-Jun)*, Dance Place, 3225 8th St, NE. **Tel** 269-1600. African dance, street markets, and concerts.

Fireworks over Washington, DC on the Fourth of July

JULY

Independence Day *(Jul 4)*, Constitution Ave & US Capitol, other areas. Concert on west front of the Capitol. A parade along Constitution Avenue, with fireworks from the base of the Washington Monument. Other areas such as Old Town Alexandria have parades, concerts, and fireworks. **Bastille Day** *(Jul 14)*, Les Halles Restaurant, 1201 Pennsylvania Ave, NW. Racing waiters and live entertainment.

Mary McLeod Bethune Celebration *(Jul 10)*, Bethune Statue, Lincoln Palk, E Capitol St, SE, between 11th St & 13th St. **Tel** 673-2402. Memorial wreath-laying, gospel music, and speeches. **Caribbean Summer in the Park** *(mid-Jul)*, RFK Stadium, 2400 E Capitol St, SE. **Tel** 547-9077. Music, food, and dancing, Caribbean style. **Hispanic-Latino Festival** *(late Jul)*, Washington Monument. **Tel** 619 7222. Music, food, and celebration of 40 Latin American Nations.

AUGUST

Arlington County Fair *(mid-Aug)*, Thomas Jefferson Center, Arlington, VA. **Tel** *(703) 920-4556.* Food, crafts, music, and fairground rides. **Georgia Avenue Day** *(end of Aug)*, Georgia Ave, NW. A parade plus food, stalls, rides, and music. **National Frisbee Festival** *(late Aug)*, Washington Monument. **Tel** 619-7222. A weekend celebrating the game of Frisbee, including a free Frisbee contest for champions and amateurs alike.

A frenzy of Frisbee throwing at Washington's National Frisbee Festival

AVERAGE MONTHLY RAINFALL

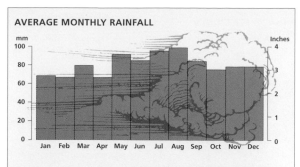

mm												Inches
100												4
80												3
60												
40												2
20												1
0	Jan	Feb	Mar	Apr	May	Jun	Jul	Aug	Sep	Oct	Nov Dec	0

Rainfall Chart
It is impossible to escape the rain completely in Washington. The heaviest rainfall occurs during the summer months of May through August, when rain can come as a welcome break from the humidity. Rainfall tails off in the fall months of September and October and reaches its lowest ebb in late winter. Rain rarely lingers for long in the city.

A school band performing in Constitution Gardens

FALL

With the air turning cooler, Labor Day (the first Monday in September) bids goodbye to the summer. The fall (autumn) season covers September, October, and November in Washington, when the temperatures steadily drop. A particularly enjoyable event at this time of year is Halloween, when children dress up as their favorite creatures or characters to go trick-or-treating.

Halloween Jack-O'-Lanterna

SEPTEMBER

Labor Day Weekend Concert *(Sun before Labor Day)*, West Lawn of the US Capitol. *Tel 619-7222.* National Symphony Orchestra performs a concert. **John F. Kennedy Center for the Performing Arts Open House** *(early Sep)*. *Tel 457-4600.* A one-day celebration with performances of blues, rock,

jazz, dance, drama, and film. **International Children's Festival**, Wolf Trap Park, Vienna, VA. *Tel (703) 255-1800.* Performers come from around the world. **18th-century Fair**, Mount Vernon, VA. *Tel (703) 780-2000.* Craft demonstrations and 18th-century entertainment.

OCTOBER

DC Open House *(first weekend)*, various venues. *Tel 661-7581.* Free walking tours and museum visits. **Taste of DC** *(Sat, Sun, and Mon of Columbus Day weekend)*, Pennsylvania Ave, NW. *Tel 789-7000.* A food and musical festival. **Columbus Day** *(second Mon)*, Columbus Memorial, Union Station. *Tel 289-1908.* Speeches and wreath-laying for the man who discovered America. **National Book Fair** *(early Oct)*, National Mall. *Tel 707-5000.* **White House Fall Garden Tours** *(mid-Oct)*. *Tel 456-2200.* A chance to walk the grounds of the President's home.

Halloween *(Oct 31)*. Young people appear on the streets trick-or-treating, dressed as ghosts, clowns, and witches. Dupont Circle and Georgetown are popular areas.

NOVEMBER

Annual Seafaring Celebration *(date varies)*, Navy Museum. *Tel 433-4882.* A maritime event for the whole family with food, music, and naval displays. **Veterans Day Ceremonies** *(Nov 11)*, Arlington National Cemetery. *Tel (703) 607-8000.* Services, parades, and wreath-layings at various memorials around the city, commemorating United States military personnel who died in war. There are special Veterans Day ceremonies also at the Vietnam Veterans Memorial, *Tel 426-6841,* and at the US Navy Memorial, *Tel 737-2300.* **Kennedy Center Holiday Festival** *(late Nov–New Year's Eve)*. *Tel 467-4600.* Free concerts.

Military guard on Veterans Day in Arlington National Cemetery

AVERAGE MONTHLY TEMPERATURE

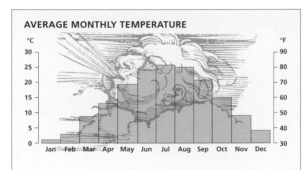

Temperature Chart

Washington's climate varies greatly. In winter the air is bitterly cold, with temperatures rising little above freezing. In July and August, however, it becomes very hot and extremely humid. The best time to visit the city is in the spring or fall, when the weather is pleasantly mild and the air is clear.

WINTER

Temperatures can plummet below freezing during the winter months of December, January, and February. Hence the city is generally quieter at this time of year, making it a good time to see the most popular sights. Over the Christmas period, Washington becomes busy again with festive events to get people into the holiday spirit. Decorations are visible across the city, and many places, including the White House, offer Christmas tours.

Toward the end of winter, a number of famous birthdays are celebrated, including those of Martin Luther King Jr. and Presidents Abraham Lincoln and George Washington.

DECEMBER

National Christmas Tree Lighting *(mid-Dec)*, Ellipse south of the White House. **Tel** *456-2200.* The President turns on the lights on the National Christmas tree.

Washington National Cathedral Christmas Services *(throughout Dec)*. **Tel** *537-6200.* Holiday celebrations with festive music.
White House Candlelight Tours *(after Christmas)*. **Tel** *456-7041.* The President's Christmas decorations are on display to the public.

JANUARY

Robert E. Lee's Birthday *(mid-Jan)*. Ceremony at Lee's house in Alexandria. **Tel** *(703) 548-1789.*
Martin Luther King Jr.'s Birthday *(third Mon)*, **Tel** *426-7222.* **Restaurant week** *(mid Jan)*, Many of Washington's top restaurants offer prix fixe lunch or dinner specials.

FEBRUARY

Chinese New Year *(first two weeks)*, N St, Chinatown. **Tel** *789-7000.* Parades, dancing, and live music. **African American History Month** *(throughout Feb)*. Various events are held across the

city: contact the Smithsonian (**Tel** *633-1000*) and the National Park Service (**Tel** *426-7222*).
George Washington's Birthday Parade *(around Feb 15)*, Old Town Alexandria, VA. **Tel** *(703) 838-4200.*
Abraham Lincoln's Birthday, *(Feb 12)*, Lincoln Memorial. **Tel** *426-7222.* There is a wreath-laying ceremony which is followed by a reading of the Gettysburg Address.

Girl Scouts watching George Washington's Birthday Parade

FEDERAL HOLIDAYS

New Year's Day (Jan 1)

Martin Luther King Jr.'s Birthday (3rd Mon in Jan)

Presidents' Day (3rd Mon in Feb)

Easter Monday (Mar or Apr)

Memorial Day (last Mon in May)

Independence Day (Jul 4)

Labor Day (1st Mon in Sep)

Columbus Day (2nd Mon in Oct)

Veterans Day (Nov 11)

Thanksgiving (4th Thu in Nov)

Christmas Day (Dec 25)

The National Christmas tree outside a snow-covered White House

WASHINGTON, DC AREA BY AREA

CAPITOL HILL 42–53

THE MALL 54–85

OLD DOWNTOWN 86–103

THE WHITE HOUSE
AND FOGGY BOTTOM 104–119

GEORGETOWN 120–127

FARTHER AFIELD 128–145

THREE GUIDED WALKS 146–151

CAPITOL HILL

S oon after the Constitution was ratified in 1788, America's seat of government began to take root on Capitol Hill. The site was chosen in 1791 from 10 acres that were ceded by the state of Maryland. Pierre L'Enfant (see p19) chose a hill on the east side of the area as the foundation for the Capitol building and the center of the new city.

In more than 200 years, Capitol Hill has developed into a bustling microcosm of modern America.

Statue of Roman Legionnaire at Union Station

Symbols of the country's cultural development are everywhere, from its federal buildings to its centers of commerce, shops, and restaurants, as well as residential areas for a wide variety of people.

The Capitol Hill area is frequented by the most powerful people in the United States, yet at the same time, ordinary citizens are able to petition their congressional representatives here, or pose for a photograph with them on the steps of the Capitol building.

SIGHTS AT A GLANCE

Historic Buildings
Folger Shakespeare Library ❷
Library of Congress pp46–7 ❶
Sewall-Belmont House ❹
Union Station ⓭
US Capitol pp50–51 ❺
US Supreme Court ❸

Museums and Galleries
National Postal Museum ⓮

Market
Eastern Market ⓬

Monuments and Memorials
National Japanese American Memorial ❼
Robert A. Taft Memorial ❻

Ulysses S. Grant Memorial ❽

Parks and Gardens
Bartholdi Park and Fountain ❿
US Botanic Garden ❾

Church
Ebenezer United Methodist Church ⓫

KEY
▨	Street-by-street map pp44–5
Ⓜ	Metro station
ⓘ	Tourist information
▣	Police
⊠	Post office
▤	Train station

GETTING THERE
The best way to get to Capitol Hill is by Metro. Take the red line to Union Station, or the blue or orange line to Capitol South, Eastern Market, or Federal Center SW. Metrobuses 30, 32, 34, 35, and 36 stop at various points on Capitol Hill.

0 meters	500
0 yards	500

Street-by-Street: Capitol Hill

The cityscape extending from the Capitol is an impressive combination of grand classical architecture and stretches of grassy open spaces. There are no skyscrapers here, only the immense marble halls and columns that distinguish many of the government buildings. The bustle and excitement around the US Capitol and US Supreme Court contrast with the calm that can be found by a reflecting pool or in a quiet residential street. Many of the small touches that make the city special can be found in this area, such as the antique lighting fixtures on Second Street, the brilliant bursts of flowers along the sidewalks, or the brightly painted façades of houses on Third Street near the Folger Shakespeare Library.

★ US Capitol
The famous dome of the nation's seat of government is one of the largest in the world ❺

Robert A. Taft Memorial
A statue of Taft (1889–1953) stands in front of the bell tower that was erected to honor his principles and achievements ❻

Ulysses S. Grant Memorial
General Grant (1822–85), the Union leader in the American Civil War, is the central figure in a remarkable group of bronze equestrian statuary ❼

US Botanic Garden
Established in 1820, the Botanic Garden contains thousands of exotic and domestic plants ❽

Sewall-Belmont House

A life-size statue of the French martyr Joan of Arc (a replica of a French sculpture), graces this 18th-century house that serves as the headquarters of the National Women's Party ❹

0 meters	150
0 yards	150

LOCATOR MAP
See Street Finder map 4

KEY

- ▬ ▬ Suggested route

Senate
Offices

US Supreme Court
The highest court in the land has been housed since 1935 in this classical marble building designed by Cass Gilbert ❸

THE TRAGEDIE OF IVLIVS CÆSAR

Folger Shakespeare Library
A tribute to the Bard's works and times, the library also doubles as a museum displaying Elizabethan treasures ❷

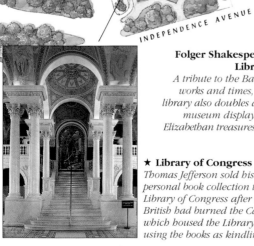

★ Library of Congress

Thomas Jefferson sold his personal book collection to the Library of Congress after the British had burned the Capitol, which housed the Library, using the books as kindling ❶

STAR SIGHTS

★ US Capitol

★ Library of Congress

Library of Congress ❶

Congress first established a reference library in the U.S. Capitol in 1800. When the Capitol was burned in 1814, Thomas Jefferson offered his own collection as a replacement, his belief in a universality of knowledge becoming the foundation for the Library's acquisition policy. In 1897 the Library of Congress moved to a new Italian Renaissance-style main building designed by John L. Smithmeyer and Paul J. Pelz. The main building, now known as the Thomas Jefferson Building, is a marvel of art and architecture, with its paintings and mosaics, and several exhibitions, including American Treasures and the Bob Hope Gallery of American Entertainment. The Library of Congress has the world's largest collection of books and special materials.

Thomas Jefferson (1743–1826)

Front façade of the Jefferson Building

★ **Main Reading Room**
Eight huge marble columns and 10-ft (3-m) high female figures personifying aspects of human endeavor dwarf the reading desks in this room. The domed ceiling soars 160 ft (49 m) above the reading room floor.

STAR SIGHTS

★ Great Hall

★ Gutenberg Bible

★ Main Reading Room

Swann Gallery

World Treasures Exhibit

African & Middle Eastern Reading Room
This is one of 10 reading rooms in the Jefferson Building where visitors can use books from the Library's collections.

Mosaic of Minerva
This beautiful marble mosaic figure of Minerva of Peace, created by Elihu Vedder, dominates the staircase landing near the Visitors' Gallery, overlooking the Main Reading Room.

Asian Reading Room

VISITORS' CHECKLIST

10 First St, SE. **Map** 4 E4.
Tel 707-5000. 707-8000.
Tel Visitor services 707-0919.
Capitol South. 32, 34, 36, 96. 10am–5:30pm Mon–Sat.
Federal hols. For access to reading rooms, visitors must be over 18 and have a user card, obtained by presenting a driver's license or passport and completing a registration form. **www**.loc.gov

★ Gutenberg Bible
The 15th-century Gutenberg Bible was the first book printed using movable metal type. This is one of only three perfect vellum copies.

American Treasures Exhibit

Main Entrance

Exhibition Area

Neptune Fountain
The bronze statue of Neptune, the Roman god of the sea, forms a striking feature at the front of the Jefferson Building.

★ Great Hall
Splendid marble arches and columns, grand staircases, imposing bronze statues, stained-glass skylights, mosaics, and murals all combine to create a magnificent entrance hall.

Folger Shakespeare Library ❷

201 E Capitol St, SE. **Map** 4 F4.
Tel 544-4600. Ⓜ *Capitol South.*
🅾 *10am–4pm Mon–Sat.* ⬤ *federal hols.* 🎫 ♿ *Tickets for plays, concerts, and readings available from box office.* **www**.folger.edu

Inspired by Shakespeare's own era, this library and museum celebrate the works and times of the Elizabethan playwright.

The research library was a gift to the American people in 1932 from Henry Clay Folger who, as a student in 1874, began to collect Shakespeare's works. Folger also funded the construction of this edifice, built specifically to house his collection. It contains 310,000 Elizabethan books and manuscripts, as well as the world's largest collection of Shakespeare's writings, including a third of the surviving copies of the 1623 First Folio (first editions of Shakespeare's works). One of these first editions is displayed in the oak-paneled Great Hall, along with books and engravings.

The Shakespeare Gallery presents the Elizabethan Age through a multimedia exhibition based around "The Seven Ages of Man" from the comedy *As You Like It* (c. 1599).

The Folger hosts many cultural events. For example, There are regular performances of Shakespeare's plays in the library's 250-seat Elizabethan theater. There is

The Great Hall in the Folger Shakespeare Library

The impressive Neoclassical façade of the US Supreme Court

also an annual series of poetry readings, as well as numerous lectures and talks throughout the year. The acclaimed Folger Consort early music ensemble, performs concerts of 12th- to 20th-century music.

US Supreme Court ❸

1st St between E Capitol St and Maryland Ave, NE. **Map** 4 E4.
Tel 479-3000. Ⓜ *Capitol South.*
🅾 *9am–4:30pm Mon–Fri.*
⬤ *federal hols.* 🅿 📷 ♿ *Lectures.*
www.supremecourtus.gov

The Supreme Court forms the judicial and third branch of the US government *(see pp28–9)*. It was established in 1787 at the Philadelphia Constitutional Convention and provides the last stop in the disposition of the nation's legal disputes and issues of constitutionality. Groundbreaking cases settled here include *Brown v. Board of Education*, which abolished racial segregation in schools, and *Miranda v. Arizona*, which declared crime suspects were entitled to a lawyer before

being interrogated. The Court is charged to guarantee "Equal Justice Under Law," the motto emblazoned over the entrance.

As recently as 1929 the Supreme Court was still meeting in various sections of the US Capitol building. Then, at Chief Justice William Howard Taft's urging, Congress authorized a separate building to be constructed. The result was a magnificent Corinthian edifice, designed by Cass Gilbert, that opened in 1935. Sculptures depicting the allegorical figures of the Contemplation of Justice and the Guardian of the Law stand beside the steps while on the pediment above the entrance are figures of Taft (far left) and John Marshall, the fourth Chief Justice (far right).

Visitors are permitted to watch the court in session Monday to Wednesday from October through April. Admission is on a first-come, first-served basis. When court is not in session, public lectures on the Supreme Court are held every hour on the half-hour in the Courtroom (contact for confirmation).

Sewall-Belmont House **4**

144 Constitution Ave, NE. **Map** 4 E4.
Tel 546-1210. Ⓜ *Capitol South,
Union Station.* ◯ *11am–3pm
Tue–Fri, noon–4pm Sat.* ● *federal
hols.* **Donations welcome.** ☑ ▯
www.sewallbelmont.org

Robert Sewall, the original
owner of this charming 18th-
century house, rented it out
to Albert Gallatin, the
Treasury Secretary under
President Thomas Jefferson,
in the early 1800s. It was here
Gallatin entertained a number
of wealthy contributors whose
financial backing brought

**Hallway of the 18th-century
Sewall-Belmont House**

about the Louisiana Purchase
in 1803, which doubled the
size of the United States. During the British invasion in
1814, the house was the only
site in Washington to resist
the attack. While the US
Capitol was burning,
American soldiers took refuge
in the house from where they
fired upon the British.
　The National Women's Party,
who won the right to vote for
American women in 1920,
bought the house in 1929
with the help of feminist
divorcee Alva Vanderbilt
Belmont. Today, the house is
still the headquarters of the
Party, and visitors can admire
the period furnishings and
suffragist artifacts. The desk
on which the, as yet unratified,
Equal Rights Amendment of
1923 was written by Alice Paul,
leader of the Party, is here.

US Capitol **5**

See pp50–51.

Robert A. Taft Memorial **6**

Constitution Ave and 1st St,
NW. **Map** 4 E4. Ⓜ *Union
Station.* ♿

This statue of Ohio senator
Robert A. Taft (1889–1953)
stands in a park
opposite the US
Capitol. The statue
itself, by sculptor
Wheeler Williams, is
dwarfed by a vast, white bell
tower that rises up behind the
figure of the politician. The
memorial, designed by
Douglas W. Orr, was erected
in 1959 as a "tribute to the
honesty, indomitable courage,
and high principles of free
government symbolized by his
life." The son of President
William Howard Taft, Robert
Taft was a Republican,
famous for sponsoring the
Taft-Hartley Act, the regulator
of collective bargaining
between labor and
management.

**Statue of
Robert Taft**

National Japanese American Memorial **7**

Louisiana and New Jersey Avenues at
D St, NW. **Map** 4 E3. Ⓜ *Union
Station.*

This memorial, designed by
Davis Buckley, commemorates
the story of the 120,000

Japanese Americans interned
during World War II and the
more than 800 Japanese
Americans who died in
military service. The
names of these service-
men are carved upon a
curving granite wall,
while etched on the
top are the names of
the ten detention camps
where Japanese American
civilians were confined.
An 18-foot long aluminum
bell may be rung by
visitors, serving as a
call to reflection and
remembrance.

Ulysses S. Grant Memorial **8**

Union Square, west side of US Capitol
in front of Reflecting Pool. **Map** 4 E4.
Ⓜ *Capitol South, Union Station.* ♿

This dramatic memorial was
sculpted by Henry Merwin
Shrady and dedicated in 1922.
With its 13 horses, it is one
of the world's most complex
equestrian statues. The bronze
groupings around General
Grant provide a graphic depiction of the suffering of
the Civil War. In the artillery
group, horses and soldiers
pulling a cannon are urged
on by their mounted leader,
the staff of his upraised flag
broken. The infantry group
storms into the heat of battle,
where a horse and rider have
already fallen under the charge.
　Shrady worked on the
sculpture for 20 years, using
soldiers in training for his
models. He died two weeks
before it was dedicated.

The artillery group in the Ulysses S. Grant Civil War Memorial

United States Capitol ❺

The US Capitol is one of the world's best-known symbols of democracy. The center of America's legislative process for 200 years, its Neoclassical architecture reflects the democratic principles of ancient Greece and Rome. The cornerstone was laid by George Washington in 1793, and by 1800 the Capitol was occupied. The British burned it down in the War of 1812, but restoration began in 1815. Many architectural and artistic features, such as the Statue of Freedom and Brumidi's murals, were added later. Construction of a massive new Capitol Visitor Center, scheduled for completion in 2005, will improve visitor access and facilities.

The Dome
Originally a wood and copper construction, the dome was designed by Thomas U. Walter.

★ **The Rotunda**
Completed in 1865, the 180-ft (55-m) high Rotunda is capped by The Apotheosis of Washington, a fresco by Constantino Brumidi.

The Hall of Columns
is lined with statues of notable Americans.

The House Chamber

Crypt with central rose denoting the city's division into quadrants

★ **National Statuary Hall**
In 1864 Congress invited each state to contribute two statues of prominent citizens to stand in this hall.

★ Old Senate Chamber
Occupied by the Senate until 1859, this chamber was then home to the Supreme Court for 75 years. Today it is used mainly as museum space.

The Senate Chamber has been the home of the US Senate since 1859.

VISITORS' CHECKLIST

Independence Mall, between 1st & 3rd Sts, and Independence and Constitution Avenues. **Map** 4 E4.
Tel 224-3121. 225-6827.
Capitol South, Union Station.
32, 34, 36, 96.
9am– 4:30pm Mon–Sat. Call or visit the web sites for further information. federal hols.
except Sun.
www.aoc.gov. www.house.gov.
www.senate.gov

The Brumidi Corridors are lined with the frescoes, bronze-work, and paintings of Italian artist Constantino Brumidi (1805–80).

The Columbus Doors, created by Randolph Rogers, are made of solid bronze and depict Christopher Columbus's life and his discovery of America – a theme echoed throughout the works of art in the Capitol.

US Capitol
Not only representative of the legislative heart of Washington, the Capitol marks the precise center of the city. The city's four quadrants radiate out from the middle of the building.

East Entrance
Carved on the pediment are Classical female representations of America, flanked by figures of Justice and Hope. Construction of the new Visitor Center in the East Capitol Grounds may still be ongoing.

STAR FEATURES

★ National Statuary Hall

★ Old Senate Chamber

★ The Rotunda

US Botanic Garden ❾

1st St and Maryland Ave, SW.
Map 4 D4. **Tel** 225-8333. Ⓜ *Federal Center SW.* ◯ *10am–5pm daily.* ♿
www.usbg.gov

After a three-year renovation, the Botanic Garden reopened with better exhibits than ever, the 80-ft (24-m) tall Palm House being the centerpiece of the Conservatory. The appearance of the 1933 building has been preserved but modernized, creating a spacious venue for the collection of tropical and subtropical plants, and the comprehensive fern and orchid collections. Other specialties are plants native to deserts in the Old and New Worlds, plants of economic and healing value, and endangered plants rescued through an international trade program.

The Botanic Garden was originally established by Congress in 1820 to cultivate plants that could be beneficial to the American people. The garden was revitalized in 1842, when the Wilkes Expedition to the South Seas brought back an assortment of plants from around the world, some of which are still are on display.

A National Garden of plants native to the mid-Atlantic region was created on three acres next to the Conservatory. It includes a Showcase Garden, a Water Garden, a Rose Garden, and an Environmental Learning Center.

Bartholdi Park and Fountain ❿

Independence Ave and 1st St, SW.
Map 4 D4. Ⓜ *Federal Center SW.* ♿
www.aco.gov/usbg/barthold.htm

The graceful fountain that dominates this jewel of a park was created by Frédéric August Bartholdi (sculptor of the Statue of Liberty) for the 1876 Centennial. Originally lit by gas, it was converted to electric lighting in 1881 and became a nighttime attraction. Made of cast iron, the sym-

The elegant Bartholdi Fountain, surrounded by miniature gardens

metrical fountain is decorated with figures of nymphs and tritons. Surrounding the fountain are tiny model gardens, planted to inspire the urban gardener. They are themed, and include Therapeutic, Romantic, and Heritage plants, such as Virginia sneezeweed, sweet william, and wild oats.

Ebenezer United Methodist Church ⓫

4th St & D St, SE. **Tel** 544-1415.
Map 4 F5. Ⓜ *Eastern Market.* ◯ *10am–2pm Mon–Fri, 9am–2pm Sun.* ● *Federal hols.*

Ebenezer Church, established in 1819, was the first black church to serve Methodists in Washington. Attendance grew

rapidly and a new church, Little Ebenezer, was built to take the overflow. After the Emancipation Proclamation in 1863 *(see p21)*, Congress decreed that black children should receive public education. In 1864, Little Ebenezer became the District of Columbia's first school for black children. The number of members steadily increased and another church was built in 1868, but this was badly damaged by a storm in 1896. The replacement church, which was constructed in 1897 and still here today, is Ebenezer United Methodist Church. A model of Little Ebenezer stands next to it.

Eastern Market ⓬

7th St and C St, SE. **Tel** 544-0043.
Map 4 F4. Ⓜ *Eastern Market.* ◯ *7am–6pm Tue–Sat, 9am–4pm Sun.* ● *Mon, Jan 1, Jul 4, Thanksgiving, Dec 25 & 26.* ♿ *at West end.*

This block-long market hall has been a fixture in Capitol Hill since 1871, and the provisions sold today still have an Old World flavor. Big beefsteaks and fresh pigs' feet are plentiful, along with gourmet sausages and cheeses from all over the world. The aroma of fresh bread, roasted chicken, and flowers pervades the hall. On Saturdays, the

The redbrick, late 19th-century Ebenezer United Methodist Church

Flowers for sale on the sidewalk outside the Eastern Market

covered stalls outside are filled with crafts and farmers' produce, while on Sundays they host a flea market.

Eastern Market was designed by local architect Adolph Cluss. It is one of the few public markets left in Washington, and the only one that is still used for its original purpose.

Union Station **⓭**

50 Massachusetts Ave, NE. **Map** 4 E3.
Tel 371-9441. Ⓜ *Union Station.*
◯ *daily.* ▢ ▥ ▨ *call 289-1908.*
⬚ www.unionstationdc.com

When Union Station opened in 1908, its fine Beaux Arts design (by Daniel H. Burnham) set a standard that influenced architecture in Washington for 40 years. The elegantly proportioned white granite structure, its three main archways modeled on the Arch of Constantine in Rome, was the largest train station in the world. For half a century, Union Station was a major transportation hub, but as air travel became increasingly popular, passenger trains went into decline.

By the late 1950s, the size of the station outweighed the number of passsengers it served. For two decades, the railroad authorities and Congress debated its fate. Finally, in 1981, a joint public and private venture set out to restore the building.

Union Station reopened in 1988, and today is the second most visited tourist attraction

in Washington. Its 96-ft (29-m) barrel-vaulted ceiling has been covered with 22-carat gold leaf. There are around 100 specialty shops and a food court to visit, and the Main Hall hosts cultural and civic events throughout the year. The building still serves its original purpose as a station, however, and over 100 trains pass through daily.

Vintage stamp depicting Benjamin Franklin

National Postal Museum **⓮**

1st St and Massachusetts Ave, NE.
Map 4 E3. *Tel* 633-5534. Ⓜ *Union Station.* ◯ *10am–5:30pm daily.*
◉ *Dec 25.* ▨ ▢ ⬚
www.postalmuseum.si.edu

Opened by the Smithsonian in 1990, this fascinating

museum is housed in the former City Post Office building. Exhibits include a stagecoach and a postal rail car, showing how mail traveled before modern airmail.

The "Art of Cards and Letters" exhibit highlights the personal and artistic nature of correspondence. "Stamps and Stories" displays some of the museum's vast stamp collection. "Binding the Nation" explains the history of the mail from the pre-Revolutionary era to the end of the 19th century. Other exhibits illustrate how the mail system works and how a stamp is created.

At postcard kiosks, you can address a postcard electronically, see the route it will take to its destination, and drop it in a mailbox on the spot.

Columbus Memorial, sculpted by Lorado Taft, in front of Union Station

THE MALL

I n L'Enfant's original plan for the new capital of the United States, the Mall was conceived as a grand boulevard lined with diplomatic residences of elegant, Parisian architecture. L'Enfant's plan was never fully realized, but it is nevertheless a moving sight – this grand, tree-lined expanse is bordered on either side by the Smithsonian museums and features the Capitol at its eastern end and the Washington Monument at its western end. This dramatic formal version of the Mall did not materialize until after World War II. Until then the space was used for everything from a zoo to a railroad

Gold mirror back, Sackler Gallery

terminal to a wood yard. The Mall forms a vital part of the history of the United States. Innumerable demonstrators have gathered at the Lincoln Memorial and marched to the US Capitol. The Pope said Mass here, African-American soprano Marian Anderson sang here at the request of first lady Eleanor Roosevelt, and Dr. Martin Luther King, Jr. delivered his famous "I have a dream" speech here. Every year on the Fourth of July (Independence Day), America's birthday party is held on the Mall, with a fireworks display. On summer evenings, teams of local employees play softball on its fields.

SIGHTS AT A GLANCE

Museums and Galleries
Arthur M. Sackler Gallery ❾
Arts and Industries Building ❹
Freer Gallery of Art ❿
Hirshhorn Museum ❸
*National Air and Space
   Museum pp62–5* ❷
National Gallery of Art pp58–61 ❶
National Museum of African Art ❺
*National Museum of American
   History pp74–7* ⓫
National Museum of the American
   Indian ❻
*National Museum of
   Natural History pp70–71* ❼
Smithsonian Castle ❽
*United States Holocaust
   Memorial Museum pp80–81* ⓭

Monuments and Memorials
Franklin D. Roosevelt
   Memorial ⓴
Jefferson Memorial ⓯
Korean War Veterans
   Memorial ⓳
Lincoln Memorial ㉑
Vietnam Veterans
   Memorial ⓲
Washington Monument ⓬
World War II Memorial ⓱

Parks and Gardens
Tidal Basin ⓰

Official Buildings
Bureau of Engraving and
   Printing ⓮

GETTING THERE
Although visitors can park at the limited parking meters on the Mall, it is easier to get to the area by Metrobus (on routes 32, 34, 36, or 52) or by Metrorail. The nearest Metrorail stops are Smithsonian and Archives-Navy Memorial.

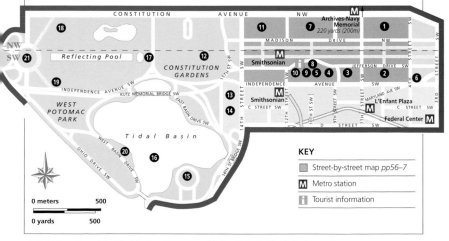

KEY

☐ Street-by-street map *pp56–7*

Ⓜ Metro station

ℹ Tourist information

0 meters 500
0 yards 500

◁ **Night-time view of the Washington Monument with the US Capitol in the background**

Street-by-Street: The Mall

This 1-mile (1.5-km) boulevard between the Capitol and the Washington Monument is the city's cultural heart; the many different museums of the Smithsonian Institution can be found along this green strip. At the northeast corner of the Mall is the National Gallery of Art. Directly opposite is one of the most popular museums in the world – the National Air and Space Museum – a soaring construction of steel and glass. Both the National Museum of American History and the National Museum of Natural History, on the north side of the Mall, also draw huge numbers of visitors.

★ National Museum of Natural History
The central Rotunda was designed in the Neoclassical style and opened to the public in 1910 ❼

Smithsonian Castle
Now the main information center for all Smithsonian activities, this building once housed the basis of the collections found in numerous museums along the Mall ❽

★ National Museum of American History
From George Washington's uniform to this 1940s Tucker Torpedo, US history is documented here ⓫

Freer Gallery of Art
Asian art, including this 13th-century Chinese silk painting, is a highlight, in addition to a superb Whistler collection ❿

Arthur M. Sackler Gallery
This extensive collection of Asian art was donated to the nation by New Yorker Arthur Sackler ❾

National Museum of African Art
Founded in 1965 and situated underground, this museum houses a comprehensive collection of ancient and modern African art ❻

Washington Monument

0 meters   100
0 yards   100

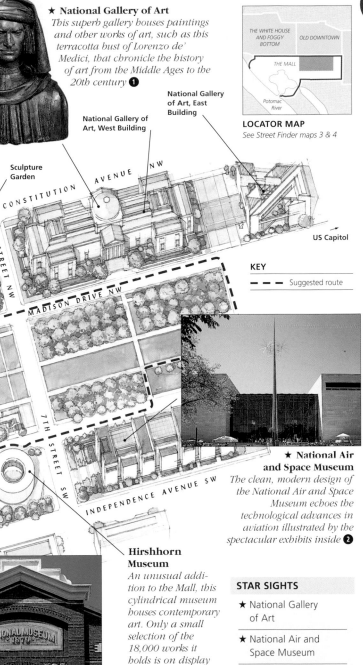

★ **National Gallery of Art**
This superb gallery houses paintings and other works of art, such as this terracotta bust of Lorenzo de' Medici, that chronicle the history of art from the Middle Ages to the 20th century ❶

National Gallery of Art, West Building

National Gallery of Art, East Building

LOCATOR MAP
See Street Finder maps 3 & 4

THE WHITE HOUSE AND FOGGY BOTTOM

OLD DOWNTOWN

THE MALL

Potomac River

Sculpture Garden

CONSTITUTION AVENUE NW

7TH STREET NW

MADISON DRIVE NW

US Capitol

KEY
— — — Suggested route

7TH STREET SW

INDEPENDENCE AVENUE SW

★ **National Air and Space Museum**
The clean, modern design of the National Air and Space Museum echoes the technological advances in aviation illustrated by the spectacular exhibits inside ❷

Hirshhorn Museum
An unusual addition to the Mall, this cylindrical museum houses contemporary art. Only a small selection of the 18,000 works it holds is on display at any one time ❸

STAR SIGHTS

★ National Gallery of Art

★ National Air and Space Museum

★ National Museum of Natural History

★ National Museum of American History

Arts and Industries Building
This masterpiece of Victorian architecture was built to contain exhibits from the Centennial Exposition in Philadelphia ❹

National Gallery of Art ❶

In the 1920s, American financier and statesman Andrew Mellon began collecting art with the intention of establishing a new art museum in Washington. In 1936 he offered his collection to the country and offered also to provide a building for the new National Gallery of Art. Designed by architect John Russell Pope, the Neo-classical building was opened in 1941. Other collectors followed Mellon's example and donated their collections to the Gallery, and by the 1960s it had outgrown the West Building. I.M. Pei designed the innovative new East Building which was opened in 1978. The building was paid for by Andrew Mellon's son and daughter.

★ Ginevra de' Benci
This depiction of a thoughtful young Florentine girl by Leonardo da Vinci (c.1474) is his only painting in the US.

The Alba Madonna
Painted c.1510 by Raphael, this work is considered one of the major achievements of the Renaissance.

West Garden Court

A Young Man with His Tutor
This charming work by French artist Nicolas de Largilliere (1656–1746) was painted in 1685.

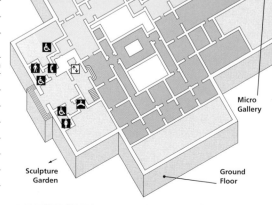

KEY TO FLOOR PLAN

- ☐ 13th-15th-century Italian
- ☐ 16th-century Italian
- ☐ 17th-century Dutch and Flemish
- ☐ 17th-18th-century Spanish, Italian, and French
- ☐ 18th-19th-century Spanish and French
- ☐ 19th-century French
- ☐ 20th-century
- ☐ American paintings
- ☐ British paintings
- ☐ Sculpture and Decorative Arts
- ☐ Special exhibitions
- ☐ Nonexhibition space

Micro Gallery

Sculpture Garden

Ground Floor

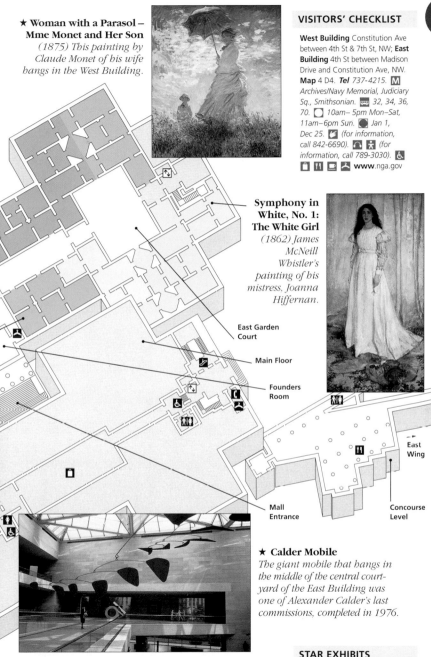

★ **Woman with a Parasol –
Mme Monet and Her Son**
*(1875) This painting by
Claude Monet of his wife
hangs in the West Building.*

VISITORS' CHECKLIST

West Building Constitution Ave
between 4th St & 7th St, NW; **East
Building** 4th St between Madison
Drive and Constitution Ave, NW.
Map 4 D4. **Tel** 737-4215. **M**
*Archives/Navy Memorial, Judiciary
Sq., Smithsonian.* 🚌 *32, 34, 36,
70.* ⬜ *10am– 5pm Mon–Sat,
11am–6pm Sun.* 🚫 *Jan 1,
Dec 25.* 📷 *(for information,
call 842-6690).* 📞 ⛓ *(for
information, call 789-3030).* ♿
🏠 🍴 🖥 🎨 www.nga.gov

**Symphony in
White, No. 1:
The White Girl**
*(1862) James
McNeill
Whistler's
painting of his
mistress, Joanna
Hiffernan.*

East Garden
Court

Main Floor

Founders
Room

East
Wing

Mall
Entrance

Concourse
Level

★ **Calder Mobile**
*The giant mobile that hangs in
the middle of the central courtyard of the East Building was
one of Alexander Calder's last
commissions, completed in 1976.*

GALLERY GUIDE
*The National Gallery of Art is divided into two main
buildings. The West Building features European
paintings and sculptures from the 13th to the 19th
centuries, including American works, a substantial
Impressionist collection, and new Sculpture Gallery.
The East Building features modern art. An underground
concourse connects the two buildings.*

STAR EXHIBITS

★ Calder Mobile

★ Ginevra de' Benci

★ Woman with a
Parasol

Exploring the National Gallery of Art

The National Gallery's West and East Buildings are an unusual pair. The West Building, designed by John Russell Pope, is stately and Classical, with matching wings flanking its rotunda. Built of Tennessee marble, it forms a majestic presence on the Mall. Its collection is devoted to Western art from the 13th through the 19th centuries. The East Building, completed in 1978, occupies a trapezoidal plot of land adjacent to the West Building. The triangular East Building is as audacious as the West one is conservative, but together they are harmonious. The interior of the East Building is a huge, fluid space, with galleries on either side housing works of modern art. The Sculpture Garden, adjacent to the West Building, has a fountain area that becomes an ice rink in winter.

Detail of *Christ Cleansing the Temple* (c.1570), by El Greco

Giotto's *Madonna and Child*, painted between 1320 and 1330

13TH- TO 15TH-CENTURY ITALIAN ART

The Italian galleries house paintings from the 13th to 15th centuries. The earlier pre-Renaissance works of primarily religious themes illustrate a decidedly Byzantine influence.

The Florentine artist Giotto's *Madonna and Child* (c.1330) shows the transition to the Classical painting of the Renaissance. *Adoration of the Magi*, painted in the early 1480s by Botticelli, portrays a serene Madonna and Child surrounded by worshipers in the Italian countryside. Around the same date Pietro Perugino painted *The Crucifixion with the Virgin, St. John, St. Jerome and St. Mary Magdalene*. Andrew Mellon bought the triptych from the Hermitage Gallery in Leningrad. Raphael's *The Alba Madonna* of 1510 was called

by one writer "the supreme compositional achievement of Renaissance painting." Leonardo da Vinci's *Ginevra de' Benci* (c.1474) is thought to be the first ever "psychological" portrait (depicting emotion) to be painted.

16TH-CENTURY ITALIAN ART

This collection includes works by Tintoretto, Titian, and Raphael. The 1500s were the height of Italian Classicism. Raphael's *St. George and the Dragon* (c.1506) typifies the perfection of technique for which this school of artists is known. Jacopo Tintoretto's *Christ at the Sea of Galilee* (c.1575/1580) portrays Christ standing on the shore while his disciples are on a storm-tossed fishing boat. The emotional intensity of the painting and the role of nature in it made Tintoretto one of the greatest of the Venetian artists.

17TH- TO 18TH-CENTURY SPANISH, ITALIAN, AND FRENCH ART

Among the 17th- and 18th-century European works are Jean-Honoré Fragonard's *Diana and Endymion* (c.1765), which was heavily influenced by Fragonard's mentor, François Boucher. El Greco's *Christ Cleansing the Temple* (pre-1570) demonstrates the influence of the 16th-century Italian schools. El Greco ("The Greek") signed his real name, Domenikos Theotokopoulos, to the panel.

17TH-CENTURY DUTCH AND FLEMISH ART

This collection holds a number of Old Masters including works by Rubens, Van Dyck, and Rembrandt. An example of Rembrandt's self-portraits is on display, which he painted

Oil painting, *Diana and Endymion* (c.1753), by Jean-Honoré Fragonard

in oils in 1659, ten years before his death.

Several paintings by Rubens in this section testify to his genius, among them *Daniel in the Lions' Den* (c.1615). This depicts the Old Testament prophet, Daniel, thanking God for his help during his night spent surrounded by lions. In 1617, Rubens exchanged this work for antique marbles owned by a British diplomat. Rubens also painted *Deborah Kip, Wife of Sir Balthasar Gerbier, and her Children* (1629–30). Not a conventional family portrait, the mother and her four children seem withdrawn and pensive, suggesting unhappiness and perhaps even foreboding tragedy. Van Dyck painted Rubens's first wife, *Isabella Brant* (c.1621) toward the end of her life. Although she is smiling, her eyes reveal an inner melancholy.

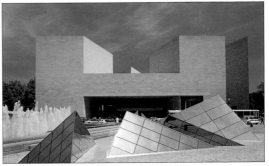

Geometric skylights in the plaza from the West Building to the East Building

19TH-CENTURY FRENCH ART

This is one of the best Impressionist collections outside Paris. Works on display include Paul Cézanne's *The Artist's Father* (1866), Edouard Manet's *Gare St Lazare* (1873), Auguste Renoir's *Girl with a Watering Can* (1876), *Four Dancers* (c.1899) by Edgar Degas, and Claude Monet's *Woman with a Parasol – Madame Monet and Her Son* (1875) and *Palazzo da Mula, Venice* (1908). Post-Impressionist works include Seurat's pointillist *The Lighthouse at Honfleur* (c.1886), in which thousands of dots are used to create the image, and Van Gogh's *Self Portrait*. The latter was painted in St Rémy in 1889 when he was staying in an asylum and shows his mastery at capturing character and emotion. Toulouse-Lautrec's painting, *Quadrille at the Moulin Rouge* (1892), depicts a dancer provocatively raising her skirts above her ankles.

Miss Mary Ellison by Mary Cassatt (1880)

AMERICAN PAINTING

This important collection of American artists shows evidence of European influence, but in themes that are resolutely American. James McNeill Whistler's *The White Girl* (1862) has a European sophistication. Mary Cassatt left America for exile in Europe and was heavily influenced by the Impressionists, especially Degas. *Boating Party* (1893–4) is an unsentimental example of one of her recurrent themes; mother and child. *Children Playing on a Beach* (1884) is also a good example of her child paintings, and *Miss Mary Eillson* of her portraiture. Winslow Homer's *Breezing Up* (1876) is a masterpiece by the pre-eminent American Realist. His painting is a charming depiction of three small boys and a fisherman enjoying sailing on a clear day.

MODERN AND CONTEMPORARY ART

The enormous East Building houses modern and contemporary art. The building's vast atrium is edged by four balconies and adjacent galleries. Architecturally, this space provides a dramatic focus and spatial orientation for visitors to the East Building. Centered in the atrium is

Untitled, a vast red, blue, and black creation by Alexander Calder. It was commissioned in 1972 for the opening of the museum in 1978. At the entrance to the East Building is Henry Moore's bronze sculpture *Knife Edge Mirror Two Piece* (1977–8). The courtyard also holds Joan Miró's 1977 tapestry *Woman*.

Also in the East Building are a research center for schools, offices for the curators, a library, and a large collection of drawings and prints.

Both the East and West buildings also host traveling exhibits. These are not limited to modern art, but have included the art of ancient Japan, American Impressionists, and the sketches of Leonardo da Vinci. The East Building's galleries are surprisingly intimate.

SCULPTURE GARDEN

Located across the street from the West Building at 7th Street, the Sculpture Garden holds 17 sculptures. Late 20th-century works sit around the perimeter of the garden, offering a display of work by Isamu Noguchi, Louise Bourgeois, Roy Lichtenstein, and Joan Miró. Although all very different, the sculptures do not compete with each other because they are spread out. Transformed into an ice rink in winter, the garden functions both as an outdoor gallery and as a pleasant oasis within the city. The pavilion houses a year round café.

National Air and Space Museum ❷

United States Air Force insignia

The Smithsonian's National Air and Space Museum opened on July 1, 1976, during the country's bicentennial. The soaring architecture of the building, designed by Hellmuth, Obata, and Kassabaum, is well suited to the airplanes, rockets, balloons, and space capsules of aviation and space flight. The Steven F. Udvar-Hazy Center *(see page 153)*, named after its primary benefactor, opened in 2003 to celebrate the 100th anniversary of the Wright brothers' first powered flight. With this new facility, the museum becomes the largest air and space museum complex in the world.

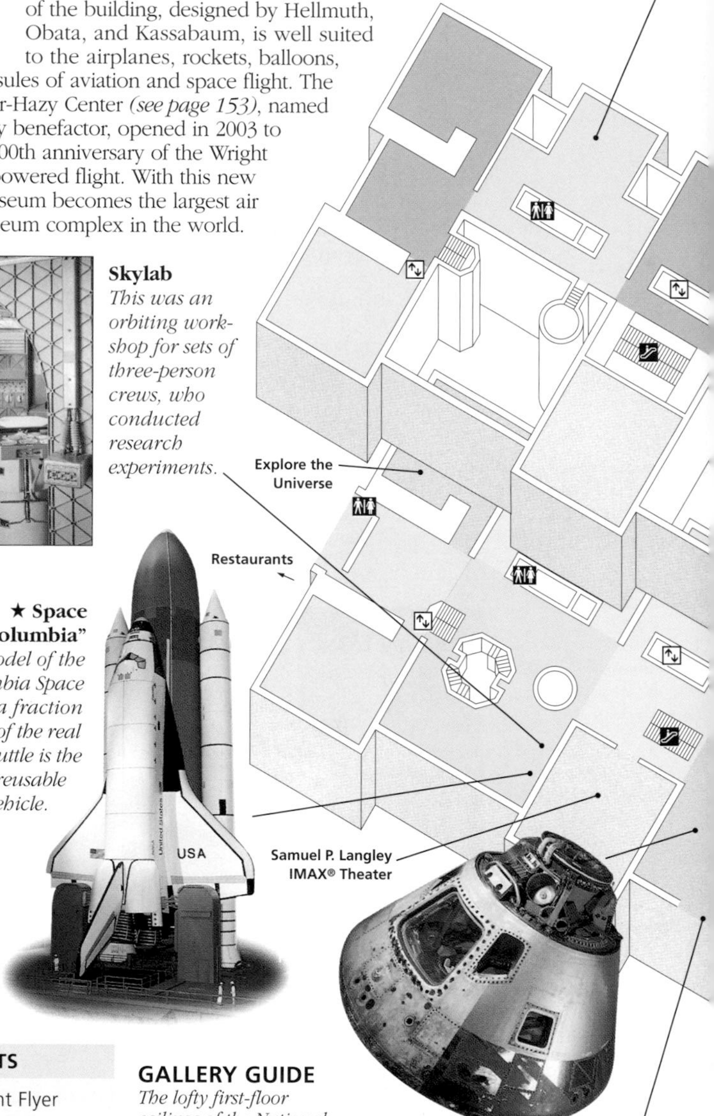

Apollo to the Moon Full of artifacts, this exhibit tells the story of how the United States put a man on the moon.

Skylab
This was an orbiting workshop for sets of three-person crews, who conducted research experiments.

Explore the Universe

Restaurants

★ Space Shuttle "Columbia"
This model of the Columbia Space Shuttle is a fraction of the size of the real one. The shuttle is the world's first reusable space vehicle.

USA

Samuel P. Langley IMAX® Theater

Mall Entrance

★ Apollo 11 Command Module
This module carried astronauts Buzz Aldrin, Neil Armstrong, and Michael Collins on their historic mission to the moon in July 1969, when Neil Armstrong took his famous first steps.

STAR EXHIBITS

★ 1903 Wright Flyer

★ Columbia Space Shuttle model

★ Apollo 11 Command Module

★ Spirit of St. Louis

GALLERY GUIDE

The lofty first-floor ceilings of the National Air and Space Museum show the history of flight, from the early days to the space age. The Museum Store and the Lockheed Martin IMAX® theater are also on the first floor. The second level houses several themed displays.

Amelia Earhart's Red Vega
Amelia Earhart was the first woman to make a solo transatlantic flight. She succeeded in her red Lockheed Vega, five years after Charles Lindbergh.

VISITORS' CHECKLIST

601 Independence Ave, SW.
Map 4 D4. **Tel** *633-1000.*
M *Smithsonian.* 🚌 *32, 34, 36, 52.* ⏰ *10am–5:30pm daily.*
🎫 *Dec 25.* 📷 *10:15am, 1pm.*
♿ 🚹 🎁 🍴 🛒
www.nasm.si.edu

KEY TO FLOOR PLAN

- ☐ Milestones of Flight
- ☐ Developments in Flight
- ☐ Aviation in World Wars I and II
- ☐ The Space Race
- ☐ Progress in Air and Space Technology
- ☐ Other exhibitions
- ☐ Explore the Universe
- ☐ Temporary exhibition space

Albert Einstein Planetarium

Supermarine Spitfire MK. VII
With more than 20,351 Spitfires built, these planes saw service on every major front and sucessfully defended England against Germany in WWII.

★ 1903 Wright Flyer
The first powered, heavier-than-air machine to achieve controlled, sustained flight.

Second Floor

★ Spirit of St. Louis
At the age of 25, pilot Charles Lindbergh made the first solo transatlantic flight in this plane, landing in France on May 21, 1927.

First Floor

Milestones of Flight Exhibition
Many of the firsts in both aviation and space travel are on display in this gallery.

Exploring the National Air and Space Museum

The National Air and Space Museum has a massive exhibition space of 23 galleries. The most visited museum in the world, it has to cope not only with millions of visitors but also with the range and sheer size of its artifacts, which include hundreds of rockets, planes, and space capsules. A single airplane, including one as small as the Wright brothers' 1903 *Flyer*, would dwarf a conventional gallery. In 2003 the museum opened a sister exhibition space: A huge new state-of-the art facility, the Steven F. Udvar-Hazy Center, near Dulles Airport so that almost the entire collection can now be displayed.

The **Pioneers of Flight** gallery celebrates the men and women who have challenged the physical and psychological barriers faced when leaving the earth. Adventurer Cal Rogers was the first to fly across the United States, but it was not non-stop. In 1911 he flew from coast to coast in less than 30 days, with almost 70 landings. His early biplane is one of the exhibits. (Twelve years later, a Fokker T-2 made the trip in less than 27 hours.)

Amelia Earhart was the first woman to fly the Atlantic, just five years after Charles Lindbergh. Her red Lockheed Vega is displayed. Close by is *Tingmissartoq*, a Lockheed Sirius seaplane belonging to Charles Lindbergh. Its unusual name is Inuit for "one who flies like a bird." Some of the greatest strides in aviation were made in the period between the two world wars, celebrated in the **Golden Age of Flight** gallery. The public's intense interest in flight resulted in races, exhibitions, and adventurous exploration. Here a visitor can see planes equipped with skis for landing on snow, with short wings for racing, and a "staggerwing" plane on which the lower wing was placed ahead of the upper.

The F4B Navy fighter, used by US Marine Corps squadrons, was developed between the world wars and is on display in the **Sea-Air Operations** gallery. Flight then progressed from propeller propulsion to

The Boeing F4B Navy fighter

MILESTONES OF FLIGHT

Entering the National Air and Space Museum from the Mall entrance, first stop is the soaring **Milestones of Flight** gallery, which gives an overview of the history of flight. The exhibits in this room are some of the major firsts in aviation and space technology, as they helped to realize man's ambition to take to the air.

The gallery is vast, designed to accommodate the large aircraft – many of which are suspended from the ceiling – and space capsules. Some of these pioneering machines are surprisingly small, however. Charles Lindbergh's *Spirit of St. Louis*, the first aircraft to cross the Atlantic with a solo pilot, was designed with the fuel tanks ahead of the cockpit so Lindbergh had to use a periscope to look directly ahead. John Glenn's Mercury spacecraft, *Friendship 7*, in which he orbited the earth, is smaller than a sports car.

Near the entrance to the gallery is a moon rock – a symbol of man's exploration of space. Also in this gallery is the *Apollo 11* Command Module, which carried the first men to walk on the moon. Overhead is the Wright brothers' *Flyer*, the first plane to sustain powered flight on December 17, 1903, at Kitty Hawk, North Carolina.

DEVELOPMENTS IN FLIGHT

Travelers now take flying for granted – it is safe, fast, and, for many, routine. The National Air and Space Museum, however, displays machines and gadgets from an era when flight was new and daring.

Early mail and cargo planes in the Air Transportation Gallery

Rockets on display in the Space Race gallery

jets. The **Jet Aviation** gallery has the first operational jet fighter, the German Messerschmitt Me 262A. *Lulu Belle*, the prototype of the first US fighter jet, was used in the Korean War of 1950–53.

The **Air Transportation** Gallery has planes from the earliest days of air mail, when open-cockpit planes made of fabric and wood flew with mail in the front cockpit and the pilot in the rear.

AVIATION IN WORLD WARS I AND II

One of the most popular parts of the museum is the **World War II Aviation** gallery, which has planes from the Allied and the Axis air forces. Nearby is an example of the Japanese Mitsubishi A6M5 Zero Model 52, which was a light, highly maneuverable fighter plane.

The maneuverability of the Messerschmitt Bf 109 made it Germany's most successful fighter. It was matched, and in some areas surpassed, by the Supermarine Spitfire of the Royal Air Force, which helped to win control of the skies over Britain in 1940–41.

SPACE HALL

The animosity that grew between the United States and the Soviet Union after World War II manifested itself in the Space Race. America was taken by surprise when

the Soviets launched *Sputnik 1* on October 4, 1957. The US attempt to launch their first satellite proved a spectacular failure when the *Vanguard* crashed in December 1957. The satellite is on display here.

In 1961, Soviet cosmonaut Yuri Gagarin became the first man to orbit the earth. The Americans countered with Alan Shepard's manned space flight in *Freedom 7* later the same year. The first space walk was from the *Gemini IV* capsule by American astronaut Edward H. White in 1965.

The history of man's desire to get into space is explored further in the **Rocketry and Space Flight** gallery, which examines concepts about space travel from the 13th century to the present. It also houses "Earth Today," a video presentation of satellite data, and the space suits worn by the first astronauts.

Gemini IV capsule

Other artifacts from the Space Race on display include a full-size mock-up of a lunar module, a Lunar Roving Vehicle, *Skylab 4* command module, and *Gemini 7*, a two-person spacecraft that successfully orbited the earth in 1965.

The Space Hall gallery shows the result of the final détente between the superpowers with the Apollo-Soyuz Test Project. When the *Apollo* module docked alongside the Soviet *Soyuz* spacecraft, it was the start of the end of the Space Race.

PROGRESS IN AIR AND SPACE TECHNOLOGY

Mankind's fascination with flight is in part a desire to see the earth from a great distance and also to get closer to other planets. In the Independence Avenue lobby is artist Robert T. McCall's interpretation of the birth of the universe, the planets, and astronauts reaching the moon.

The Hubble Telescope, launched from the *Discovery* shuttle in April 1990, provides pictures of extremely distant astronomical objects. Launched in 1964, the *Ranger* lunar probe also took high-quality pictures of the moon, and then transmitted them to Cape Canaveral.

Beyond the Limits explains how computers have revolutionized flight technology and displays some of the recent achievements in aircraft design, a process that has been transformed by the arrival of CAD (Computer-Aided-Design).

The spacesuit worn by Apollo astronauts in 1969

Fountain in the central plaza of the Hirshhorn Museum

Hirshhorn Museum ❸

Independence Ave and 7th St, SW.
Map 3 C4. **Tel** 633-1000. **Tel** 357-1618 for recorded information evenings and weekends. Ⓜ Smithsonian. ◯ 10am–5:30pm daily (Sculpture Garden 7:30am–dusk). ◯ Dec 25. ☑ ♿ 🚻 🖥 summer only. ✈ www.smithsonian.org

When the Hirshhorn Museum was in its planning stages, S. Dillon Ripley, then Secretary of the Smithsonian Institution, told the planning board that the building should be "controversial in every way" so that it would be fit to house contemporary works of art.

The Hirshhorn fulfilled its architectural mission. It has been variously described as a doughnut or a flying saucer,

but it is actually a four-story, not-quite-symmetrical cylinder. It is also home to one of the greatest collections of modern art in the United States.

The museum's benefactor, Joseph H. Hirshhorn, was an eccentric, flamboyant immigrant from Latvia who amassed a collection of 6,000 pieces of contemporary art. Since the museum opened in 1974, the Smithsonian has built on Hirshhorn's original donation, and the collection now consists of 3,000 pieces of sculpture, 4,000 drawings and photographs, and approximately 5,000 paintings. The works of art are arranged chronologically. The main floor and second floor house 19th- and 20th-century art, including works by Matisse and Degas; the third floor has contemporary works by artists such as Bacon, de Kooning, John Singer Sargent, and Cassatt. The outdoor sculpture garden, across the street from the museum, includes pieces by Auguste Rodin, Henry Moore, and many others. In addition to the permanent collection, the Hirshhorn has at least three major temporary exhibitions every year. These are usually arranged thematically, or as tributes to individual artists, such as Lucien Freud, Alberto Giacometti, or Francis Bacon. An

outdoor café in the circular plaza at the center of the building provides light lunches during the summer.

Arts and Industries Building ❹

900 Jefferson Drive, SW. **Map** 3 C4.
Tel 357-3030. Ⓜ Smithsonian. ◯ call for information. ◯ Dec 25. 📷 for Discovery Theater only. ☑ by appt.
♿ 🚻 www.smithsonian.org

The ornate, vast galleries and rotunda of the Victorian Arts and Industries Building were designed by Montgomery Meigs, architect of the National Building Museum (see p103). The Arts and Industries Building is extraordinary because of its expanse of open space (17 uninterrupted exhibition areas) and abundance of natural light.

The museum has served many functions since its completion on March 4, 1881. In its opening year it was the site of President James Garfield's inaugural ball; it displayed artifacts from Philadelphia's 1876 Centennial Exposition, including a complete steam train; and it was home to a collection of the First Ladies' Gowns, as well as Lindbergh's famous airplane the *Spirit of St. Louis*, before these exhibits were moved to other Smithsonian museums on the Mall.

The Arts and Industries Building hosts a series of temporary exhibitions, many of which focus on African-American and Native American culture. It is currently closed for renovation work. On weekday mornings throughout most of the year, the Discovery Theater in the S. Dillon Ripley Center has a children's program of live acts by singers, dancers, actors, and puppeteers presenting classic stories for children, folk tales from around the world, and American history and cultures. There are also workshops at various times.

Arts and Industries Buildings's fountain

Two Disks (1965) by Alexander Calder, in the Hirshhorn plaza

Airy rotunda of the Arts and Industries Building

National Museum of African Art ⑤

950 Independence Ave, SW.
Map 3 C4. **Tel** 357-4600.
Ⓜ Smithsonian. ◯ 10am–5:30pm daily. ⬤ Dec 25. 🎫 ♿ 🏪 ⛩
www.nmafa.si.edu

The National Museum of African Art is one of the quietest spots on the Mall. Perhaps because it is mostly underground, with a relatively low above-ground presence, it is often missed by visitors. The small entrance pavilion at ground level leads to three subterranean floors, where the museum shares space with the adjacent Ripley Center (which houses the Smithsonian administration offices) and the Arthur M. Sackler Gallery (see pp72–3).

The museum was founded in 1965 by Warren Robbins, a former officer in the American Foreign Service (he was a cultural attaché and public affairs officer), and was the first museum in the US to concentrate entirely on the art and culture of Africa. It was first situated in the home of Frederick Douglass (see p145), on Capitol Hill. For several years Robbins had to finance the museum himself, but gradually financial support was forthcoming as the importance of the collection was recognized. Eventually, the Smithsonian acquired Robbins' collection in 1979, and the works were finally moved to their new home in 1987.

The 7,000-piece permanent collection includes both modern and ancient art from Africa, although the majority of pieces date from the 19th and 20th centuries. Traditional African art of bronze, ceramics, and gold is on display, along with an extensive collection of masks. There is also a display of *kente* cloth from Ghana – brightly colored and patterned cloth used to adorn clothing as a symbol of African nationalism. The Eliot Elisofon Photographic Archives (Eliot Elisofon was a famous photographer for *Life* magazine) contain 300,000 prints and some 120,000 ft of edited and unedited film footage, as well as videos and documentaries on African art and culture. The Warren M. Robbins

A Benin bronze head at the NMAA

Library has approximately 25,000 books in its collection, mainly on African art, history, and culture. The library, however, also has children's literature and videos. It is open to the public by appointment only.

There are several permanent exhibitions at the museum, such as "The Ancient West African City of Benin, 1300–1897," which details the history of this culture prior to the intervention by the European powers, particularly the British. The "Images of Power and Identity" exhibition brings together a diverse collection of masks and sculpture from the museums huge archives. While "The Art of the Personal Object" examines the great artistic qualities and aesthetic merit that can be found in even the most mundane and everyday objects, old and new.

HISTORY OF THE MALL

In September, 1789, French-born Pierre L'Enfant (1754–1825) asked George Washington for permission to design the capital of the new United States. While the rest of the city developed, the area planned by L'Enfant to be the Grand Avenue, running west from the Capitol, remained swampy and undeveloped. In 1850, landscape gardener Andrew Jackson Downing was employed to develop the land in accordance with L'Enfant's plans. However, the money ran out, and the work was abandoned. At the end of the Civil War in 1865, President Lincoln, eager that building in the the city should progress, instructed that work on the area should begin again, and the Mall began to take on the park-like appearance it has today. The addition of many museums and memorials in the latter half of the 20th century established the Mall as the cultural heart of Washington.

Aerial view, showing the Mall stretching down from the Capitol

National Museum of the American Indian ❻

Built from Minnesota Kasota limestone, the National Museum of the American Indian was established in collaboration with Native American communities throughout the western hemisphere. It is the only national museum dedicated to the Native peoples of the Americas, and is the eighteenth museum of the Smithsonian Institution. The original collections of artifacts were assembled by George Gustav Heye (1874–1957), a wealthy New Yorker, at the turn of the 20th century. The exhibitions showcase the spiritual and daily lives of diverse peoples and encourage visitors to look beyond stereotypes.

★ Our Peoples
American Indians, including the Seminole and Kiowa, tell their own stories and histories, focusing on both the destruction of their culture and their resilience.

George Heye (1874–1957)
Collector and world traveler, George Gustav Heye and his wife, Thea, accompanied a Zuni delegation in New York c.1923.

Lelawi Theater
In this circular theater a spectacular multimedia presentation is shown every 15 minutes. "Who We Are" highlights the diversity of American Indian life from the Arctic, to the Northwest Coast, to Bolivia.

★ Our Universes
Eight groups of American Indians, from the Pueblo in New Mexico to the Lakota in South Dakota, share their world-views, philosophies of creation, and spiritual relationship with nature.

Window on Collections: Many Hands, Many Voices
Over 3,000 objects are on display, including dolls, beaded objects, and artwork.

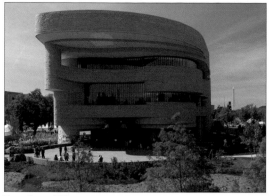

Exterior of Museum
The museum's curvilinear limestone exterior gives it a natural, weathered effect. It is set in a landscape of flowing water, hardwood forest, meadowland, and croplands, to reflect the American Indian's connection to the land.

Window on Collections
Interactive technology allows for a self-guided tour of the exhibits. Shown here is a peace medal that once belonged to Powder Face, an Arapaho.

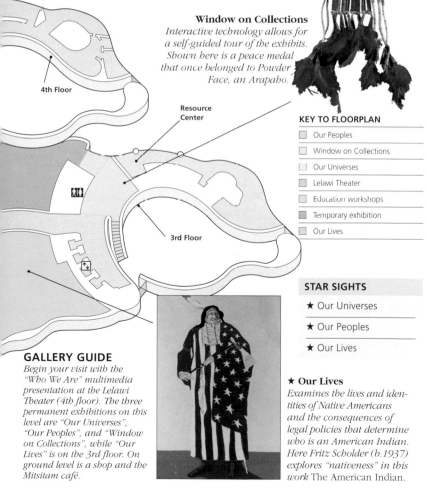

4th Floor

Resource Center

KEY TO FLOORPLAN

- ☐ Our Peoples
- ☐ Window on Collections
- ☐ Our Universes
- ☐ Lelawi Theater
- ☐ Education workshops
- ☐ Temporary exhibition
- ☐ Our Lives

3rd Floor

STAR SIGHTS

★ Our Universes

★ Our Peoples

★ Our Lives

GALLERY GUIDE
Begin your visit with the "Who We Are" multimedia presentation at the Lelawi Theater (4th floor). The three permanent exhibitions on this level are "Our Universes", "Our Peoples", and "Window on Collections", while "Our Lives" is on the 3rd floor. On ground level is a shop and the Mitsitam café.

★ Our Lives
Examines the lives and identities of Native Americans and the consequences of legal policies that determine who is an American Indian. Here Fritz Scholder (b.1937) explores "nativeness" in this work The American Indian.

National Museum of Natural History ❼

The National Museum of Natural History, which opened in 1910, preserves artifacts from the earth's diverse cultures and collects samples of fossils and living creatures from land and sea. Visiting the museum is a vast undertaking. The trick is to sample the best of the exhibits and leave the rest for return visits. The O. Orkin Insect Zoo, with its giant hissing cockroaches and large leaf-cutter ant colony, is popular with children, while the newly renovated Dinosaur Hall delights young and old. The stunning new Hall of Mammals displays 274 creatures, telling the story of how they evolved and adapted to changes in habitat and climate over millions of years.

★ O. Orkin Insect Zoo
This popular exhibit explores the lives and habitats of the single largest animal group on earth and features many live specimens.

The Johnson IMAX® Theater
shows 2-D and 3-D films on a range of fascinating subjects.

African Elephant
The massive African Bush elephant is one of the highlights of the museum. It is the centerpiece of the Rotunda and creates an impressive sight as visitors enter the museum.

The Kenneth E. Behring Family Hall of Mammals
was opened in 2003 and has 25,000 sq ft of displays explaining the diversity of mammals.

Mall Entrance

Ground Floor

STAR SIGHTS

★ Dinosaur Hall

★ Insect Zoo

★ Hope Diamond

GALLERY GUIDE

The first floor's main exhibitions feature mammals from different continents and habitats. Dinosaurs and myriad cultural exhibits are also displayed on this level. The Gems and Minerals collection and the Insect Zoo are on the second floor.

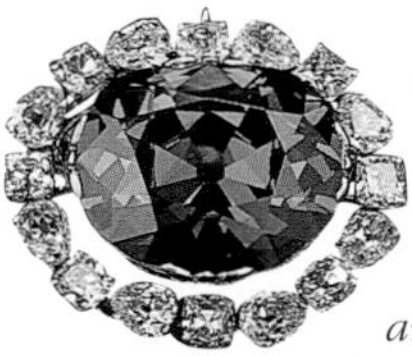

Second Floor

★ **Hope Diamond**
At 45.52 carats, the Hope Diamond is the largest deep blue diamond in the world and is famed for its stunning clarity and color. It is more than one billion years old and once belonged to King Louis XVI of France in the 18th century.

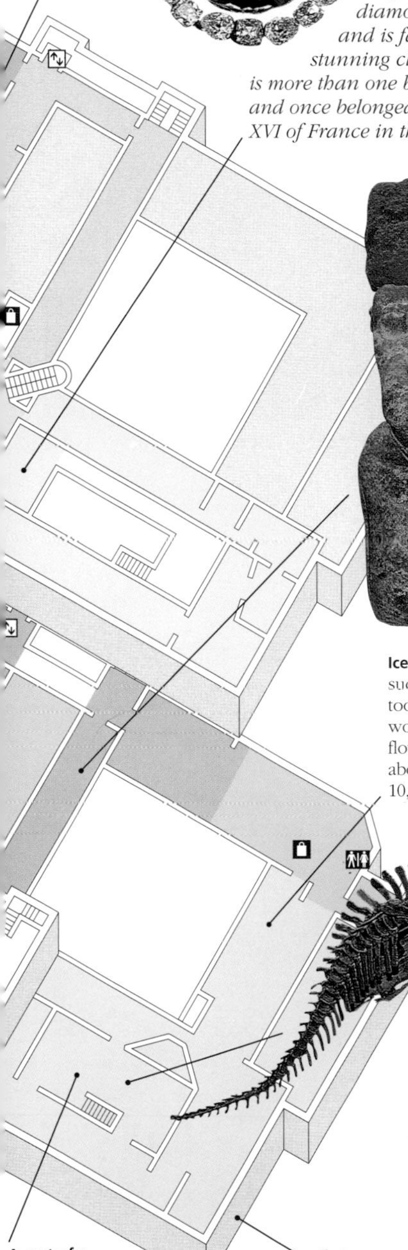

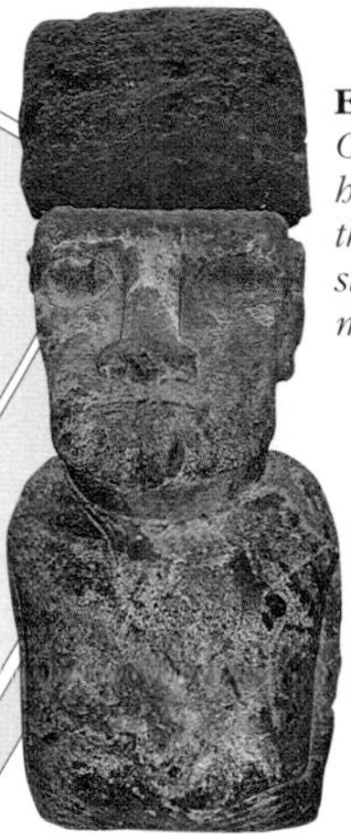

Easter Island Stone Head
Originally erected by the hundreds on Easter Island in the South Pacific, these huge stone statues were built in memory of the dead.

KEY TO FLOOR PLAN

☐	Fossils, Dinosaurs, and Early Life
☐	Kenneth E. Behring Family Hall of Mammals
☐	Native American Cultures, and Pacific and Asian Cultures
☐	South American Culture
☐	Western Cultures
☐	Geology, Gems, and Minerals
☐	Bones, Reptiles, and the Insect Zoo
☐	Discovery Room
☐	Rotunda Gallery
☐	Special Exhibition space
☐	Nonexhibition space

Ice Age Mammals,
such as the saber-toothed cat and the woolly mammoth, flourished between about 1.6 million and 10,000 years ago.

A cast of a nest of dinosaur eggs sheds light on the life of *Troodon*, a relative of *Tyrannosaurus*, who lived around 70 million years ago.

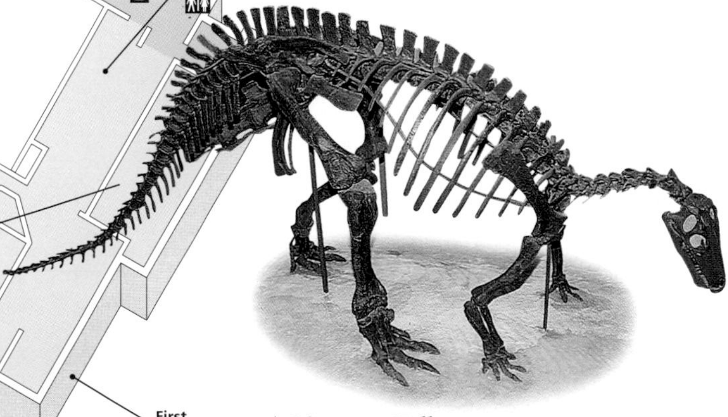

First Floor

★ **Dinosaur Hall**
Featuring reconstructions of fossils that lived up to 200 million years ago, including this skeleton of Camptosaurus dispar, *the Dinosaur Hall is one of the most popular areas of the museum.*

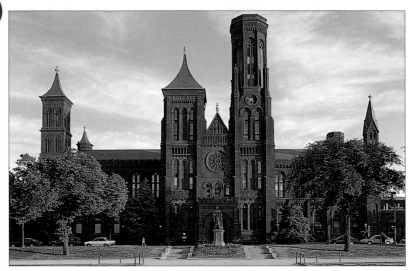

The elegant Victorian façade of the Smithsonian Castle, viewed from the Mall

Smithsonian Castle ❽

1000 Jefferson Drive, SW. **Map** 3 C4.
Tel 633-1000. Ⓜ Smithsonian.
◯ 9am–5:30pm daily. ⬤ Dec 25.
▨ ⬥ ◻ www.si.edu

This ornate Victorian edifice served as the first home of the Smithsonian Institution, and was also home to the first Secretary of the Smithsonian, Joseph Henry, and his family. A statue of Henry stands in front of the building.
Constructed of red sandstone in 1855, the Castle was designed by James Renwick,

The tomb of James Smithson

architect of the Renwick Gallery *(see p113)* and St Patrick's Cathedral in New York. It is an outstanding example of the Gothic Revival style. Inspired also by 12th-century Norman architecture, the Castle has nine towers and an elaborate cornice.
Today it is the seat of the Smithsonian administration and houses its Information Center. Visitors can visit the Crypt Room and see the tomb of James Smithson, who bequeathed his fortune to the United States. The South Tower Room was the first children's room in a Washington museum. The ceiling and colorful wall

stencils that decorate the room were restored in 1987.
Outside the castle is the Smithsonian rose garden, filled with beautiful hybrid tea roses. The garden was a later addition that now connects the Castle to the equally ornate Arts and Industries Building *(see p66)*.

Arthur M. Sackler Gallery ❾

1050 Independence Ave, SW.
Map 3 C4. **Tel** 633-1000. Ⓜ Smithsonian. ◯ 10am–5:30pm daily.
⬤ Dec 25. ▨ 12:15pm. ⬥ ◻
▨ www.asia.si.edu

Dr. Arthur M. Sackler, a New York physician, started collecting Asian art in the 1950s. In 1982, he

JAMES SMITHSON (1765–1829)

Although he never once visited the United States, James Smithson, English scientist and philanthropist, and illegitimate son of the first Duke of Northumberland, left his entire fortune of half a million dollars to "found at Washington, under the name of the Smithsonian Institution, an establishment for the increase and diffusion of knowledge among men." However, this was only if his nephew and heir were to die childless. This did happen and hence, in 1836, Smithson's fortune passed to the government of the United States, which did not quite know what to do with such a vast bequest. For 11 years Congress debated various proposals, finally agreeing to set up a government-run foundation that would administer all national museums. The first Smithson-funded collection was shown at the Smithsonian Castle in 1855.

James Smithson

Sculpture of the goddess Uma in the Arthur M. Sackler Gallery

donated more than 1,000 artifacts, along with $4 million in funds, to the Smithsonian Institution to establish this museum. The Japanese and Korean governments also contributed $1 million each toward the cost of constructing the building, and the museum was completed in 1987.

The entrance to the gallery is a small pavilion at ground level that leads down to two subterranean floors of exhibits. Among its 3,000 works of Asian art, the Sackler has paintings from Iran and India, and Chinese ceramics from the 7th to the 10th centuries AD. There are also textiles and village crafts from South Asia, and stunning displays of Chinese bronzes and jades, some dating back to 4000 BC.

Over the years the gallery has built on Arthur Sackler's original collection. In 1987 it acquired the impressive Vever Collection from collector Henri Vever, which includes such items as Islamic books from the 11th to the 19th centuries, 19th- and 20th-century Japanese prints, Indian, Chinese, and Japanese paintings, and modern photography.

The Sackler is one of two underground museums in this area; the other is the National Museum of African Art (see p67), which is part of the same complex. The Sackler is also connected by underground exhibition space to the Freer Gallery of Art. The two

galleries share a director and administrative staff as well as the Meyer Auditorium, which hosts dance performances, films, and chamber music concerts. There is also a research library in the Sackler devoted to Asian art.

Freer Gallery of Art ❿

Jefferson Drive and 12th Street, SW. **Map** 3 C4. **Tel** 633-1000. Ⓜ Smithsonian. ◯ 10am–5:30pm daily. ● Dec 25. 🎟 12:15pm. ♿ 📷 **www**.asia.si.edu

The Freer Gallery of Art is named after Charles Lang Freer, a railroad magnate who donated his collection of 9,000 pieces of American and Asian art to the Smithsonian, and funded the building of a museum to house the works. Freer died in 1919 before the building's completion. When the gallery opened in 1923 it became the first Smithsonian museum of art.

Constructed as a single-story building in the Italian Renaissance style, the Freer has an attractive courtyard with a fountain at its center. There are 19 galleries, most with skylights that illuminate a superb collection of Asian

Detail of a screen by Thomas Wilmer Dewing

and American art. Since Freer's original donation, the museum has tripled its holdings. In the Asian Art collection are examples of Chinese, Japanese, and Korean art, including sculpture, ceramics, folding screens, and paintings. The gallery also has a fine selection of Buddhist sculpture, and painting and calligraphy from India.

There is a select collection of American art in the Freer as well, most of which shows Asian influences. Works by the artists Childe Hassam (1859–1935), John Singer Sargent (1865–1925), and Thomas Wilmer Dewing (1851–1938) are all on display.

The most astonishing room in the museum is James McNeill Whistler's "The Peacock Room." Whistler (1834–1903) was a friend of Freer's who encouraged his art collecting. Whistler painted a dining room for Frederick Leyland in London, but Leyland found that it was not to his taste. Freer purchased the room in 1904; it was later moved to Washington and installed here after his death. In contrast to the subtle elegance of the other rooms, this room is a riot of blues, greens, and golds. Whistler's painted peacocks cover the walls and ceiling.

The attractive courtyard of the Freer Gallery of Art

National Museum of American History ⓫

The National Museum of American History is a collection of artifacts from the nation's past. Among the 3 million holdings are the first ladies' gowns, a mid-19th-century post office, computers, a 280-ton steam locomotive, and the ruby slippers from the *Wizard of Oz*. The original Star-Spangled Banner that flew over Fort McHenry in 1814 is currently being preserved but is still on view. The museum's expanding, eclectic collection grew from the 1876 Philadelphia Centennial Exhibition and items held in the US Patent Office.

The Ruby Slippers, worn by Dorothy (Judy Garland) in the *Wizard of Oz*, are just one of the myriad exhibits from American popular culture.

Redware and Blackware Pottery
These pots, by various Santa Clara artists, are decorated with serpent patterns. They can be seen in the American Encounters exhibit.

Second Floor

Mall Entrance

★ **Star-Spangled Banner**
Currently being preserved, the flag is the symbol of America. It inspired Francis Scott Key to write the poem that became the US national anthem. Visitors can view the flag through a window wall.

KEY TO FLOOR PLAN

☐	First floor
☐	Second floor
☐	Third floor
☐	Temporary and non-exhibition space

STAR EXHIBITS

- ★ Star-Spangled Banner
- ★ First Ladies
- ★ Model T
- ★ Headsville Post Office

★ **First Ladies:**
Political Role and Public Image
Giving an insight into the lives of the presidents' wives, this exhibit contains over 800 items, including a collection of inaugural ball gowns and designer dresses.

GALLERY GUIDE

The first floor features the transportation and science exhibits and the Palm Court restaurant. Highlights of the second floor include the First Ladies exhibit and the Star-Spangled Banner. The third floor offers an eclectic selection including textiles, the American Presidency: A Glorious Burden, and military displays.

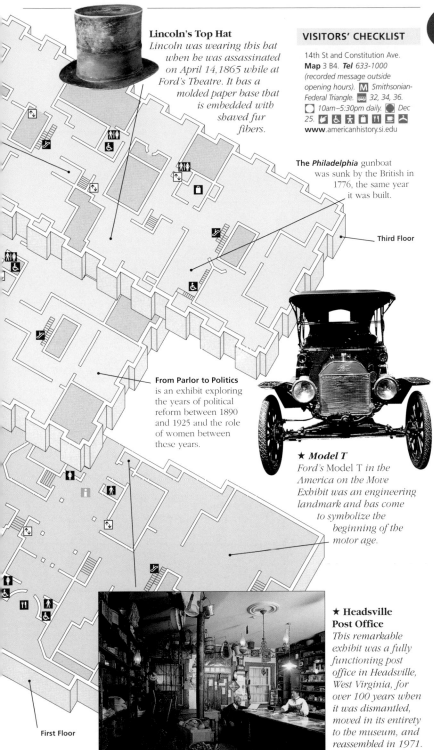

Lincoln's Top Hat
Lincoln was wearing this hat when he was assassinated on April 14, 1865 while at Ford's Theatre. It has a molded paper base that is embedded with shaved fur fibers.

The *Philadelphia* gunboat was sunk by the British in 1776, the same year it was built.

Third Floor

From Parlor to Politics
is an exhibit exploring the years of political reform between 1890 and 1925 and the role of women between these years.

★ **Model T**
Ford's Model T *in the* America on the Move *Exhibit was an engineering landmark and has come to symbolize the beginning of the motor age.*

First Floor

★ **Headsville Post Office**
This remarkable exhibit was a fully functioning post office in Headsville, West Virginia, for over 100 years when it was dismantled, moved in its entirety to the museum, and reassembled in 1971. It is still a working post office.

Exploring the National Museum of American History

The collections at the National Museum of American History is so diverse that a visitor could ricochet from exhibit to exhibit, running out of time and patience before seeing the entire collection. The best approach is to be selective; there is simply too much to take in during one visit. Whether you head straight for the first ladies' gowns or spend time viewing the collections of money, medals, musical instruments, and presidential artifacts, planning is the key to a successful visit.

The museum's modern façade on Madison Drive

FIRST FLOOR

From the Constitution Avenue entrance, visitors to the museum first encounter the reassembled post office from Headsville, West Virginia. First established in 1861, the post office was transferred in its entirety to the Smithsonian in 1971. Visitors can mail letters from here with a special postmark.

Galleries in the East Wing are devoted to artifacts of the Industrial Age. From agriculture to railroads, electricity to road transportation, heavy machinery such as *Old Red*, the International Harvester cotton picker, and powerful engines, feature widely here.

America on the Move is the museum's largest single exhibition and tells the story of how trains, streetcars, ships, and automobiles have shaped American lives. Exhibits include the locomotive that pulled Franklin D. Roosevelt's funeral train, a section of pavement from the legendary Route 66, Ford's *Model T*, and a hot rod driven by Elvis Presley.

In the West Wing, lovers of American popular culture will enjoy seeing the items from vintage television shows, such as the leather jacket worn by the Fonz in *Happy Days*, on display near the escalators, and TV puppet star Howdy Doody. There are also exhibits of a scientific nature. **The Information Age** deals with the history of telecommunications, from the telegraphs of the 1840s and the invention of the telephone (1876) to the rise of the Internet.

The **Science in American Life** exhibition explores the impact of scientific discovery on everyday life, allowing visitors to explore concepts such as DNA fingerprinting and phenomena such as global warming and radioactivity.

SECOND FLOOR

Dominating the East Wing of the second floor is one of the museum's most popular exhibits, **First Ladies: Political Role and Public Image**. This display includes gowns worn to the presidents' inaugural balls. Candidates for the most elegant dress are those worn by Nancy Reagan and Jackie Kennedy, but Rosalynn Carter's dress is noteworthy as she bought it "off the rack." Next to the gowns is a re-creation of Cross Hall, the ceremonial front entrance to the White House. Furniture and accessories that were once used in the White House are exhibited here. In the third floor exhibit "The American Presidency" is a delightful teddy bear. The name of the bear was inspired by President Theodore "Teddy" Roosevelt, who, while out hunting one day, refused to shoot a bear cub that had been captured for him. A cartoon appeared in the *Washington Post* the next day, which inspired the production of a range of bears, named Teddy Bears.

Staying in the East Wing, visitors can discover the role played by women in early 20th-century reform in **From Parlor to Politics**. Symbols of philanthropy, such as pamphlets on education and banners demanding the end of child

Interior of a Spanish home from Taos, New Mexico, on the second floor

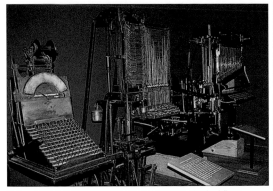

Early examples of printing equipment, on display on the third floor

THIRD FLOOR

The largest exhibition on this floor is **The Price of Freedom** in the East Wing. It explores the nation's military history, from the French and Indian War in the 1750s to recent conflicts in Afghanistan and Iraq. The exhibition features a restored Vietnam-era Huey helicopter, and a World War II jeep.

American Presidency: A Glorious Burden displays objects that represent the lives and office of the presidency in 11 sections. Artifacts include the portable desk on which Thomas Jefferson wrote the Declaration of Independence, and the top hat worn by President Lincoln the night he was shot.

The **Price of Freedom** exhibition explores American military exploits from the Revolution to the present. The display includes flags, weapons and uniforms, as well as decorations from Saddam Hussein's palaces.

The **Hall of Musical Instruments** sometimes includes a violoncello made by Stradivari in 1701. A small popular culture display features the ruby slippers worn by Judy Garland in the *Wizard of Oz*.

labor, are on display. Nannie Helen Burroughs founded the National Training School for Women and Girls in 1909 to provide African-American women with vocational skills and an education in the liberal arts. Her ground-breaking work is remembered here.

The Star-Spangled Banner that flew over Fort McHenry in 1814 and inspired Francis Scott Key to write the poem that was later to become the national anthem is undergoing conservation and stabilization. Visitors can learn about the flag and preservation process in an exhibit in the West Wing.

The **American Encounters** exhibit examines how Anglo-Americans, American Indians, and Hispanics struggled to live alongside one another in the American Southwest. The display includes such exhibits as photographs, textiles, jewelry, and religious items, all of which illustrate how the communities learned to co-exist in the new united nation.

Field to Factory traces the migration of hundreds of thousands of African Americans from the South to the North between 1915 and 1940, also examining some of the new technologies that the migrants found in their changed environment. Artifacts include a cotton gin, a Klu Klux Klan robe, and a portion of a tenant farmer's home, as well as objects from a beauty salon

run by the successful African American entrepreneur, Marjorie Stewart Joyner.

One of the biggest draws on this floor is the **Hands on Science Room**. This exhibition has many interactive displays and is popular with all ages. Here you can investigate various scientific subjects, such as unraveling some of the mysteries of DNA, measuring the intensity of radioactive hotspots, how to use lasers for incredibly accurate measuring of distances, how to transmit the human voice, and, as mentioned, all about the techniques used in the conservation of the Star-Spangled Banner.

Activities in the Hands on Science Room correlate to exhibits in the rest of the museum. It is museum policy that all children must be accompanied by an adult, and no children under five are admitted. Tickets are required on weekends and other busy times (it is best to check the times with the museum first). The Science Room is open from noon to 3pm Tuesday to Sunday.

Teddy Bear, dating from 1903

Detail of the Pocahontas Quilt

Washington Monument ⑫

Constructed of 36,000 pieces of marble and granite, the Washington Monument remains one of the most recognizable monuments in the capital. Funds for this tribute to the first president of the United States initially came from individual citizens. A design by Robert Mills was chosen and construction began in 1848. When the money ran out the building work stopped for over 20 years. Then, in 1876, public interest revived the cause of completing the project. (A slight change in the color of stone marks the point where construction resumed.) The Monument has recently undergone a massive renovation; it has been thoroughly cleaned, cracks have been sealed, chipped stone patched, and the 192 commemorative stones repaired.

VISITORS' CHECKLIST

Independence Ave at 17th St, SW. **Map** 2 F5 & 3 B4.
Tel 426-6841.
Ⓜ Smithsonian. 🚌 13, 52.
🕘 9am–4:45pm daily.
Ⓒ Dec 25.
♿ 🛈 *Interpretive talks.*
www.nps.gov/wamo

Viewing window

The Marble Capstone
The capstone weighs 3,300 pounds (2,000 kg) and is topped by an aluminum pyramid. Restoration of the monument was carried out in 1934 as part of President Roosevelt's Public Works Project (see p23).

Elevator taking visitors to top

The Original Design
Although the original design included a circular colonnade around the monument, lack of funds prohibited its construction.

The two-tone stonework indicates the point at which construction stopped in 1858 and then began again in 1876.

Commemorative stones inside the monument are donations from individuals, societies, states, and nations.

50 flagpoles surrounding monument

Restoration
Specially designed scaffolding encased the monument during its two year program of repair and cleaning.

View of the Monument
The gleaming white stone of the newly restored monument makes it clearly visible from almost all over the city. The views from the top of the monument across Washington are stunning.

The colonnaded domed Jefferson Memorial, housing the bronze statue

United States Holocaust Memorial Museum ⑬

See pp80–81.

Bureau of Engraving and Printing ⑭

14th and C St, SW. **Map** 3 B5. *Tel 874-3019 or 2330.* M *Smithsonian.* 📷 *10am–1:45pm Mon–Fri (May–Aug: 5– 6:40pm additional tours).* ⬤ *Sat & Sun, week after Christmas, federal hols.* 🅱📷 *www.moneyfactory.com*

Until 1863, individual banks were responsible for printing American money. A shortage of coins and the need to finance the Civil War led to the production of standardized bank notes, and the Bureau of Engraving and Printing was founded. Initially housed in the basement of the Treasury Building *(see p112),* the bureau was moved to its present location in 1914. It prints over $140 billion a year, as well as stamps, federal documents, and White House invitations. Coins are not minted here, but in a federal facility in Philadelphia.

The 40-minute tour includes a short film, and a walk through the building to view the printing processes and checks for defects. Also on display are bills that are out of circulation, counterfeit money, and a special $100,000 bill. The Visitor Center has a gift shop, videos, and exhibits.

Jefferson Memorial ⑮

South bank of the Tidal Basin. **Map** 3 B5. *Tel 426-6841.* M *Smithsonian.* 🕐 *8am–midnight.* ⬤ *Dec 25.* **Interpretive talks.** 🅱 📷 *www.nps.gov/thje*

Thomas Jefferson *(see p166)* was a political philosopher, architect, musician, book collector, scientist, inventor and the third American president, from 1801 to 1809. He also played a significant part in drafting the Declaration of Independence in 1776.

The idea for the memorial came from President Franklin Delano Roosevelt, who felt that Jefferson was as important as Lincoln. Designed by John Russell Pope, this Neo-Classical memorial was dedicated in 1943 and covers an area of 2.5 acres. At the time, metal

Statue of Jefferson

was being strictly rationed so the standing statue of Jefferson had to be cast in plaster. After World War II, the statue was recast in bronze and the plaster version was moved.

Etched on the walls of the memorial are Jefferson's words from the Declaration of Independence as well as other writings. The impressive bronze statue of Jefferson is 19 ft (6 m) high and weighs 10,000 lb.

Tidal Basin ⑯

Boathouse: 1501 Maine Ave, SW. **Map** 2 F5 & 3 A5. M *Smithsonian.* **Paddle-boats:** *Tel 479-2426.* 🕐 *Mar–Oct: 10am–6pm.* 🅱

The Tidal Basin was built in 1897 to catch the overflow from the Potomac River and prevent flooding. In 1912, hundreds of cherry trees, given by the Japanese government, were planted along the shores of the man-made lake. However, during the two weeks when the cherry trees bloom (between mid-March and mid-April) chaos reigns around the Tidal Basin. The area is filled with cars and busloads of people photographing the sight. The only way to avoid this gridlock is to see the blossoms at dawn. The Tidal Basin reverts to a relatively quiet park after the blossoms have fallen and the hordes depart. Paddle-boats can be rented from the boathouse on Maine Ave.

The banks of the Tidal Basin, with Jefferson Memorial in the distance

United States Holocaust Memorial Museum ⑬

The US Holocaust Memorial Museum, opened in 1993, bears witness to the systematic persecution and murder in Europe of six million Jews and others deemed undesirable by the Third Reich, including homosexuals and the disabled. The exhibition space ranges from the intentionally claustrophobic to the soaringly majestic. The museum contains 2,500 photographs, 1,000 artifacts, 53 video monitors, and 30 interactive stations that contain graphic and emotionally disturbing images of violence, forcing visitors to confront the horror of the Holocaust. While Daniel's Story is suitable for children of eight years and up, the Permanent Exhibition is recommended for children over 12.

★ Hall of Remembrance
The Hall of Remembrance houses an eternal flame that pays homage to the victims of the Holocaust.

Second Floor

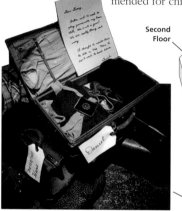

★ Daniel's Story
This exhibit, aimed at children between the ages of eight and 12, tells the history of the Holocaust from the point of view of an eight-year-old Jewish boy in 1930s Germany.

First Floor

KEY TO FLOOR PLAN

- ☐ Concourse Level
- ☐ First Floor
- ☐ Second Floor
- ☐ Third Floor
- ☐ Fourth Floor

GALLERY GUIDE

The Holocaust Museum is meant to be experienced, not just seen. Starting from the top, footage, artifacts, photographs, and testimonies of survivors can be seen from the fourth to the second floors. The first floor has an interactive display, and the Concourse Level houses the Children's Tile Wall.

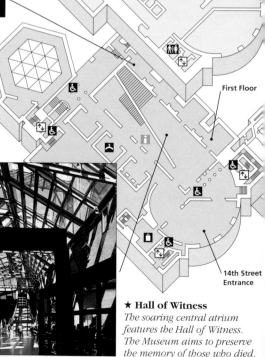

14th Street Entrance

★ Hall of Witness
The soaring central atrium features the Hall of Witness. The Museum aims to preserve the memory of those who died.

The Nazi Assault
On April 1, 1933 the boycott announced by the National Socialist party began. This placard at the Jewish Tietz store in Berlin reads, "Germans, defend yourselves! Do not buy from Jews."

VISITORS' CHECKLIST

100 Raoul Wallenberg Place, SW.
Map 3 B4. **Tel** 488-0400.
M Smithsonian. 13 (Pentagon shuttle). Mid-Jun–Mar: 10am–5:30pm daily; Apr–mid-Jun: 10am–8pm Tue & Thu. Dec 25 & Yom Kippur. Time pass required for Permanent Exhibit: Same-day from Pass Desk; advance passes: Tickets.com (800) 400-9373.
www.ushmm.org

Fourth Floor
Documenting the early years of the Nazi regime, these exhibits expose the ruthless and methodical persecution of the Jews.

Third Floor
The third floor permanent exhibits are devoted to the "Final Solution," the killing of 11 million "undesirable" people. Artifacts include a boxcar used to carry prisoners to the concentration camps.

Children's Tile Wall
Children painted over 3,000 tiles on this memorial to commemorate the lives of the one-and-a-half million children murdered in the Holocaust.

Concourse Level

STAR EXHIBITS

★ Daniel's Story

★ Hall of Remembrance

★ Hall of Witness

The National WWII Memorial looking west towards the Lincoln Memorial

National WWII Memorial 🔟

17th St, NW, between Constitution Ave & Independence Ave. **Map** 2 E5. **Tel** 426-6841. Ⓜ Smithsonian or Federal Triangle. ◗ 8am–midnight daily. ◖ Dec 25. ◪ on request. ⚫ **www**.nps.gov/nwwm
The online Registry of Remembrances: **www**.wwiimemorial.com

Sixteen million Americans served in World War II and of them 400,000 died. The 4,000 gold stars, the "Field of Stars," on the Freedom Wall commemorate these war dead, and in front of the wall is the inscription: "Here We Mark the Price of Freedom." Millions more ordinary citizens contributed in some way to the war effort. The National World War II Memorial on the National Mall honors their service and sacrifice.

The establishment of the memorial, however, was not without controversy as to both location and scale. After a bill was first introduced in 1987 it took a further six years before the legislation made its way through Congress. President Clinton signed the bill into law on May 25, 1993 and then there followed a great debate over where it should be located. The Rainbow Pool site was chosen in October 1995 with the condition that the east-west vista from the Washington Monument to the Lincoln Memorial be preserved. Further delays followed because the Commission of Fine Arts criticized the mass and scale of the initial plans and asked that further consideration be given to preserving the vista. Work finally began in September 2001.

Design and construction was awarded to the firm of

Ceremonial entrance shield

Leo A. Daly, and the design architect was Friedrich St. Florian (former dean of Rhode Island School of Design). Two 43-ft (13-m) pavilions stand on either side of the Rainbow Pool, marking the north and south entrances, and represent the Atlantic and Pacific theaters of war. Fifty-six granite pillars, one for each of the country's states and territories, are adorned with bronze wreaths of oak and wheat, which symbolize the nation's agricultural and industrial strength. Bas-relief panels created by sculptor Ray Kaskey line both sides of the 17th St entrance. They depict the many contributions Americans made to the war effort: from enlistment and embarkation to the Normandy landings, from Rosie the Riveter to medics in the field.

Words spoken by presidents and generals are inscribed throughout the memorial, including these by General Douglas MacArthur marking the war's end: "Today the guns are silent...The skies no longer rain death – the seas bear only commerce – men everywhere walk upright in the sunlight. The entire world is quietly at peace."

The memorial was officially opened to the public in April 2004 and on May 29 some 150,000 people, many of them veterans, joined in the dedication ceremony.

The Freedom Wall lined with 4,000 stars commemorating the US war dead

Vietnam Veterans Memorial ⓲

21st St & Constitution Ave, NW. **Map**
2 E4. **Tel** 426-6841. Ⓜ Smithsonian.
◯ 8am– midnight daily. 📷 on
request. ♿ www.nps.gov/vive

Maya Lin, a 21-year-old
student at Yale University,
submitted a design for the
proposed Vietnam Veterans
Memorial as part of her architecture course. One of 1,421
entries, Maya Lin's design was
simple – two triangular black
walls sinking into the earth at
an angle of 125 degrees, one
end pointing to the Lincoln
Memorial, the other to the
Washington Monument. On
the walls would be inscribed
the names of the Americans
who died in the Vietnam
war, in chronological order,
from the first casualty
in 1959 to the last
in 1975.

Lin received only
a B grade on the
course, but she
won the com-
petition. Her
design, called by
some a scar on
the earth, has
become
one of the most
moving monuments
on the Mall. Veterans and their
families leave tokens of remembrance – soft toys, poems,

pictures, and flowers – at the
site of the fallen soldier's name.
To mollify those opposed
to the abstract memorial, a
statue of three soldiers,
sculpted by Frederick Hart,
was added in 1984. Further
lobbying led to the Vietnam
Women's Memorial, erected
close by in 1993.

Korean War Veterans Memorial ⓳

21st St & Independence Ave, SW.
Map 2 E5. **Tel** 426-6841. Ⓜ
Smithsonian. ◯ 8am–midnight daily.
📷 on request. ♿
www.nps.gov/kwvm

The Korean War Veterans
Memorial is a
controversial tribute to
a controversial war.
Although 1.5 million
Americans served in
the conflict, war was
never officially
declared. It is often
known as "The
Forgotten War."
Intense debate
preceded the
selection of the
memorial's
design. On July 27,
1995, the 42nd
anniversary of the armistice
that ended the war, the
memorial was dedicated.

**The Vietnam Women's
Memorial**

Touching names on the wall at
the Vietnam Veterans Memorial

Nineteen larger-than-life
stainless steel statues, a squad
on patrol, are depicted moving
towards the American flag as
their symbolic objective. The
soldiers are wearing ponchos
because the Korean War was
notorious for being fought in
miserable weather conditions.
On the south side is a
polished black granite wall
etched with the images of
more than 2,400 veterans. An
inscription above the Pool of
Remembrance reads: "Our
nation honors her sons and
daughters who answered the
call to defend a country they
never knew and a people they
never met."

The poignant statues of the Korean War Veterans Memorial

Franklin D. Roosevelt Memorial 🔟

Franklin Roosevelt once told Supreme Court Justice
Felix Frankfurter, "If they are to put up any memorial
to me, I should like it to be placed in the center of
that green plot in front of the Archives Building. I
should like it to consist of a block about the size
of this," pointing to his desk. It took more than 50
years for a fitting monument to be erected, but
Roosevelt's request for modesty was not heeded.
Opened in 1997, this memorial is a mammoth park
of four granite open-air rooms, one for each of
Roosevelt's terms, with statuary and waterfalls. The
president, a polio victim, is portrayed in a chair,
with his dog Fala by his side.

The statue of Roosevelt,
*by Neil Estern, is one of the
memorial's most controversial
elements as it shows the disabled
president sitting in a wheelchair
hidden by his Navy cape.*

Third
room

The fourth room honors
Roosevelt's life and legacy.
A statue of his wife, Eleanor,
stands in this room.

A relief of Roosevelt's funeral cortège
*was carved into the granite wall by artist
Leonard Baskin. It depicts the coffin on a
horse-drawn cart, followed by the crowds of
mourners walking behind.*

Dramatic waterfalls *cascade
into a series of pools in the fourth
room. The water reflects the peace
that Roosevelt was so keen to
achieve before his death.*

**Hunger, a sculpture of
figures in the breadline,**
*by George Segal, recalls
the hard times of the Great
Depression, during which
Roosevelt was elected and
reelected three times.*

The first room commemorates
FDR's first term and
includes a bas-relief of his
inaugural parade.

**Second
room**

The Visitor Center
includes an information
area and a bookstore.
The leg braces that FDR
wore after he had polio
are also on display.

President Roosevelt
*initiated the New Deal in the 1930s to create jobs
and provide immediate relief during the Great
Depression: "...treating the task as we would treat
the emergency of war."*

Lincoln
Memorial ㉑

Many proposals were made
for a memorial to President
Abraham Lincoln. One of the
least promising was for a
monument on a swampy piece
of land to the west of the
Washington Monument. Yet
this was to become one of the
most awe-inspiring sights in
Washington. Looming over
the Reflecting Pool is the
seated figure of Lincoln in his
Neoclassical "temple," which
has 36 Doric columns, one for
each state at the time of
Lincoln's death.

Before the monument could
be built in 1914, the site had
to be drained. Solid concrete
piers were poured for the
foundation so that the building
could be anchored in bedrock.
Architect Henry Bacon
realized that the original 10-ft
(3-m) statue by Daniel Chester
French would be dwarfed
inside the building, so it was
doubled in size. As a result, it
had to be carved from 28
blocks of white marble.

Engraved on the south wall is
Lincoln's Gettysburg Address
(see p163). Above it is a mural
painted by Jules Guerin
depicting the angel of truth
freeing a slave. This was the
site of Dr. Martin Luther King,
Jr.'s famous address, "I Have a
Dream *(see p97)."*

**Lincoln Memorial, reflected in the
still waters of the pool**

OLD DOWNTOWN

Bordered by the Capitol to the east and the White House to the west, Washington's Downtown was the heart of the city one hundred years ago. F Street, the city's first paved road, bustled with shops, newspaper offices, bars, and churches, as well as horses and carriages. Downtown was also an important residential neighborhood. The upper classes maintained elegant homes, while middle-class merchants lived above their shops. But by the 1950s suburbia had lured people away from the area, and in the 1980s Downtown had become a mixture of boarded-up buildings and discount shops. However, the 1990s saw a dramatic change in the area and the beginnings of regeneration, as the MCI Center attracted new restaurants and stores.

Sculpture outside the National Museum of American Art

SIGHTS AT A GLANCE

Museums and Galleries
Carnegie Library Building **14**
International Spy Museum **19**
National Building Museum **22**
Smithsonian American Art Museum and National Portrait Gallery pp98–101 **18**
National Museum of Women in the Arts **13**

Statues and Fountains
Benjamin Franklin Statue **8**
Mellon Fountain **1**

Aquarium
National Aquarium **10**

Historic and Official Buildings
FBI Building **5**
Ford's Theatre **15**
Martin Luther King Memorial Library **16**
MCI Center **20**
National Archives **2**
National Theater **12**
Old Post Office **7**
Ronald Reagan Building **6**
Willard Hotel **11**

Districts, Streets, and Squares
Chinatown **17**
Freedom Plaza **9**
Pennsylvania Avenue **4**

Memorials
National Law Enforcement Officers' Memorial **21**
US Navy Memorial **3**

0 meters   500
0 yards   500

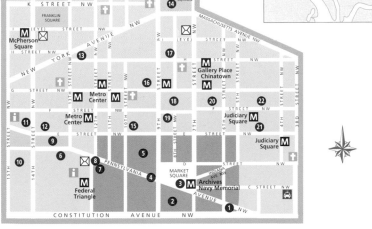

GETTING THERE
Old Downtown is well served by several Metrorail stops: McPherson Square, Gallery Place-Chinatown, Metro Center, Judiciary Square, Archives-Navy Memorial, and Federal Triangle. The 32, 34, and 36 bus lines run along Pennsylvania Avenue.

KEY

▨ Street-by-street map *pp88–9*	🏛 Police station
M Metro station	⊠ Post office
ℹ Tourist information	✚ Church

◁ **Statue of Benjamin Franklin outside the flag-festooned Old Post Office**

Street-by-Street: Old Downtown

In the mid-20th century, Pennsylvania Avenue, the main route for presidential inaugural parades, was tawdry and run down. It is now a grand boulevard worthy of L'Enfant's original vision. The FBI Building, a concrete structure built in a challenging, modern style, is one of its most prominent features. Opposite the nearby US Navy Memorial is the US National Archives, housing original copies of the Constitution and the Declaration of Independence. To the east are the Mellon Fountain and the National Gallery of Art. The Ronald Reagan Building was the site of the 1999 NATO summit, and the Old Post Office has been wonderfully restored.

★ FBI Building
The headquarters of the Federal Bureau of Investigation was built in the austere Brutalist style between 1967 and 1972 to resemble a "central core of files" **5**

Pennsylvania Avenue
Part of L'Enfant's original plan for the city, Pennsylvania Avenue was the first main street to be laid out in Washington. It joins the US Capitol to the White House **4**

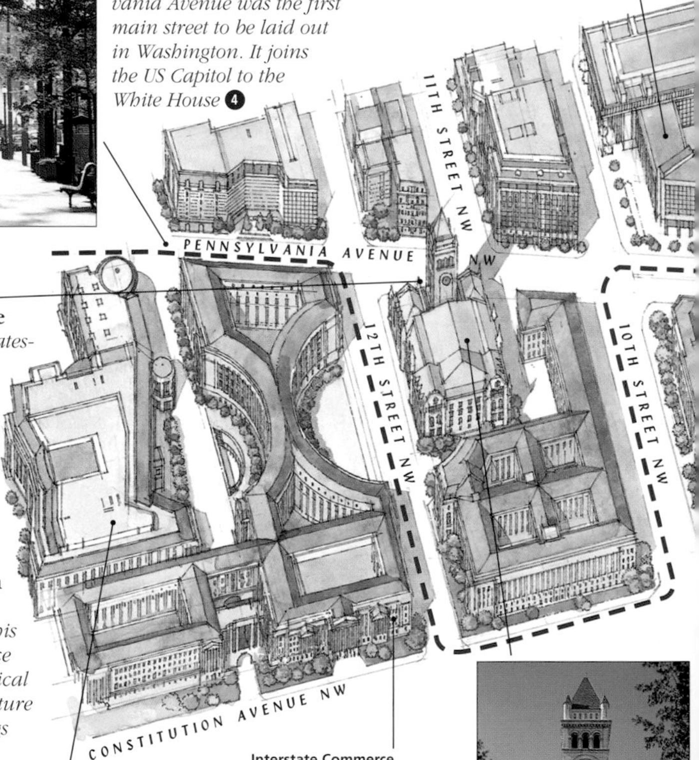

Benjamin Franklin Statue
This inventor, statesman, writer, publisher, and man of genius is remembered as "printer, philosopher, philanthpoist, patriot" **8**

Ronald Reagan Building
Built in 1997, this impressive edifice echoes the Classical Revival architecture of other buildings in the Federal Triangle **6**

11TH STREET NW

PENNSYLVANIA AVENUE

12TH STREET NW

10TH STREET NW

CONSTITUTION AVENUE NW

Interstate Commerce Commission

★ Old Post Office
This majestic granite building was completed in 1899. It now houses shops and a food court. The elegant clock tower measures 315 ft (96 m) in height **7**

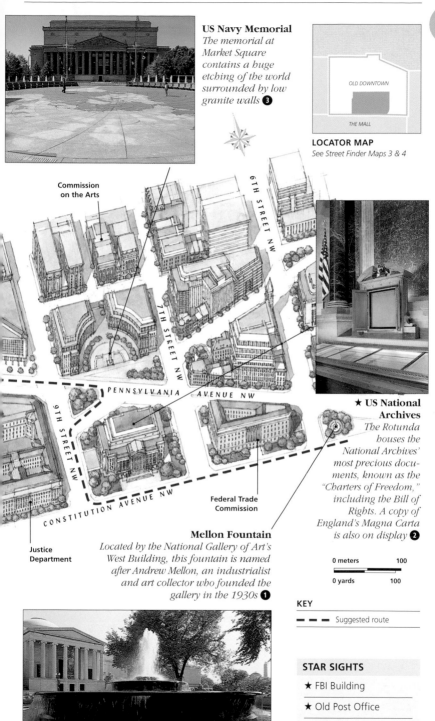

US Navy Memorial
The memorial at Market Square contains a huge etching of the world surrounded by low granite walls ❸

LOCATOR MAP
See Street Finder Maps 3 & 4

OLD DOWNTOWN

THE MALL

Commission
on the Arts

6TH STREET NW

7TH STREET NW

PENNSYLVANIA AVENUE NW

9TH STREET NW

CONSTITUTION AVENUE NW

★ US National Archives
The Rotunda houses the National Archives' most precious documents, known as the "Charters of Freedom," including the Bill of Rights. A copy of England's Magna Carta is also on display ❷

Federal Trade Commission

Justice Department

Mellon Fountain
Located by the National Gallery of Art's West Building, this fountain is named after Andrew Mellon, an industrialist and art collector who founded the gallery in the 1930s ❶

| 0 meters | 100 |
| 0 yards | 100 |

KEY

– – – Suggested route

STAR SIGHTS

★ FBI Building

★ Old Post Office

★ US National Archives

The cascading water of the Classical-style Mellon Fountain

Mellon Fountain ❶

Constitution Ave & Pennsylvania Ave, NW. **Map** 4 D4. M *Archives-Navy Memorial.*

Situated opposite the National Gallery of Art *(see pp58–61),* this fountain commemorates the man who endowed the gallery with its collection. Andrew Mellon was Secretary of the Treasury and a financier and industrialist. At his death, his friends donated $300,000 to build the fountain, which was dedicated on May 9, 1952.

The three bronze basins with their cascades of water were inspired by a fountain

seen in a public square in Genoa, Italy. On the bottom of the largest basin, the signs of the Zodiac are engraved in bas-relief. The Classical lines of the fountain echo the architectural style of the National Gallery of Art West Building.

National Archives ❷

Constitution Ave, between 7th St & 9th St, NW. **Map** 3 D3. *Tel* 501-5000. M *Archives-Navy Memorial.* ◯ *Apr 1–Labor Day: 10am–9pm daily; Sep–Mar: 10am–5:30pm daily.* ● *Sun, Dec 25.* 🅿 🎫 ♿ **www.**nara.gov

In the 1930s, Congress recognized the need to preserve the country's paper records before they deteriorated, were lost or were destroyed. The National Archives building, created for this purpose, was designed by John Russell Pope, architect of the National Gallery of Art and the Jefferson Memorial; it opened in 1934. This impressive library houses the most important historical and legal documents in the United States.

The National Archives' Building Rotunda has reopened to the public after major improvements. For the

first time, on display are all four pages of the *Constitution of the United States*, as well as the *Declaration of Independence*, the *Bill of Rights*, and a 1297 copy of the *Magna Carta*, which is on indefinite loan from Ross Perot.

Also in the National Archives are millions of documents, photographs, motion picture film, and sound recordings going back over two centuries. There is enough material, in fact, to fill around 250,000 filing cabinets. The National Archives and Records Administration (NARA) is the body responsible for cataloging, managing, and conserving all this material. Much of the Archives' information is now stored on computer. A permanent exhibition, "Public Vaults," offers people an opportunity to explore a representative sample of the Archives' vast collection.

Statue outside the US National Archives

The National Archives is of great importance as a research center. The Central Research Room is reserved for scholars, who can order copies of rare documents for study purposes. Copies of military records, immigration papers, slave transit documents, death certificates, and tax information are also available.

The impressive Neoclassical façade of the National Archives Building

The Constitution of the United States

In 1787, delegates from the 13 original American states convened in the city of Philadelphia to redraft the Articles of Confederation *(see p18).* It soon became clear that an entirely new document was required, rather than a revised one. Weeks of debate grew into months, as delegates drafted the framework for a new country. Cooperation and compromise finally led to the creation of the Constitution, a document that outlines the powers of the central

Original flag of the 13 US states

government and the makeup of Congress. One of the main issues, how to elect the representatives, was finally determined to be by direct voting by the people. Once signed, the new Constitution was sent to the states for review. Federalists and anti-Federalists debated fervently over its content in pamphlets, speeches, and articles. In the end, the majority of states ratified the Constitution, giving up some of their power in "order to form a more perfect union."

The Preamble of the Constitution of the United States

Signatures on the US Constitution

SIGNING OF THE CONSTITUTION
After many months of debate by the delegates to the Federal Convention, the Constitution was completed and signed by 39 of the 55 state delegates on September 17, 1787, at Assembly Hall in Philadelphia. The oldest delegate was 81-year-old Benjamin Franklin. James Madison, another signatory, played a major role in achieving the ratification of the new Constitution during the two years after it was signed.

James Madison

THE CONSTITUTION TODAY
The seven articles of the Constitution (of which the first three lay out the principles of government; *see pp28–9*) still determine the laws of the United States today. In addition there are Amendments. The first ten form the Bill of Rights, which includes such famous issues as the right to bear arms and the freedom of religion and of speech.

Swearing Allegiance
The pledge of allegiance to the flag was written in 1892 to mark the 400th anniversary of Columbus's discovery of America. Today it is recited daily by schoolchildren and by immigrants taking up American citizenship.

Public Demonstration
Citizens demonstrate their right to free speech by protesting against the Persian Gulf War.

A view down tree-lined Pennsylvania Avenue toward the US Capitol

US Navy Memorial ❸

Market Square, Pennsylvania Ave between 7th St & 9th St, NW. **Map** 3 C3. Ⓜ *Archives-Navy Memorial.* ♿ **Naval Heritage Center** 701 Pennsylvania Ave, NW. *Tel* 737-2300. ◯ *9:30am–5pm Mon–Sat.* ◯ *Sun; Nov 1–Mar 1: Mon.* 🖥 www.lonesailor.org

The memorial to the US Navy in Market Square centers on the statue of a single sailor. Sculpted in bronze by Stanley Bleifeld in 1990, the figure provides a poignant tribute to the men and women who have served in the US Navy.

The sculpture stands on a vast map of the world – the outlines of the countries are laid into the ground and protected by low walls. Four waterfalls and a group of flagpoles complete the memorial.

There are free summer concerts by military bands in the square. Behind the memorial is the **Naval Heritage Center**, with historical exhibits and portraits of famous naval personnel, including John F. Kennedy. A free film "At Sea," is shown daily at noon.

The lone sailor of the US Navy Memorial

Pennsylvania Avenue ❹

Pennsylvania Ave. **Map** 3 A2 to 4 D4. Ⓜ *Federal Triangle, Archives-Navy Memorial.*

When Pierre L'Enfant drew up his plans in 1789 for the capital city of the new United States, he imagined a grand boulevard running through the center of the city, from the presidential palace to the legislative building.

For the first 200 years of its history, Pennsylvania Avenue fell sadly short of L'Enfant's dreams. In the early 19th century it was simply a muddy footpath through the woods. Paved in 1833, it became part of a neighborhood of boarding houses, shops, and hotels.

During the Civil War, the area deteriorated quickly into "saloons, gambling dens, lodging houses, quick-lunch rooms, cheap-jack shops, and catch penny amusement places" according to the *Works Progress Administration Guide to Washington*. When President John F. Kennedy's inaugural parade processed down Pennsylvania Avenue in 1961, Kennedy took one look at "America's Main Street" with its shambles of peep shows, pawn shops, and liquor stores and said, "It's a disgrace – fix it." This command by Kennedy provided the impetus to reevaluate the future of Pennsylvania Avenue.

Almost 15 years later, Congress established the Pennsylvania Avenue Development Corporation – a public and private partnership that developed a comprehensive plan of revitalization. Today, Pennsylvania Avenue is a

PRESIDENTIAL INAUGURAL PARADES

The tradition of inaugural parades to mark the occasion of a new president's coming-to-office started in 1809 when the military accompanied President James Madison from his Virginia home to Washington, DC. Military bands have been a part of the inaugural parades ever since, and the Army Band traditionally leads the procession down Pennsylvania Avenue from the US Capitol to the White House. The first parade to include floats was held in 1841 for President William Henry Harrison. In 1985, the freezing January weather forced Ronald Reagan's inaugural ceremony indoors to the Capitol Rotunda.

President Franklin D. Roosevelt's third inaugural parade in 1941

The authoritative exterior of the FBI Building on Pennsylvania Avenue

clean, tree-lined street. Parks, memorials, shops, theaters, hotels, museums, and assorted government buildings border the street on either side, providing a suitably grand and formal setting for all future presidential inaugural parades.

FBI Building **❺**

935 Pennsylvania Ave, NW. **Map** 3 C3. **Tel** 324-3447. Ⓜ Archives-Navy Memorial, Gallery Place. ⬤ 9am – 4:15pm Mon–Fri. ♿ 🏠 **www**.fbi.gov

The headquarters of the Federal Bureau of Investigation was started in 1964 and dedicated in 1975. The official name of the building is the J. Edgar Hoover FBI Building, in honor of the Bureau's long-time head.

Established in 1908 with the motto Fidelity, Bravery, and Integrity, the FBI has jurisdiction over federal crime. The Bureau, as it is commonly known, made its name in the 1920s and 1930s when it enforced Prohibition – the federal law that made the sale of alcohol a criminal offense.

The tour of the FBI building is one of the most popular in Washington, made even more so by the success of the cult TV show *The X Files*, starring two fictional FBI agents. Once inside, visitors are led through the exhibits by a tour guide. Criminal artifacts on display include pipe bombs, assault rifles, and handguns, some of which were owned by famous criminals such as Pretty Boy Floyd and John Dillinger. Visitors learn about the history

of the FBI and the "Ten Most Wanted" list of fugitives. The future of crime detection is highlighted with a look at DNA analysis and advanced fingerprinting techniques. The tour ends with a display of FBI firearms, though these are rarely used on duty.

Sculpture from the Oscar Straus Memorial Fountain

Ronald Reagan Building **❻**

1300 Pennsylvania Ave, NW. **Map** 3 B3. **Tel** 312-1300. Ⓜ Federal Triangle. ⬤ 7am –7am Mon–Fri, 11am–6pm Sat, Mar 31–Aug 31: 12–6pm Sun. ⬤ Federal hols. 🎟 call 312-1470. 🍴 🏠 ♿ **www**.itcdc.com and **www**.dcvisit.com

The Ronald Reagan Building is a modern 3.1 million sq ft limestone structure that is Classical in appearance on the

outside and modern on the inside, and the huge complex is only slightly smaller than Vatican City in Rome. Completed in 1997, it was the most expensive federal building project ever undertaken. Designed by Pei Cobb Freed & Partners, architects of the US Holocaust Memorial Museum (*see pp80–81*) and the National Gallery of Art's East Wing, the building houses a mix of federal, trade, and public spaces.

On the east end of the atrium is the largest neon sculpture in North America – "Route Zenith" is a creation of Keith Sonnier. Outside the building is the Oscar Straus Memorial Fountain, with sculpture by Adolph Alexander Weinman.

In summer the four-acre Woodrow Wilson Plaza, graced by sculptures by such artists as Martin Puryear and Stephen Rodin, is the venue for free concerts from noon to 1:30pm every weekday.

The building is the home of the Washington DC Visitor Information Center due to its location in the heart of the capital. The Center provides tour information and tickets to shows and events, and is open 8am to 6pm, Monday through Saturday.

Mock-Classical entrance to the immense Ronald Reagan Building

Food court in the spectacular galleried hall of the Old Post Office

Postmaster general, writer, and scientist, Benjamin Franklin was also a key member of the committee that drafted the 1776 Declaration of Independence. As a diplomat to the court of Louis XVI of France, he went to Versailles in 1777 to gain support for the American cause of independence from Britain. Franklin returned to France in 1783 to negotiate the Treaty of Paris that ended the American Revolution (see p18).

Stately figure of Benjamin Franklin

Old Post Office ❼

1100 Pennsylvania Ave, NW. **Map** 3 C3.
Tel 289-4224. Ⓜ Federal Triangle.
Ⓒ Mar–Aug: 10am–9pm Mon–Sat;
Sep–Feb: 10am–7pm Mon–Sat,
noon–6pm Sun all year. Ⓒ Jan 1,
Thanksgiving, Dec 25. 🎫 tower only
(call 606-8691). ♿ ▯ ☐ ⚑
www.oldpostofficedc.com

Built in 1899, the Old Post Office was Washington's first skyscraper. Soaring 12 stories above the city, it was a fireproof model of modern engineering with a steel frame covered in granite. The huge interior had 3,900 electric lights and its own generator, the first one to be used in the city. Its fanciful Romanesque architecture was fashionable at the time it was built, and the breathtaking hall, with its glass roof and balconies, remains a spectacular mixture of light, color, and gleaming metal.

In the 15 years following its construction, the Post Office became an object of controversy. Its turrets and arches, once praised by critics, were derided. The *New York Times* newspaper said the building looked like "a cross between a cathedral and a cotton mill." Government planners thought the Post Office building clashed with the Neoclassical architecture that dominated the rest of Washington. When the postal system moved its offices in 1934, there seemed

to be no reason to keep the architectural relic. Only a lack of funds during the Great Depression of the 1930s (see p23) prevented the Old Post Office from being torn down.

The building was occupied intermittently by various government agencies until the mid-1960s, when its decrepit condition again drew a chorus in favor of demolition. A Washington preservation group, Don't Tear It Down, promoted the historical significance of the Old Post Office, and it was spared once more.

The renovated building, commonly known as the Pavilion, is now home to a broad range of shops and restaurants. The Post Office tower has an observation deck rising 270 ft (82 m) above the city, giving one of the best views of Washington.

Benjamin Franklin Statue ❽

Pennsylvania Ave & 10th St, NW.
Map 3 C3. Ⓜ Federal Triangle.

Donated by publisher Stilson Hutchins (1839–1912), it was unveiled by Benjamin Franklin's great-granddaughter in 1889. The words "Printer, Philosopher, Patriot, Philanthropist" are inscribed on the four sides of the statue's pedestal in tribute to this man of diverse talents.

Freedom Plaza ❾

Pennsylvania Ave between 13th St & 14th St, NW. **Map** 3 B3. Ⓜ Federal Triangle, Metro Center.

Freedom Plaza was conceived as part of a Pennsylvania Avenue redevelopment plan in the mid-1970s. Designed by Robert Venturi and Denise Scott Brown, and completed in 1980, the plaza displays Pierre L'Enfant's original plan for Washington in black and white stone embedded in the ground. Around the edge are engraved quotations about the new city from Walt Whitman and President Wilson, among others.

Freedom Plaza provides a dramatic entry to Pennsylvania Avenue (see pp92–3). On the

The large-scale reproduction of L'Enfant's city plans, Freedom Plaza

north side of the plaza, where Pennsylvania Avenue leads into E Street, are the **Warner Theatre** and the **National Theatre**. South of the plaza is the Beaux Arts **District Building** (housing government employees). Throughout the year, Freedom Plaza hosts festivals and open-air concerts.

National Aquarium

Commerce Building, 14th St & Constitution Ave, NW. **Map** 3 B3. **Tel** 482-2825. Ⓜ *Federal Triangle.* ⭘ *9am–5pm daily.* ⬤ *Thanksgiving, Dec 25.* **www**.nationalaquarium.com

Originally located in 1873 at Woods Hole, Massachusetts (a major center for marine biology), the National Aquarium was moved to Washington in 1888 in order to make it more accessible. Since 1931 it has been located in the US Department of Commerce Building, and today the aquarium is home to around 1,200 specimens and 200 different species.

Green Turtle at the National Aquarium

The Aquarium has a wide range of freshwater and saltwater fish on display, such as nurse sharks, piranhas, and moray eels, and also a number of reptiles and various species of amphibians, all displayed in simulated "natural environments."

There is a touch tank that allows visitors to handle some of the creatures.

Willard Hotel ⓫

1401 Pennsylvania Ave, NW. **Map** 3 B3. **Tel** 628-9100, (800) 327-0200. Ⓜ *Metro Center.* **www**.washington.interconti.com

There has been a hotel on this site since 1816. Originally called Tennison's, the hotel was housed in six adjacent two-story buildings. Refurbished in 1847, it was managed by hotel keeper Henry Willard, who gave his name to the hotel in 1850. Many famous people stayed here during the Civil War (1861–65), including the writer Nathaniel Hawthorne, who was covering the conflict for a magazine, and Julia Ward Howe who wrote the popular Civil War standard *The Battle Hymn of the Republic*. The word "lobbyist" is said to have been coined because it was known by those seeking favors that President Ulysses S. Grant went to the hotel's lobby to smoke his after-dinner cigar.

The present 340-room building, designed by the architect of New York's Plaza Hotel, Henry Hardenbergh, was completed in 1904. It was the most fashionable place to stay in the city until the end of World War II, when the surrounding neighborhood fell into decline. For 20 years it was boarded up and faced demolition. A coalition, formed of preservationists and the Pennsylvania Avenue Development Corporation, worked to restore the Beaux Arts building, and it finally reopened in renewed splendor in 1986.

No other hotel can rival the Willard's grand lobby, with its 35 different kinds of marble, polished wood, and petal-shaped concierge station. There is a style café, a bar, and a restaurant called The Willard Room.

Peacock Alley, one of the Willard Hotel's luxuriously decorated corridors

Façade of the National Theatre on E Street

National Theatre ⓬

1321 Pennsylvania Ave, NW. **Map** 3 B3. **Tel** 628-6161, 800-447-7400. Ⓜ *Metro Center, Federal Triangle.* **www**.nationaltheatre.org

The present National Theatre is the sixth theater to occupy this Pennsylvania Avenue site and the oldest cultural institution in the city. The first four theaters burned down, and the fifth one was replaced by the current building in 1922. Extensively renovated in 1984, it hosts Broadway-bound productions and touring groups, including such major shows as "Les Miserables." The National is known as an "actor's theater" because of its excellent acoustics (even a whisper on stage can be heard in the top balcony). It is haunted by the ghost of 19th-century actor John McCullough, murdered by a fellow actor and buried in the cellar under the stage.

National Museum of Women in the Arts ⑬

1250 New York Ave, NW. **Map** 3 C3.
Tel 783-5000, 800-222-7270. Ⓜ
Metro Center. ◯ *10am–5pm*
Mon–Sat, noon–5pm Sun. ◉
Thanksgiving, Dec 25, Jan 1.
🎟 *for groups (call 783-7996).* ♿
♿ 🖥 📷 **www**.nmwa.org

This museum of women's art houses works that span five centuries, from the Renaissance to the present day. The collection was started in the 1960s by Wilhelmina Holladay and her husband, who gathered paintings, sculpture, and photography from all over the world.

The museum operated out of the Holladays' private residence for several years, until it acquired a more permanent home in this Renaissance Revival landmark building, formerly a Masonic Temple. The collection has as its highlights masterpieces by female American artists. Some of the outstanding works on display from the 19th century include *The Bath* (1891) by Mary Cassatt and *The Cage* (1885) by Berthe Morisot. Among the works by 20th-century artists are *Bacchus 3* (1978) by Elaine de Kooning and *Self-Portrait Between the Curtains, Dedication to Trotsky* (1937) by Mexican artist Frida Kahlo. The museum shop sells a range of gifts, also created by women.

Carnegie Library Building ⑭

801 K St (Mount Vernon Sq) NW. **Map**
3 C2. *Tel 383-1800.* Ⓜ *Gallery*
Place–Chinatown, Mt Vernon Sq.
◯ *by appointment, depending on*
the event ♿ 🖥 📷
www.citymuseumdc.org.

The Carnegie Library Building was once Washington's central library. It hosts various events and exhibitions, and in 2003 the Washington Historical Society moved its headquarters to the building and the City Museum of Washington, DC was created. However, the museum is temporarily closed while

Impressive exterior of the National Museum of Women in the Arts

it undergoes extensive reorganization. The state-of-the-art Research Library and Reading Room house extensive collections of historic materials, including rare publications, prints, maps, photographs, manuscripts, and memorabilia. There are also lectures, workshops, and videos. Washington Perspectives, an overview exhibit, features a giant map of the city set into the floor.

Painting of John Wilkes Booth poised to shoot Abraham Lincoln

Ford's Theatre ⑮

511 10th St between E St & F St, NW.
Map 3 C3. *Tel 426-6924.* Ⓜ
Gallery Place-Chinatown, Metro
Center. ◯ *9am–5pm daily (except*
matinee or rehearsal days - call
ahead). ♿ ◉ *Dec 25.* **Petersen**
House ◯ *9am–5pm daily.* ◉ *Dec*
25. 📷 **www**.nps.gov/foth

John T. Ford, a theatrical producer, built this small jewel of a theater in 1863. Washington was a Civil War boomtown, and the theater, located in the thriving business district, enjoyed great popularity.

The fate of the theater was sealed, however, on April 14, 1865, when President Abraham Lincoln was shot here by John Wilkes Booth while watching a performance. Across the road from the theater, **Petersen House**, where the wounded president died the next morning, has been preserved as a museum.

After the tragedy, people stopped patronizing the theater, and Ford was forced to sell the building to the federal government a year later. It was left to spiral into decay for nearly a century until the government decided to restore it to its original splendor.

Maintained by the National Park Service, the theater now stages small productions. The Presidential Box is permanently decorated in Lincoln's honor.

Exterior of Ford's Theatre, site of the shooting of President Lincoln

Martin Luther King Memorial Library ⑯

901 G St at 9th St, NW. **Map** 3 C3.
Tel 727-1111. Ⓜ *Gallery Place–
Chinatown, Metro Center.* ◯
9:30am–9pm Mon–Thu, 9:30am–
5:30pm Fri & Sat. ◑ *Federal hols.*
♿ www.dclibrary.org/mlk

Washington's Martin Luther King Memorial Library is the only example of the architecture of Ludwig Mies van der Rohe in the city. A prominent figure in 20th-century design, van der Rohe finalized his plans for the library shortly before his death in 1969. It was named in honor of Dr. Martin Luther King Jr. at the request of the library's trustees when it opened in 1972, replacing the small and out-dated Carnegie Library as the city's central public library.

Architecturally, the building is a classic example of van der Rohe's theory of "less is more." It is an austere, simple box shape with a recessed entrance lobby. Inside, there is a mural depicting the life of Dr. Martin Luther King Jr., the leader of the Civil Rights Movement, painted by artist Don Miller.

The library sponsors concerts and readings, as well as a program of children's events.

The "Friendship Archway" spanning H Street in the heart of Chinatown

Chinatown ⑰

6th St to 8th St & G St to H St, NW.
Map 3 C3 & 4 D3. Ⓜ *Gallery Place-
Chinatown.*

The small area in Washington known as Chinatown covers just six square blocks. Formed around 1930, it has never been very large and today houses about 500 Chinese residents. The area has been reinvigorated by the arrival of the adjacent MCI Center *(see p102)* in 1997. Although rents are up, and a few well-established restaurants have been forced to close, the increased number of visitors has brought new prosperity. H Street is particularly lively, with many shops and a selection of good restaurants.

The "Friendship Archway," a dramatic gateway over H Street at the junction with 7th Street, marks the center of the Chinatown area. Built in 1986, it was paid for by Washington's sister city, Beijing, as a token of esteem, and is based on the architecture of the Qing Dynasty (1649–1911). Its seven roofs, topped by 300 painted dragons, are balanced on a steel and concrete base, making it the largest single-span Chinese arch in the world. It is lit up at night.

DR. MARTIN LUTHER KING, JR.

A charismatic speaker and proponent of Mahatma Gandhi's theories of non-violence, Dr. Martin Luther King, Jr. was a black Baptist minister and leader of the the civil rights movement in the United States.

Born in Atlanta, Georgia in 1929, King's career in civil rights began with the 1955 Montgomery, Alabama bus boycott – a protest of the city's segregated transit system. The movement escalated to protests at schools, restaurants, and hotels that did not admit blacks. King's methods of non-violence were often met with police dogs and brutal tactics.

The culmination of the movement was the March on Washington on August 28, 1963, when 200,000 people gathered at the Lincoln Memorial in support of civil rights. The highlight of this event was King's "I Have a Dream" speech, calling for support of the movement. A direct result was the passing by Congress of the civil rights legislation in 1964, and King was awarded the Nobel Peace Prize the same year. In 1968 he was assassinated in Memphis, Tennessee, triggering riots in 100 American cities, including Washington.

Dr. King speaking at the Lincoln Memorial

Smithsonian American Art Museum and National Portrait Gallery ⑱

Nowhere in Washington is the city's penchant to copy Greek and Roman architecture more obvious than in the former US Patent Office Building, now the home of the Smithsonian American Art Museum and the National Portrait Gallery. The wonderfully ornate Patent Office building (designed in 1836) was converted into the twin museums in 1968. The Classical space now provides a complementary backdrop to these collections. The National Portrait Gallery is America's family album, featuring paintings, photographs, and sculptures of thousands of famous Americans. The American Art Museum contains a wealth of works by American artists.

Façade of the former US Patent Office, now home to the galleries

★ ACHELOUS AND HERCULES

This painting (1947) by Thomas Hart Benton (1889–1975) is a mythological analogy of early American life. Interpreted in many ways, it is widely accepted that Hercules is man taming the wild, then enjoying the results of his labors.

Hercules tries to capture the bull.

Achelous, the river god, appears as a bull being wrestled by Hercules, representing the struggle of the American people.

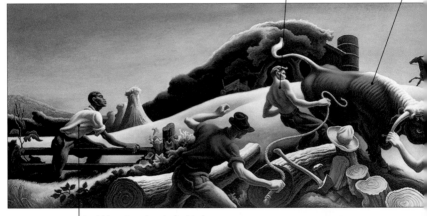

An African-American is depicted climbing over a fence to the idealized equality of America.

★ Cliffs of the Upper Colorado River

This dramatic work, created in 1882, captures the vastness of the American West. It is just one of several landscapes in the museum by artist Thomas Moran.

Old Bear, a Medicine Man
This vibrant painting by George Caitlin dates from 1832. Native Americans were a popular choice of subject matter for this artist.

Mary Cassatt
This portrait by Edgar Degas, painted c.1882, depicts his fellow artist Mary Cassatt playing cards.

"Casey" Stengel
This bronze sculpture of the baseball great was created by Rhoda Sherbell in 1981 from a 1965 cast.

John Singleton Copley
This self-portrait of the artist, who was largely known for his depictions of others, was painted c.1780.

VISITORS' CHECKLIST

☐ An extensive renovation program has just been completed, so call the museum for opening times.

Smithsonian American Art Museum: 8th St & G St, NW. *Tel* 633-1000. **Map** 3 C3.
Ⓜ *Gallery Place-Chinatown.*
www.americanart.si.edu

National Portrait Gallery: 8th St & F St, NW. *Tel* 357-2700.
Ⓜ *Gallery Place-Chinatown.*
www.npg.si.edu

The man working in the field represents the people of America, enjoying the fruits of the land after laboring.

Hercules is about to break off the bull's horn.

The horn is transformed into a cornucopia, or horn of plenty, symbolizing America as a land of abundance and opportunity.

★ Technology
In a cabinet that is both Gothic and futuristic, this "altar" of the moving image contains 25 video monitors and three laser disc players. The artist is Nam June Paik.

In the Garden
This charming depiction of the poet Celia Thaxter is by the artist Childe Hassam and was painted in 1892.

STAR SIGHTS

★ Achelous and Hercules

★ Technology

★ Cliffs of the Upper Colorado River

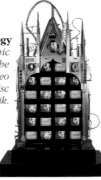

Exploring the Smithsonian American Art Museum

The Smithsonian American Art Museum was established in 1829 and is the first federal art collection. The museum began with gifts from private collections and art organizations that existed in Washington, DC before the founding of the Smithsonian in 1846. The American Art Museum has become a center for America's cultural heritage, and has a collection of more than 40,000 artworks spanning 300 years. The building has been recently renovated.

A bottlecap giraffe

AMERICAN FOLK ART

The collection of American folk art includes some truly amazing pieces of work, created from a wide range of materials. James Hampton's *Throne of the Third Heaven of the Nations' Millennium General Assembly* (c. 1950–1964) is one of the star pieces in the collection. Hampton, a janitor in Washington, created this wonderful piece of visionary art in his garage. His media were gold and tin foil, old furniture, and light bulbs. Over the course of many years he fashioned a throne, pulpits, crowns, and other devotional objects, all of which are included in this unusual yet beautiful work.

19TH- AND EARLY 20TH-CENTURY ART

Some of the highlights in this collection from the last two centuries are the Thomas Moran Western landscapes. Moran's paintings are monumental; he was one of the few artists who captured the scale of the Grand Canyon and the Colorado River. Especially moving is *Cliffs of the Upper Colorado River, Wyoming Territory* (1882).

Many of the American artists such as Albert Pinkham Ryder, Winslow Homer, and John Singer Sargent, were contemporaries to the Impressionist artists. Homer's *High Cliffs, Coast of Maine* (1894) is a dramatic meeting of land and sea. Seascapes were also a popular subject for Ryder. *Jonah*, painted c.1885, illustrates the Bible story of Jonah and the whale, depicting Jonah floundering in the sea during a storm, overlooked by God. Frederick Remington's *Fired On*, an impressive oil painting, is another highlight. The artist was best known as a sculptor, rather than a painter, of cowboys and horses.

The museum holds hundreds of paintings of Native Americans, many of them works by anthropologist George Caitlin. This was also a popular subject for Charles Bird King and John Mix Stanley.

American Impressionists are also well represented in the gallery, including Mary Cassatt, William Merritt Chase, John Henry Twachtman, and Childe Hassam. Hassam's paintings, inspired by the French Impressionists, are refreshing yet tranquil. The calm seascape of *The South Ledges, Appledore* (1913) is typical of his style.

Robert Rauschenberg's *Reservoir* (1961), mixed media on canvas

AMERICAN MODERNISTS

The enormous canvases of the Modernists provide a dramatic contrast to the landscapes and portraits of the 19th and 20th centuries. Franz Kline's black slashes on a white canvas in *Merce C* (1961), which was inspired by his involvement with dancer Merce Cunningham, are the antithesis of the delicacy of the Impressionists. Kenneth Noland's geometrical compositions resemble firing targets. Other Modernists here include Robert Rauschenberg, Jasper Johns, Andy Warhol, Hans Hofman, and David Hockney.

THE GREAT HALL

The third floor Great Hall is a crazy quilt of tiles and ceiling medallions. A frieze showing the evolution of technology in America also runs around the room. Once a display area for new inventions, it is a reminder of the building's past as the Patent Office.

Throne of the Third Heaven of the Nations' Millennium General Assembly

Exploring the National Portrait Gallery

The American nation has set aside a place to keep generations of remarkable Americans in the company of their fellow citizens – the National Portrait Gallery. Its mission is to collect and display images of "men and women who have made significant contributions to the history, development and culture of the people of the United States." Through the visual and performing arts the lives of leaders such as George Washington and Martin Luther King Jr., artists such as George Gershwin and Mary Cassatt, and activists such as Rosa Parks and Sequoyah are celebrated.

Ronald Reagan, painted in oils
by Henry C. Casselli, Jr. in 1989

OVERVIEW OF THE COLLECTION

The National Portrait Gallery illuminates America's family album, magnificently combining history, biography, and art in its collections. The portraits are fascinating not only because they reveal their subjects but also because they illustrate the times in which they were produced. There are 18,600 images in the permanent collection – which includes portraits, photographs, sculptures, etchings, and drawings – and both heroes and villains are represented. Portraits taken from life sittings are favored by the gallery.

Portrait of Pocahontas
by an unidentified artist

Cagney. There are also bronze busts of the poet T.S. Eliot and the humorist Will Rogers. Religious leaders, business magnates, pioneers in women's rights and civil rights (such as Dr. Martin Luther King Jr.), explorers, and scientists are portrayed in a whole range of media, including oils, clay, and bronze. There are also many photographic portraits, including some recent acquired pictures of Marilyn Monroe, which were taken during a morale-boosting visit the actress made to soldiers during the Korean War.

THE HALL OF PRESIDENTS

The chronologically ordered portrayal of all of the country's leaders remains the heart of the National Portrait Gallery's collections. In 1857, Congress commissioned

George Peter Alexander Healy to paint portraits of the presidents. The likenesses were to be installed in the White House as an artistic chronicle of its occupants. A large number of paintings remain in the White House. The portraits of George and Martha Washington are featured prominently in the Portrait Gallery.

The most famous painting is Gilbert Stuart's "Landsdowne" portrait of George Washington, painted from life in 1796. The likeness is the basis for the image of the President on the one-dollar bill. Abraham Lincoln posed for photographer Alexander Gardener several months before he was assassinated *(see p96)*. He looks careworn and weary. President Clinton's image is represented in a sculptured bust and a photograph. A painter has been selected and a portrait is in the process of being painted.

NOTABLE AMERICANS

The National Portrait Gallery's collection is not limited to the political history of the country. There is also a large collection of portraits of American people, notable for their achievements in the arts, sports, or in the country's religious or cultural history. Athletes honored include the famous baseball player Babe Ruth and baseball manager Casey Stengel. Among figures from the world of entertainment are portraits of actresses Judy Garland, Tallulah Bankhead, and Mary Pickford. John Wayne also features among the Hollywood stars, as does Buster Keaton, Clark Gable, and James

Diana Ross and The Supremes, photographed by Bruce Davidson in 1965

The unique and innovative International Spy Museum

International Spy Museum ⑲

800 F St, NW. **Map** 3 C3. **Tel** 393-7798, EYE-SPY-U. Ⓜ *Gallery Place-Chinatown, National Archives-Navy Memorial.* ◯ *Apr–Oct: 10am–8pm; Nov–Mar: 10am–6pm.* 🦽 📷 📷 *group tours by reservation.* **www**.spymuseum.org

The Spy Museum is the first museum in the world devoted to international espionage. Its huge collection includes the German Enigma cipher machine from World War II, a Soviet shoe transmitter, a wristwatch camera, and a lipstick pistol, displayed in a variety of themed exhibits.

A visit to the museum begins with a film on the real life of a spy, revealing what motivates people to enter this clandestine world. The "Trick of the Trade" exhibit displays over 200 artifacts used by spies to disguise and protect themselves during operations. "The Secret History of Histories" traces the art of spying from

World War II cipher machine, essential for breaking enemy codes

biblical times to the early 20th century. "Spies Among Us" examines the making and breaking of codes during World War II, and highlights famous spies such as Marlene Dietrich, John Ford, and Josephine Baker. Other permanent exhibits explore espionage from the Cold War to the present day, featuring spy planes, listening and tracking devices, and the lives of spies, such as Aldrich Ames and Robert Hanssen.

MCI Center ⑳

601 F St, NW. **Map** 4 D3. **Tel** 628-3200. Ⓜ *Gallery Place-Chinatown.* **Modell's Sports Store** ◯ *10am–5:30pm daily (later on event days).* 🎫 *for National Sports Gallery.* 🦽 🍴 📷 **www**.mcicenter.com

Opened in 1997, the MCI Center is a sports and entertainment complex that houses many shops and restaurants.

The 20,000-seat MCI stadium is the brainchild of Abe Pollin, owner of Washington's basketball teams, The Wizards (men's team) and The Mystics (women's), as well as the hockey team, The Capitals. The complex has been very successful, and its presence has revived the surrounding area beyond recognition. Half of the arena's seats are below ground level, in a vast but harmonious structure. It hosts rock concerts as well as sports events and exhibitions.

OLD DOWNTOWN RENAISSANCE

During the 1990s, Washington's Old Downtown was transformed from a derelict historic area to prime real estate. The construction of the MCI Center and renewed appreciation for the restoration of dilapidated Victorian buildings helped to accelerate this process. As a result of losing its shabby image, Old Downtown also lost many of the artists who carved studios out of the high-ceilinged, low-rent spaces, but their influence can still be seen in the large number of art galleries and exhibitions in the area. Some of the non-profit organizations and small businesses that leased offices in the big, aging buildings were forced to relocate due to an increase in rent. Soaring prices also closed a number of traditional Chinese restaurants around the MCI Center, which have been replaced by upscale eateries. Today Old Downtown is a safer area for those on foot, with a buzzing selection of nightly activities available, including sports events, theater shows, concerts, and lively restaurants.

A contemporary office building linking two Victorian façades on 7th Street

IN VALOR
THERE IS HOPE

Majestic lion statue alongside a marble wall at the police memorial

National Law Enforcement Officers Memorial ㉑

E St, NW, between 4th St & 5th St, NW. **Map** 4 D3. **Tel** 737-3400 or 737-3213. Ⓜ Judiciary Square. **Visitor Center** 605 E St, NW. ◯ 8:30am–5:30pm Mon–Fri, 10am–5pm Sat, noon–5pm Sun. ◯ Thanksgiving, Dec 25, Jan 1. ⬛ ⬛ ⬛ **www**.nleomf.com

Dedicated by President George Bush in 1991, the National Law Enforcement Officers Memorial honors the 15,000 police officers who have been killed since the founding of the United States. Spread over three acres in the center of Judiciary Square, the memorial's flower-lined pathways are spectacular in springtime. The names of the fallen officers are inscribed on marble walls. Each path is guarded by a statue of an adult lion shielding its cubs, symbolic of the US police force's protective role.

National Building Museum ㉒

401 F St at 4th St, NW. **Map** 4 D3. **Tel** 272-2448. Ⓜ Judiciary Square, Gallery Place-Chinatown. ◯ 10am–5pm Mon–Sat, 11am–5pm Sun. ◯ Jan 1, Thanksgiving, Dec 25. ⬛ ⬛ ⬛ ⬛ **www**.nbm.org

It is fitting that the National Building Museum, dedicated to the building trade, should be housed in the architecturally audacious former Pension Bureau building. Civil War

General, Montgomery C. Meigs, saw Michelangelo's Palazzo Farnese on a trip to Rome and decided to duplicate it as a Washington office building, albeit twice as big and in red brick as opposed to the stone masonry of the Rome original.

Completed in 1887, the building is topped by a dramatic terracotta frieze measuring 3 ft (1 m) in height. The daring exterior of the building is matched by its flamboyant interior. The vast concourse, measuring 316 ft by 116 ft (96 m by 35 m), is lined with balconies containing exhibitions. The roof is supported by huge columns, constructed of brick, plastered, and fauxpainted to give the appearance of marble. The Great Hall has been the impressive venue for many presidential balls.

In 1926 the Pension Bureau relocated to different offices, and there was a move to demolish Miegs' building.

Ornamental plinth in the grounds of the museum

Instead it was occupied by various government agencies for a time and was even used as a courthouse for a while.

The building was eventually restored, and in 1985 opened in renewed splendor as the National Building Museum. A privately owned collection, the museum has a display on the architectural history of the city – "Washington: Symbol and City." It includes an excellent illustration of Pierre L'Enfant's original plans for the capital, as well as other photographs, models, and interactive exhibits demonstrating how the city grew and changed. The temporary exhibits in the museum often highlight controversial issues in the field of design and architecture, and facets of the building trade. There is a small café in the courtyard, and a gift shop. Free tours offer access to the restricted areas of the building. Donations are requested.

The splendid, colonnaded Great Hall in the National Building Museum

THE WHITE HOUSE AND FOGGY BOTTOM

The official residence of the President, the White House is one of the most distinguished buildings in DC and was first inhabited in 1800. Although burned by the British during the War of 1812, most of today's building remains as it was planned. Other buildings surrounding the White House are worth a visit, such as the Daughters of the American Revolution building and the Corcoran Gallery. East of the White House is the Foggy Bottom area, which was built on swampland. Notable edifices here include the Kennedy Center, the State Department building, and the notorious Watergate Complex, focus of the 1970s Nixon scandal.

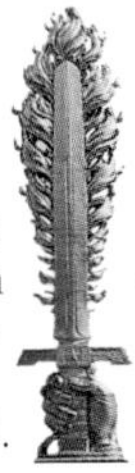

Second Division Memorial

SIGHTS AT A GLANCE

Galleries
Corcoran Gallery of Art 7
Renwick Gallery 5

Squares
Lafayette Square 3
Washington Circle 17

Historic Buildings
Daughters of the American Revolution 9
Eisenhower Old Executive Office Building 6
George Washington University 15
Hay-Adams Hotel 4
Octagon 8
Watergate Complex 18

Official Buildings
Department of the Interior 11
Federal Reserve Building 12
National Academy of Sciences 13
Organization of the American States 10
State Department 14
Treasury Building 2
The White House pp108–11 1

Performing Arts Center
Kennedy Center pp118–19 19

Church
St. Mary's Episcopal Church 16

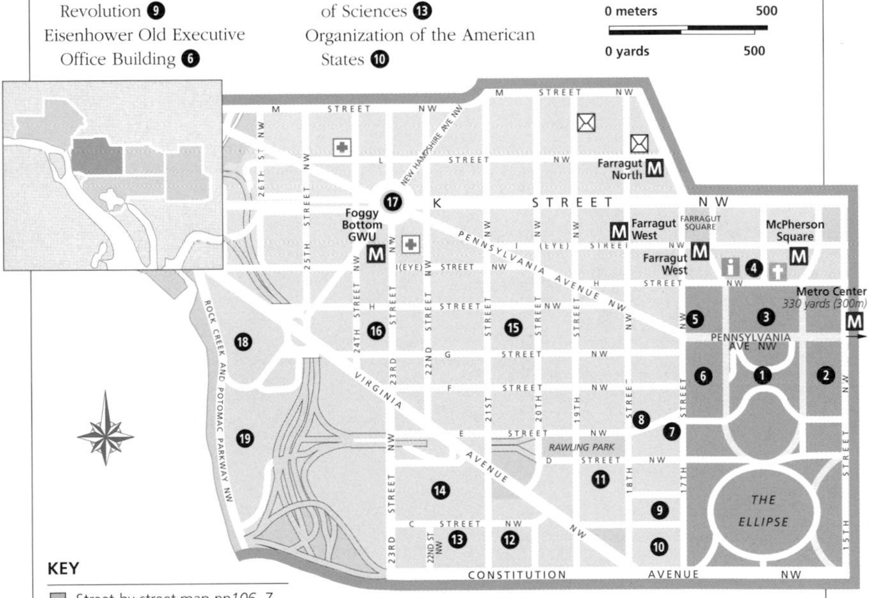

KEY
- Street-by-street map *pp106–7*
- Metro station
- Tourist information
- Hospital emergency room
- Post office
- Church

GETTING THERE

The closest Metrorail stations to the White House and Foggy Bottom area are Metro Center, McPherson Square, Farragut West and Foggy Bottom-GWU station. Also, Metrobuses 32, 34, and 36 travel east to west and will take you to most of the major sights within the area.

◁ The First Division Monument in front of Eisenhower Old Executive Office Building

Street-by-Street: Around The White House

The area surrounding the White House is filled with grand architecture and political history, and the vistas from the Ellipse lawn are breathtaking. It is worth spending a day exploring the area and visiting some of its buildings (by appointment only), such as the Treasury Building with its statue of Alexander Hamilton (the first Secretary of the Treasury) and the Eisenhower Old Executive Office Building. The buildings of the Daughters of the American Revolution and the OAS both offer the visitor an insight into the pride the nation takes in its past.

Eisenhower Old Executive Office Building
Although it was poorly received on its completion in 1888, this attractive building now houses staff of the Executive branch **6**

Renwick Gallery of the Smithsonian American Art Museum
The inscription above the entrance of this 19th-century building reads "Dedicated to Art." **5**

Octagon
At one time James Madison's home, this building has had a varied history functioning as a hospital and a school, among other things **8**

★ Corcoran Gallery of Art
A treasure trove of fine art, the Corcoran Gallery counts works by Rembrandt, Monet, Picasso, and de Kooning among its many exhibits **7**

0 meters 100
0 yards 100

DAR Building
This beautiful Neoclassical building is one of three founded by the historical organization, the Daughters of the American Revolution **9**

KEY

– – – Suggested route

OAS Building
The central statue of Queen Isabella of Spain stands in front of this Spanish Colonial-style mansion. Built in 1910, it houses the Organization of American States **10**

Hay-Adams Hotel
Formed by the joining of two town houses, this luxurious hotel has been the scene of political activity since it opened in the 1920s ❹

LOCATOR MAP
See Street Finder map 3

Lafayette Square
Named after the Marquis de Lafayette, a Revolutionary War hero, this leafy square has at its center this statue of Andrew Jackson, the seventh president, sculpted by Clark Mills ❸

★ Treasury Building
Widely regarded as the most impressive Neoclassical structure in the city, this building took over 60 years to complete ❷

★ The White House
One of the most famous sights in Washington, DC, this has been the President's official residence since the 1800s ❶

STAR SIGHTS

★ Corcoran Gallery of Art

★ Treasury Building

★ The White House

The White House ❶

In 1790 George Washington chose this site as the location for the new President's House. Irish-born architect James Hoban was selected to design the building, known as the Executive Mansion. In 1800, President and Mrs. John Adams became the first occupants, even though the building was not yet completed. Burned by the British in 1814, the partially rebuilt edifice was occupied again in 1817, by James Monroe. In 1901, President Theodore Roosevelt changed the name of the building to the White House and in 1902 ordered the West Wing to be built. The East Wing was added in 1942 on the instruction of President Franklin D. Roosevelt, completing the building as it is today.

The White House
The official residence of the US president for 200 years, the White House façade is familiar to millions of people around the world.

★ State Dining Room
Able to seat as many as 140 people, the State Dining Room was enlarged in 1902. A portrait of President Abraham Lincoln, by George P.A. Healy, hangs above the mantel.

The West Terrace leads to the West Wing and the Oval Office, the President's official office.

The stonework has been painted over and over to maintain the building's white façade.

STAR ROOMS

★ Red Room
─────────────────
★ State Dining Room
─────────────────
★ Vermeil Room

★ Red Room
One of four reception rooms, the Red Room is furnished in red in the Empire Style (1810–30). The fabrics were woven in the US from French designs.

Lincoln Bedroom
President Lincoln used this room as his Cabinet Room, then turned it into a bedroom, furnishing it wib Lincoln-era decor. Today it is used as a guest room.

VISITORS' CHECKLIST

1600 Pennsylvania Ave, NW.
Map 3 B3. ⬜ *Tue–Sat: 10am–11am only for groups with congressional or embassy appointments. Contact Visitor Center for information.* ⬛ *federal hols and official functions* ◨ *obligatory.* **www**.nps.gov
White House Visitor Center
1450 Pennsylvania Ave, NW.
Tel *208 1631.* Ⓜ *Federal Triangle.* ⬜ *daily 7:30am–4pm.* ⬛ *Jan 1, Thanksgiving, Dec 25.*
🔲 🔲 🔲 **www**.nps.gov/whho

The East Terrace leads to the East Wing.

The East Room is used for large gatherings, such as dances and concerts.

Treaty Room

The Green Room was first used as a guest room before Thomas Jefferson turned it into a dining room.

★ **The Vermeil Room**
This yellow room houses seven paintings of first ladies, including this portrait of Eleanor Roosevelt by Douglas Chandor.

Blue Room

Diplomatic Reception
This room is used to welcome friends and ambassadors. It is elegantly furnished in the Federal Period style (1790–1820).

WHITE HOUSE ARCHITECTS

After selecting the site, George Washington held a design competition to find an architect to build the residence where the US president would live. In 1792 James Hoban, an Irish-born architect, was chosen for the task. It is from Hoban's original drawings that the White House was initially built and all subsequent changes grew. In 1902 President Teddy Roosevelt hired the New York architectural firm of McKim, Mead, and White to check the structural condition of the building and refurbish areas as necessary. The White House underwent further renovations and refurbishments during the administrations of Truman and Kennedy.

James Hoban, architect of the White House

Exploring the White House

The White House rooms are beautifully decorated in period styles and are filled with valuable antique furniture, china, and silverware. Hanging on its walls are some of America's most treasured paintings, including portraits of past presidents and first ladies. Until fairly recently, more than a million and a half visitors each year would wander through the home of the President on the free tour. This is now suspended.

THE LIBRARY

Originally used as a laundry area, this room was turned into a "gentleman's ante-room" at the request of President Theodore Roosevelt in 1902. In 1935 it was re-modeled into a library. Furnished in the style of the late Federal period (1800–1820) the library was redecorated in 1962, and then again in 1976. Today, its soft gray and rose-colored tones make it a perfect room for informal gatherings, such as afternoon teas.

Portraits of four native-American chiefs, painted by Charles Bird King, are displayed in the library. The chandelier was crafted in the early 1800s and was originally owned by the family of James Fenimore Cooper, author of *The Last of the Mohicans.*

THE VERMEIL ROOM

Often called the Gold Room, the Vermeil Room was redecorated in 1991. It is named after the collection of vermeil, or gilded silver, that is on display in the cabinets. On show are 18th-, 19th-, and

20th-century tableware crafted by English Regency silver-smith Paul Storr (1771–1836) and French Empire silver-smith Jean-Baptist Claude Odiot (1763–1850). The collection was bequeathed to the White House in 1956.

Seven portraits of first ladies hang on the walls: Elizabeth Shoumatoff's painting of Claudia (Lady Bird) Johnson, Aaron Shikler's portraits of Nancy Reagan and of Jackie Kennedy in her New York apartment, and an unusual portrait of Eleanor Roosevelt, caught in various moods, by Douglas Chador. Also on display are portraits of Ellen Wilson, Patricia Ryan Nixon and Lou Henry Hoover.

THE CHINA ROOM

Used by Mrs. Woodrow Wilson in 1917 to display the White House China, this room was redecorated in 1970. Today it is used as a reception room. The rich red color scheme is suggested by the stunning portrait of Mrs. Calvin Coolidge, painted in 1924 by Howard Chandler Christy. The Indo-Isfahan rug dates from the early 20th century.

The red and cream color scheme of the China Room

THE BLUE ROOM

President James Monroe chose the French Empire-style decor for this magnificent, oval-shaped room in 1817. The Classically inspired furniture and accompanying motifs, such as urns, acanthus leaves, and imperial eagles, typify the style. The settee and seven chairs were created by Parisian cabinetmaker, Pierre-Antoine Bellangé.

A portrait of Thomas Jefferson by Rembrandt Peale, dating from 1800, hangs in this elegant room, along with a portrait of President John Adams, painted in 1793 by artist John Trumball. The Blue Room has always been used as a reception room, except for a brief period during the John Adams administration.

THE RED ROOM

This room was decorated in the Empire style by Jackie Kennedy in 1962 and was refurbished in 1971 and again in 2000. Much of the wooden furniture in the room, including the beautiful inlaid round table, was created by cabinetmaker Charles-Honoré Lannuier in his New York workshop. Above the mantel hangs a portrait of Angelica Singleton Van Buren, the daughter-in-law of President Martin Van Buren, which was painted by Henry Inman in 1842. The room was used as a parlor or sitting room; in recent times it has been used for small dinner parties.

THE STATE DINING ROOM

As a result of the growing nation and its international standing, the size of official dinners in the White House increased. Finally in 1902 the architects McKim, Mead, and White were called in to enlarge the State Dining Room. The plaster and paneling was modeled on the style of 18th-century Neoclassical English houses. The mahogany dining table was created in 1997. The pieces of French giltware on the table were bought by President Monroe in 1817.

The dining room was redecorated in 1998. The Queen Anne-style chairs date from 1902 and were reupholstered in 1998.

THE LINCOLN BEDROOM

Used today as the guest room for the friends and family of the President, the Lincoln Bedroom is decorated in the American Victorian style, dating from 1850–70. Used by Lincoln as an office and cabinet room, this room became the Lincoln Bedroom when President Truman decided to fill it with furniture from Lincoln's era. In the center is a 6 ft- (1.8 m-) wide rosewood bed with an 8 ft- (2.5 m-) high headboard. The portrait of General Andrew Jackson next to the bed is said to have been one of President Lincoln's favorites. A painting of Lincoln's wife, Mary Todd Lincoln, also hangs here.

THE TREATY ROOM

Beginning with Andrew Johnson's presidency in 1865, the Treaty Room served as the Cabinet Room for 10 presidential Administrations. The room contains many Victorian pieces bought by President Ulysses S. Grant, including the original table used by the Cabinet. The cut-glass chandelier that hangs here was made in Birmingham, England around 1850. The chandelier has 20 arms, each one fitted with a frosted-glass globe.

THE WHITE HOUSE VISITOR CENTER

The White House Visitor Center has interesting exhibits about the history of the White House and its décor, as well as royal gifts on display. There are also seasonal lectures by renowned speakers on aspects of history in and out of the White House. The Center has a monthly Living History program with actors portraying historic figures. The gift shop carries an extensive range, including the annual White House Christmas ornament. Tours of the presidential official residence in the White House, conducted by the National Park Service are extremely limited at this time. In fact, guided tours can only be booked by special arrangement through a member of Congress or an embassy.

Façade of the White House Visitor Center

THE EAST WING

The East Wing houses offices rather than ceremonial rooms and was built in 1942. The walls of the Lobby are adorned with portraits of presidents. Both the Garden Room and the East Colonnade, which fronts the East Terrace, look out onto the Jacqueline Kennedy Garden. The Terrace, which links the East Wing to the Residence, houses the White House Movie Theater.

THE WEST WING

In 1902, the West Wing, including the Oval Office, was built by the architectural firm McKim, Mead, and White for a total cost of $65,196. In

The interior of the Oval Office, located in the West Wing

this wing, the former Fish Room was renamed the Roosevelt Room by President Nixon, in honor of presidents Theodore and Franklin Roosevelt who created this wing. Their portraits still hang in the room today.

Also in the West Wing are the Cabinet Room, where government officials meet with the president, and the Oval Office, where the president meets with visiting heads of state. Many presidents have personalized this room in some way; President George W. Bush uses a desk given to President Rutherford B. Hayes by Queen Victoria in 1880.

Detail of *The Peacemakers* by George Healy, located in the Treaty Room

The colonnaded portico of the Neoclassical Treasury Building

Treasury Building ❷

15th St & Pennsylvania Ave, NW.
Map 3 B3. *Tel* 622-0896. Ⓜ
McPherson Square. 🞖 *Tours by appointment only.* 🞖
www.ustreas.gov

The site of this massive, four-story Greek Revival building, home to the Department of the Treasury, was chosen by President Andrew Jackson. The grand, sandstone-and-granite edifice was designed by architect Robert Mills, who also designed the Washington Monument *(see p78)*. A statue of Alexander Hamilton, the first Secretary of the Treasury, stands in front of the southern entrance to the building.

Now suspended, the official guided tour used to show visitors the restored historic rooms, including the 1864 burglar-proof vault, the Andrew Johnson suite (Johnson's temporary office after the assassination of President Lincoln in 1865), and the marble Cash Room.

Between 1863 and 1880, US currency was printed in the basement, and during the Civil War it was used as storage space for food and arms. Today, the building is home to the Department of the Treasury, which manages the government's finances and protects US financial systems.

Liberty Bell in front of the Treasury

Lafayette Square ❸

Map 2 F3 & 3 B3. Ⓜ *Farragut West, McPherson Square.*

Set behind the White House is Lafayette Square, named after the Marquis de Lafayette (1757–1834), a hero of the American Revolutionary War *(see p19)*. Due to its proximity to the White House, this public park is often the scene of peaceful demonstrations. It is home to 19th-century former mansions and the historic church of St. John's (the "Church of the Presidents"), built in 1816 by Benjamin Latrobe, who designed Decatur House, 748 Jackson Place, which was home to famous figures such as Henry Clay and Martin Van Buren,

Federal-style 19th-century houses overlooking tranquil Lafayette Square

and is open to the public. In the center of the Square is a huge statue of President Andrew Jackson (1767–1845) seated on a horse. Cast in bronze by Clark Mills, it was the first equestrian statue of its size to be built in the US and was dedicated in 1853.

At each of the square's four corners stand statues of men who took part in America's struggle for liberty. The southeast corner has the bronze figure of French compatriot Lafayette. In the southwest corner is a statue of another Frenchman, Jean-Baptiste Donatien de Vimeur, Comte de Rochambeau (1725–1807). This was a gift from France to the American people and accepted by Theodore Roosevelt in 1902. A statue of Polish general, Thaddeus Kosciuszko (1746–1817), who fought with the American colonists in the Revolutionary War, stands in the northeast corner. Baron von Steuben (1730–94), a German officer and George Washington's aide at the Battle of Valley Forge, is honored at the northwest end.

Hay-Adams Hotel ❹

1 Lafayette Square, NW. **Map** 2 F3 & 3 B3. *Tel* 638-6600, 1-800-424-5054. Ⓜ *Farragut North, Farragut West.* **www**.hayadams.com

Situated close to the White House, the historic Hay-Adams Hotel is an Italian Renaissance landmark in Washington. Its plush interior is adorned with European and Oriental antiques.

It was originally two adjacent houses, built by Henry Hobson Richardson in 1885, belonging to statesman and author John Hay and diplomat and historian Henry Adams. A popular hotel since its conversion in 1927 by developer Harry Wardman, the exclusive Hay-Adams remains one of Washington's top establishments *(see p175)*, well situated for all the major sights. Afternoon tea and drinks are available in the Lafayette Restaurant.

Renwick Gallery ❺

Pennsylvania Ave at 17th St, NW. **Map** 2 F3 & 3 A3. *Tel* 633-1000. Ⓜ *Farragut West.* ◯ 10am–5:30pm *daily.* ⬤ *Dec 25.* ⬛ ⬛ ⬛
www.americanart.si.edu

Forming part of the Smithsonian American Art Museum *(see pp98–101)*, this red-brick building was designed and constructed by James Renwick Jr. in 1858. It originally housed the art collection of William Wilson Corcoran until this was moved to the current Corcoran Gallery of Art in 1897.

After efforts by First lady Jacqueline Kennedy saved the building from destruction, it was bought by the Smithsonian. Refurbished and renamed, the Renwick Gallery opened in 1972. It is dedicated primarily to 20th-century American arts, crafts, and design, and houses some impressive exhibits in every medium including metal, clay, and glass. *Game Fish* (1988) by Larry Fuente is a stunning example of mixed media art.

Eisenhower Old Executive Office Building ❻

17th St at Pennsylvania Ave, NW. **Map** 2 F4 & 3 A3. *Tel* 395-5895. Ⓜ *Farragut West.* ⬛ *Sat by appt.* ⬛
www.whitehouse.gov/history/eeobtour

Formerly known simply as the Old Executive Office Building, this structure stands on the

Imposing façade of Eisenhower Old Executive Office Building

The magnificent Renwick Gallery, a fine example of French Empire style

West side of the White House. It was once the home of the War, Navy, and State Departments. Built between 1871 and 1888 by Alfred B. Mullett, its French Second Empire design, which was inspired by the 1852 expansion of the Louvre in Paris, generated much criticism at the time.

The building has long been the site of historic events, such as the meeting between Secretary of State Cordell Hull and the Japanese after the bombing of Pearl Harbor.

Lion statue guarding the Corcoran Gallery

Today the building houses government agencies, including the White House Office, the Office of the Vice President, and the National Security Council.

Corcoran Gallery of Art ❼

500 17th St, NW. **Map** 2 F4 & 3 A3. *Tel* 639-1700. Ⓜ *Farragut West, Farragut North.* ◯ 10am–5pm Mon–Wed, 10am–9pm Thu (except Thanksgiving). ⬤ *Tue, Dec 25, Jan 1.* ⬛ ⬛ ⬛ ⬛ ⬛ ⬛ ⬛
www.corcoran.org

One of the first fine art museums in the country, the Corcoran Gallery of Art opened in 1874. It outgrew its original home (what is now the Renwick Gallery building) and moved to this massive

edifice designed in 1897 by Ernest Flagg. A privately funded art collection, the Corcoran was founded by William Wilson Corcoran – a banker whose main interest was American art. Many of the European works in the collection were added in 1925 by art collector and US senator William A. Clark.

The Corcoran Gallery of Art is filled with works by European and American masters that span the centuries. These include 16th-century paintings by Titian, 17th-century works by Rembrandt, and 19th-century French Impressionist paintings by Monet and Renoir. The gallery also contains the largest collection of paintings by Jean-Baptiste Camille Corot outside France. There is a fine collection of modern and African American art, which includes sculpture, paintings, textiles, and photographs. Paintings from the 20th century include a selection by Picasso, Singer Sargent, and de Kooning.

Within the building is the only accredited art school in Washington. A gospel brunch takes place every Sunday in the beautiful atrium, with live music and singing. The Corcoran also has a shop selling an excellent selection of books, postcards, and other items.

Octagon ❽

1799 New York Ave, NW. **Map** 2 F4
& 3 A3. **Tel** 638-3221. Ⓜ Farragut
West and Farragut North.
🔵 10am–4pm Tue–Sun. 🔴 Mon,
Thanksgiving, Christmas, New Year's
Day. 🈺 ✓ ♿ (first floor only).
www.theoctagon.org

Actually hexagonal in shape,
the Octagon is a three-story
red-brick building, designed
in the late-Federal style by
Dr. William Thornton
(1759–1828), first architect of
the US Capitol. The Octagon
was completed in 1801 for
Colonel John Tayloe III, a rich
plantation owner from Richmond County, Virginia, and a
friend of George Washington.

When the White House was
burned in the War of 1812
against Britain *(see p19)*, President James Madison and his
wife, Dolley, lived here from
1814 to 1815. The Treaty of
Ghent that ended the war was
signed by Madison on the
second floor of the house on
February 17, 1815.

In the early 1900s, the building was taken over by the
American Institute of Architects,
which is now headquartered
in the large building behind
the Octagon. The American
Architectural Foundation,
established in 1970, set up a
museum of architecture in the
Octagon. Following renovation in 1996, the building has
been restored to its historically
accurate 1815 appearance, and
has some original furnishings
and fine architectural features,
such as a circular entrance hall.

**The circular main entrance to the
attractive Octagon building**

South portico of the DAR Memorial Continental Hall

Daughters of the American Revolution ❾

1776 D St, NW. **Map** 2 F4 & 3 A3.
Tel 879-3241. Ⓜ Farragut West.
🔵 9:30am–4pm Mon–Fri, 9am–5pm
Sat. 🔴 Sun, 2 weeks in April, Federal
hols. ✓ 10am–3pm Mon–Fri, 10am–
4pm Sat (book in advance for groups
of 5 or more). ♿ ⚐ **www**.dar.org

Founded in 1890 as a non-
profit organization, the
Daughters of the American
Revolution (DAR) is dedicated
to historic preservation and
promoting education and
patriotism. In order to become
a member, you must be a
woman with blood relations to
any person, male or female,
who fought in or aided the
Revolution. There are
currently over 170,000 members in 3,000 regional
branches throughout the USA
and in nine other countries.

The DAR museum is located
in the Memorial Continental
Hall, designed for the organi-
zation by Edward Pearce
Casey and completed in 1910.
The 13 columns in the south

portico symbolize the 13
original states of the Union.
Entrance to the museum is
through the gallery, which
displays an eclectic range of
pieces from quilts to glassware
and china.

The 33 period rooms that
form the State Rooms in the
museum house a collection
of over 50,000 items, from
silver to porcelain, ceramics,
stoneware, and furniture. Each
room is decorated in a unique
style particular to an American
state from different periods
during the 18th and 19th
centuries. An attic room filled
with 18th- and 19th-century
toys will delight children. Also,
there is a huge genealogical
library, consisting of approximately 125,000 publications.

**DAR Museum banners proclaiming
Preservation, Patriotism, Education**

Fountain in the courtyard of the OAS building

Organization of American States ❿

17th St & Constitution Ave, NW. **Map** 2 F4 & 3 A4. **Tel** 458-3000. ⭘ 9am– 5:00pm Mon–Fri. Sat–Sun, Federal hols. **Art Museum of the Americas** 201 18th St NW. ⭘ 10am–5pm Tue–Sun. ◉ Good Friday, Federal hols. Ⓜ Farragut West. ✍ call 458-3327. **www**.oas.org

Dating back to the First International Conference of the American States, held from October 1889 to April 1890 in Washington, the Organization of American States (OAS) is the oldest alliance of nations dedicated to reinforcing the peace and security of the continent, and maintaining democracy. The Charter of the OAS was signed in Bogotá, Colombia, in 1948 by the United States and 20 Latin American republics. Today there are 35 members. The building dates from 1910 and houses the Columbus Memorial Library and the **Art Museum of the Americas**, which exhibits 20th-century Latin American and Caribbean art.

Department of the Interior Building ⓫

1849 C St, between 18th St & 19th St, NW. **Map** 2 F4 & 3 A3. **Tel** 208-4743. Ⓜ Farragut West. ⭘ 8:30am–4:30pm Mon–Fri. ◉ Federal hols. ✍ call ahead. To enter the building you need a photo ID. ♿ **www**.doi.gov/museum

Designed by architect Waddy Butler Wood and built in 1935, this huge limestone building is the headquarters of the Department of the Interior. The building has a long central section, with six wings that extend off each side. In total it covers more than 16 acres of floor space, and has 2 miles (3 km) of corridors.

The Department of the Interior was originally formed of only the Departments of Agriculture, Labor, Education, and Energy, but it expanded to oversee all federally owned land across the United States. Visible inside, but only when taking the official guided tour, are 36 murals painted by Native American artists in the 1930s, including one of the singer Marian Anderson performing at the Lincoln Memorial in 1939 *(see pp84–5)*.

The small **Department of the Interior Museum**, located on the first floor, opened in 1938. The displays include an overview of the Department's history, dioramas of American wildlife and important historical events as well as paintings by 19th-century surveyors, and crafts by Native Americans. There is a visitor shop selling a selection of gifts including Native American crafts.

The south façade of the immense Department of the Interior Building

THE TAYLOE FAMILY

Portrait, in crayon, by Saint Memin of Colonel John Tayloe III

John Tayloe III (1771–1828), a colonel in the War of 1812, was responsible for the construction of the unusual Octagon building. He and his wife Ann, the daughter of Benjamin Ogle (the governor of Maryland), had their primary residence at Mount Airy, an estate and tobacco plantation in Richmond County, Virginia. The Tayloes decided they wanted to build a second house where they could spend the inclement winter seasons. President George Washington, a close friend of Tayloe and his father, was at the time overseeing the building of the US Capitol and was eager for people to move into the new city. The president encouraged Tayloe and his family to choose a plot in Washington rather than in the more popular Philadelphia. The family heeded his advice and the triangular-shaped corner plot for the Octagon was chosen. Tayloe's vast wealth enabled him to employ the services of William Thornton, the original designer of the US Capitol building, and spend a total of $35,000 on the construction of the house.

Federal Reserve Building ⑫

Constitution Ave & 20th St NW. **Map**
2 E4 & 3 A4. **Tel** 452-3778, for art
exhibitions. Ⓜ Foggy Bottom. ◯
11am–2pm Mon–Fri. ⬤ federal hols.
🗓 by appointment, call 452-3149 for
details. ♿ **www**.federalreserve.gov

Known to most people as
"the Fed," this building is
home to the Federal Reserve
System. This is the US banking
system under which 12 Federal
Reserve banks in 12 districts
across the country regulate
and hold reserves for member
banks in their districts. Dollar
bills are not printed here,
however, but at the
Bureau of Engraving
and Printing (see p79).

The four-story,
white marble edifice
was designed by Paul
Philippe Cret,
architect for the OAS
building (see p115)
and the Folger
Shakespeare
Library (see p48). The
building opened in 1937.

Visitors can take a brief tour
of the Board Room and watch
a film about the building and
the institution. Small art exhibitions are also held
throughout the year.

The gleaming, white marble exterior of the Federal Reserve Building

Marble eagle above the
entrance to "the Fed"

National Academy of Sciences ⑬

2101 Constitution Ave, NW. **Map** 2
E4. **Tel** 334-2000. Ⓜ Foggy Bottom.
◯ 8:30am–5pm Mon–Fri.
⬤ federal hols. ♿
www.nationalacademies.org

Established in 1863, the
National Academy of
Sciences is a non-
profit organization
that conducts
over 200
studies a
year on
subjects

such as health, science, and
technology, and educates the
nation by providing news of
scientific discoveries. Among
the past and present
Members of the
Academy are more
than 120 Nobel Prize
winners, notably
Albert Einstein.

The three-story
white marble build-
ing, designed by
Bertram Grosvenor
Goodhue, was
completed in 1924. Inside is a
gold dome adorned with portraits of Greek philosophers
and panels illustrating various
scientists. A 700-seat auditorium hosts a series of free
chamber recitals throughout
the year, and there are also
occasional, temporary science
exhibitions. On the building's
upper floors are the offices
of the National Research
Council, the National Academy
of Sciences, and the National
Academy of Engineering.

Nestled among the trees in
front of the Academy is the
much-admired bronze statue
of Albert Einstein, sculpted
by Robert Berks. The same
artist created the bust of
President John F. Ken-
nedy, which can be seen
in the Grand Foyer of the
Kennedy Center
(see pp118–9).
The huge
statue of

Albert Einstein reaches 12 ft
(6 m) in height and weighs
7,000 pounds (4 tons). It was
erected in 1979.

State Department ⑭

23rd St & C St, NW. **Map** 2 E4 & 3
A3. **Tel** 647-3241. Ⓜ Foggy
Bottom-GWU. 🗓 by appointment;
must show photo ID; call 4–6 weeks
in advance to reserve a place.
⬤ Federal hols. ♿ **www**.state.gov

As the oldest executive
department of the United
States government, established
in 1781, the State Department
handles all foreign policy.

Covering an expanse of 2.5
million sq ft (232,250 sq m)
over four city blocks, the
State Department building
rises eight stories high. Work-
place of the Secretary of State,
the State Department, and the
United States Diplomatic
Corps, the building is host
to 80,000 guests and 60,000
visitors every year. The State
Department's Diplomatic
Reception Rooms were
lavishly refurbished in the
late 1960s, and now contain
antiques worth over $90
million dollars.

George Washington University ⑮

2121 I (Eye) St, NW. **Map** 2 E3.
Tel 994-1000. Ⓜ Foggy Bottom-
GWU. **Lisner and Betts Auditoriums**
Tel 994-6800. **www**.gwu.edu

Founded in 1821, George
Washington University,
known as "GW" to many
people, is named after the
first president of the United

Sculpture of Albert Einstein outside the National Academy of Sciences

States. George Washington is the largest university in Washington, DC. There are nine schools offering both undergraduate and graduate studies. Strong subjects on offer include International Affairs, Business Administration, Medicine, Law, and Political Science.

As a result of its location, the university has many famous alumni, including Colin Powell (US Secretary of State in George W. Bush's administration) and Jacqueline Bouvier (who married John Kennedy) as well as a number of children of past presidents, including Lynda Johnson, Margaret Truman, and D. Jeffrey Carter.

The on-campus Lisner, Morton and Betts auditoriums host a series of plays, dances, lectures, and concerts.

St. Mary's Episcopal Church, built for freed slaves

St. Mary's Episcopal Church ⑯

728 23rd St, NW. **Map** 2 E3.
Tel 333-3985. Ⓜ Foggy Bottom-GWU. ◷ 10am–3pm Mon–Fri.
✝ 8am, 11am Sun, 12:10 Wed. ♿

Opened on January 20, 1887, the red-brick, Gothic St. Mary's Episcopal Church was the first church in Washington to be built specifically for freed slaves.

St Mary's was designed by James Renwick, who was the architect of the Renwick Gallery (see p113), the Smithsonian Castle (see p72), and St. Patrick's Cathedral in

The distinctive curved walls of the infamous Watergate Complex

New York City. The church was placed on the city's register of protected historic buildings in 1972.

Washington Circle ⑰

Map 2 E3. Ⓜ Foggy Bottom-GWU.

One of several circles and squares created by Pierre L'Enfant's original design of the city (see p19), Washington Circle lies at the northern edge of Foggy Bottom. It forms the point where Pennsylvania Avenue and New Hampshire Avenue meet K Street and 23rd Street. The circle boasts an imposing bronze statue of George Washington astride his horse, designed by artist Clark Mills and unveiled in 1860. The statue faces east, looking toward the White House and the US Capitol.

Watergate Complex ⑱

Virginia Ave between Rock Creek Parkway and New Hampshire Ave, NW. **Map** 2 D3. Ⓜ Foggy Bottom-GWU. ♿

Located next to the Kennedy Center (see pp118–9), on the bank of the Potomac River, the impressive, Italian-designed Watergate Complex was completed in 1971. The four rounded buildings that make up the complex were designed to contain shops, offices, apartments, hotels, and diplomatic missions.

In the summer of 1972 the complex found itself at the center of international news. Burglars, linked to President Nixon, broke into the offices of the Democratic National Committee, sparking off the Watergate scandal that led to the president's resignation.

THE WATERGATE SCANDAL

On June 17, 1972, during the US presidential campaign, five men were arrested for breaking into the Democratic Party headquarters in the Watergate Complex. The burglars were employed by the re-election organization of President

President Nixon addressing the nation while still in office

Richard Nixon, a Republican. Found guilty of burglary and attempting to bug telephones, the men were not initially linked to the White House. However, further investigation, led by Washington Post reporters Woodward and Bernstein, uncovered the extent of the president's involvement, including the possession of incriminating tapes and proven bribery. This led to an impeachment hearing, but before Nixon could be impeached, he resigned. Vice-President Gerald Ford succeeded him.

The Kennedy Center ⑲

In 1958, President Dwight D. Eisenhower signed an act to begin fund-raising for a national cultural center that would attract the world's best orchestras, opera, and dance companies to the US capital. President John F. Kennedy was an ardent supporter of the arts, taking the lead in fund-raising for it. He never saw the completion of the center, which was named in his honor. Designed by Edward Durrell Stone, it was opened on September 8, 1971. This vast complex houses three huge theaters; the Opera House, the Eisenhower Theater, and the Concert Hall, and on the roof is the Terrace Theater, the Theater Lab, and the Film Theater.

African sculpture

Don Quixote Statue
This bronze and stone statue by Aurelio Teno was a gift to the center from Spain.

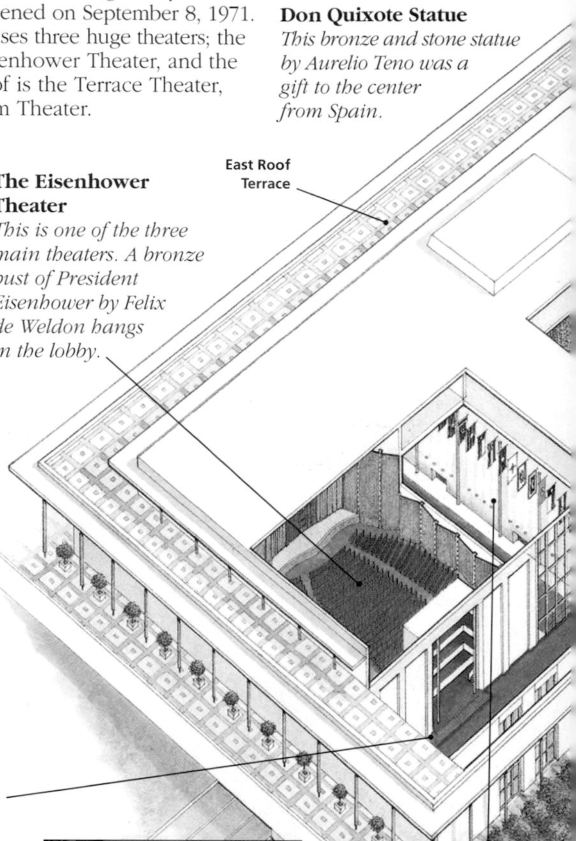

The Eisenhower Theater
This is one of the three main theaters. A bronze bust of President Eisenhower by Felix de Weldon hangs in the lobby.

East Roof Terrace

Millennium Stage
The Millennium Stage provides free performances put on in the Grand Foyer every afternoon at 6 pm.

The Hall of States
The flags of each of the 50 American states hang here. The sculptural tapestry by Jacques Douchez above the stairwell was a gift from Brazil.

STAR FEATURES

★ Bust of JFK

★ The Grand Foyer

★ The Opera House

The Hall of Nations
houses the flag of
every country with
which the US has
diplomatic relations.

★ **The Opera House**
*The Opera House seats 2,300 people.
The vast chandelier is made of
Lobmeyr crystal and was a
gift from Austria.*

VISITORS' CHECKLIST

New Hampshire Ave & Rock
Creek Parkway, NW. **Map** 2 D4.
Tel 467-4600 or (800) 444-1324.
Ⓜ *Foggy Bottom.* 🚌 *80.*
◯ *10am–9pm daily; 10am–9pm
Mon–Sat, noon– 9pm Sun and
hols (box office).* 🎟 *10am–5pm
Mon–Fri, 10am– 1pm Sat–Sun
(call 416-8340).* ♿ 🛍 🍽 🎭
www.kennedy-center.org

The Concert Hall is the largest
auditorium, seating 2,450 people.
It is the home of the
National Symphony
Orchestra.

★ **Bust of JFK**
*Created by sculptor Robert
Berks, this bronze bust stands
in the Grand Foyer. Berks
was chosen by Kennedy's family
to create the masterpiece.*

★ **The Grand Foyer**
*This enormous
room stretches 630
feet (192 m) and provides
an impressive entrance
into the Opera House, the
Concert Hall, and the
Eisenhower Theater.*

The JFK Terrace
*This stretches the length
of the Center and over-
looks the Potomac and
has glorious views
up and down the river.
Quotes by John F.
Kennedy are engraved
into the marble walls.*

GEORGETOWN

Georgetown developed well before Washington, DC. Native Americans had a settlement here, and in 1703 a land grant was given to Ninian Beall, who named the area the Rock of Dumbarton. By the mid-18th century immigrants from Scotland had swelled the population, and in 1751 the town was renamed George Town. It grew rapidly into a wealthy tobacco and flour port and finally, in 1789, the city of Georgetown was formed. The harbor and the Chesapeake and Ohio

John Carroll,
University founder

Canal were built in 1828, and the streets were lined with town-houses. The birth of the railroad undercut Georgetown's econ-omy, which by the mid-1800s was in decline. But by the 1950s the cobblestone streets and charming houses were attracting wealthy young cou-ples, and restaurants and shops sprang up on Wisconsin Avenue and M Street. Today Georgetown retains its quiet distinction from the rest of the city, and is a pleasant area in which to stroll for a few hours *(see pp148-9)*.

SIGHTS AT A GLANCE

Historic Buildings
Dumbarton Oaks **13**
Georgetown University **9**
Old Stone House **5**
Tudor Place **10**
Washington Post Office **7**

Churches and Cemeteries
Grace Church **3**
Mt. Zion Church **11**
Oak Hill Cemetery **12**

Streets, Canals, and Harbors
Chesapeake and Ohio Canal **4**
M Street **6**
N Street **8**
Washington Harbor **1**
Wisconsin Avenue **2**

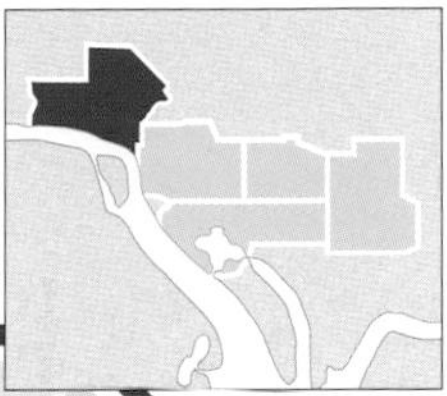

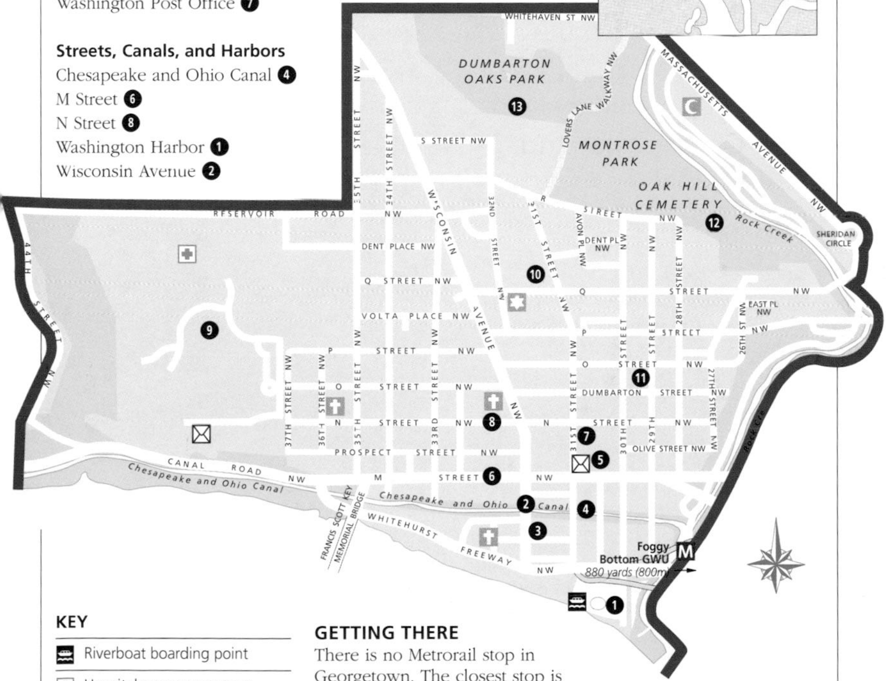

KEY

🚢 Riverboat boarding point

➕ Hospital emergency room

✉ Post office

⛪ Church

🕌 Mosque

✡ Synagogue

GETTING THERE
There is no Metrorail stop in Georgetown. The closest stop is Foggy Bottom (**Map 2 E3**). The Georgetown Metro Connection serves all Georgetown Metrobus stops and connects with Foggy Bottom-GWU, Rosslyn, and Dupont Circle Metro stations. Bus routes 32, 34, and 36 run on Wisconsin Avenue and M Street.

0 meters 500
0 yards 500

◁ **Typical colorful house in Georgetown**

Fountain at Washington Harbor

Washington Harbor ❶

3000-3020 K Street, NW. **Map** 2 D3.

Washington is a city where few architectural risks have been taken. However, the approach used by architect Arthur Cotton Moore for Washington Harbor, which is a combination residential and commercial building on the Potomac River, is unusually audacious.

Built on a site that was once filled with factories and warehouses, Moore's creation is a structure that hugs the waterfront and surrounds a semi-circular pedestrian plaza. The architect borrowed motifs from almost every type of design, such as turrets, columns, and even flying buttresses. The harbor has a pleasant boardwalk, a huge fountain, and tall, columned lamp-posts. Under the ground are steel gates that can be raised to protect the building from floods. The top floors of the harbor are apartments. On the bottom floors are office complexes, restaurants, and shops. Sightseeing boats dock at the river's edge for trips to the Mall and back.

Wisconsin Avenue ❷

Wisconsin Ave. **Map** 1 C2.
Ⓜ *Tenleytown, Friendship Heights.*

Wisconsin Avenue is one of two main business streets in Georgetown and is home to a wide variety of shops and restaurants. It is also one of the few streets in Washington that pre-dates L'Enfant's grid plan *(see p67)*. Once called High Street and then 32nd Street, it starts at the bank of the Potomac River and runs north through Georgetown right up to the city line, where

The Chesapeake and Ohio Canal ❸

When it was constructed in 1828, the C&O Canal featured an ingenious and revolutionary transportation system of locks, aqueducts, and tunnels that ran along its 184 miles (296 km) from Georgetown to Cumberland, Maryland. With the arrival of the railroad in the late 19th century, the canal fell out of use. It was only as a result of the efforts of Supreme Court Justice William Douglas that the Chesapeake and Ohio Canal was finally declared a protected national park in 1971. Today visitors come to enjoy its recreational facilities and also to study its fascinating transportation system.

Georgetown
The attractive federal houses of Georgetown line the banks of the canal for about 1.5 miles (2 km).

The Francis Scott Key Memorial Bridge was named after the composer of the American national anthem, *The Star-Spangled Banner.*

Canal Trips
Rides in mule-drawn canal clippers guided by park rangers dressed in period costumes are popular with visitors to the canal.

it continues as Rockville Pike. On the junction of Wisconsin Avenue and M Street is the landmark gold dome of Riggs National Bank.

During the French and Indian Wars, George Washington marched his troops up the avenue on his way to Pittsburgh to engage the British.

The gold dome of Riggs National Bank

Grace Church ❸

1041 Wisconsin Avenue, NW. **Map** 1 C3. *Tel* 333-7100. ☐ *call office in advance (office open by appointment 10am–6pm Mon, Tue, Fri).* ♿ **www**.gracedc.org

Built in 1866, Grace Church was designed to serve the religious needs of the boatmen who worked on the Chesapeake and Ohio Canal and the sailors of the port of Georgetown. Set on a tree-filled plot south of the canal and M Street, the Gothic Revival church, with its quaint exterior, is an oasis in Georgetown.

The building has undergone few extensive alterations over the years and has a certain timeless quality. The church's multi-ethnic congregation makes great efforts to reach out to the larger DC commu-

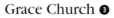

Sign for Grace Church

nity and works with soup kitchens and shelters for the homeless. The church also sponsors the "Thank God It's Friday" lunchtime discussion group, and holds a poetry coffee house on the third Tuesday of the month. Classical concerts, including chamber pieces, organ, and piano works, are held here regularly. There is also a popular annual festival devoted to the music of the German composer J.S. Bach.

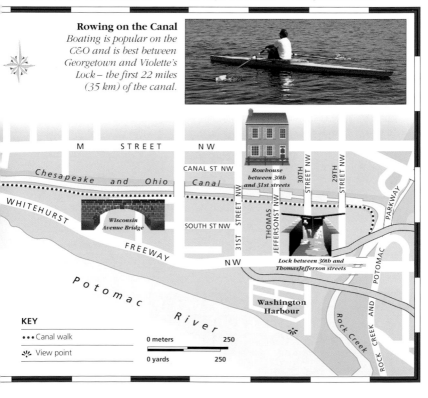

Rowing on the Canal
Boating is popular on the C&O and is best between Georgetown and Violette's Lock – the first 22 miles (35 km) of the canal.

M STREET N W

Chesapeake and Ohio Canal

CANAL ST NW

Rowhouse between 30th and 31st streets

WHITEHURST

Wisconsin Avenue Bridge

FREEWAY

SOUTH ST NW

31ST STREET NW

THOMAS JEFFERSON ST NW

30TH STREET NW

29TH STREET NW

PARKWAY

Lock between 30th and Thomas Jefferson streets

N W

POTOMAC

Washington Harbour

P o t o m a c   R i v e r

ROCK CREEK AND

Rock Creek

KEY

••• Canal walk

🔆 View point

0 meters   250

0 yards   250

Old Stone House ❺

3051 M St, NW. **Map** 2 D2.
Tel 426-6851. ○ noon–4pm
Sat–Sun. ▥ 30, 32, 34, 36, 38.
▣ call 895-6070. ♿ limited.
www.nps.gov/rocr/oldstonehouse

The Old Stone House may be
the only building in Washington that pre-dates the American
Revolution. It was built in
1765 by Christopher Layman,
and the tiny two-story cottage
has a large garden, which is a
welcome respite from the
shops of busy M Street.

There is a legend that still
persists about the Old Stone
House – that it was the Suter's
Tavern where Washington and
Pierre L'Enfant made their

plans for the city. However,
most historians today now
believe that they met in a
tavern located elsewhere in
Georgetown.

Over the years, the building
has housed a series of artisans,
and in the 1950s it even served
as offices for a used-car deal-
ership. In 1960 the National
Park Service restored it to its
pre-Revolutionary War appearance. Today park rangers give
talks about what Georgetown
would have been like during
the Colonial days. The Old
Stone House is technically the
oldest house in DC, although
The Lindens, which is now in
Kalorama, was built in Massachusetts in the mid-1750s and
later moved to Washington.

The picturesque Old Stone House

M Street ❻

M Street, NW. **Map** 1 C2. ▥ 30,
32, 34, 36, 38.

One of two main shopping
streets in Georgetown,
M Street is also home to some
of the most historic spots in
the city. On the northeast
corner of 30th and M Streets,
on the current site of a bank,
stood Union Tavern. Built in
1796, the tavern played host
to, among others, Presidents
George Washington and John
Adams, Napoleon's younger
brother Jerome Bonaparte,
author Washington Irving, and
Francis Scott Key, the composer of the "Star Spangled
Banner." During the Civil War,
the inn was turned into a temporary hospital where Louisa
May Alcott, the author of *Little
Women,* nursed wounded soldiers. In the 1930s the tavern
was torn down and replaced
by a gas station. Dr. William
Thornton, architect of the US
Capitol and Tudor Place *(see
p126)* lived at 3219 M Street.

On the south side of M
Street is Market House, which
has been the location of
Georgetown's market since
1751. In 1796 a wood frame
market house was constructed
and later replaced by the

**Only the two end
houses** *in this group
of fine Federal homes
(numbers 3327–3339) are
still in their original state.*

N Street ❽

1215 31st St, NW. **Map** 1 C2. ▥ 30,
32, 34, 36.

N Street is a sampler of
18th-century American
Federal architecture – a style
favored by leaders of the new
nation as being of a lighter
and more refined design than
the earlier Georgian houses.

At the corner of 30th and N
Streets is the Laird-Dunlop
House. Today it is owned by
Benjamin Bradlee, the former

editor of the *Washington Post.*

An excellent example of a
Federal house is the Riggs-
Riley House at 3038 N Street,
most recently owned by
Averill and Pamela Harriman.
At 3041–3045 N Street is
Wheatley Row. These houses
were designed to provide not
only maximum light from
large windows but also maximum privacy as they were
placed above street level.

Known as Wheatley Row,
these three well-designed
Victorian town homes were
built in 1859.

current brick market in 1865. In the 1930s the market became an auto supply store, and in the 1990s the New York gourmet food store Dean and Deluca opened a branch here.

Today M Street is home to a collection of fashionable stores and restaurants. Young buyers shop for alternative music at Smash and alternative clothing at Urban Outfitters. National chainstores such as Barnes and Noble, Pottery Barn, and Starbucks have branches along M Street.

Clyde's restaurant at number 3236 is a Georgetown institution, famous for its "happy hour." Bill Danoff, of the Starland Vocal Band, wrote his song "Afternoon Delight" about Clyde's; his gold disc hangs in the bar.

The elegant façade of the Post Office in Georgetown

Washington Post Office, Georgetown Branch ❼

1215 31st St, NW. **Map** 2 D2.
🚌 30, 32, 34, 36.

Built in 1857 as a customhouse, the still-functioning Georgetown Branch of the Washington Post Office is interesting both historically and architecturally. A customhouse was a money-producing venture for the Federal government, and the US government's investment in such an expensive building provides evidence of Georgetown's importance

as a viable port for many years. Architect Ammi B. Young, who was also responsible for the design of the Vermont State Capitol building in 1832 and the Boston Custom House in 1837, was called to Washington in 1852. He designed several other Italianate buildings in the capital, but this post office is his finest work. The granite custom-house was converted to a post office when Georgetown's fortunes declined.

The building underwent a renovation in 1997 that increased its efficiency and accessibility but retained the integrity of Young's simple, functional design.

Attractive houses lining the bustling M Street

The Thomas Beall House *(number 3017) was built in 1794 by one of Georgetown's most prominent families. It has since been occupied by the Secretary of War during World War I, and by Jackie Kennedy, who lived here for a year after the death of JFK.*

Number 3025–3027, with its raised mansard roof, shows the influence of the French during this period.

The Laird-Dunlop House *(number 3014) was built by John Laird who owned many of Georgetown's tobacco warehouses. Laird modeled his home on those in his native Edinburgh. It was subsequently owned by President Lincoln's son, Robert.*

Unusual flat roof

Georgetown University **9**

37th St & O St, NW. **Map** 1 B2.
Tel 687-0100. ☐ *varies,*
depending on university schedule.
☑ *call 687-3600 for details.* ♿
www.georgetown.edu

Georgetown University was
the first Catholic college to be
established in America.
Founded in 1789 by John
Carroll, and affiliated with the
Jesuit Order, the university
now attracts students of all
faiths from over 100 countries
around the world.

The oldest building on
the campus is the Old North
Building, completed in 1872,
but the most recognizable
structure is the Healy Building,
a Germanic design topped by
a fanciful spiral. The university's most famous graduate
is President Bill Clinton.

**The Gothic-inspired Healy
Building, Georgetown University**

Tudor Place **10**

1644 31st St, NW. **Map** 1 C2.
Tel 965-0400. ☐ *10am–4pm Tue–*
Sat, 10am–3pm Sun. ● *Jan, Jul 4,*
Thanksgiving, Dec 25. ☑ ☑ ☑
www.tudorplace.org

The manor house and large
gardens of this Georgetown
estate, designed by William
Thornton, offer a unique
glimpse into a bygone era.

Martha Washington, the
First Lady, gave $8,000 to her
granddaughter, Martha Custis
Peter, and her granddaughter's
husband. With the money, the
Peters purchased eight acres
and commissioned Thornton,
the architect of the Capitol

Stone dog in the garden of Tudor Place

(see pp50–51) and the Octagon
(see p114), to design a house.
Generations of the Peters
family lived here from 1805
to 1984. It is a mystery as to
why this stuccoed, two-story
Georgian structure with a
"temple" porch is called Tudor
Place, but it was perhaps
illustrative of the family's
English sympathies at the time.

The furniture, silver, china,
and portraits provide a glimpse
into American social and
cultural history; some of the
pieces on display come from
Mount Vernon *(see pp160–61)*.

Mt. Zion Church **11**

1334 29th St, NW. **Map** 2 D2.
Tel 234-0148. ✝ *11am Sun.* ☑ ♿

This church is thought to
have had the first black
congregation in DC. The first
church, at 27th and P Streets,
was a "station" on the city's
original Underground Railroad.

Altar in Mt. Zion church

It provided shelter for runa-
way slaves on their journey
north to freedom. The present
redbrick building was completed in 1884 after the first
church burned down.

Mt. Zion Cemetery, the
oldest black burial ground in
Washington, is located a short
distance away, in the middle
of the 2500 block of Q Street.

Oak Hill Cemetery **12**

3001 R St, NW. **Map** 2 D1.
Tel 337-2835. ☐ *10am–4pm*
Mon–Fri. ● *Sat & Sun, Federal hols.*

William Wilson Corcoran *(see
p113)* bought the land for the
cemetery and Congress then
established Oak Hill Cemetery
in 1849. Today there are
around 18,000 graves covering
the 25-acre site, which is
planted with groves of huge
oak trees.

Members of some of the
city's most prominent
families are buried
here, their names
featuring throughout
Washington's history,
including Magruder,
Thomas, Beall, and
Marbury.

At the entrance to
the cemetery is an
Italianate gatehouse
that is still used as the
superintendent's lodge
and office. Northeast
of the gatehouse is
the Spencer family
monument, designed
by Louis Comfort
Tiffany. The granite
low-relief of an angel
is signed by Tiffany.

The conference members in the music room of Dumbarton Oaks

THE FOUNDING OF THE UNITED NATIONS

In 1944, a conference held at the Dumbarton Oaks estate laid the groundwork for establishing the United Nations. President Franklin Roosevelt and the British Prime Minister, Winston Churchill, wanted to create a "world government" that would supervise the peace at the end of World War II. Roosevelt proposed that a conference be held in Washington, but at the time the State Department did not have a room big enough to accommodate all the delegates. As a solution, Robert Woods Bliss offered the use of the music room in his former home, Dumbarton Oaks, for the event.

The structure of the United Nations was settled at the Dumbarton Oaks Conference and then refined at the San Francisco Conference a year later when the United Nations' charter was ratified. The UN Headquarters building, the permanent home of the organization, was built in New York on the East River site after John D. Rockefeller donated $8.5 million toward its construction.

Also notable is the Gothic chapel designed by James Renwick. Nearby is the grave of John Howard Payne, composer of "Home, Sweet Home," who died in 1852. The bust that tops Payne's monument was originally sculpted with a full beard, but Corcoran requested a stonemason to "shave the statue" and so now it is clean shaven.

Dumbarton Oaks ⑬

1703 32nd St, NW. **Map** 2 D2. *Tel* *339-6401.* ◯ **House** 2–5pm Tue – Sun. **Gardens** 2–5pm daily. ◐ Mon, *Federal hols.* 🎨 💶 *for groups call* *339-6409* 🚻 ♿ *house only.* **www**.doaks.org

In 1703, a Scottish colonist named Ninian Beall was granted around 800 acres of land in this area. In later years the land was sold off and in 1801, 22 acres were bought by Senator William Dorsey of Maryland, who proceeded to build a Federal-style brick home here. A year later, financial difficulties caused him to sell it, and over the next century the property changed hands many times.

By the time pharmaceutical heirs Robert and Mildred Woods Bliss bought the rundown estate in 1920, it was overgrown and neglected. The Blisses altered and expanded the house, with the architectural advice of the

prestigious firm McKim, Mead and White *(see p109)*, to meet 20th-century family needs, and set to work on the garden. They engaged their friend, Beatrix Jones Farrand, one of the few female landscape architects at the time, to lay out the grounds. Farrand designed a series of terraces that progress from the formal gardens near the house to the more informal landscapes farther away from it.

In 1940 the Blisses moved to California and donated the whole estate to Harvard University. It was then converted into a library, research institution, and museum. Many of the 1,400 pieces of Byzantine Art on display were collected by the

Fountain in Dumbarton Oaks

Blisses themselves. Examples of Greco-Roman coins, late Roman and early Byzantine bas-reliefs, Egyptian fabrics, and Roman glass and bronzeware are just some of the highlights. In 1962 Robert Woods Bliss donated his collection of pre-Columbian art. In order to house it, architect Philip Johnson designed a new wing, consisting of eight domes surrounding a circular garden. Although markedly different from the original house, the new wing is well suited to the dramatic art collection it houses, which includes masks, stunning gold jewelry from Central America, frescoes, and Aztec carvings.

Swimming pool in the grounds of Dumbarton Oaks

FARTHER AFIELD

Zoo sign

North of the White House is Dupont Circle, a neighborhood of museums, galleries, and restaurants. The Embassy Row, Kalorama, Adams-Morgan, and Cleveland Park neighborhoods are a walker's paradise, especially for visitors interested in architecture.

Arlington, Virginia, across the Potomac River, was one of DC's first suburbs. Arlington National Cemetery was founded in 1864 to honor those who died for the Union. The Pentagon was built 80 years later by Franklin D. Roosevelt and is the area's most famous landmark.

SIGHTS AT A GLANCE

Museums and Galleries
African American Civil War
  Museum and Memorial **7**
Anacostia Museum **27**
Hillwood Museum **17**
Mary McLeod Bethune
  Council House **16**
National Geographic Society **8**
Phillips Collection **10**
Textile Museum **11**

**Historic Districts,
Streets, and Buildings**
Adams-Morgan **15**
Dupont Circle **9**
Embassy Row **13**
Frederick Douglass House **26**
Heurich Mansion **6**
Howard University **25**

Kalorama **14**
Lincoln Theatre **18**
*Washington National Cathedral
  pp142–3* **20**
The Pentagon **2**
Southwest Waterfront **3**
Woodrow Wilson House **12**

Monuments
Basilica of the National Shrine
  of the Immaculate
  Conception **23**
Iwo Jima Statue **4**

Parks and Gardens
Cleveland Park **21**
National Arboretum **24**
*National Zoological Park
  pp138–9* **19**
Rock Creek Park **22**

Roosevelt Island **5**

Cemetery
*Arlington National Cemetery
  pp130–31* **1**

KEY

▨	Central Washington
▢	District of Columbia
▢	Greater Washington
✈	Domestic airport
—	Metro line
═	Freeway (motorway)
═	Major road
═	Minor road

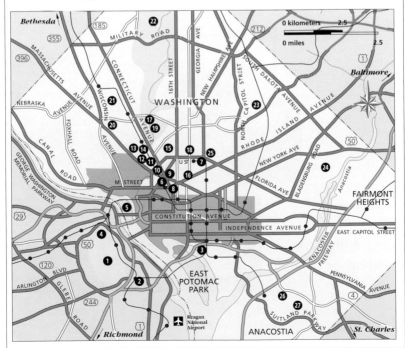

◁ **Chinese-style pagoda in the Asian collection at the National Arboretum**

Arlington National Cemetery ❶

For 30 years, Confederate General Robert E. Lee (1807–70) lived at Arlington House. In 1861 he left his home to lead Virginia's armed forces, and the Union confiscated the estate for a military cemetery. By the end of the Civil War in 1865, 16,000 soldiers were interred in the newly consecrated Arlington National Cemetery. Since then, around another 250,000 veterans have joined them. Simple headstones mark the graves of soldiers who died in every major conflict from the Revolution to the present. The focus of the cemetery is the Tomb of the Unknowns, which honors the thousands who have died in battle but have no known resting place.

Soldier on guard

Confederate Memorial
This bronze and granite monument honors the Confederate soldiers who died in the Civil War. It was dedicated in 1914.

Sea of Graves
Amost 300,000 servicemen and their families are buried on the 624 acres of Arlington Cemetery.

★ Tomb of the Unknowns
This tomb contains four vaults – for World War I and II, Vietnam, and Korea. Each vault held one unidentified soldier until recently when the Vietnam soldier was identified by DNA analysis and reburied in his home town.

| 0 meters | 200 |
| 0 yards | 200 |

STAR FEATURES

★ Arlington House

★ Grave of John F. Kennedy

★ Tomb of the Unknowns

Memorial Amphitheater
This marble amphitheater is the setting of the annual services on Memorial Day (see p36) when the nation's leaders pay tribute to the dead who served their country. It has also hosted many state funerals.

★ Arlington House

Once home to Robert E. Lee, this Georgian-Revival house is now a memorial to the general and his family. It is possible to tour the house during cemetery visiting hours.

Iwo Jima Statue (p126)

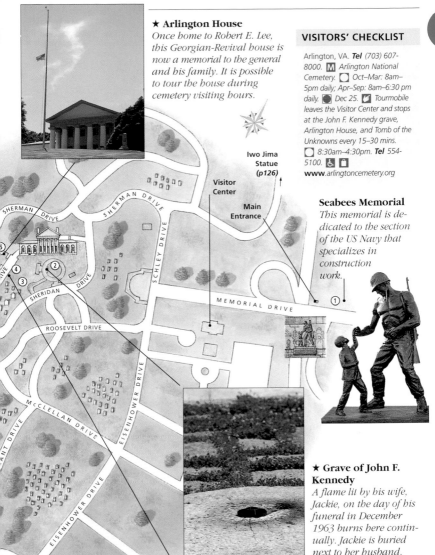

Visitor Center

Main Entrance

VISITORS' CHECKLIST

Arlington, VA. **Tel** (703) 607-8000. **M** *Arlington National Cemetery.* Oct–Mar: 8am–5pm daily; Apr–Sep: 8am–6:30 pm daily. Dec 25. *Tourmobile leaves the Visitor Center and stops at the John F. Kennedy grave, Arlington House, and Tomb of the Unknowns every 15–30 mins.* 8:30am–4:30pm. **Tel** 554-5100. www.arlingtoncemetery.org

Seabees Memorial

This memorial is dedicated to the section of the US Navy that specializes in construction work.

★ Grave of John F. Kennedy

A flame lit by his wife, Jackie, on the day of his funeral in December 1963 burns here continually. Jackie is buried next to her husband.

Tomb of Pierre L'Enfant

The architect responsible for planning the city of Washington has a suitably grand burial site in the cemetery (see p67).

KEY TO TOMBS AND SITES

Arlington House ⑤
Challenger Shuttle Memorial ⑨
Confederate Memorial ⑦
Grave of John F. Kennedy ②
Grave of Robert F. Kennedy ③
Lockerbie Memorial ⑥
Memorial Amphitheater ⑩
Rough Riders Memorial ⑧
Seabees Memorial ①
Tomb of Pierre L'Enfant ④
Tomb of the Unknowns ⑪

View of the Pentagon building's formidable concrete façade from the Potomac River

The Pentagon ❷

1000 Defense Pentagon, Hwy 1-395, Arlington, VA. **Tel** *(703) 697-1776.* Ⓜ *Pentagon. Tours by appointment only. For the latest information call the above number.* **www**.*defenselink.mil*

President Franklin Roosevelt decided in the early 1940s to consolidate the 17 buildings that comprised the Department of War (the original name for the Department of Defense) into one building. Designed by army engineers, and built of gravel dredged from the Potomac River and molded into concrete, the Pentagon was started on September 11, 1941 and completed on January 15, 1943, at a cost of $83 million. As the world's largest office building, it is almost a city in itself. Yet despite its size, the unique five-sided design is very efficient, and it takes only seven minutes to walk between any two points.

Fish stall at the waterfront's market

The Pentagon is the headquarters of the Department of Defense, a Cabinet-level organization consisting of three military departments, the Army, Navy, and Air Force, as well as 14 defense agencies. Leading personnel are the Secretary of Defense and the Chairman of the Joint Chiefs of Staff.

On September 11, 2001, the building was damaged in a terrorist attack. A memorial to the 184 people who died in the Pentagon and on Flight 77 is to be constructed.

Southwest Waterfront ❸

Ⓜ *Waterfront.* **Fish Market** ☐ *7:30am–8pm daily.*

In the 1960s, urban planners tested their new architectural theories on Washington's southwest waterfront along the Potomac River. Old neighborhoods were torn down, and apartment high-rises put up in their place. Eventually new restaurants developed along the waterfront, and Arena Stage, a popular regional theater company, built an experimental theater here. The area enjoyed a regeneration, and today it is a relaxed place to eat or just take a stroll.

The fish market off Maine Avenue, a remnant of the old waterfront culture, still thrives and draws customers from all over Washington and is one of the most vibrant spots in the area. Customers can buy lobster, crabs, oysters, and all kinds of fresh fish

from the vendors selling from their barges on the river. There are also several good restaurants along the waterfront that specialize in freshly caught local fish and seafood.

Iwo Jima Statue (US Marine Corps Memorial) ❹

Meade St, between Arlington National Cemetery & Arlington Boulevard. **Map** 1 B5. Ⓜ *Rosslyn.* ♿

The horrific battle of Iwo Jima that took place during World War II was captured by photographer Joe Rosenthal. His Pulitzer Prize-winning picture of five Marines and a Navy Corpsman raising the American flag on the tiny Pacific island came to symbolize in the American psyche the heroic struggle of the American forces in the war against Japan. This image was magnificently translated into bronze by sculptor Felix DeWeldon and paid for

A poignant memorial to the men who died in the battle of Iwo Jima

SEPTEMBER 11

On September 11, 2001, one of four airplanes hijacked by terrorists was flown into the Pentagon, resulting in huge loss of life and causing the side of the building to collapse. Crews at the Pentagon worked tirelessly to rebuild the damaged 10 percent of the building (400,000 to 500,000 square feet). It was estimated that repairs would take three years to finish but they were completed in less than a year. The west wall has a dedication capsule and a single charred capstone. A memorial is also planned.

The damaged Pentagon after the September 11 attack

by private donations. The three surviving soldiers from Rosenthal's photograph actually posed for DeWeldon; the other three men, however, were killed in further fighting on the islands. The Iwo Jima Memorial was dedicated on November 10, 1954, to coincide with the 179th birthday of the Marine Corps.

Roosevelt Island ❺

GW Memorial Pkwy, McLean, VA. **Map** 1 C4. **Tel** (703) 289-2500. Ⓜ Rosslyn. ◷ 7am–dusk daily. ♿ by appt only. www.nps.gov/this

A haven for naturalists, Roosevelt Island's 91 acres of marshlands and two and a half miles (4 km) of nature trails are home to red-tailed hawks, great owls, groundhogs, wood ducks, and many species of trees and plants. President Theodore Roosevelt (1858–1919), a great naturalist himself, is honored

with a 17-ft (5-m) tall memorial in bronze, and four granite tablets, each inscribed with quotes by the president.

Roosevelt Island is accessible by car via the George Washington Memorial Parkway or by canoe, which can be rented from Thompson's Boathouse (see p205) near the Watergate Complex.

Heurich Mansion ❻

1307 New Hampshire Ave, NW. **Tel** 429-1894. Ⓜ Dupont Circle. ◷ Wed for tours: 12:15pm and 1:15pm. ◷ Sun, Federal Holidays. 🎟 donation. ♿ www.heurichhouse.org

Brewer Christian Heurich built this wonderful Bavarian fantasy for his family just south of Dupont Circle in 1894. The turreted mansion built in the Romanesque Revival architectural style was home to the Historical Society of Washington, DC until 2003,

when it relocated to the City Museum in the Carnegie Library Building (see p96). The Heurich Mansion is a fine example of an upper-middle-class family house in Washington in the late 1800s.

The ornate carving in Heurich's Beer Hall

African American Civil War Museum and Memorial ❼

Museum 1200 U St, NW. **Memorial** 10th St, NW and Vermont Ave, NW. **Tel** 667-2667. Ⓜ U Street. ◷ 10am–5pm Mon–Fri, 10am–2pm Sat (call for tours). www.afroamcivilwar.org

Opened in January 1999, the African American Museum uses photographs, documents and audiovisual equipment to explain the still largely unknown story of African Americans' long struggle for freedom. The Museum's permanent exhibition is entitled "Slavery to Freedom; Civil War to Civil Rights." Interactive kiosks bring together historic documents, photographs, and music in a powerful and evocative way. There is also a service for anyone interested in tracing relatives who may have served with United States Colored Troops during the Civil War. At the center of a paved plaza is situated the "Spirit of Freedom," a sculpture by Ed Hamilton, which was unveiled on July 18, 1998. It is the first major art piece by a black sculptor on federal land in the District of Columbia. It stands 10ft tall and features uniformed black soldiers and a sailor poised to leave home.

The statue of President Roosevelt and granite tablets on Roosevelt Island

Giant globe in the Explorers Hall at the National Geographic Society

National Geographic Society ❽

1145 17th St at M St, NW.
Map 2 F2 & 3 B2. **Tel** 857-7588.
Ⓜ *Farragut North.* ◯ *9am–5pm Mon–Sat & federal hols, 10am–5pm Sun.* ◉ *Dec 25.* ⓖ ▯
www.nationalgeographic.com

The National Geographic Society has been funding explorers and producing a monthly newsletter, the precursor to its famous yellow-bordered magazine, since 1888.

In 1964 the Society moved into its present headquarters, designed by Edward Durrell Stone, the architect who also designed the Kennedy Center. The upper floors house staff working on magazines and other educational projects.

On the first floor is Explorers Hall, a compact museum that illustrates the Society's mission to explore the earth's land, water, and air masses. Highlights include a simulated tornado that can be touched, holograms that look so lifelike visitors try to reach out and grab them, and Earth Station One, an amphitheater that simulates orbital flight. There are also supermicroscopes (or cyberscopes), which visitors can use to look at minerals and plants.

The Explorers Hall has an 10-ft (3-m) high globe, which has become a symbol for the Society. Geographica is an interactive exhibit that allows visitors to experience vicariously undersea exploration,

the force of a tornado, and the land of dinosaurs. The National Geographic's bookstore is a treasure trove of all things related to geography; atlases, videos, books, and maps.

Dupont Circle ❾

Map 2 F2 & 3 A1. Ⓜ *Dupont Circle.*

This area to the north of the White House gets its name from the fountain and is at the intersection of Massachusetts, Connecticut, and New Hampshire Avenues, and 19th Street, NW. At the heart of this traffic island is the Francis Dupont Memorial Fountain, named for the first naval hero of the Civil War, Admiral Samuel Francis Dupont. Built by his family, the original memorial was a

Playing chess in Dupont Circle

bronze statue that was moved eventually to Wilmington, Delaware. The present marble fountain, which was constructed in 1921, has four figures (which represent the sea, the wind, the stars, and the navigational arts) supporting a marble basin.

The park area around the fountain draws a cross section of the community – chess players engrossed in their games, cyclists pausing at the fountain, picnickers eating alfresco, and tourists taking a break from sightseeing. Do not stray into the Circle after dark as it may not be safe at night.

In the early 20th century the Dupont Circle area was a place of grand mansions. Its fortunes then declined until the 1970s, when Washingtonians began to buy the decaying mansions. The district is now filled with art galleries, bars, restaurants, and bookstores. The old Victorian buildings have been divided into apartments, restored as single family homes, or converted into small office buildings.

Dupont Circle is also the center of Washington's gay community. The bars and clubs on the section of P Street between Dupont Circle and Rock Creek Park are the most popular area for gay men and women to meet. The area east along P Street, and past 14th Street, changes dramatically for the worse, so is best avoided.

The elaborate fountain at the heart of the Dupont Circle intersection

Auguste Renoir's masterpiece, *The Luncheon of the Boating Party* (1881)

Phillips Collection ⑩

1600 21st St at Q St, NW. **Map** 2 E2
& 3 A1. *Tel* 387-2151. Ⓜ *Dupont
Circle.* ◯ *10am–5pm Tue–Sat (10am–
8:30pm Thu), 12–5pm Sun.* ⬤ *Mon,
Jan 1, Jul 4, Thanksgiving, Dec 25,
federal hols.* 🎟 📷 *2pm Wed & Sat.*
♿ www.*phillipscollection.org*

This is one of the finest
collections of Impressionist
works in the world and the
first museum devoted to
modern art of the 19th and
20th centuries in the United
States. Duncan and Marjorie
Phillips, who founded the
collection, lived in the older
of the museum's two adjacent
buildings. Following the
death of his father in 1917,
Duncan Phillips decided to
open two of the mansion's
rooms as The Phillips
Memorial Gallery.

The couple spent their time
traveling and adding to their
already extensive collection.
During the 1920s they acquired
some of the most important
modern European paintings,
including *The Luncheon of the
Boating Party* (1881) by Renoir,
for which they paid $125,000
(one of the highest prices ever
paid at the time). The collection continued to grow to
more than 2,000 pieces of art
over the next 50 years.

In 1930 the Phillips family
moved to a new home on
Foxhall Road in northwest
Washington and converted
the rest of their former 1897
Georgian Revival residence

into a private gallery. The
Phillips Gallery was then
reopened to the public in
1960 as the newly named
Phillips Collection.

The elegant Georgian
Revival building that was
the Phillips' home
makes for a more
intimate and personal
gallery than the big
Smithsonian art
museums.

The Collection is
best known for its
wonderful selection
of Impressionist and
Post Impressionist paintings;
Dancers at the Barre by
Degas, *Self-Portrait* by
Cézanne and *Entrance to the
Public Gardens in Arles* by Van
Gogh are just three examples.
The museum also has one of
the largest collections in the
world of pieces by French
artist Pierre Bonnard, including
The Open Window (1921).

Other great paint-
ings to be seen
in the collection
include El Greco's
*The Repentant Saint
Peter* (1600), *The
Blue Room* (1901) by
Pablo Picasso, Piet
Mondrian's *Composi-
tion No. III* (1921-25),
and *Ochre on Red
on Red* (1954) by
Mark Rothko.

In addition to the
permanent exhibits,
the museum supports
traveling exhibitions,
which start at the
Phillips Collection
before appearing

in galleries around the
country. The exhibitions often
feature one artist (such as
Georgia O'Keeffe) or one
particular topic or period
(such as the *Twentieth-Century
Still-Life Paintings* exhibition).

The Phillips Collection en-
courages enthusiasts of modern
art to visit the museum for a
number of special events. On
Thursday evenings the
museum hosts "Artful Evenings." These include gallery
talks, live jazz music, and
light refreshments, and give
people the opportunity to
discuss the issues of the
art world in a relaxed, social
atmosphere. On Sunday after-
noons from September through
May, a series of concerts are
staged in the gallery's Music
Room. Running since
1941, these popular
concerts are free to
anyone who has pur-
chased a ticket for the
gallery on that day.
They range from
piano recitals and
string quartets to
performances by
established singers
of world renown,
such as the famous
operatic soprano
Jessye Norman

**Collector Duncan
Phillips (1886–1966)**

The gallery shop sells merchandise linked to permanent
and temporary exhibitions.
Books, posters, and prints can
be found as well as ceramics,
glassware, and other creations
by contemporary artists. There
are also hand-painted silks and
artworks based on the major
paintings in the collection.

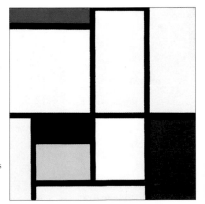

Composition No. III (1921–25) by Piet Mondrian

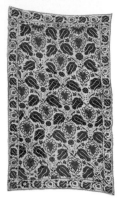

18th-century Turkish embroidery on silk in the Textile Museum

Textile Museum ⓫

2320 S St, NW. **Map** 2 E1.
Tel 667-0441. Ⓜ Dupont Circle.
◯ 10am–5pm Mon–Sat, 1–5pm
Sun. ● Dec 24, Dec 25, federal
hols. 🈂 donation. 🗐 introductory
tours Sep–May: 1:30pm Wed, Sat &
Sun. **Library** ◯ 10am–2pm
Wed–Fri, 10am–4pm Sat.
🗐 ♿ call in advance.
www.textilemuseum.org

George Hewitt Myers, the
founder of the Textile
Museum, began collecting
oriental rugs while he was at
college. In 1925 he opened
a museum in his home to
display his collection of 275
rugs and 60 textiles. It was a
private museum, open only
by appointment, until Myers'
death in 1957.

Today the museum is still
housed in Myers' home, which
was designed by John Russell
Pope, architect of the Jefferson
Memorial *(see p79)*. The
collection is also now
in an adjacent building
by Waddy B. Wood,
architect of Woodrow
Wilson's house.

There are around
17,000 objects in the
collection from all over
the world, including
textiles from Peru, India,
Indonesia, and Central
America. The museum
has a collections data-
base, as well as a
library of over 17,000
books on the subject
of textiles. Visitors must
make an appointment
to use the database.

Woodrow Wilson House ⓬

2340 S St, NW. **Map** 2 E1.
Tel 387- 4062. Ⓜ Dupont Circle.
◯ 10am–4pm Tue–Sun.
● Mon, federal hols. 🈂 🗐 ♿
www.woodrowwilsonhouse.org

Located in the beautiful
Kalorama neighborhood,
the former home of Woodrow
Wilson (1856–1924), who
served as president from 1913
to 1921, is the only presidential museum within the
District of Columbia.

Wilson led the US through
World War I and advocated
the formation of the League of
Nations, the precursor to the
United Nations. Although ex-
hausted by the war effort,
Wilson campaigned tire-
lessly for the League
across America.

In 1919 he collapsed
from a stroke and
became an invalid for
the rest of his life. Many
believe that Wilson's second wife, Edith Galt,
assumed many of the
presidential duties herself
(she guided his hand when
he signed documents).
Unable to leave his
sickbed, Wilson saw his
dream, the League of
Nations, defeated in
the Senate. In 1920 he
was awarded the
Nobel Peace Prize –
small consolation for the
failure of the League.

Wilson and his wife moved
to this townhouse, designed
by Waddy B. Wood, at the end

**Statue of
Churchill, British
Embassy**

of his second term in 1921.
Edith Galt Wilson arranged for
the home to be bequeathed to
the nation. Since then the
building has been maintained
as it was during the President's
lifetime, containing artifacts
from his life and reflecting the
style of an upper-middle-class
home of the 1920s. The house
today belongs to the National
Trust for Historic Preservation.

Embassy Row ⓭

Massachusetts Avenue. **Map** 2 E1.
Ⓜ Dupont Circle. See also pp146-7.

Embassy Row stretches along
Massachusetts Avenue from
Scott Circle toward Observatory
Circle. It developed during
the Depression when many
of Washington's wealthy
families were forced to
sell their mansions to
diplomats, who bought
them for foreign mis-
sions. Since then, many
new embassies have
been built, often in
the vernacular style
of their native country,
making Embassy Row
architecturally fascinating.

At No. 2315 Massachu-
setts Avenue, the Embassy
of Pakistan is an opu-
lent mansion built in
1908, with a mansard
roof (four steep sloping
sides) and a rounded
wall that hugs the corner.

Farther down the road, at
No. 2349, is the Embassy of
the Republic of Cameroon,
one of the Avenue's great

An elaborately decorated room in the Georgian Revival Woodrow Wilson House

early 20th-century Beaux Arts masterpieces. This romantic, Norwegian chateau-style building was commissioned in 1905 to be the home of Christian Hauge, first Norwegian ambassador to the United States, before passing to Cameroon.

Situated opposite the Irish Embassy stands a bronze statue of the hanged Irish revolutionary Robert Emmet (1778–1803). The statue was commissioned by Irish Americans to commemorate Irish independence.

At No. 2536 is the India Supply Mission. Two carved elephants stand outside as symbols of Indian culture and mythology. In the park in front of the Indian Embassy is an impressive bronze sculpture of Mahatma Gandhi.

The British Embassy, at No. 3100, was designed by Sir Edwin Lutyens in 1928. The English-style gardens were planted by the American wife of the then British ambassador, Sir Ronald Lindsay. Outside the embassy is an arresting statue of Sir Winston Churchill by William M. McVey.

Façade of the Croatian Embassy on Massachusetts Avenue

Kalorama ⓪

Map 2 D1 & 2 E1. Ⓜ *Woodley Park or Dupont Circle.*

The neighborhood of Kalorama, situated north of Dupont Circle, is an area of stately private homes and elegant apartment buildings. From its development at the turn of the 20th century as a suburb close to the city center, Kalorama (Greek for "beautiful view") has been home to the wealthy and upwardly mobile.

The apartments at 2311 Connecticut Avenue, Kalorama

Five presidents had homes here: Herbert Hoover, Franklin D. Roosevelt, Warren Harding, William Taft, and Woodrow Wilson. Only Wilson's home served as his permanent postpresidential residence.

Some of the most striking and ornate apartment buildings in Washington are found on Connecticut Avenue, south of the Taft Bridge that crosses Rock Creek Park. Most notable are the Georgian Revival-style Dresden apartments at No. 2126, the Beaux Arts-inspired Highlands building at number 1914, and the Spanish Colonial-style Woodward apartments at No. 2311 Connecticut Avenue. Also worth viewing is the Tudor-style building at No. 2221 Kalorama Road.

The best views of nearby Rock Creek Park *(see p141)* are from Kalorama Circle at the northern end of 24th Street.

Adams-Morgan ⓯

North of Dupont Circle, east of Rock Creek Park, and south of Mt. Pleasant. **Map** 2 E1 & 2 F1. Ⓜ *Dupont Circle or Woodley Park.*

Adams-Morgan is the only racially and ethnically diverse neighborhood in the city. It was given its name in the 1950s when the Supreme Court ruled that Washington must desegregate its educational system, and forced the combination of two schools in the area – Adams (for white children) and Morgan (an all-black school).

Packed with cafés, bookstores, clubs, and galleries, the district is a vibrant and eclectic mix of African, Hispanic, and Caribbean immigrants, as well as white urban pioneers, both gay and straight. People are attracted by the neighborhood's lively streets and its beautiful, and relatively affordable, early 20th-century houses and apartments.

The area has a thriving music scene and, on any night, rap, reggae, salsa, and Washington's indigenous go-go can be heard in the clubs and bars. The cosmopolitan feel of Adams-Morgan is reflected in its wide variety of restaurants *(see p190)*. Cajun, New Orleans, Ethiopian, French, Italian, Caribbean, Mexican, and Lebanese food can all be found along 18th Street and Columbia Road, the two main streets.

Although the area is becoming increasingly modern and trendy, its 1950s Hispanic roots are still evident. They are loudly celebrated in the Hispanic-Latino Festival that takes place every July and spreads from the Mall up to Adams-Morgan *(see p37)*.

It should be noted that this area can be dangerous after dark, so be wary if you are walking around at night. The area is not served by Metrorail and parking, especially on weekends, can be difficult.

Colorful mural on the wall of a parking lot in Adams-Morgan

National Zoological Park ⑲

Micronesian Kingfisher

Established in 1887 as the Smithsonian's Department of Living Animals and sited on the Mall, the National Zoo moved to its present location in 1891. The park, which covers 163 acres, was designed by Frederick Law Olmstead, the landscape architect responsible for New York's Central Park. Today, the zoo has more than 4,500 animals and is a dynamic "biopark" where animals are studied in environments that replicate their natural habitat. It has a number of breeding programs, one of the most successful of which is the Sumatran tiger program.

Giant Panda Exhibit
Tian Tian and Mei Xiang were given by the Chinese government and arrived in the zoo on December 6, 2001. The giant pandas are one of the zoo's most popular attractions.

↗ Rock Creek Park (see p135)

★ **Prairie Exhibit**
This exhibit features plants and creatures, including bison and prairie dogs, from a typical American Prairie.

Main Entrance

Flight Exhibit
Endangered species such as the Guam rail and Bali Mynah can be seen in the Bird House.

KEY TO ANIMAL ENCLOSURES

Amazonia ⑩	Hippos and Rhinos ㉒
Bat Cave ⑪	Invertebrate Exhibit ⑰
Bears ⑬	Lions and Tigers ⑫
Beavers and Otters ⑥	Monkey Island ⑭
Bird House and Flight Exhibit ⑤	Prairie Exhibit ㉔
Birds ④	Red Wolves ⑦
Bongos (rare antelope) ②	Reptile Discovery Center ⑯
Camels ㉑	Seals and Sea Lions ⑧
Cheetahs and Zebras ㉕	Servals ⑮
Elephants, Giraffes, and Pandas ㉓	Small Mammal House ⑳
Gibbon Ridge ⑲	Spectacled Bears ⑨
Great Ape House ⑱	Tapirs ①
	Wetlands Exhibit and Eagles ③

Bald Eagle
The only eagle unique to North America, the bald eagle is named for its white head, which appears to be "bald" against its dark body.

0 meters   100

0 yards   100

Golden Lion Tamarins

These endangered mammals are protected by an international conservation program which includes breeding and conservation education.

VISITORS' CHECKLIST

3001 Connecticut Ave, NW.
Tel 673-4800. Ⓜ Cleveland Park, Woodley Park-Zoo.
◯ Apr–Oct: 10am–6pm daily (buildings), 6am–8pm daily (grounds); Oct–Apr: 10am–4:30pm daily (buildings), 6am–6pm daily (grounds).
◯ Dec 25. ✆ call 673-4671.
♿ ⚘ 🏠 📷
www.natzoo.si.edu

★ Great Ape House

Lowland gorillas – males can weigh up to 400 pounds (180 kg) – can be seen in the Great Ape House. Other occupants include arboreal (tree-dwelling) orangutans.

★ Komodo Dragons

These rare lizards can grow up to 10 ft (3 m) in length, and weigh up to 200 lbs (90 kg). They are the first to be born in captivity outside Indonesia

Red Wolves

Related to the gray wolf, the endangered red wolf is native to America. There are only around 300 in existence and of these, 220 live in captivity.

Amazonia

This exhibit re-creates the Amazonian habitat. Visitors can see many creatures from poison arrow frogs to giant catfish.

STAR EXHIBITS

★ Great Ape House

★ Komodo Dragons

★ Prairie Exhibit

Mary McLeod Bethune Council House National Historic Site ⑯

1318 Vermont Ave, NW. **Map** 3 B1.
Tel 673-2402. Ⓜ *McPherson Square/U Street.* ◯ *10am–4pm Mon–Sat.* ● *Sun.* ✔ *plus interactive tour for children.* ▣
www.nps.gov/mamc

Born in 1875 to two former slaves, Mary McLeod Bethune was an educator and civil and women's rights activist. In 1904 she founded a college for impoverished black women in Florida, the Daytona Educational and Industrial School for Negro Girls. Renamed the Bethune-Cookman College, it is still going strong.

In the 1930s, President Franklin D. Roosevelt asked her to be his special advisor on racial affairs, and she later became director of the Division of Negro Affairs in the National Youth Administration. As part of Roosevelt's cabinet, Bethune enjoyed the highest position ever held by a black woman in the US government.

Bethune went on to found the National Council of Negro Women, which gives voice to the concerns of black women. The Council grew to have a membership of 10,000, and

Entrance to the Mary McLeod Bethune Council House

Mary McLeod Bethune

this house on Vermont Avenue was bought by Bethune and the Council as its headquarters.

It was not until November 1979, 24 years after Bethune's death, that the original Council House was opened to the public, with photographs, manuscripts, and other artifacts from her life on display. In 1982 the house was declared a National Historic Site and was bought by the National Park Service.

Hillwood Museum and Gardens ⑰

4155 Linnean Avenue, NW. *Tel* 1/877 HILLWOOD, 686-5807. Ⓜ *Van Ness/ UDC.* ◯ *10am–5pm Tue–Sat.* ● *January, Federal hols. Visits must be booked in advance.* ▨ ✔ ▣
▣ **www**.hillwoodmuseum.org

Hillwood was owned by Marjorie Merriweather Post, and it was opened to the public in 1977. The Museum contains the most comprehensive collection of 18th- and 19th-century Russian imperial costume to be found outside of Russia. It also has a renowned collection of French decorative arts from the 18th century. The Gardens are set within a 25-acre estate, surrounded by woodlands in the heart of Washington, and have important collections of azaleas and orchids.

The stunning interior of the restored Lincoln Theatre

Lincoln Theatre ⑱

1215 U St, NW. **Map** 2 F1. *Tel* 328-6000. Ⓜ *U Street-Cardozo.* ◯ *10am– 6pm Mon–Fri.* ● *Federal hols.* ✔ *groups by appt.* ⓓ

Built in 1922, the Lincoln Theatre was once the centerpiece of cultural life for Washington's downtown African American community. Like the Apollo Theater in New York, the Lincoln presented big-name entertainment, such as jazz singer and native Washingtonian Duke Ellington and his orchestra, Ella Fitzgerald, and Billie Holiday.

By the 1960s the area around the theater began to deteriorate, and the 1968 riots turned U Street into a corridor of abandoned and burned-out buildings and attendance at the theater dropped dramatically. By the 1970s the theater had closed down. Then, in the early 1980s fundraising began for the $10 million renovation. Even the original, highly elaborate plasterwork was carefully cleaned and repaired, and the theater reopened in 1994.

Today the Lincoln Theatre is a center for the performing arts, and one of the linchpins of U Street's renaissance. The magnificent auditorium hosts a program of concerts, stage shows, and events including the DC Film Festival *(see p202)*.

National Zoological Park ⑲

See pp138–9.

Washington National Cathedral ⑳

See pp142–3.

Cleveland Park ㉑

Ⓜ *Cleveland Park.*

Cleveland Park is a beautiful residential neighborhood that resembles the picture on a postcard of small-town America. It was originally a summer community for those wanting to escape the less bucolic parts of the city. In 1885, President Grover Cleveland (1885–9) bought a stone farmhouse here as a summer home for his bride.

The town's Victorian summer houses are now much sought after by people wanting to be close to the city but live in a small-town environment. There are interesting shops and good restaurants, as well as a grand old Art Deco movie theater, called the Uptown.

Rock Creek Park ㉒

Ⓜ *Cleveland Park.* **Rock Creek Park Nature Center** 5200 Glover Rd, NW. **Map** 2 D1–D3. **Tel** 895-6070. Ⓜ *Friendship Heights.* ◯ 9am–5pm *Wed–Sun.* ● *federal hols* ⊠ *by appointment.* **www**.nps.gov/rocr

Named after the creek that flows through it, Rock Creek Park bisects the city of Washington. This 1800-acre

Pierce Mill, the 19th-century gristmill in Rock Creek Park

THE SHAW NEIGHBORHOOD

This neighborhood is named after Union Colonel Robert Gould Shaw, the white commander of an all-black regiment from Massachusetts. He supported his men in their struggle for the same rights as white soldiers. Until the 1960s, U Street was the focus of black-dominated businesses and organizations. Thriving theaters, such as the Howard and the Lincoln, attracted top-name performers, and Howard University was the center of intellectual life for black students. The 1968 riots, sparked by the assassination of Dr. Martin Luther King Jr., wiped out much of Shaw's business district, and many thought the area could never be revived. However, the restoration of the Lincoln Theatre, the renewal of the U Street business district, and an influx of homebuyers renovating historic houses, have all contributed to the rejuvenation. In the part of U Street closest to the U Street-Cardoza metro stop, many fashionable bars and clubs have recently opened.

Mural in the Shaw neighborhood depicting Duke Ellington

stretch of land runs from the Maryland border south to the Potomac River and constitutes nearly five percent of the city. Unlike the crowded lawns of Central Park, Rock Creek Park has a feeling of the wilderness. Although the elk, bison, and bears that used to roam the park have vanished, raccoons, foxes, and deer can still be found here in abundance.

The park was endowed in 1890 and is now run by the National Park Service. In addition to hiking and picnicking, the park has a riding stable and horse trails, tennis courts, and an 18-hole golf course. On Sundays, a portion of Beach Drive – one of the main roads running through the park – is closed to cars to allow cyclists and in-line skaters freedom of the road. The creek itself is inviting, with little eddies

and waterfalls, but visitors are advised not to go into the water because it is polluted.

The **Rock Creek Park Nature Center** is a good place to begin an exploration of the park. It includes a small planetarium, and a 1-mile (1.6-km) nature trail, which is very manageable for children.

Pierce Mill near Tilden Street was an active gristmill which was restored by the National Park Service in 1936. It was kept working as a visitor exhibit until 1993 when it was deemed unsafe to work any more. Plans are underway to carry out a second restoration but only once sufficient funding is acquired. The Carter Barron Amphitheater, near 16th Street and Colorado Avenue, stages free performances of Shakespeare's plays and summer jazz concerts.

Washington National Cathedral ⑳

The building of the Church of Saint Peter and Saint Paul (its official name) was financed entirely by donations. It is the world's sixth largest cathedral, measuring 518 ft (158 m) in length and 301ft (94.8 m) from grade to the top of the central tower. Constructed from Indiana limestone, using labor-intensive building techniques of the Gothic style of architecture, evident in the pointed arches, rib vaulting, stained glass windows, and exterior flying buttresses. Inside, carvings, sculpture, needlework, wrought iron and wood carving depict the nation's history and biblical scenes. The cathedral welcomes all people regardless of faith and daily services are conducted in the Episcopal tradition. The Cathedral is the seat of the Bishop of the Episcopal Diocese of Washington.

Exterior
A masterpiece of Gothic-style architecture, the towers of the cathedral dominate the skyline.

★ Creation
Above the west entrance is "Creation," by artist Frederick Hart, carved by Vincent Palumbo, depicting mankind being formed from chaos.

Pilgrim Observation Gallery

Main Entrance
Three huge Gothic arches dominate the west façade, with pierced bronze gates depicting stories from the book of Genesis.

George Washington Bay

Space Window
Mankind's achievements in science and technology are commemorated in this window with the flight of Apollo 11 and a piece of moon rock.

The pinnacles on the cathedral towers are decorated with leaf-shaped ornaments and topped by elaborately carved finials.

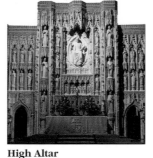

High Altar
Carved on the high altar are 110 figures, surrounding the central statue of Christ. Encased in the floor in front of the altar is stone from Mt. Sinai.

VISITORS' CHECKLIST

Massachusetts Ave & Wisconsin Ave, NW. *Tel* 537-6200. 📠 364-6616. Ⓜ *Tenley Town, Red Line.* 🚌 *32, 34, 36.* ⬜ *10am–3:30pm Mon–Fri, 10:00am–3:15pm Sat, 12:45pm–2:30pm Sun.* 📷 📹 *Group reservations call 537-6207.* 🅿 ♿ 🖬 📖 ✝ *Evening service 5:30pm Mon–Fri, 4:0pm Sat, Sun; noon Mon–Sat; hourly 8am–11am, 4pm, & 6:30pm Sun.* **www**.nationalcathedral.org

Children's Chapel
A statue of Jesus as a boy stands by this chapel built to the scale of a six-year-old. There are also motifs of baby and mythical animals.

★ South Rose Window
The theme of this window by Joseph Reynolds and Wilbur Burnham is "The Church Triumphant."

Nave
From the West Portal to the High Altar, the iconography tells the story of humanity to redemption.

STAR FEATURES

★ South Rose Window

★ Creation

Basilica of the National Shrine of the Immaculate Conception ㉓

400 Michigan at 4th St, NE.
Tel 526-8300. **M** Brookland-CUA.
◐ Apr 1–Oct 31: 7am–7pm daily;
Nov 1–Mar 31: 7am–6pm daily.
🔾 📷 🖥 🚻 &
www.nationalshrine.com

Completed in 1959, this enormous Catholic Church is dedicated to the Virgin Mary. The church was designed in the shape of a crucifix and has many stained-glass windows. The building can seat a congregation of 2,500 people or more.

In the early 1900s, Bishop Thomas Shahan, rector of the Catholic University of America, proposed building a national shrine in Washington. Shahan gained the Pope's support in 1913, and in 1920 the cornerstone was laid. The Great Upper Church was dedicated on November 20, 1959. An unusual and striking combination of Romanesque and Byzantine styles, the shrine boasts classical towers as well as minarets in its design. The basilica's large interior includes a number of chapels, each with a distinctive design of its own.

Visitors can also enjoy the peaceful and extensive Prayer Garden which covers almost an acre (4,050sq m).

Entrance to the Chinese Pavilion at the National Arboretum

National Arboretum ㉔

Bladensburg Road and R St, NE.
Tel 245-2726. **M** Stadium Armory.
◐ 8am–5pm daily. Museum
10am–3:30pm daily. ◑ Dec 25.
📷 by appointment only. 🚻 &
limited. **www.**usna.usda.gov

Tucked away in a corner of northeast Washington is the 446-acre National Arboretum – a center for research, education, and the preservation of trees, shrubs, flowers, and other plants. The many different collections here mean that the Arboretum is an ever-changing, year round spectacle.

The Japanese Garden, which encompasses the National Bonsai and Penjing Museum, has bonsai that are from 20 to 380 years old. The 2-acre herb garden has ten specialty gardens, where herbs are grouped according to use and historical significance. At the entrance to the garden is an elaborate 16th-century European-style "knot garden," with about 200 varieties of old roses. The Perennial Collection includes peonies, daylilies, and irises, which bloom in late spring and summer. The National Grove of State Trees has trees representing every state.

Bonsai tree in the Arboretum

Howard University ㉕

2400 Sixth St, NW. **Tel** 806-6100.
M Shaw-Howard. **www.**howard.edu

In 1866 the first Congregational Society of Washington considered establishing a seminary for the education of African-Americans – a school intended for "teachers and preachers." The concept expanded to include a multi-purpose university, and within two years the Colleges of Liberal Arts and Medicine of Howard University were founded. Named for General Oliver O. Howard (1830–1909), an abolitionist and Civil War hero who later became a commissioner of the Freedman's Bureau. The impetus for establishing such a university was the arrival of newly-freed men from the South who were coming to the North seeking education to improve their lives. The university's charter was enacted by Congress and approved by President Andrew Jackson.

Famous graduates include Thurgood Marshall, who championed desegregation of public schools and was the first African-American Supreme Court Justice, Carter Woodson, Toni Morrison, Ralph Bunche, Stokely Carmichael, and Ossie Davis.

View down the nave to the Basilica's altar

FREDERICK DOUGLASS (1817–95)

Born a slave around 1818, Frederick Douglass became the leading voice in the abolitionist movement that fought to end slavery in the United States. Douglass was taught to read and write by his white owners. At the age of 20 he fled to Europe. British friends in the anti-slavery movement purchased him from his former masters, and he was at last a free man. For most of his career he lived in New York, where he worked as a spokesman for the abolitionist movement. A brilliant speaker, he was sent by the American Anti-Slavery Society on a lecture tour and won added fame with the publication of his autobiography in 1845. In 1847 he became editor of the anti-slavery newspaper *The North Star*, named after the constellation point followed by escaping slaves on their way to freedom. During the Civil War *(see p21)*, Douglass was an advisor to President Lincoln and fought for the constitutional amendments that guaranteed equal rights to freed blacks.

Frederick Douglass

Frederick Douglass House ㉖

1411 W St, SE. **Tel** 426-5961.
Ⓜ *Anacostia.* ◯ *9am–4pm Mon–Sun.* ⬤ *Jan 1, Thanksgiving, Dec 25.* 🏷 ☑ ♿ *call ahead.*
www.nps.gov/frdo

The abolitionist leader Frederick Douglass lived in Washington only toward the end of his illustrious career. After the Civil War he moved first to a townhouse on Capitol Hill, and then to Anacostia. In 1877 he bought this white-framed house, named it Cedar Hill, and lived here, with his family, until his death in 1895. Douglass's widow opened Cedar Hill for public tours in 1903, and in 1962 the house was donated to the National Park Service, which is now responsible for maintaining it. Most of the furnishings are original to the Douglass family and include gifts to Douglass

"The Growlery" in the garden of the Frederick Douglass House

from President Lincoln and the writer Harriet Beecher Stowe, author of *Uncle Tom's Cabin* (1852).

In the garden is a small stone building that Douglass used as an alternative study, and which he nicknamed "The Growlery." From the front steps of the house there is a magnificent view across the Anacostia River.

Anacostia Museum ㉗

1901 Fort Place, SE. **Tel** 357-2700.
Ⓜ *Anacostia.* ◯ *10am–5pm daily.* ⬤ *Dec 25.* ☑ *by appointment only; call 287-3369.* ♿
www.si.edu/anacostia

The full name of this museum is the Anacostia Museum and Center for African-American History and Culture. It is part of the Smithsonian Institution *(see p72)*, and is dedicated to increasing public understanding and awareness of the history and culture of people of African descent and heritage living in the Americas.

Basic needs such as housing, transportation, healthcare, and employment were long denied to members of the African-American community, and the Anacostia Museum sponsors exhibits addressing these concerns. Two of its major initiatives have been *Black Mosaic*, a research project on Washington's diverse Afro-Caribbean culture, and *Speak to My Heart: African American Communities of Faith and Contemporary Life*.

After a recent renovation of its library and computers, the museum is now as much a resource center as it is a space for art and history exhibitions. Its collections include historical objects, documents, videos, and works of art. A nationally traveling exhibit, *Reflections in Black*, traces the history of African-American photography from 1840 to the present.

Façade of Cedar Hill, the Frederick Douglass House

THREE GUIDED WALKS

The best way to discover Washington's historic neighborhoods, diverse architecture, parks and gardens is on foot. The first walk takes you up and down Massachusetts Avenue, past many of the city's larger embassies and grand, imposing mansions into Kalorama, a pretty area that's home to many of the smaller embassies. Afterwards, you may wish to spend more time exploring. You'll find at least one hidden gem; the Embassy area also houses the Phillips Collection *(see p135)* and several art galleries. On the walks through Georgetown and Old Town Alexandria you'll notice that many of the historic buildings you pass are open to the public.

Fountain at Dumbarton Oaks

A CLOSER LOOK

In Georgetown you could tour Dumbarton Oaks, Tudor Place, or Georgetown University *(see pp120–7)*. In Alexandria you might look inside churches, the Lyceum (the local history museum), the Lee-Fendall House, Gadsby's Tavern Museum, or the Carlyle House *(see pp158–9)*.

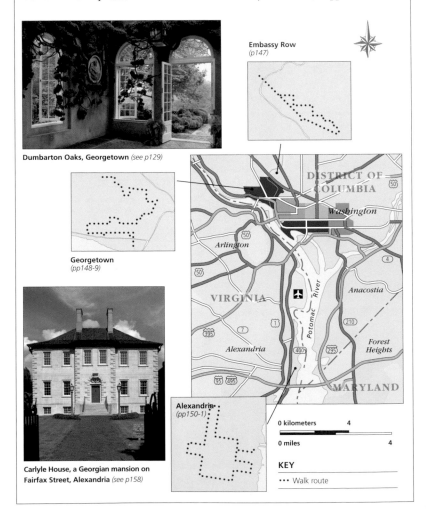

Dumbarton Oaks, Georgetown *(see p129)*

Embassy Row
(p147)

Georgetown
(pp148-9)

Carlyle House, a Georgian mansion on Fairfax Street, Alexandria *(see p158)*

Alexandria
(pp150-1)

DISTRICT OF COLUMBIA

Washington

Arlington

VIRGINIA

Potomac River

Anacostia

Alexandria

Forest Heights

MARYLAND

| 0 kilometers | 4 |
| 0 miles | 4 |

KEY

••• Walk route

A Walk Around Embassy Row

For those fans of eclectic architecture this walk is a fascinating experience. Starting from Dupont Circle west it takes you along Massachusetts Avenue, past many of the larger embassies to the Italian Embassy and then back along Massachusetts Avenue to Kalorama, a quiet residential area where smaller embassies and museums are tucked away in its tree-lined streets.

Ornate Embassy of Indonesia ①

organization set up by George Washington. A statue of Civil War General Philip T. Sheridan on his horse greets you at Sheridan Circle ③. Walk around the circle to the left, passing the Irish and Romanian embassies. You'll see the Turkish Embassy ④, an ornate mansion that boasts a mixture of Romanesque and Turkish styles on the exterior, while inside there are Doric columns, marble floors, mosaic tiles, bronze statues, stained glass windows, and frescoes. It was built by Washington architect George Oakley Totten, who was

Islamic Center's striking minaret ⑦

copper eaves are reminiscent of a Renaissance palazzo. Cross Massachusetts Avenue and turn back toward Dupont Circle. Keep walking until you come to the the Islamic Center ⑦, a mosque with a 160-ft (48-m) minaret. Wander inside to see the exquisite tile work and Persian carpets. (Head coverings for women are provided.) Turn left on California Street, right onto 24th Street and left onto S Street past the Woodrow Wilson House ⑧ (the unpretentious home of the 28th president) and the Textile Museum ⑨. Go right onto 22nd Street, walking down the Spanish Steps to R Street. Turn left on R and right on 21st Street, passing the Phillips

At Dupont Circle Metro head northwest on the south side of Massachusetts Avenue. Look for the Indonesian Embassy ①. This Beaux Arts mansion was built at the turn of the century by an Irish immigrant from Tipperary who made his fortune in the gold mines. The house later became the property of Evalyn Walsh McLean, who also owned the 44-carat Hope Diamond, which is at the Smithsonian. Farther on, there's an Italianate palace, now home to the Society of Cincinnati ②, a charitable

inspired by palaces in Istanbul, for wealthy industrialist Edward Hamlin Everett. Known as the "bottle top king" (he obtained the patent for corrugated bottle tops), Everett staged elaborate musical evenings here. As you stroll along Massachusetts Avenue, take a look at the garden behind the gate of the Japanese Embassy ⑤, a simple and graceful Georgian Revival building. After crossing the bridge over Rock Creek Park, you reach the Italian Embassy ⑥, a stunning contemporary structure that was designed by Piero Sartogo Architetti in Rome and Leo A. Daly in Washington. Its cantilevered

Collection ⑩, one of the country's most delightful modern art museums. Turn left on Q Street to make your way back to your start at the Dupont Circle Metro.

TIPS FOR WALKERS

Starting point: *Dupont Circle Metro.*
Length: *2.5 miles (4 km)*
Stopping off points: *Choose from one of several good restaurants near the Dupont Circle Metro stop.*

0 meters   400
0 yards   400

KEY

••• Walk Route

❀ Good viewing point

Ⓜ Metro station

A 90-Minute Walk in Georgetown

Renowned for its beautiful and historic architecture, eclectic shops, and delightful restaurants, Georgetown has it all. Starting in upper Georgetown, this walk takes you along residential streets past grand homes and Federal-style rowhouses, past early churches and cemeteries, parks and river vistas, quiet lanes and crowded streets. The walk ends on M Street in the commercial heart of Georgetown at the oldest house built in the district. Details of many sights mentioned are in the section on Georgetown *(see pp120–7)*.

come to O Street. Turn right on O Street and then left on 29th Street. Mt. Zion Church ⑧, on your right at 1334, was Washington's first African-American church, and has a tin ceiling that shows a West African influence *(see p126)*.

At the corner, turn right on Dumbarton Street, left on 30th Street, and right on N Street, which is full of elegant

Dumbarton House, beautifully designed inside and out ⑥

Francis Scott Key Memorial Bridge

Start at Wisconsin Avenue and S Street where you head east and then right on to 32nd Street. Dumbarton Oaks ① at 1703, a Federal-style mansion owned by Harvard University, contains a huge collection of pre-Columbian and Byzantine art, and may be worth returning to explore at length one afternoon *(see p127)*.

Turn left on R Street and right onto 31st Street. Admire Tudor Place ②, designed by the Capitol architect William Thornton on the right *(see p126)*. Turn left onto Avon Lane and left again on Avon Place. Walk across R Street to Montrose Park ③, which has a maze where you might like to meander for a bit, and then return to R Street. Head east and go

into Oak Hill Cemetery ④. James Renwick, architect of New York's St. Patrick's Cathedral, designed the chapel inside *(see p126)*.

Back on R Street, head east to 28th Street. Turn right past Evermay ⑤, a Georgian manor, built by Scotsman Samuel Davidson in 1792. Turn left on Q Street. On your left, the Federal-style Dumbarton House ⑥, is noted for its beautiful 18th- and 19th-century furnishings. Make a left at the corner on 27th Street. Facing you is the Mt. Zion cemetery ⑦ where African Americans were buried before the Civil War.

Turning around, walk back on 27th Street until you

TIPS FOR WALKERS

Starting point: *Wisconsin Avenue & S Street.*
Length: *3 miles (5 km).*
Getting there: *Take the Metro Connection express bus service from Foggy Bottom metro stop to Wisconsin Ave & R Street.*

Smith Row, American Federal-style architecture on N Street ⑪

Montrose Park, a tranquil space for city relaxation ③

18th-century architecture. On your right you pass 3017 N Street, the house where Jackie Kennedy once lived ⑨. At Wisconsin Avenue you can take a break at Martin's Tavern (est. 1933) or one of many cafés here. Turn right on Wisconsin and then left on O Street. Note the old streetcar tracks and St. John's Episcopal Church ⑩ at 3240, once attended by Thomas Jefferson. Turn left on Potomac Street then right and

walk along N Street for several blocks. You'll pass Smith Row ⑪ with its brick Federal-style houses at 3255-63, John and Jackie Kennedy's home ⑫ from 1957 to 1961 at 3307, and Cox's Row ⑬ at 3327-39, built by Colonel Cox, a former merchant and mayor. Farther along N Street

is Georgetown University ⑭ (*see p126*). Turn left on 36th Street to find The Tombs bar, a favorite haunt of students. On Prospect Street ⑮ next to the Car Barn (once used to house trolleys and now part of the university), go down three flights of steep steps (where a scene from *The Exorcist* was filmed) to M Street (the city's busiest and most colorful street) and the Potomac River.

Cross M Street and turn left, passing the Key Bridge and the Francis Scott Key Park ⑯, named for the author of "The Star-Spangled Banner". Still on M Street, look for the sign to Cady's Alley at 3316, make a right, and go down the steps. Turn left on Cady's Alley ⑰, browse in the high-end home furnishing shops, left again on 33rd Street to return to M Street. Turn right and you may want to stop at Dean & DeLuca ⑱, a lively café and gourmet market built in 1866. Stroll past the Victorian-style Georgetown Park ⑲, a former tobacco warehouse that now houses over 100 shops. Cross Wisconsin Avenue and go along M Street to 31st Street. Turn right then left onto the towpath by the C & O Canal ⑳ for a block, turning right on Thomas Jefferson Street and head toward Washington Harbor ㉑ (*see pp122–3*). Walk through this large complex of shops to the waterfront. After admiring the magnificent river view, retrace your steps to M Street and visit the Old Stone House ㉒, which dates from pre-Revolutionary days.

Georgetown University ⑭

0 meters 300

0 yards 300

KEY

••• Walk Route

⚡ Good viewing point

Ⓜ Metro station

Passenger barge on the C & O Canal, a reminder of 19th-century shippers ⑳

A 90-Minute Walk in Alexandria

Stroll along cobblestone streets to see historic Alexandria, settled in the 18th century. This walk through the Old Town will take you by many historic homes, two of the oldest churches (George Washington attended both of them at one time or another), Gadsby's Tavern, and an old firehouse. The walk ends at the Torpedo Factory, now a thriving art center where over 200 artists exhibit their work. Afterward, go around to the back of the Torpedo Factory for a view of the Potomac River.

Historic Farmer's Market in Market Square ②

Start at the Ramsay House Visitor Center ①, once the home of a Scottish merchant and city founder, William Ramsay. Built in 1724, it is the oldest house in Alexandria. Outside Ramsay House, you'll see Market Square ② where farmers have sold their produce for over 250 years. At the corner of Fairfax and King Streets turn left onto South Fairfax Street. Walk past the Stabler-Leadbeater Apothecary Shop ③ *(see p158)*, built in 1792 and now under renovation. This was formerly run by Edward Stabler who worked with the "Society for the Relief of People Illegally Held in Bondage" to free enslaved African Americans.

Turn left on Prince Street to find 211, which was the former home of Dr. Elisha Cullen Dick, the doctor who attended George Washington on his deathbed. At the corner is the Athenaeum ④, a Greek Revival building dating from 1851, once the Bank of the Old Dominion. Cross Lee Street and continue walking on Prince Street. This block, dubbed Captain's Row ⑤, is still paved with cobblestones and was once home to sea captains and shipbuilders. Turn right

on Union Street. You'll pass several art galleries and catch a glimpse of the river on your left. Turn right on Duke Street to see the Federal-style homes and pretty gardens. Turn left on South Fairfax Street. The Old Presbyterian Meeting House ⑥ *(see p158)*, a brick church built by Scottish settlers in 1775 and rebuilt in 1837 after a fire, is on your right. On George Washington's death the bell of the Old Presbyterian tolled for four days. You'll find the Tomb of the Unknown Soldier of the American Revolution in the churchyard.

Go to the corner of

South Fairfax Street and turn right onto Wolfe Street. This cuts through what was once a neighborhood called Hayti, home to many prominent African-American leaders in the early 1800s. Continue until you reach Royal Street. The house at 404 South Royal Street ⑦ is the home of George Seaton, a black master carpenter whose

TIPS FOR WALKERS

Starting point: The Ramsay House Visitor's Center.
Length: 2.5 m (4 km).
Getting there: Take the Dash bus from the King Street Metro stop to the Ramsay House Visitor's Center.
Stopping Off Points: The Friendship Firehouse is open Fri–Sun. For lunch try Gadsby's Tavern or one of the restaurants on King Street.

Ramsay House, the oldest building in Alexandria ①

mother was freed by Martha Washington. Continue for three blocks. At 604 Wolfe Street is the Alexandria Academy ⑧, built with the support of George Washington and others. This free school was attended by white children before it became a school for African Americans in the first half of the 19th century.

Cross South Washington Street and turn right. After two blocks you'll come to the Lyceum ⑨, a building inspired by a Doric temple, which was originally a library, then a hospital for Union troops during the Civil War, and now a local history museum. A statue of a Confederate soldier, "Appomattox," stands in the center of the Prince and Washington Streets intersection, marking the spot where troops left Alexandria to join

Gadsby's Tavern, where President Jefferson's inaugural banquet was held ⑯

Portrait of Robert E. Lee ⑭

the Confederate army on May 24, 1861. Turn left on Prince Street and walk two blocks to South Alfred Street. Turn right to see the Friendship Firehouse ⑩ at 107. Turn right on King Street where you'll find colorful shops and restaurants. Turn left on Washington Street. Christ Church ⑪ will be on your left. Wander through the historic cemetery and into the church – this is where every year presidents have come to honor George Washington on his birthday. Continue on Washington Street past Lloyd House ⑫, a Georgian home built in 1796, once a station on the underground railroad.

After two blocks turn right on Oronoco Street at the Lee-Fendall House ⑬ *(see p159)*. The house, now a museum, was built by Philip Fendall who then married the sister of "Light Horse" Harry (Robert E. Lee's father and a Revolutionary hero). Across the road at 607 Oronoco Street is Robert E. Lee's boyhood home ⑭ *(see p158)*, which is now closed to the public.

Alexandria loves its dogs and they are all welcome at the Olde Towne School of Dogs on the corner of Oronoco and St. Asaph Streets. Turn right on St. Asaph and cross Princess Street with its cobblestones that were laid in the 1790s. Cross Cameron Street and turn left. A replica of the small house built by George Washington in 1769 is at 508 Cameron Steet ⑮.

Turning right on Royal Street, you'll find Gadsby's Tavern ⑯ *(see p158)*, where Jefferson's inaugural banquet was held. Across the street is the City Hall ⑰. Continue on Cameron Street and cross Fairfax Street. The Bank of Alexandria, the city's oldest bank, established in 1792, stands on the corner. Next door is Carlyle House ⑱ *(see p158)*, a Georgian mansion modeled after the Scottish estate Craigiehall. Go around to the rear to see the gardens. Back on Fairfax Street, continue on King Street and turn left. Enjoy the shop windows for two blocks to The Torpedo Factory on Union Street ⑲ *(see p159)*, a dynamic arts center.

The Torpedo Factory, with riverview studios, art galleries, and archaelogy museum ⑲

0 meters 300

0 yards 300

KEY

••• Walk Route

🔅 Good viewing point

Ⓜ Metro station

ℹ️ Tourist information

FOUNDERS PARK

NORTH UNION ST

WATERFRONT PARK

Potomac River

MARKET SQUARE

NORTH ROYAL STREET

NORTH FAIRFAX ST

NORTH LEE STREET

SOUTH FAIRFAX ST

SOUTH LEE STREET

SOUTH UNION STREET

EXCURSIONS BEYOND WASHINGTON, DC

OLD TOWN ALEXANDRIA 158–159

MOUNT VERNON 160–161

GUNSTON HALL • ANNAPOLIS • BALTIMORE
GETTYSBURG • FREDERICK 162–163

ANTIETAM • HARPER'S FERRY
GREAT FALLS PARK • MIDDLEBURG
SKYLINE DRIVE 164–165

CHARLOTTESVILLE • FREDERICKSBURG
RICHMOND • CHESAPEAKE BAY
CHINCOTEAGUE AND ASSATEAGUE 166–167

WILLIAMSBURG • YORKTOWN
AND JAMESTOWN 168–169

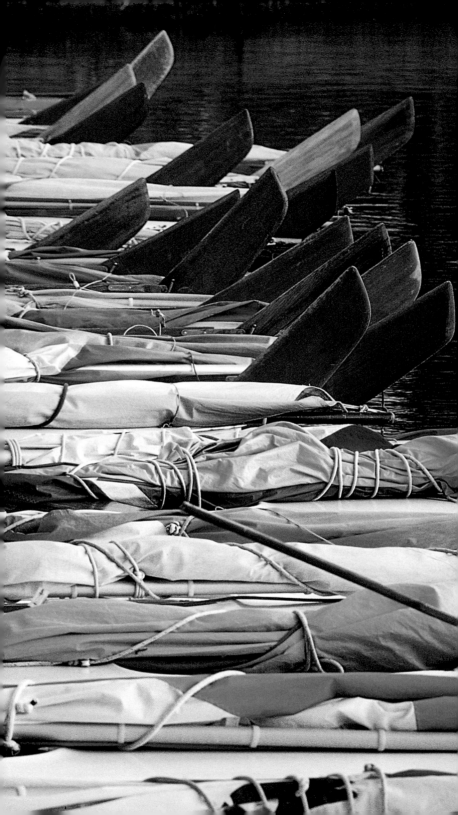

BEYOND WASHINGTON, DC

W ithin a half-day's drive of Washington lies enough history and natural beauty to satisfy the most insatiable sightseer. Alexandria and Williamsburg are a must for history buffs, while Chesapeake Bay and the islands of Chincoteague and Assateague offer a wealth of natural beauty. This area of Virginia and Maryland, along with parts of West Virginia and Pennsylvania, has been at the center of 400 years of turbulent American history.

Founded in 1623, Jamestown was the first permanent English settlement in America. In the 18th century, Williamsburg became the capital of Virginia and the first colony to declare independence from England. Today, Williamsburg is a living museum of the Colonial era.

A Civil War Howitzer cannon

The cultural influence of Europe is clearly seen in the architecture of this region. The two presidents largely responsible for crafting the character of the early republic lived in Virginia – George Washington at Mount Vernon, and Thomas Jefferson at Monticello. These homes reveal the lives their occupants led, at once imaginative, agrarian, inventive, comfortable – and, like many wealthy landowners, relying on slavery.

Cities and towns throughout the area have attractive historic districts that are a welcome contrast to the modern commercial strips on their outskirts.

Annapolis, for example, is a pleasant Colonial and naval port city. Baltimore also has a diverse charm, combining working-class neighborhoods and Old World character, and the town of Richmond blends the Old South's Victorian gentility with the luxuries of modern life.

Civil War battlefields are spread over the map as far as Gettysburg and tell the war's painful story with monuments, museums, cemeteries, and the very contours of the land itself.

The 105-mile (170-km) Skyline Drive through Shenandoah National Park, situated west of DC, makes the beautiful Blue Ridge Mountains accessible to hikers, cyclists, and drivers alike. To the east of the city, the Chesapeake Bay region attracts sailors and fishermen, as well as seafood lovers who can indulge in the delicious local specialty – blue crabs.

Farm fields in front of the treading barn at Mount Vernon

◁ **Colorful furled sails at the Dangerfield Island marina**

Exploring Beyond Washington, DC

Just minutes outside the bustling center of Washington is a striking and varied area of mountains, plains, and historic towns. To the west are Virginia's Blue Ridge Mountains, the setting for Shenandoah National Park. To the south is the Piedmont, an area of gently rolling hills that supports the vineyards of Virginia's burgeoning wine industry. To the east, the Chesapeake Bay divides Maryland almost in two, and to the south it travels the length of the Virginia coastline. To the north is the big port city of Baltimore, with its pleasant waterfront promenade, shops, museums, and stunning National Aquarium.

The Philadelphia Brigade Monument at Gettysburg

A re-created fort in Jamestown

SIGHTS AT A GLANCE

Alexandria Old Town pp158–9 **1**
Annapolis **4**
Antietam **8**
Baltimore **5**
Charlottesville **14**
Chesapeake Bay **17**
Chincoteague and Assateague **18**
Frederick **7**
Fredericksburg **15**
Gettysburg **6**
Great Falls Park **10**
Gunston Hall **3**
Harpers Ferry **9**
Middleburg **11**
Mount Vernon pp160–61 **2**
Richmond **16**
Steven F. Udvar-Hazy Center **12**
Skyline Drive **13**
Williamsburg pp168–9 **19**
Yorktown and Jamestown **20**

The dramatic Bearfence Mountain, part of Shenandoah National Park

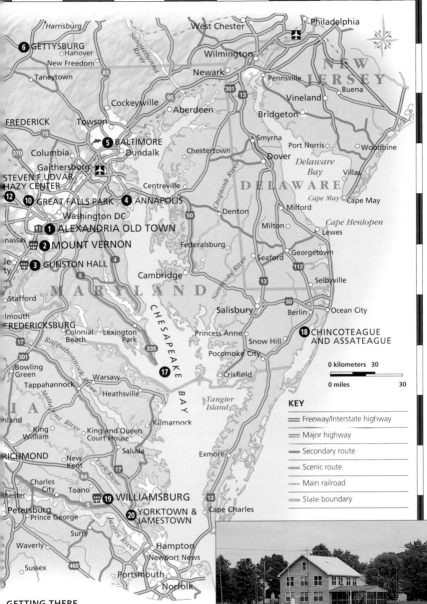

Harrisburg

West Chester

Philadelphia

6 GETTYSBURG
Hanover
New Freedom

Wilmington

Newark

Pennsville

NEW
JERSEY

Taneytown

83

301

13

Vineland

Buena

Cockeysville

95

Aberdeen

Bridgeton

FREDERICK

70

Towson

Smyrna

Port Norris

Woodbine

270

Columbia

5 BALTIMORE
Dundalk

Chestertown

Dover

*Delaware
Bay*

Villas

Gaithersburg

STEVEN F. UDVAR-
HAZY CENTER

12

Centreville

DELAWARE

Cape May

Cape May

10 GREAT FALLS PARK **4** ANNAPOLIS

Washington DC

Denton

50

Milford

Milton

Cape Henlopen

Lewes

1 ALEXANDRIA OLD TOWN

nassas

2 MOUNT VERNON

Federalsburg

Georgetown

113

Je
ty

3 GUNSTON HALL

4

Seaford

Selbyville

35

5

Cambridge

MARYLAND

13

Stafford

50

Salisbury

Berlin

Ocean City

Imouth
FREDERICKSBURG

Colonial
Beach

Lexington
Park

Princess Anne

Snow Hill

18 CHINCOTEAGUE
AND ASSATEAGUE

17

301

Pocomoke City

Bowling
Green

235

Tappahannock

17

Crisfield

0 kilometers   30

Warsaw

Heathsville

C
H
E
S
A
P
E
A
K
E

0 miles   30

I
A

*Tangier
Island*

KEY

hland

Mattaponi River

Kilmarnock

B
A
Y

Freeway/Interstate highway

King
William

King and Queen
Court House

Saluda

Major highway

RICHMOND

New
Kent

Exmore

Secondary route

chester

Charles
City

Toano

64

York River

Scenic route

Petersburg

5

19 WILLIAMSBURG

13

Cape Charles

Main railroad

Prince George

James River

20 YORKTOWN &
JAMESTOWN

State boundary

Surry

Waverly

Hampton

Newport News

Sussex

460

Portsmouth

Norfolk

GETTING THERE

Four good interstate highways lace the area: I-95
runs south and north on the eastern side of Virginia;
I-81 runs south and north in western Virginia; I-66
heads west from Washington; and I-270 goes toward
Frederick. Trains depart from Union Station to most
of the main towns, such as Baltimore, Alexandria,
Richmond, Williamsburg, and Harpers Ferry, which
is also served by the MARC *(see pp218–19)*. Virginia
Railway Express goes from Union Station to Alexandria and Fredericksburg. Greyhound buses also
travel to most towns.

Boats moored in the Chesapeake Bay area

Old Town Alexandria ❶

Detail from the Apothecary Shop

Old Town Alexandria has kept a special historical flavor, dating back to its incorporation in 1749. It is still a busy seaport and offers many historic sights, as well as shops selling everything from antique hat racks to banana splits. Restaurants are abundant, art thrives here, and the socializing goes on day and night, in and around Market Square.

Exploring Alexandria

Alexandria's tree-lined streets are filled with elegant, historic buildings and make for a pleasant stroll (see pp150-51). Alternatively, a boat tour offers an attractive prospect as does a leisurely lunch on the patio overlooking the waterfront. Nearby Founder's Park is the perfect place to bask on the grass by the river.

Façade of the elegant Carlyle House

🏛 Carlyle House

121 N Fairfax St. **Tel** (703) 549-2997. ⏰ 10am–5pm Tue–Sat, noon–5pm Sun; Nov–Mar: Last tour at 4pm. ● Mon, Thanksgiving, Dec 25, Jan 1. ♿ ✆ ♿ (call in advance.) 📷 www.carlylehouse.org

This elegant Georgian Palladian mansion was built by wealthy Scottish merchant John Carlyle in 1753. The house fell into disrepair in the 19th century but was bought in 1970 by the Northern Virginia Regional Park Authority; it has since been beautifully restored. A guided tour provides fascinating details about 18th-century daily life. One room, known as the "architecture room," has been deliberately left unfinished to show the original construction of the house. The back garden is planted with 18th-century plant species.

🏛 Stabler-Leadbeater Apothecary Shop

105 S Fairfax St. **Tel** (703) 836-3713. ⏰ 10am–4pm Mon–Sat, 1–5pm Sun. ● Thanksgiving, Dec 25, Jan 1. ♿ ✆ 📷

Established in 1792, this family apothecary was in business for 141 years. When it closed in 1933, the doors were locked with all of the contents intact. Now reopened as a museum, the shop's mahogany drawers still contain the potions noted on their labels. Jars containing herbal remedies line the shelves. Huge mortars and pestles and a collection of glass baby bottles are among the shop's 8,000 original objects. George Washington was a patron, as was Robert E. Lee, who bought the paint for his Arlington house here.

🏛 Gadsby's Tavern Museum

134 N Royal St. **Tel** (703) 838-4242. ⏰ Apr–Oct: 10am–5pm Tue–Sat, 1–5pm Sun, Mon; Nov–Mar: 11am–4pm Wed–Sat, 1–4pm Sun. ● federal hols. ♿ ✆ 📷 🍽

Dating from 1770, this tavern and the adjoining hotel, owned by John Gadsby, were the Waldorf-Astoria of their day. Now completely restored, they evoke the atmosphere of a hostelry in this busy port.

You can see the dining room with buffet and gaming tables, the bedrooms where travelers reserved not the room but a space in a bed, and the private dining room for the wealthy. The hotel's ballroom, where George and Martha Washington were fêted on his last birthday in 1799, can be rented out. This is also a working restaurant.

Interior of the Old Presbyterian Meeting House

🏛 Old Presbyterian Meeting House

321 S Fairfax St. **Tel** (703) 549-6670. ⏰ 9am–4:30pm Mon–Fri. ✆ ♿

Memorial services for George Washington were held in this meeting house, founded in 1772. In the churchyard are buried Dr. John Craig, a close friend of Washington, merchant John Carlyle, the Reverend Muir, who officiated at Washington's funeral, and the American Revolution's unknown soldier.

🏛 Boyhood Home of Robert E. Lee

Unfortunately, the boyhood home of Robert E. Lee is currently a private residence and not open to the public. General Lee lived in this 1795 Federal townhouse from the age of 11 until he went to West Point Military Academy. The drawing room was the setting for the marriage of Mary Lee Fitzhugh to Martha Washington's grandson, George Washington Parke Custis. The house is elegantly furnished with antiques.

Bedroom of Robert E. Lee

Lee-Fendall House Museum

614 Oronoco St. ***Tel*** *(703) 548-1789.* *10am–4pm Tue–Sat, 1–4pm Sun.* *Dec 25–Jan 31 (except 3rd Sun, Lee's birthday celebration).*

Philip Fendall built this stylish house in 1785, then married the sister of Revolutionary War hero "Light Horse" Harry Lee. Lee descendants lived here until 1904. Restored to its early Victorian motif, the house is rich with artifacts from the Revolution to the 1930s Labor Movement.

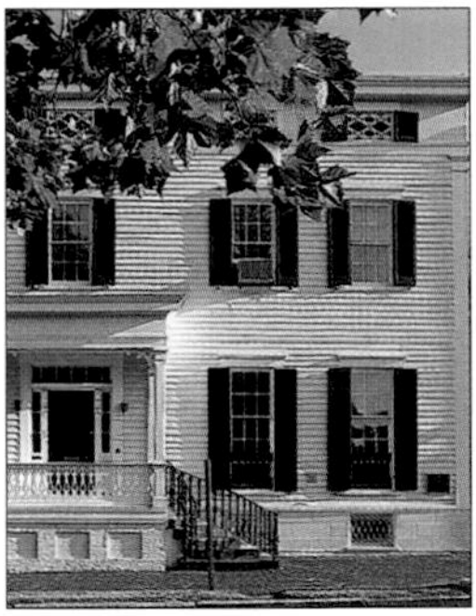

Lee-Fendall House Museum

Torpedo Factory Art Center

105 N. Union St. ***Tel*** *(703) 838-4565.* *10am–5pm daily.* *Easter, July 4, Thanksgiving, Dec 25, Jan 1.*

www.torpedofactory.org

Originally a real torpedo factory during World War II, it was converted into an arts center by a partnership between the town and a group of local artists in 1974. Today there is gallery and studio space for over 150 artists to create and exhibit their work. Visitors can watch a potter at his wheel, sculptors, print-makers, and jewelry-makers.

Christ Church

Cameron & N Washington Sts. ***Tel*** *(703) 549-1450.* *9am–4pm Mon–Fri, 9–4pm Sat, 2–4:30pm Sun.* *Thanksgiving, Dec 25, Jan1.*

The oldest church in continuous use in the town, this Georgian edifice was completed in 1773. George Washington's square pew is still preserved with his nameplate, as is that of Robert E. Lee.

On the other side of this Episcopalian church, a label reads "William E. Cazenove. Free pew for strangers." In the churchyard 18th-century gravestones wear away under the weather of the centuries.

VISITORS' CHECKLIST

Alexandria. *119,000.* *Union Station, 110 Callahan St.* *King Street.* *Ramsay House Visitor Center, 221 King St (703-838-4200.)*

www.FunSide.com

Farmers Market

Market Square, King & Fairfax Sts. ***Tel*** *(703) 838-0960, 4770.* *5:30am–10am Sat.*

This market dates back to the city's incorporation in 1749. George Washington, a trustee of the market, regularly sent produce to be sold at the market from his farm at Mount Vernon *(see pp160–61)*. A very pleasant aspect of the market square today is its central fountain. Shoppers can find fresh fruits and vegetables, cut flowers, herbs, baked goods, meats, and crafts.

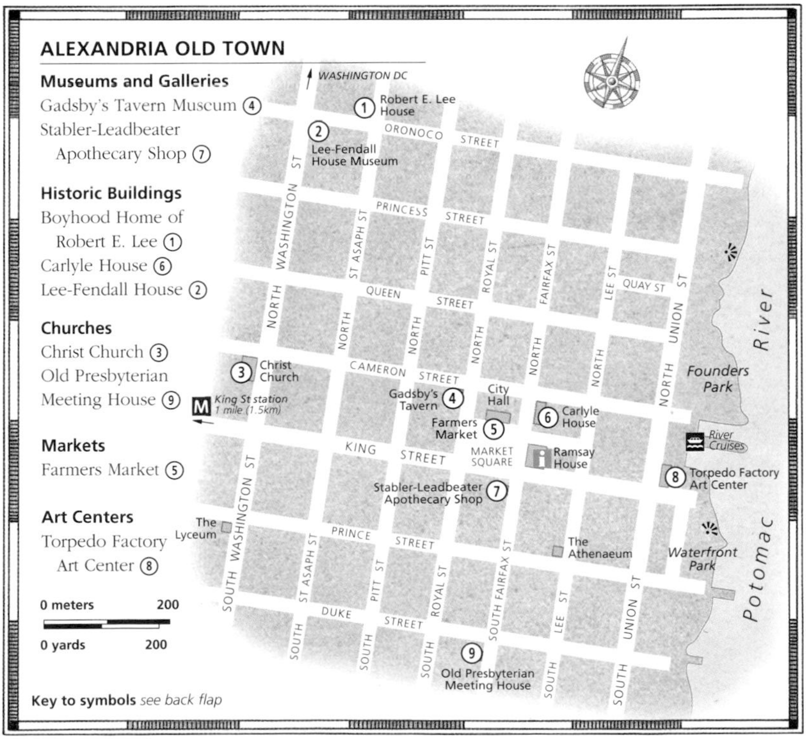
ALEXANDRIA OLD TOWN
Museums and Galleries
Gadsby's Tavern Museum ④
Stabler-Leadbeater Apothecary Shop ⑦
Historic Buildings
Boyhood Home of Robert E. Lee ①
Carlyle House ⑥
Lee-Fendall House ②
Churches
Christ Church ③
Old Presbyterian Meeting House ⑨
Markets
Farmers Market ⑤
Art Centers
Torpedo Factory Art Center ⑧
0 meters 200
0 yards 200
Key to symbols see back flap
WASHINGTON DC
Robert E. Lee House
Lee-Fendall House Museum
ORONOCO STREET
PRINCESS STREET
QUEEN STREET
CAMERON STREET
KING STREET
PRINCE STREET
DUKE STREET
QUAY ST
NORTH WASHINGTON ST
ST ASAPH ST
PITT ST
ROYAL ST
FAIRFAX ST
LEE ST
NORTH UNION ST
SOUTH WASHINGTON ST
SOUTH FAIRFAX ST
UNION ST
Christ Church
King St station 1 mile (1.5km)
Gadsby's Tavern
City Hall
Farmers Market
Carlyle House
MARKET SQUARE
Ramsay House
River Cruises
Torpedo Factory Art Center
Stabler-Leadbeater Apothecary Shop
The Lyceum
The Athenaeum
Founders Park
Waterfront Park
Old Presbyterian Meeting House
Potomac River

Mount Vernon ❷

Cameo of Washington

This country estate on the Potomac River was George Washington's home for 45 years. Originally built as a farmhouse by his father, Augustine, Washington made many changes, including adding architectural elements such as the cupola and curving colonnades. The house is furnished as it would have been during Washington's presidency (1789–97) and the 500-acre grounds (8,000 acres in his time) still retain aspects of Washington's farm, such as the flower and vegetable gardens, the sheep paddock, and quarters for the many slaves who worked the plantation.

Kitchen
Set slightly apart from the main house, the kitchen has been completely restored.

★ **Mansion Tour**
Visitors can see the study and the large dining room, as well as Washington's bedroom and the bed in which he died.

The Museum displays belongings of George and Martha Washington, as well as Houdon's famous bust of Washington.

Overseer's House

Slave Quarters
Washington freed all his slaves in his will. A memorial to them, erected in 1983, stands near Washington's tomb.

★ **Upper Garden**
The plants in this colorful flower garden are known to have grown here in Washington's time.

Wharf
Daytrip boats from central DC bring visitors to this wharf, which is on the same site as it was in Washington's time. Potomac cruise boats also stop off here.

Pioneer Farm

Stable

Coach House

The Lower Garden was used for growing vegetables and berries. The boxwood bushes surrounding it were planted in Washington's time.

★ Pioneer Farm
This exhibit demonstrates farming techniques that were pioneered by George Washington. There is also a replica of his unique 16-sided treading barn, which was created using authentic tools.

STAR SIGHTS

★ Mansion Tour

★ Pioneer Farm

★ Upper Garden

Washington's Tomb
In his will, Washington requested that a new brick tomb be built for his family at Mount Vernon. Washington died in 1799 but the tomb was not completed until 1831.

The Bowling Green was added to the estate by George Washington.

Gunston Hall ❸

10709 Gunston Road, Mason Neck, VA. **Tel** (703) 550-9220.
◯ 9:30am–5pm daily. ◯ Jan 1, Thanksgiving, Dec 25. 🖼 🗹 ♿ 🅿
www.gunstonhall.org

This Georgian house, built in 1755, was the home of George Mason, author of the 1776 Virginia Declaration of Rights. Situated 20 miles (32 km) south of Washington, DC, it is an exquisite example of careful historic restoration.

Of particular interest is the finely carved woodwork in the entrance hall, the chinoiserie mantel and fireplace in the formal dining room, and the servants' staircase which was used by the slaves so that they wouldn't be seen by guests. Outside are the beautiful boxwood gardens.

Annapolis ❹

Anne Arundel County, MD. 🏘 33,300. 🚊 Annapolis and Anne Arundel County Visitors Bureau, 26 West St. (410) 280-0445. ◯ 9am–5pm. **www**.visit-annapolis.org

The capital of Maryland, Annapolis is the jewel of Chesapeake Bay. It is defined by the nautical character that comes with 17 miles (27 km) of shoreline and the longtime presence of the US Naval Academy.

A walk down Main Street takes you past the 200-year-old Maryland Inn, and the shops and restaurants, to the City Dock lined with boats. It is then a short walk to the 150-year-old **US Naval Academy**. Inside the visitor center is the Freedom 7 space capsule that carried the first American, Alan Shepard, into space. The US Naval Academy Museum in Preble Hall is also worth visiting, especially to see the gallery of detailed ship models. The

The beautiful formal gardens of the William Paca House, in Annapolis

Tiffany window in the Naval Academy, Annapolis

Maryland State House is the oldest state capitol in continuous use. Its Old Senate Chamber is where the Continental Congress (delegates from each of the American colonies) met when Annapolis was briefly the capital of the United States in 1783–4.

Annapolis teems with Colonial-era buildings, most still in everyday use. The **William Paca House**, home of Governor Paca, who signed the Declaration of Independence, is a fine Georgian house with an enchanting garden, both of which have been lovingly restored recently. The **Hammond Harwood House** has also been restored. This masterpiece of Georgian design was named after the Hammond and Harwood families, both prominent in the area. Cornhill and Duke of Gloucester streets are beautiful examples of the city's historic residential streets.

Many tours are offered in Annapolis, including walking, bus, and boat tours. It is particularly enjoyable to view the city from the water, be it by sightseeing boat, chartered schooner, or even by kayak.

🏛 **US Naval Academy**
Corner of King George, east of Randall St. **Tel** (410) 263-6933.
◯ 9am–5pm daily. Photo ID needed. ◯ Thanksgiving, Dec 25, Jan 1. & 7 **www**.usna.edu

🏫 **Maryland State House**
State Circle. **Tel** (410) 974-3400.
◯ 9am–5pm (call ahead). Photo ID needed. ◯ Dec 25. 8 11am & 3pm. ♿

🏫 **William Paca House**
186 Prince George St. **Tel** (410) 263-5553. ◯ 10am–5pm Mon–Sat, noon–4pm Sun. ◯ Thanksgiving, Dec 24, Dec 25. 🖼 🅿

🏫 **Hammond Harwood House**
19 Maryland Ave. **Tel** (410) 269-1714.
◯ 10am–4pm Mon–Sat, noon–4pm Sun (Jan–Feb: Fri–Sun only). ◯ Thanksgiving, Dec 25, Jan 1. 🖼

Baltimore ❺

Chesapeake Bay, MD. 🏘 675,500.
🚊 Inner Harbor West Wall (410) 837-4636 or (800) 282-6632. Visitor services (877) BALTIMORE. 🚆 🚌 **www**.baltimore.org

There is much to do and see in this pleasant city. A good place to start is the Inner Harbor, the city's redeveloped waterfront, with the harborside complex of shops and restaurants. The centerpiece is the **National Aquarium**, which has many exhibits, including a seal pool and dolphin show. The Harbor is home to the **Maryland**

People walking along Baltimore's pleasant Inner Harbor promenade

Science Center, where "do touch" is the rule. The planetarium and an IMAX® theater thrill visitors with images of earth and space.

The **American Visionary Art Museum** houses a collection of extraordinary works by self-taught artists whose materials range from matchsticks to faux pearls.

Uptown is the **Baltimore Museum of Art**, with its world-renowned collection of modern art, including works by Matisse, Picasso, Degas, and Van Gogh. There is also a large collection of Warhol pieces and two sculpture gardens featuring work by Rodin and Calder.

The collection in the **Walters Art Gallery**, on Mount Vernon Square, features pieces by Fabergé, Rubens, and Monet and houses the beautiful painting *Sappho and Alcaeus* (1881) by Alma-Tadema.

The Little Italy area is worth a visit for its knock-out Italian restaurants and also for the games of bocce ball (Italian lawn bowling) played around Pratt or Stiles Streets on warm evenings.

🐬 National Aquarium
501 E Pratt St, Pier 3, N side of Inner Harbor. *Tel (410) 576-3800.* ⬜ *Mar–Jun, Sep–Oct: 9am–5pm Sun–Thu, 9–8pm Fri; Jul–Aug: 9–7:30pm Sun–Thu, 9–9:30pm Fri–Sat.* ⬤ *Thanksgiving, Dec 25.* 📷 ♿ 🅿 www.aqua.org

🏛 Maryland Science Center
601 Light St. *Tel (410) 685-5225.* ⬜ *10am–5pm Tue–Fri, 10am–6pm Sat, noon–5pm Sun.* ⬤ *Thanksgiving, Dec 25.* 📷 ♿ 🅿 www.mdsci.org

🏛 American Visionary Art Museum
800 Key Highway at Inner Harbor. *Tel (410) 244-1900.* ⬜ *10am–6pm Tue–Sun.* ⬤ *Mon, Thanksgiving, Dec 25.* 📷 ♿ 🍴 🅿

🏛 Baltimore Museum of Art
N Charles St & 31st St. *Tel (410) 396-7100.* ⬜ *11am–5pm Wed–Fri, 11–6 Sat–Sun.* ⬤ *Mon, Tue, Jul 4, Thanksgiving, Dec 25, Jan 1.* 📷 ♿ 🍴 🅿

🏛 Walters Art Museum
600 N Charles St. *Tel (410) 547-9000.* ⬜ *10am–5pm Wed–Sun; 1st Thu each month 10–8pm.* ⬤ *Mon, Tue, Thanksgiving, Dec 24, Dec 25, Jan 1, Jul 4.* 📷 *weekends.* ♿ 🅿

Gettysburg National Military Park ❻

97 Taneytown Rd, Gettysburg, Adams County, PA. *Tel (717) 334-1124.* **Park** ⬜ *6am–10pm daily.* **Visitor Center** ⬜ *8am–5pm daily (6pm in summer).* ⬤ *Jan 1, Thanksgiving, Dec 25.* 📷 ♿ 🔊 🅿 www.nps.gov/gett

This 6,000-acre park, south of the town of Gettysburg, Pennsylvania, marks the site of the three-day Civil War battle on July 1–3, 1863. It was the bloodiest event ever to take place on American soil,

The eye-catching architecture of the National Aquarium, Baltimore

with 51,000 fatalities. A two- or three-hour driving tour begins at the visitor center. The National Cemetery, where Abraham Lincoln gave his Gettysburg Address, is opposite. Other sights include the Eternal Light Peace Memorial.

Frederick ❼

Frederick County, MD. 👥 *50,000.* ℹ *19 E Church St (800) 999-3613, (301) 228-2888.* ⬜ *9am–5pm daily.* ⬤ *Jan 1, Easter, Thanksgiving, Dec 25.* www.fredericktourism.org

Dating back to the mid-18th century, Frederick's historic center was renovated in the 1970s.

This charming town is a major antique center and home to hundreds of antique dealers. Its shops, galleries, and eateries are all in 18th- and 19th-century settings. Francis Scott Key, author of "The Star Spangled Banner," is buried in Mt. Olivet Cemetery.

Antietam National Battlefield ⑧

Route 65, 10 miles (16 km) S of Hagerstown, Washington County, MD. **Tel** *(301) 432-5124.* ◯ *Jun–Aug: 8:30am–6pm daily; Sep–May: 8:30am–5pm.* ● *Thanksgiving, Dec 25, Jan 1.* 🈂 🏠 ♿ **www.**nps.gov/anti

One of the worst battles of the Civil War was waged here on September 17, 1862. There were 23,000 casualties but no decisive victory.

An observation tower offers a panoramic view of the battlefield. Antietam Creek runs peacefully under the costly Burnside Bridge. General Lee's defeat at Antietam inspired President Lincoln to issue the Emancipation Proclamation. The Visitors' Center movie recreating the battle is excellent.

John Brown's Fort in Harpers Ferry National Historic Park

Harpers Ferry ⑨

Route 340, Harpers Ferry, Jefferson County, WV. **Tel** *(304) 535-6298.* ◯ *8am–5pm daily.* ● *Thanksgiving, Dec 25, Jan 1.* 🈂 🎬 *Spring–Fall.* **www.**nps.gov/hafe

Nestled at the confluence of the Shenandoah and Potomac rivers in the Blue Ridge

Mountains is Harpers Ferry National Historical Park. The town was named after Robert Harper, a builder from Philadelphia who established a ferry across the Potomac here in 1761. There are stunning views from Maryland Heights to the foot of Shenandoah Street, near abolitionist John Brown's fort. Brown's ill-fated raid in 1859 on the Federal arsenal, established by George Washington, became tinder in igniting the Civil War.

The great importance of the town led to the area being designated a national park in 1944. It has been restored by the National Park Service.

Great Falls Park ⑩

Georgetown Pike, Great Falls, Fairfax County, VA. **Tel** *(703) 285-2966.* ◯ *daily.* ● *Dec 25.* 🈂 🎬 ♿ **www.**nps.gov/gwmp/grfa

The first view of the falls, near the visitor center, is absolutely breathtaking. The waters of the Potomac roar through a gorge of jagged rock over a 76-ft (23-m) drop at the point that divides Virginia's undulating Piedmont from the coastal plain. Only experienced kayakers are permitted to take to the tubulent whitewater below, which varies with rainfall upstream.

The park is crisscrossed by 15 miles of hiking trails, some showing evidence of the commerce from the early 19th-century Patowmack, America's first canal. Guided history and nature walks are offered.

Situated just across the river, in Maryland, is the C&O Canal National Historical Park, entry to which is free for visitors to Great Falls Park.

The Red Fox Inn in Middleburg

Middleburg ⑪

Route 50, Loudoun County, VA. 🏇 *600.* 🛈 *Visitors' Center, 12 N Madison St.* **Tel** *(540) 687-8888.* ◯ *11am–3pm Mon–Fri, 11am–4pm Sat–Sun.* **www.**middleburgonline.com

Horse and fox are king in this little piece of England in the Virginia countryside. Middleburg's history began in 1728, with Joseph Chinn's fieldstone tavern on the Ashby's Gap Road, still operating today as the Red Fox Inn. Colonel John S. Mosby and General Jeb Stuart met here to plan Confederate strategy during the Civil War.

The exquisite countryside has thoroughbred horse farms, some opening during the Hunt Country Stable Tour in May.

Foxcroft Road, north of the town, winds past immaculate horse farms. East of Route 50 is **Chrysalis Vineyard and Winery**. On the Plains Road at the west end of town is **Piedmont Vineyards**, and a mile east of Middleburg is **Swedenburg Winery**. All three have tours and tastings.

🍷 **Chrysalis Vineyard**
23876 Champe Ford Rd (Off Route 50). **Tel** *(540) 687-8222, 800-235-8804.* ◯ *10am–5pm daily.* ● *Thanksgiving, Dec 25, Jan 1.* **www.**chrysaliswine.com

🍷 **Piedmont Vineyards**
Off Route 626. **Tel** *(540) 687-5528.* ◯ *daily.* ● *Thanksgiving, Dec 24, 25, 31, Jan 1.* **www.**piedmontwines.com

🍷 **Swedenburg Winery**
23595 Winery Lane. **Tel** *(540) 687-5219.* ◯ *daily.* ● *Thanksgiving, Dec 25, Jan 1.* **www.**swedenburgwines.com

The roaring waterfalls in Great Falls Park

Steven F. Udvar-Hazy Center ⑫

Dulles International Airport, near intersection of Rtes 28 and 50, Chantilly, VA.
Tel 703-572-4118. 🚌 *Shuttle from National Air and Space Museum $7.*
⬜ *10am–5:30pm daily.* ⬤ *Dec 25.* 🍴
www.nasm.si.edu/udvarhazycenter

This is a must for anyone who would like to view the Space Shuttle "Enterprise," or who wants to find out about rockets and satellites, or is eager to see a rare Boeing B-29 Stratoliner.
Opened in December 2003 to celebrate the 100th anniversary of the Wright brothers' first powered flight, and named in honor of its major donor, this museum was built to display and also preserve historic aviation and space artifacts. The vast building of over 760,000 sq ft (7,000 sq m) houses exhibit hangars with more than 300 aircraft and spacecraft. Visitors can walk among exhibits, view hanging aircraft from elevated walkways, and go up an observation tower to watch air traffic at Dulles Airport. As well as an education center and Imax® theater, a Wall of Honor offers a permanent memorial to those men and women who contributed to America's space exploration and aviation heritage.

Skyline Drive ⑬

Skyline Drive runs along the backbone of the Shenandoah National Park's Blue Ridge Mountains. Originally farmland, the government designated the area a national park in 1926. Deer, wild turkey, bears, and bobcats inhabit the park, and wildflowers, azaleas, and mountain laurel are abundant. The park's many hiking trails and its 75 viewpoints offer stunning natural scenery.

Pinnacles Overlook ①
The view of Old Rag Mountain with its outcroppings of granite is spectacular.

Whiteoak Canyon ②
The Whiteoak Canyon Trail passes six waterfalls on its route.

North entrance station

0 kilometers 10

0 miles 10

Camp Hoover ④
At the end of Mill Prong Trail, this 160-acre resort was President Hoover's weekend retreat until 1933, when he donated it to the Park.

Big Meadows ③
Close to the Visitor Center, this meadow is kept in its centuries-old state. It was probably kept clear by fire from lightning or Indians. Deer can easily be seen here.

Bearfence Mountain ⑤
Although it is a bit of a climb up this mountain, partly on rock scramble, it is not too difficult, and the reward is a breathtaking 360-degree view of the surrounding landscape.

Lewis Mountain ⑥
This awe-inspiring view from Lewis Mountain shows Shenandoah Valley in spring, when the lush scenery is interspersed with beautiful wildflowers.

KEY

- - - Walk route

🔆 Lookout point

━━ Road

TIPS FOR DRIVERS

Starting points: *north at Front Royal, central at Thornton Gap, south at Rockfish Gap.*
Length: *105 miles (168 km), duration of 3–8 hrs depending on how many stops are taken.*
When to go: *Fall leaf colors draw crowds in mid-October. Wildflowers bloom through spring and summer. .*
What it costs: *toll charge of $10 per car (valid for 7 days).*

Charlottesville ⓮

Virginia. 🏛 *40,700.* 🚗 🚌 ℹ️
*Charlottesville-Albemarle Convention
and Visitors Bureau, Monticello Visitors
Center, Route 20 South.* **Tel** *(434) 977-
1783, (877) 386-1102 (toll free).*
www.charlottesvilletourism.org

Charlottesville was Thomas
Jefferson's hometown. It is
dominated by the University
of Virginia, which he founded
and designed, and also by his
home, **Monticello**.

Jefferson was a Renaissance
man – author of the Declaration
of Independence, US president,
farmer, architect, inventor, and
vintner. It took him 40 years
to complete Monticello, beginning in 1769 when he was 25.
It is now one of the most celebrated houses in the country.
The entrance hall doubled as
a private museum, and the
library held a collection of
around 6,700 books.

The grounds include a large
terraced vegetable garden
where Jefferson grew and
experimented with varieties.

The obelisk over Jefferson's
grave in the family cemetery
lauds him as "Father of the

University of Virginia." Tours
of the university are available
year round.

Vineyards and wineries sur-
round Charlottesville. Michie
Tavern, joined to the Virginia
Wine Museum, has been re-
stored to its 18th-century appearance, and serves a buffet
of typical Southern food.

Montpelier, on a 2,500 acre
site 25 miles (40 km) to the
north, was the home of former
US president James Madison.

🏯 Monticello
Route 53, 3 miles (5 km) SE of
Charlottesville. **Tel** *(434) 984-9822.*
⬜ *Mar–Oct: 8am–5pm; Nov–Feb:
9am– 4:30pm.* ⬤ *Dec 25.* 🔖 📷
♿ 📷 **www.**monticello.org

Fredericksburg ⓯

Virginia. 🏛 *22,600.* 🚗 🚌 ℹ️ *Fredericksburg Visitor Center, 706 Caroline
St.* **Tel** *(800) 678-4748, (800) 654-4118.*
⬜ *9am–5pm daily, Memorial Day,
Labor Day until 7pm.* ⬤ *Dec 25.*
www.fredericksburgvirginia.net

Fredericksburg's attractions are
its historic downtown district,
and four Civil War battlefields,

**The elegant dining room at
Kenmore House**

including The Wilderness and
Chancellorsville. The Rising
Sun Tavern and Hugh Mercer
Apothecary Shop offer living
history accounts of life in a
town that began as a port on
the Rappahannock River.
Kenmore Plantation is famous
for its beautiful rooms.

The visitor center offers useful maps as well as horse-and-
carriage or trolley tours.

🏯 Kenmore Plantation
and Gardens and George
Washington's Ferry Farm
1201 Washington Ave, Fredericksburg.
Tel *(540) 373-3381.* ⬜ *Jan–Feb:
11am–5pm Sat; Mar–May, Sep–Dec:
11–5pm daily; Jun–Sep: 10–5pm
daily.* ⬤ *Thanksgiving, Dec 24, 25,
31.* **www.**kenmore.org

MONTICELLO, CHARLOTTESVILLE

*Situated in the leafy foothills of the Blue Ridge
Mountains, this Palladian masterpiece was built
between 1769 and 1809
by Thomas Jefferson.*

East portico

The greenhouse
was used by
Jefferson to
cultivate
a variety
of plants.

**North
piazza**

The entrance hall, where
guests and visitors were
greeted, is also a museum.

Jefferson's bed
straddles his cabinet
(office) and bed
chamber.

Richmond 16

Virginia. 198,300. Metropolitan Richmond Convention and Visitors Bureau, 405 N. Third St. **Tel** (804) 783-7450. Toll free 888-RICHMOND. 8:30am–5pm Mon–Fri. **www**.richmondva.org

Richmond, the old capital of the Confederacy (see p19), still retains an Old South aura. Bronze images of Civil War generals punctuate Monument Avenue. Brownstones and Victorian houses testify to this area's postwar prosperity.

The Museum of the Confederacy contains Civil War artifacts, including Robert E. Lee's coat and sword. The restored White House of the Confederacy is next door. Another popular museum is the fascinating **Science Museum of Virginia**.

The Neoclassical State Capitol, inside which is the life-sized Houdon sculpture of George Washington, was designed by Charles-Louis-Clérisseau. Hollywood Cemetery is the resting place of presidents John Tyler and James Monroe, and also 18,000 Confederate soldiers.

Statue of Robert E. Lee in Richmond

Museum of the Confederacy
1201 E Clay St. **Tel** (804) 649-1861. 12–5pm Mon–Sat, noon–5pm Sun. Thanksgiving, Dec 25, Jan 1. **www**.moc.org

Science Museum of Virginia
2500 W Broad St. **Tel** (804) 864-1400. Memorial Day to Labor Day: 9:30am–5pm Sun–Thu, 9:30am–9pm Fri & Sat. Rest of year: 9:30am–5pm, Mon–Sat, noon–5pm Sun. Thanksgiving, Dec 25. **www**.smv.org

Chesapeake Bay 17

www.wwlandmarks.com

Known as "the land of pleasant living," Chesapeake Bay offers historic towns, fishing villages, bed-and-breakfasts, seafood restaurants, beaches, wildlife, and farmland. Much of its Colonial history is preserved

in towns such as Cambridge and Easton. The Chesapeake Bay Maritime Museum, in the town of St. Michael's, depicts life on the bay, both past and present. Watermen unload the catch in Crisfield, where cruises depart for Smith Island. The place really feels like a step back in time, particularly with the local Elizabethan dialect.

Chincoteague and Assateague 18

Chincoteague, Accomack County, VA. 4,000. Assateague, Accomack County, VA and MD (unpopulated). Chincoteague Chamber of Commerce, 6733 Maddox Blvd. (757) 336-6161. **www**.nps.gov/asis **www**.chincoteaguechamber.com

These sister islands offer a wealth of natural beauty. Chincoteague is a town situated on the Delmarva (Delaware, Maryland and Virginia) Peninsula. Assateague is an unspoiled strip of nature with an ocean beach and hiking trails that wind through woods and marshes. It is famously populated by wild ponies, thought to be descended from animals grazed on the island by 17th-century farmers. The woodlands and salt marshes of Assateague attract over 300 species of birds, and in fall peregrine falcons and snow geese fly in. Monarch butterflies migrate here in October. There are several campgrounds

in the area, and the ocean beach is ideal for swimming and surf fishing. **Toms Cove Visitor Center** and **Chincoteague Refuge Visitor Center** can provide extra information.

Toms Cove Visitor Center
Tel (757) 336-6577.

Chincoteague Refuge Visitor Center
Tel (757) 336-6122.

Yorktown and Jamestown 20

York County, VA, and James City County, VA. York County Public Information Office (757) 890-3300.

Established in 1607, Jamestown was the first permanent English settlement in America. It has 1,500 acres of marshland and forest, threaded with tour routes. There are ruins of the original English settlement and a museum. There is a re-creation of James Fort, and full-scale reproductions of the ships that brought the first colonists to America. An Indian village invites visitors to experience traditional Indian culture.

Yorktown was the site of the decisive battle of the American Revolution in 1781. **Colonial National Historical Park**'s battlefield tours and exhibits explain the siege at Yorktown.

Settlement
Tel (757) 253-4838. 9am–5pm daily. Dec 25 and Jan 1.

Colonial National Historical Park
Tel (757) 898-2410 or (757) 229-1733. 9am–5pm daily. Dec 25. **www**.nps.gov/colo

Jamestown Settlement, a re-creation of Colonial James Fort

Colonial Williamsburg ⑲

As Virginia's capital from 1699 to 1780, Williamsburg was the hub of the loyal British colony. After 1780 the town went into decline. Then in 1926, John D. Rockefeller embarked on a massive restoration project. Today, in the midst of the modern-day city, the 18th-century city has been re-created. People in colonial dress re-enact the lifestyle of the original townspeople; blacksmiths, silversmiths, cabinet makers, and bakers show off their skills while horse-drawn carriages pass through the streets, providing visitors with a fascinating insight into America's past.

Colonial couple

Courthouse
Built in 1770–71 this was the home of the county court for more than 150 years.

NASSAU STREET

PALACE STREET

PALACE STREET

NORTH ENGLAND ST

QUEEN ST

★ **Governor's Palace**
Originally built in 1720 by Governor Alexander Spotswood, the palace has been reconstructed in its full pre-Revolution glory.

0 meters	200
0 yards	200

Nursery
Costumed living-history interpreters work the land in Colonial Williamsburg using replica tools and the same techniques as the original settlers.

STAR SIGHTS

★ Governor's Palace

★ Robertson's Windmill

★ Capitol

★ **Robertson's Windmill**
The windmill has daily demonstrations of the settlers' crafts, such as basket-making and barrel-making. The cart was a traditional means of transporting materials.

Print Office
This store stocks authentic 18th-century foods, including wine, Virginia ham, and peanuts.

Milliner
Owned by Margaret Hunter, the milliner shop stocked a wide range of items. Imported clothes for women and children, jewelry, and toys could all be bought here.

Raleigh Tavern
The Raleigh was once an important center for social, political and commercial gatherings. The original burned in 1859, but this reproduction has its genuine flavor.

★ Capitol
The capitol is a 1945 reconstruction of the original 1705 building. The government resided in the West Wing, while the General Court was in the East Wing.

KEY

– – – Suggested route

TRAVELERS' NEEDS

WHERE TO STAY 172–181

RESTAURANTS, CAFES, AND BARS 182–191

SHOPPING IN WASHINGTON, DC 196–199

ENTERTAINMENT IN
WASHINGTON, DC 200–207

WHERE TO STAY

If you plan to be doing the sights in Washington from dawn until midnight, you may simply need a roof over your head and a bed for your weary body. If you intend to take your time and relax, you may want to have a hotel with all the amenities: pool, health club, deluxe restaurant, room service. Washington can offer a wide range of accommodations. Generally, hotels that are closer to downtown and the Mall are more expensive, and those in the city suburbs are more affordable. Being a tourist destination as well as a business center, Washington's room rates are the second highest in the United States next to New York City. However, there are bargains to be had, especially during the off season and on weekends. Package deals are advertised regularly in the Sunday travel sections of *The New York Times* and the *Washington Post*.

Hotel doorman

Lobby of the plush Hilton Hotel

HOW TO RESERVE

Many hotels have toll-free numbers for making reservations. It is also often possible to preview the accommodations on the hotel's website. If you want to stay at a bed-and-breakfast, either reserve one through an agent or pick one from the phone book. Many hotels sell unreserved rooms at a discount, just as airlines sell unsold tickets. Some companies specialize in offering hotel discounts, including **Capitol Reservations/Discounter** and **Washington DC Accommodations**.

HOTEL GRADING AND FACILITIES

A five-star hotel will offer everything the visitor could wish for. Room service, health facilities, bathrooms with a jacuzzi, valet parking, and 24-hour maid and butler service are just some of the luxury services provided, but at a price. At the opposite end of the spectrum, a one-star hotel will have a television and a telephone in the bedroom but may have shared bathrooms. Hotels of all price ranges are available in the city.

DISCOUNTS

Washington has different "seasons" from other cities. When the cherry blossoms around the Tidal Basin bloom in April, it is impossible to find a reasonably priced room in the city. Then in June the city is full of school groups taking end-of-the-year trips. Despite often broiling temperatures, families are lured to the capital in the summer. Labor Day in September is very big for tourists as is, of course, the Fourth of July.

However, you can find bargains during the winter months from November through March. Washington is a Monday-through-Friday convention town, so the best prices are on the weekend, often at a fraction of the vacation season, midweek rate.

HIDDEN EXTRAS

Beware the hefty 14.5% tax levied on hotels in Washington. Also note that most hotels will invariably charge you extra for parking in the hotel's parking lot. There is no way to escape the tax, but you can shop around for a hotel with free parking. If you have to park your car in a garage, you can expect to have another $7 to $15 added to each night's tab.

CHAINS AND BOUTIQUE HOTELS

Staying at either a **Hilton, Best Western, Marriott**, or **Howard Johnson** hotel will guarantee a level of service and cleanliness mandated by the chain. An alternative to the large chain hotels are the increasingly popular boutique hotels. These small, unique places all have their own personalities. The Hotel George in Old Downtown has undergone a sleek modern renovation. It also houses Bis, one of the city's most talked-about new restaurants. The Henley Park has the décor of a British aristocratic home and serves afternoon tea. The Morrison

The George, a boutique hotel

Clark Inn on Massachusetts Avenue is a restored mansion filled with Victorian antiques. The Phoenix Park Hotel on Capitol Hill has an Irish theme and staff – and a pub popular with Irish nationals and Irish-American politicians.

BUSINESS TRAVELERS

Washington hotels increasingly accommodate the sophisticated communications needs of the business traveler. Modems and fax machines are often installed in rooms, and secretarial services are available through the (often multilingual) concierge. **Meeting Solutions** (a division of Washington DC Accommodations) can help arrange block bookings for a business convention.

Entrance to the Hay-Adams hotel

BED-AND-BREAKFASTS

Although bed-and-breakfast accommodations are not as popular or as plentiful in the United States as they are in Europe, both American and foreign travelers are starting to seek them out as an alternative to the more sterile and expensive hotels. **Bed-and-Breakfast Accommodations Ltd.** tries to match visitors with the perfect room in a bed-and-breakfast, an apartment or small hotel, or even a private home. They have 85 properties in the city and suburbs, and charge a one-time booking fee of $10.

BUDGET OPTIONS

The best value accommodation option for young travelers in Washington is the Youth Hostel. It is located in the center of the city in an area that is currently being rehabilitated. Young travelers are advised to be cautious when returning after dark. The rate is around $25 per night for a bunk bed in a single-sex dormitory room.

Camping is another inexpensive alternative. There are no campgrounds in the city itself, but camping facilities are available in the outer suburbs. The closest facility approved by Kampgrounds of America is in Millersville, Maryland, 17 miles (27 km) from central DC.

DISABLED TRAVELERS

Nearly all the large, modern hotels are wheelchair accessible, but the independent hotels and bed-and-breakfasts may not be. Call in advance to ask about stairs, elevators, and door widths if you have special needs.

CHILDREN

Traveling with children may dictate your hotel reservations. There are many hotels such as Embassy Suites *(see p177)* and **Washington Suites Georgetown** that have kitchens or kitchenettes and living rooms with sofabeds that provide space and privacy for parents. The Washington Courtyard by Marriott NW *(see p179)* has a safe outdoor pool and free cookies every afternoon. After walking around the Mall, children may crave a hotel with a pool or a game room. Consider a more expensive room in town rather than a less expensive room in the suburbs. The suburban rates may look appealing until you face a long drive back to your hotel during Washington's unpleasant rush hour.

Some hotels may ban children completely, but these are few and far between. More often than not hotels will be very accommodating toward young guests.

Doormen at the Willard Hotel

DIRECTORY

DISCOUNT COMPANIES

Capitol Reservations/ Discounter
Tel (800) 847-4832.
www.visitdc.com

Washington DC Accommodations; Meeting Solutions
Tel (800) 554-2220.
www.wdcahotels.com

CHAIN HOTELS

Best Western
Tel (800) 528-1234.
www.bestwestern.com

Hilton
Tel (800) 445-8667.
www.hilton.com

Howard Johnson
Tel (800) 406-1411.
www.hojo.com

Marriott
Tel (800) 228-9290.
www.marriott.com

BED-AND-BREAKFAST

Bed-and-Breakfast Accommodations Ltd.
*Tel (202) 328-3510,
(877) 893-3233 (toll free).*
www.bedandbreakfastdc.com

CHILDREN

Washington Suites Georgetown
2500 Pennsylvania Ave, NW.
Tel (202) 333-8060.
www.washingtonsuites.com

Choosing a Hotel

These hotels have been selected across a wide price range for facilities, good value, and location. They are listed by area and within these by price, both for central Washington, DC and the surrounding areas. All hotel rooms have air conditioning and private bathrooms, unless stated otherwise.

PRICE CATEGORIES
For a standard double room per night, inclusive of breakfast, service charges and any additional taxes such as VAT:

$ Under $125
$$ $125–$175
$$$ $175–$275
$$$$ $275–$375
$$$$$ over $375

CAPITOL HILL

Bull Moose Bed-and-Breakfast on Capitol Hill
$$$
101 5th St, NE (at A St), 20002 **Tel** *547-1050* **Fax** *548-9741 Rooms 10*   **Map** *4 F4*

Five blocks from the Capitol and the Mall, this turn-of-the-19th-century bed-and-breakfast has kept the original woodwork and given each room a Teddy Roosevelt theme. Some rooms come with shared bath. On-street parking is available. The hotel serves gourmet European breakfasts. **www.bullmoose-b-and-b.com**

Holiday Inn on the Hill
$$$
415 New Jersey Ave, NW, 20001 **Tel** *638-1616* **Fax** *638-0707 Rooms 343*   **Map** *4 E3*

Walking distance from the Smithsonian, this newly renovated hotel is a great choice for families, while it also appeals to business travelers. Some of the rooms have internet access. There is an outdoor pool. The fitness center here is open 24 hours. Children 12 and under dine free when accompanied by an adult. **www.holidayinnonthehill.com**

Capitol Hill Suites
$$$$
200 C St, SE (at 2nd St), 20003 **Tel** *543-6000* **Fax** *547-2608 Rooms 152*   **Map** *4 F5*

Located two blocks from the Capitol, this boutique-style all-suites hotel was recreated from an apartment building. It has a large, but cozy lobby. It offers free Continental breakfast. Each room comes with a spacious kitchen or kitchenette. Some rooms have high-speed internet. **www.capitolhillsuites.com**

Hyatt Regency Capitol Hill
$$$$
400 New Jersey Ave, NW (at D St), 20002 **Tel** *737-1234* **Fax** *942-1512 Rooms 834*   **Map** *4 E3*

Entrance to the Hyatt is through a five-story atrium. Rooms have wireless internet, while many suites offer views of the Capitol. You'll find here the Park Promenande restaurant as well as Perks coffee shop, and Networks lobby bar. Children under 18 stay for free. Two and a half blocks from Union Station. **www.hyattregencywashington.com**

Phoenix Park Hotel
$$$$
520 N Capitol St, NW (at F St & N Capitol), 20001 **Tel** *638-6900* **Fax** *393-3236 Rooms 149*   **Map** *4 E3*

Located one block from Union Station, this historic hotel features rooms furnished in an 18th-century Irish manor style. Three of the suites have spiral staircases and three have balconies. Irish entertainers perform nightly at The Dubliner, a pub with good Irish and American food. **www.phoenixparkhotel.com**

The Hotel George
$$$$$
15 E St, NW, 20001 **Tel** *347-4200* **Fax** *347-4213 Rooms 139*   **Map** *4 E3*

This modern boutique hotel, located one and a half blocks away from Union Station, is one of the most fashionable in the city. The large, airy rooms with wide desks will appeal to business travelers. There is a trendy French restaurant called Bistro Bis *(see p186)*. **www.hotelgeorge.com**

THE MALL

Holiday Inn Capitol
$$$$
550 C St, SW, 20024 **Tel** *479-4000* **Fax** *479-4353 Rooms 532*   **Map** *4 D5*

The hotel is conveniently located near L'Enfant Plaza Metro and one block from the National Air and Space Museum. There is an outdoor pool on the roof. American food is served at the Smithson restaurant, where children under 12 eat free when accompanied by an adult. **www.holidayinncapitol.com**

Loews L'Enfant Plaza Hotel
$$$$
480 L'Enfant Plaza, SW, 20024 **Tel** *484-1000* **Fax** *646-5060 Rooms 370*   **Map** *3 C4*

Many of the rooms in this 3-star luxury hotel have spectacular views. Conveniently located near the Smithsonian with easy access to the metro station. The American Sea Grill features steaks and seafood. A good choice for families, the hotel has an indoor pool and is pet friendly. **www.loewshotels.com**

Key to Symbols *see back cover flap*
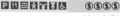

Mandarin Oriental

1330 Maryland Ave, SW, 20024 **Tel** 554-8588 **Fax** 554-8999 Rooms 400

Map 3 C5

A new luxury hotel with exotic decor and impeccable service. Enjoy live music and cocktails, accompanied by dim sum or sushi, in the Empress Lounge. Café Mozu offers an Asian-inspired menu as well as afternoon tea. It is located three blocks from the Smithsonian museums. **www.mandarinoriental.com**

OLD DOWNTOWN

Washington International Youth Hostel

1009 11th St, NW (at K St), 20001 **Tel** 737-2333 **Fax** 737-1508 Rooms 270

Map 3 C2

Attracting an international clientele, it is located three blocks away from Metro Center. The rooms are clean, spacious, and air conditioned. Amenities include a community kitchen, laundry, TV lounge, and luggage storage. Free Continental breakfast provided. Only MasterCard and Visa are accepted. **www.hiwashingtondc.org**

The Wyndham Washington, DC

1400 M St, NW (at Thomas Circle), 20005 **Tel** 429-1700 **Fax** 785-0786 Rooms 400

Map 3 B2

Four blocks from the McPherson Metro, the Wyndham has a large central atrium and all the amenities one would expect for a largely business clientele. The Veranda restaurant here offers American cuisine. The hotel also provides a 24-hour fitness center. **www.wyndham.com**

Hotel Washington

514 15th St, NW, 20004 **Tel** 638-5900 **Fax** 638-4275 Rooms 340

Map 3 B3

A registered historic landmark and one of the oldest hotels in Washington, this hotel was recently renovated. The Sky Terrace on the rooftop offers breathtaking views of the monuments. Conveniently located one block from the White House and three blocks from Metro Center. **www.hotelwashington.com**

Henley Park Hotel

926 Massachusetts Ave, NW, 20001 **Tel** 638-5200 **Fax** 638-6740 Rooms 96

Map 3 C2

The hotel, built in 1918 as an upscale apartment building, was once home to senators and Congressmen. The bar here features live jazz on weekends, and the Coeur de Lion restaurant is top-notch. Four blocks from Metro Center. **www.henleypark.com**

J. W. Marriott

1331 Pennsylvania Ave, NW (at 14th St), 20004 **Tel** 393-2000 **Fax** 626-6991 Rooms 772

Map 3 B3

The columned lobby has several cozy sitting areas. The rooms are plush with wireless internet access. Many rooms offer a beautiful view of the city and the Washington Monument. Close to the White House, National Theater, shops, and Metro Center. **www.marriott.com/wasjw**

Morrison-Clark Inn

1015 L St, NW (at Massachusetts Ave), 20001 **Tel** 898-1200 **Fax** 289-8576 Rooms 54

Map 3 C2

This historic 1864 inn was originally two separate townhouses. The Victorian-style rooms are beautifully appointed, some with marble fireplaces. One and a half blocks from the Convention Center and four blocks from the metro. **www.morrisonclark.com**

The Madison

1177 15th & M Sts, NW, 20005 **Tel** 862-1600 **Fax** 785-1255 Rooms 353

Map 3 B2

The Georgian Federal-style rooms of this elegant hotel are comfortable and luxurious, with oversize desks. Don't miss the mural District in 1812 in the The Federalist restaurant. Four blocks north of the White House. **www.themadison.net**

Grand Hyatt Washington

1000 H St, NW (at 11th St), 20001 **Tel** 582-1234 **Fax** 637-4797 Rooms 888

Map 3 C3

The Grand Hyatt's fanciful interior includes a waterfall-fed lagoon, surrounding an island where a pianist plays. Facilities include a sports bar, atrium café, martini lounge, and a restaurant. Wireless access in every room. Underground entrance to Metro Center. **www.grandwashington.hyatt.com**

Hotel Monaco Washington DC

700 F St, NW, 20004 **Tel** 628-7177 **Fax** 628-7277 Rooms 182

Map 3 C3

This magnificent hotel is housed in the Old General Post Office, built in 1836. The architect was Robert Mills who also designed the Washington Monument. Conveniently located near the National Portrait Gallery and the MCI Center. Pet friendly. The restaurant, Poste Brasserie, is delightful. **www.monaco-dc.com**

Willard Inter-Continental Hotel

1401 Pennsylvania Ave, NW (at 14th St), 20004 **Tel** 628-9100 **Fax** 637-7390 Rooms 341

Map 3 B2

A grand historic hotel (see p95) offers Edwardian-style rooms with marble bathrooms and high-speed internet. Mark Twain, Abraham Lincoln, and Walt Whitman were once guests and it was here that Martin Luther King wrote his "I Have a Dream" speech. Located two blocks from the White House. **www.washington.interconti.com**

THE WHITE HOUSE AND FOGGY BOTTOM

Beacon Hotel
P 🍽 🍸 ⛱ $$$

1615 Rhode Island Ave, NW (at 17th St), 20036 **Tel** *296-2100* **Fax** *331-0227 Rooms 199*   **Map** *3 B2*

The comfortable rooms are decorated with cosmopolitan flair. Eight deluxe turret suites and 60 corporate suites come with fully equipped kitchens, high-speed internet and web TV. The Beacon Bar & Grill restaurant serves American food. **www.beaconhotelwdc.com**

Hotel Lombardy
P 🍽 🍸 $$$

2019 Pennsylvania Ave, NW (at I St), 20002 **Tel** *828-2600* **Fax** *872-0503 Rooms 132*   **Map** *2 E3*

This European-style boutique hotel has an accommodating multilingual staff. Café Lombardy serves American food and a limited menu is available in the Venetian Room lounge. Two blocks from the Farragut West Metro and three blocks from the White House. **www.hotellombardy.com**

Lincoln Suites
P ≅ 🍸 ⛱ $$$

1823 L St, NW, 20036 **Tel** *223-4320* **Fax** *223-8546 Rooms 99*   **Map** *3 A2*

A modern boutique hotel with studio apartments, some with full-size kitchens. The tariff includes Continental breakfast, a free daily *Washington Post* and freshly baked cookies. Room service from Luigi's Italian restaurant. Free passes to Bally Fitness with gym and pool. **www.lincolnhotels.com**

One Washington Circle
P 🍽 ≅ 🍸 ⛱ $$$

1 Washington Circle, NW, 20037 **Tel** *872-1680* **Fax** *887-4989 Rooms 151*   **Map** *2 E3*

Frequented by business and leisure travelers, this recently renovated hotel has rooms with private balconies. There is an outdoor pool. The Circle Bistro serves Mediterranean food. Convenient for George Washington University and Hospital. **www.thecirclehotel.com**

Capital Hilton
P 🍽 🍸 ⛱ $$$$

1001 16th St, NW (at K St), 20036 **Tel** *393-1000* **Fax** *639-5784 Rooms 544*   **Map** *3 B2*

A large, bustling hotel. The inviting lobby has several seating areas and a sports bar. The nicest rooms are on the top floors. The Twigs Grill restaurant serves American cuisine. Two blocks from the White House and near several metro stops. **www.capitalhilton.com**

Embassy Suites Hotel
P 🍽 ≅ 🍸 ⛱ $$$$

1250 22nd St, NW, 20037 **Tel** *857-3388* **Fax** *293-3173 Rooms 318*   **Map** *2 E2*

With a swimming pool and suites that accommodate up to five people, this hotel is very suitable for families. The modern atrium has a waterfall, columns, and palm trees. A full breakfast is included in the tariff. Close to Dupont Circle shops and restaurants. **www.embassysuites.com**

Fairmont Washington Hotel
P 🍽 ≅ 🍸 ⛱ $$$$

2401 M St, NW (at 24th St), 20037 **Tel** *429-2400* **Fax** *457-5010 Rooms 410*   **Map** *2 E2*

Guests will enjoy the plant-filled atrium and luxurious rooms, some overlooking the central courtyard and gardens. The service is impeccable. The newly renovated Juniper serves American cuisine. Walking distance from Georgetown. **www.fairmont.com**

George Washington University Inn
P 🍽 ⛱ $$$$

824 New Hampshire Ave, NW, 20037 **Tel** *337-6620* **Fax** *298-7499 Rooms 95*   **Map** *2 E3*

This boutique-style hotel has a marble lobby. All rooms, with a Williamsburg-inspired decor, come with a refrigerator, microwave, and coffee-maker, while some of them have complete kitchens. High-speed internet available. Conveniently located, near the university, Kennedy Center, and metro. **www.gwuinn.com**

Hay-Adams Hotel
P 🍽 ⛱ $$$$

800 16th St, NW (at H St), 20006 **Tel** *638-6600* **Fax** *638-2716 Rooms 145*   **Map** *3 B2*

This historic Italian Renaissance-style hotel overlooking Lafayette Square and the White House combines the two homes of John Hay and Henry Adams, both renowned authors and diplomats. Beautifully renovated rooms feature antiques and ornamental ceilings. **www.hayadams.com**

Renaissance Mayflower
P 🍽 🍸 ⛱ $$$$

1127 Connnecticut Ave, NW, 20036 **Tel** *347-3000* **Fax** *776-9182 Rooms 657*   **Map** *2 F3*

The elegant and stately Mayflower, built in 1925, is on the National Register of Historic Places. Town & Country bar features live piano between 6 and 8pm. Elegant dining in the Café Promenade. Near Farragut North Metro and the White House. **www.renaissancemayflowerhotel.com**

St. Regis Washington
P 🍽 🍸 ⛱ $$$$

923 16th St, NW (at K St), 20006 **Tel** *638-2626* **Fax** *638-4231 Rooms 193*   **Map** *3 B2*

A historic, luxury hotel with a warm, European ambience. Elegantly furnished with antiques, chandeliers, and exquisite tapestries, reminiscent of a Renaissance palace. Guests will enjoy the romantic setting and American cuisine in the St. Regis restaurant. **www.stregis.com**

Key to Price Guide *see p174* **Key to Symbols** *see back cover flap*

The Jefferson: A Loew's Hotel
1200 16th St, NW (at M St), 20036 **Tel** *347-2200* **Fax** *331-7982 Rooms 100* **Map** *2F2*

Built in 1923, and popular with celebrities, this hotel is part of the America Hotel Historic Association. The Federal-style rooms are decorated with antiques and original art. The Jefferson restaurant, serving superb American cuisine, has a warm, elegant atmosphere. **www.thejeffersonhotel.com**

The Melrose Hotel
2430 Pennsylvania Ave, NW, 20037 **Tel** *955-6400* **Fax** *955-5765 Rooms 240* **Map** *2 E3*

A modern hotel, this is often the choice of artists performing at the Kennedy Center. The decor is contemporary European in style, with fine furnishings and textiles in all the rooms. The Landmark Restaurant serves seafood and steak. **www.melrosehotel.com**

The Westin Grand
2350 M St, NW, 20037 **Tel** *429-0100* **Fax** *429-9759 Rooms 263* **Map** *2 E2*

CD players, coffee makers, minibars, and luxurious marble bathrooms with extra-deep bathtubs are just a few of the amenities in the rooms of this well-appointed hotel. The Westin Café serves American food. There is an outdoor pool. **www.westin.com**

The Watergate Hotel
2650 Virginia Ave, NW, 20037 **Tel** *965-2300 Rooms 248* **Map** *2 D3*

Despite the notoriety of the Watergate name *(see p117)*, the views of the Potomac River, the genteel decor and the subdued lighting lend the hotel a peaceful air. The Aquarelle offers a superb dining experience. Across the street from the Kennedy Center. **www.watergatehotel.com**

GEORGETOWN

Georgetown Suites
1111 30th St NW (at M St) & 1000 29th St NW, 20007 **Tel** *298-7800* **Fax** *333-5792 Rooms 218* **Map** *2 D2*

This establishment provides one- and two-bedroom suites, studios, two-story townhomes, and penthouses. Each suite has fully-equipped kitchens with microwave, dishwasher, and ice-maker. The tariff includes a complimentary Continental breakfast. Free local calls. **www.georgetownsuites.com**

Hotel Monticello
1075 Thomas Jefferson St, NW, 20007 **Tel** *337-0900* **Fax** *333-6526 Rooms 47* **Map** *2 D3*

Located below M Street, near the C&O Canal, this Georgian-style boutique hotel has a lobby furnished with 18th-century antiques. It has spacious rooms, one-bedroom suites, and two-story penthouses. Continental breakfast is included in the tariff. Parking is limited to small and midsize cars. **www.hotelmonticello.com**

The Georgetown Inn
1310 Wisconsin Ave, NW, 20007 **Tel** *333-8900* **Fax** *333-8308 Rooms 96* **Map** *1 C2*

A small, boutique hotel built in the style of historic Georgetown. The large rooms have Colonial-style decor and luxurious bathrooms. The Daily Grill restaurant displays scenes of old Washington on the walls. Located in the heart of Georgetown. **www.georgetowninn.com**

The Latham Hotel
3000 M St, NW (at 30th St), 20007 **Tel** *726-5000* **Fax** *337-4250 Rooms 142* **Map** *2 D2*

This is an upscale European-style, boutique hotel with a luxurious lobby. There is an outdoor pool, four poolside bungalows, and quaint two-story carriage suites. The service is top-notch. Guests have access to an off-site fitness center. Its excellent five-star French restaurant, Citronelle, serves French cuisine. **www.thelatham.com**

Four Seasons Hotel
2800 Pennsylvania Ave, NW, 20007 **Tel** *342-0444* **Fax** *944-2076 Rooms 212* **Map** *2 D3*

A modern exterior belies the old-world elegance of this hotel, which prides itself on its excellent service. Rooms are spacious, with mahogany paneling, antiques, and flowers. Afternoon tea is served in the Garden Terrace. Near shops, restaurants and the Washington Harbor. **www.fourseasons.com**

FARTHER AFIELD

ADAMS MORGAN Adam's Inn
1744 Lanier Pl, NW, 20009 **Tel** *745-3600* **Fax** *319-7958 Rooms 26*

This European-style inn is located in three 100-year-old brick townhouses on a quiet residential street. Some of the newly renovated rooms have an "urban country" look; others are Victorian. Sixteen rooms have private baths. Five reserved parking spaces are available. Near the National Zoo and many restaurants. **www.adamsinn.com**

ADAMS MORGAN Kalorama Guest Hotel   🅿 $$

1854 Mintwood Pl, NW (near Columbia Rd & 19th St), 20009 **Tel** *667-6369* **Fax** *319-1262* *Rooms 29* **Map** *2 E1*

A Victorian townhouse in a charming residential neighborhood. The rooms are tastefully decorated in period decor. Children under six are not allowed. Parking spaces are limited. Many restaurants are close by. **www.washingtonpost.com/yp/kgh**

DUPONT CIRCLE Braxton Hotel $

1440 Rhode Island Ave, NW, 20005 **Tel** *232-7800* **Fax** *265-3725* *Rooms 48*   **Map** *3 B1*

This small hotel is located close to Logan Circle and within walking distance of Dupont Circle and U Street. Rooms come with cable TV and some have refrigerators. Continental breakfast is included in the tariff. All major credit cards, except Diners, are accepted. **www.braxtonhotel.com**

DUPONT CIRCLE Jurys Normandy Inn   🅿🚻 $

2118 Wyoming Ave, NW (Connecticut Ave & 23rd St), 20008 **Tel** *483-1350* **Fax** *387-8241* *Rooms 75* **Map** *2 E1*

Converted from a dormitory in a private school, this is a small, cozy hotel. Books can be borrowed from the hotel library and read by the fireside. Continetal breakfast is provided. The building is surrounded by stately apartments and historic townhouses. **www.jurysdoyle.com**

DUPONT CIRCLE Tabard Inn   🍽🚻 $$

1739 N St, NW, 20036 **Tel** *785-1277* **Fax** *785-6173* *Rooms 40*   **Map** *2 F2*

This country-style inn, named after the inn in Chaucer's *The Canterbury Tales*, is converted from three townhouses. The rooms are charming and eclectic; some are Victorian. Several of the rooms have a shared bath. The restaurant serves superb American-Continental cuisine. Passes to a gym are available. **www.tabardinn.com**

DUPONT CIRCLE The Churchill Hotel   🅿🍽🚻 $$

1914 Connecticut Ave, NW, 20009 **Tel** *797-2000* **Fax** *462-0944* *Rooms 144*   **Map** *2 E1*

A luxury hotel with a predominantly European clientele, the Churchill Hotel was opened as an apartment building in 1906. Its rooms are huge and tastefully furnished. The Chartwell Grill restaurant features American cuisine. **www.thechurchillhotel.com**

DUPONT CIRCLE Dupont at the Circle Inn   🅿 $$$

1604 19th St, NW (at Dupont Circle), 20009 **Tel** *332-5251* **Fax** *332-3244* *Rooms 8*   **Map** *2 F2*

This comfortable bed-and-breakfast is located in two Victorian townhouses just off Dupont Circle. Rooms have period antiques and high-speed internet. The Continental breakfast includes homemade granola. Daily passes to a nearby gym are available. Parking is limited. **www.dupontatthecircle.com**

DUPONT CIRCLE Jurys Washington Hotel   🅿🍽🚻 $$$

1500 New Hampshire Ave, NW, 20036 **Tel** *483-6000* **Fax** *328-3265* *Rooms 314*   **Map** *2 F2*

An Irish hotel, the Jurys offers four-star accommodations and appeals to both business and leisure travelers. The Dupont Grill restaurant features American food, while the Irish pub, Biddy Mulligan's, is quite popular. **www.jurysdoyle.com**

DUPONT CIRCLE Topaz Hotel   🅿🍽🚻 $$$

1733 N St, NW, 20036 **Tel** *393-3000* **Fax** *785-9581* *Rooms 99*   **Map** *2 F2*

This European-style inn provides stylish accommodation with modern facilities in an atmosphere of Eastern-inspired calm. A yoga program is available. The Topaz bar and restaurant serve Asian-inspired cocktails and food. Children under 17 stay for free. **www.topazhotel.com**

DUPONT CIRCLE Washington Courtyard by Marriott   🅿🍽🏊🚻 $$$

1900 Connecticut Ave, NW, 20009 **Tel** *332-9300* **Fax** *328-7039* *Rooms 147*   **Map** *2 E1*

This hotel features a dark wood-paneled lobby, standard rooms, and an outdoor pool. The rooms are designed with the business traveler in mind. Free cookies and coffee are available in the afternoon. The Clarets restaurant serves American cuisine. **www.marriott.com**

DUPONT CIRCLE Hotel Madera   🅿🍽🚻 $$$$

1310 New Hampshire Ave, NW (at 13th St), 20036 **Tel** *296-7600* **Fax** *293-2476* *Rooms 82*   **Map** *2 E2*

This small boutique hotel, recently renovated with dramatic lighting, is close to Dupont Circle. The hotel restaurant, The Firefly, is a modern American bistro. There is a complimentary wine hour from 5:30 to 6:30 pm. Daily passes to a gym can be arranged. **www.hotelmadera.com**

DUPONT CIRCLE Swann House   🅿🏊🚻 $$$$

1808 New Hampshire Ave, NW, 20009 **Tel** *265-7677* **Fax** *265-6755* *Rooms 9*   **Map** *2 F1*

This bed-and-breakfast, in a Romanesque-style house built in 1883, is filled with beautiful antiques, as well as "modern treasures." There is an outdoor pool in the courtyard and rooms are equipped with wireless internet access. **www.swannhouse.com**

DUPONT CIRCLE The Hilton Washington   🅿🍽🏊🚻 $$$$

1919 Connecticut Ave, NW, 20009 **Tel** *483-3000* **Fax** *939-3271* *Rooms 1,119*   **Map** *2 E1*

This is a large convention hotel with comfortable, bright rooms and all the amenities. It's situated on the fashionable upper Connecticut Ave. The magnificent Olympic-size pool and outdoor setting are extremely pleasant and relaxing. **www.hiltonwashington.com**

Key to Price Guide *see p174* **Key to Symbols** *see back cover flap*

DUPONT CIRCLE Westin Embassy Row
 $$$$

*2100 Massachusetts Ave, NW, 20008 **Tel** 293-2100 **Fax** 293-0641 Rooms 206* | **Map** *2 E2*

A posh hotel with an elegant decor. Its prime location on Embassy Row attracts diplomats. It is located close to the Phillips Gallery and Dupont Circle. The 2100 Restaurant and the Fax Lounge both serve French/Californian cuisine. **www.westin.com**

DUPONT CIRCLE Mansion on O Street
 $$$$$

*2020 O Street, NW (at 20th St), 20036 **Tel** 496-2000 **Fax** 659-0547 Rooms 20* | **Map** *2 E2*

The decor is eclectic and charming – part Victorian, part avant-garde. Suites come with wireless internet connections. Breakfast is included in the tariff. Passes to a sports club are available. The hotel takes all major credit cards except Diners. **www.omansion.com**

WISCONSIN AVE Holiday Inn Georgetwon
$$$

*2101 Wisconsin Ave, NW, 20007 **Tel** 338-4600 **Fax** 338-4458 Rooms 296* | **Map** *1 C1*

Conveniently located just north of Georgetown, this seven-story hotel was recently renovated in a rich traditional decor. It has an outdoor pool. The rooms are standard. John F's Café features American fare and Italian dishes. Close to several specialty shops and restaurants. **www.higeorgetown.com**

WISCONSIN AVE Embassy Suites Hotel at the Chevy Chase Pavilion
$$$

*4300 Military Rd, NW (at Wisconsin & Western Aves), 20015 **Tel** 362-9300 **Fax** 686-3405 Rooms 198*

Situated in the popular Chevy Chase shopping district, the all-suite hotel accesses a wide range of shops, as well as the Friendship Heights Metro, all within the Pavilion. The renowned Cheesecake Factory restaurant and a food court are also located here. **www.embassysuitesdc.com**

WOODLEY PARK/CLEVELAND PARK Days Inn Connecticut Avenue
$$

*4400 Connecticut Ave, NW, 20008 **Tel** 244-5600 **Fax** 244-6794 Rooms 155*

A convenient, inexpensive place, north of Cleveland Park near the Van Ness Metro. The Days Inn has clean rooms and has been recently renovated. Several restaurants are nearby and the Tesoro, the hotel's own restaurant, serves authentic Italian cuisine. **www.dcdaysinn.com**

WOODLEY PARK/CLEVELAND PARK Marriott Wardman Park Hotel
 $$$$

*2660 Woodley Rd, NW, 20008 **Tel** 328-2000 **Fax** 234-0015 Rooms 1334*

Surrounded by 16 acres of parkland, the original apartment building has been extended to include a modern glass complex. This large convention hotel has two pools, several restaurants, and spacious, comfortable rooms. The grounds are well maintained. The Woodley Park Metro is adjacent. **www.marriott.com**

WOODLEY PARK/CLEVELAND PARK Omni Shoreham Hotel
 $$$$

*2500 Calvert St, NW, 20008 **Tel** 234-0700 **Fax** 765-5145 Rooms 836*

This four-diamond hotel features a grand Art Deco-style lobby, spacious rooms, and marble-floored bathrooms. Set in 11 acres of beautifully landscaped grounds overlooking Rock Creek Park. The outdoor pool has splendid views and poolside service. **www.omnihotels.com**

BEYOND WASHINGTON, DC

ALEXANDRIA, VA Morrison House
$$$

*116 S Alfred St, 22314 **Tel** 703-838-8000 **Fax** 703-684-6283 Rooms 45*

Modeled after a Federal manor home, this hotel has attractive rooms with four-poster beds, armoires, and Italian marble bathrooms. The Grille restaurant offers fine dining and a varied menu in elegant surroundings. **www.morrisonhouse.com**

ALEXANDRIA, VA Holiday Inn Select Old Town
$$$$

*480 King St (at S Pitt St), 22314 **Tel** 703-838-8000 **Fax** 703-684-6508 Rooms 227*

A huge, old-fashioned lobby greets guests at this hotel, situated in the heart of Old Town. The refurbished rooms are Victorian in style. The hotel provides transportation to and from Reagan National Airport. **www.hiselect.com**

ANNAPOLIS, MD Maryland Inn
$$$

*16 Church Circle, 21401 **Tel** 410-263-2641 **Fax** 410-268-3613 Rooms 124*

This lovely, award-winning brick inn near the water was built in the 1760s. The Victorian-style rooms are comfortable and The Treaty of Paris is a warm, inviting restaurant. Reservations are made through the Historic Inns of Annapolis, which also runs the Governor Calvert House and the Robert Johnson House. **www.historicinnsofannapolis.com**

ARLINGTON, VA Arlington Crystal City Marriott
$$$

*1999 Jefferson Davis Hwy (at S 20th St), 22202 **Tel** 703-413-5500 **Fax** 703-413-0192 Rooms 343*

The lobby has a marble floor and Art Deco fixtures. Recently renovated rooms are quite elegant. The hotel, minutes from Reagan National Airport, provides complimentary airport shuttle service. The CC Bistro features American and Italian dishes. **www.crystalcitymarriott.com**

ARLINGTON, VA Ritz-Carlton Pentagon City

1250 S Hayes St, 22202 **Tel** *703-415-5000* **Fax** *703-415-5061* *Rooms 366*

The rooms in this posh hotel are furnished with antiques and art inspired by Virginia horse country. Afternoon tea is served 2–4:30pm daily. The hotel is conveniently located next to the metro and Pentagon City Mall, one mile from Reagan National Airport. **www.ritzcarlton.com**

BALTIMORE, MD Ann Street Bed-and-Breakfast

804 South Ann St, 21231 **Tel** *410-342-5883* *Rooms 3*

Originally two separate townhouses, built in 1780, this bed-and-breakfast has a Colonial atmosphere and antique furniture. Two of the guest rooms have fireplaces. A full breakfast is included in the tariff. Located in the historic neighborhood of Fells Point.

BALTIMORE, MD Peabody Court, a Clarion Hotel

612 Cathedral St, 21201 **Tel** *410-727-7101* **Fax** *410-789-3312* *Rooms 104*

A boutique-style hotel, with a Renaissance façade and a well-appointed lobby, provides an excellent service. Located close to the Walters Art Museum in a charming neighborhood. The George's restaurant offers casual fine dining. **www.peabodycourthotel.com**

BALTIMORE, MD Renaissance Harborplace Hotel

202 E Pratt St, 21202 **Tel** *410-547-1200* **Fax** *410-539-5780* *Rooms 622*

The rooms in this hotel have a view either of the harbor, or the indoor courtyard. The staff are attentive and cordial. Windows restaurant has a beautiful view of the water and specializes in excellent seafood from Chesapeake Bay. **www.renaissancehotels.com**

BERKELEY, WV Cacapon Resort State Park

818 Cacapon Lodge Dr, 25411 **Tel** *304-258-1022* **Fax** *304-258-5323* *Rooms 48*

Choose from modern rooms or rustic cabins in the lodge with hiking, fishing, and golf facilities. The Park is located two hours from Washington and 10 miles (16 km) from Berkeley Springs, a historic town known for its spa that dates back to Colonial times. **www.cacaponresort.com**

BERLIN, MD Merry Sherwood Plantation

8909 Worcester Highway, 21811 **Tel** *410-641-2112* *Rooms 8*

This bed-and-breakfast is a restored 1850s Italianate Revival-style mansion, set on 21 acres. The rooms have Victorian-style furniture and working fireplaces. The gourmet breakfast includes homemade muffins. TV and phone are not provided. Near Assateague and Ocean City. **www.merrysherwood.com**

BETHESDA, MD Hyatt Regency Bethesda

1 Bethesda Metro Center, 20814 **Tel** *301-657-1234* **Fax** *657-6453* *Rooms 390*

This luxurious hotel is in a close suburb, directly above a Metrorail stop on the Red Line for easy access into central Washington. Movie theaters, a wide variety of restaurants, bookstores, and an ice-skating rink are all within walking distance. **www.bethesda.hyatt.com**

CHARLOTTEVILLE, VA The Boar's Head Inn

Route 250 West, 22903 **Tel** *434-296-2181* **Fax** *434-972-6024* *Rooms 171*

A romantic and charming inn in a beautiful country setting near the foothills of the Blue Ridge Mountains with two lakes on the grounds. Facilities include an 18-hole golf course, tennis, fishing, biking, four pools, and a spa. The Old Mill Room, built from the timbers of an old gristmill, offers fine dining. **www.boarsheadinn.com**

CHINCOTEAGUE, VA Refuge Inn

7058 Maddox Blvd, 23336 **Tel** *757-336-5511* **Fax** *757-336-6134* *Rooms 72*

This recently renovated inn is only half a mile away from the National Wildlife Refuge and close to the National Seashore. The convenient location, inexpensive rooms, and friendly atmosphere make it a good choice for families. Two of the suites are equipped with kitchens. **www.refugeinn.com**

FREDERICKSBURG, VA Dunning Mills Inn All-Suite Hotel

2305-C Jefferson Davis Highway, 22401 **Tel** *540-373-1256* **Fax** *540-899-9041* *Rooms 54*

This hotel is set in the woods near Civil War cemeteries and five major battlefields. George Washington's boyhood home is also close by. Each suite includes a queen-size bed, a sofa bed, a kitchen, and a dining area, while some also have jacuzzis. Picnic areas, barbecues, and facilities for pets are also provided. **www.dunningmills.com**

FREDERICKSBURG, VA Kenmore Inn

1200 Princess Anne St, 22401 **Tel** *540-371-7622* **Fax** *540-371-5480* *Rooms 9*

Built in 1812, this inn is restored with Colonial furnishings and is two blocks from downtown Fredericksburg. Many of the rooms have working fireplaces. The candle-lit dining room features Virginia specialties and the English-style pub provides lighter fare. **www.kenmoreinn.com**

GETTYSBURG, VA Baladerry Inn

40 Hospital Rd, 17325 **Tel** *717-337-1342* *Rooms 9*

The cozy Baladerry Inn dates back to 1812. It later served as a hospital in the Civil War *(see p21).* There are four rooms in the original house and five in the carriage houses, some with fireplaces. Serves a three-course country-style gourmet breakfast. **www.baladerryinn.com**

Key to Price Guide *see p174* **Key to Symbols** *see back cover flap*

LURAY, VA Big Meadows Lodge

P 🍴 🚹 ♿ Ⓢ

P O Box 727 (Skyline Drive), 22835 Tel 540-999-2221 Fax 540-999-2011 Rooms 97

Located at Milepost 51 on the scenic Skyline Drive in the Shenandoah National Park. The rustic accommodations, which include cabins, suites or guest rooms in the chestnut-paneled lodge, offer attractive views of the forest and the valley. Closed November to early April. **www.visitshenandoah.com**

MIDDLEBURG, VA The Red Fox Inn

P 🍴 ♿ ⓈⓈⓈ

2 East Washington St, 20117 Tel 540-687-6301 Fax 540-687-3528 Rooms 16

This inn, on the main street of Middleburg, was built in 1728. The motif is Virginia hunt country. Each guest room is different and decorated with antiques – several with four-poster canopy beds. Continental breakfast included. The dimly-lit romantic restaurant is reminiscent of an 18th-century tavern. The food is superb. **www.redfox.com**

MIDDLETOWN, VA The Wayside Inn

P 🍴 ♿ ⓈⓈ

7783 Main St, 22645 Tel 540-869-1797 Fax 540-869-5519 Rooms 24

This charming inn has been in operation since 1797. Each room is appointed with beautiful antiques. The firelit dining room serves Southern regional dishes. The Wayside Theater, a block away, provides evening entertainment. Located in the Shenandoah Valley, one and a half hours away from DC. **www.alongthewayside.com**

PARIS, VA The Ashby Inn and Restaurant

P 🍴 🚹 ⓈⓈⓈ

692 Federal St, 20130 Tel 540-592-3900 Fax 540-592-3781 Rooms 16

Built in 1829, this attractive inn has rooms with views of the foothills of the Blue Ridge Mountains, and some with private porches. The restaurant here is excellent. Located in a small village, 12 miles (19 km) from Middleburg and an hour's drive from Washington. Only MasterCard and Visa are accepted. **www.ashbyinn.com**

RICHMOND, VA The Jefferson Hotel

 ⓈⓈⓈ

101 W Franklin St, 23220 Tel 804-788-8000 Fax 804-225-0334 Rooms 264

The oldest hotel in the area, the Jefferson was built in 1895. It has a European feel and Southern charm. The lobby boasts a magnificent stained-glass ceiling. There are two excellent restaurants. Located in downtown Richmond, close to the historic and business districts. **www.jeffersonhotel.com**

RICHMOND, VA The Berkeley Hotel

 ⓈⓈⓈⓈ

1200 East Cary St, 23219 Tel 804-780-1300 Fax 804-648-4728 Rooms 55

A warm welcome is given at this gracious hotel, with its lavish, traditional furnishings. The most popular rooms are those with balconies. Situated in the heart of downtown Richmond. Jackets are required at the Berkeley's four-diamond restaurant, The Dining Room. **www.berkeleyhotel.com**

SHEPHERDSTOWN, WV Bavarian Inn

P 🍴 🏊 📺 ♿ ⓈⓈⓈ

164 Shepherd Grade Road, 25443 Tel 304-876-2551 Fax 304-876-9355 Rooms 73

The inn is located in a picturesque town, 15 miles (24 km) from Harper's Ferry. Rooms are individually decorated with Old World elegance – some with fireplaces, canopy beds, and magnificent views of the Potomac. Excellent Continental cuisine is served here. The room rates go up on the weekend. **www.bavarianinnwv.com**

TILGHMAN ISLAND, MD Chesapeake Wood Duck Inn

P ⓈⓈⓈ

Gibsontown Rd, at Dogwood Harbor, 21671 Tel 410-886-2070 Fax 413-677-7526 Rooms 7

Winner of the AAA and 3-star Mobil awards, this waterfront bed-and-breakfast, built in 1890, offering great hospitality and innovative cuisine. A three-course gourmet breakfast and a four-course dinner is served Saturday evenings for inn guests by reservation only. **www.woodduckinn.com**

TREVILIANS, VA Prospect Hill

 ⓈⓈⓈⓈ

2887 Poindexter Rd (near Charlottesville), 23093 Tel 540-967-0844 Fax 540-967-0102 Rooms 13

This inn is situated on a 50-acre former plantation in beautiful countryside, 15 miles (24 km) east of Charlottesville. The house dates back to 1732. All of the rooms have fireplaces. Breakfast and dinner are included in the tariff. Limited rooms have been provided with facilities for the disabled. **www.prospecthill.com**

WASHINGTON, VA Inn at Little Washington

P 🍴 ♿ ⓈⓈⓈⓈ

Middle & Main Sts, 22747 Tel 540-675-3800 Fax 540-675-3100 Rooms 15

No two rooms are alike at this imaginatively furnished, lovely inn, set in the beautiful Shenandoah Valley. The world-renowned restaurant on the premises offers an excellent and generously proportioned fixed price multicourse meal. Weekday rates are less expensive. Only MasterCard and Visa are accepted. **www.theinnatlittlewashington.com**

WILLIAMSBURG, VA Colonial Houses

 ⓈⓈⓈⓈ

136 East Francis St, 23187 Tel 757-229-1000 Fax 757-220-7096 Rooms 26

Rent a room or an entire house at this restored 18th-century place with modern amenities, except a kitchen. Facilities of the nearby Williamsburg Inn, including restaurant, room service, parking, and swimming pool, are available to the guests of the Colonial houses. Wheel-chair access in only three rooms. **www.colonialwilliamsburg.com**

WILLIAMSBURG, VA The Williamsburg Inn

P 🍴 🏊 ♿ ⓈⓈⓈⓈ

136 East Francis St, 23187 Tel 757-229-1000 Fax 757-220-7096 Rooms 68

This famed hotel offers all the luxuries of a modern hotel in a Regency-style setting inside the historic district. The formal Regency Room provides fine dining, while afternoon tea is served in the Terrace Room. Golf, croquet, and tennis courts are located on the premises. **www.colonialwilliamsburg.co**

RESTAURANTS, CAFES, AND BARS

Joseph Alsop, a renowned Washington host of the early 1960s, routinely gave lavish dinner parties in his Georgetown home. When asked why he gave so many parties, Alsop replied that it was because Washington had no good restaurants. Today the capital rivals New York, offering restaurants of every cuisine and price range. It is largely due to

Façade of Ben's Chili Bowl

Washington's cosmopolitan population that the city offers such a wide array of cuisines, from Ethiopian to Vietnamese, with many new styles of "fusion food" in between. The seafood is also superb, freshly caught from the nearby waters of Chesapeake Bay. Crab and shellfish feature regularly on menus, especially in coastal areas outside the city.

The elegant Matisse restaurant

PLACES TO EAT

Washington's restaurants are a reflection of its neighborhoods. Adams-Morgan has a mix of ethnic establishments, especially Salvadoran and Ethiopian, and cutting-edge cuisine. Perry's, Cashion's Eat Place, and Felix Restaurant and Bar offer inventive fusion food with Asian and French influences, and the crowd is young and hip. An easy walk from the Mall, Washington's compact Chinatown has some of the best bargains for families. Meals are inexpensive and often served family style. Next to Chinatown is the restored Old Downtown district on Seventh Street. Chic restaurants like The Mark, Coco Loco, and the District Chophouse are in restored early 19th-century buildings. Georgetown has a mix of expensive and inexpensive places. Good value can be

found at its many Indian and Vietnamese restaurants. North of the White House and south of Dupont Circle, Downtown restaurants cater to business travelers and high-powered lobbyists. More reasonable places, again mostly ethnic restaurants, are found closer to the Circle.

With very few exceptions, all restaurants in Washington are air conditioned. This has changed the city from one where most of the population used to escape in the summer to a lively, year-round capital.

RESERVATIONS

Reservations may be necessary for popular restaurants; the most fashionable can get booked up weeks in advance. Call ahead if there is somewhere you really want to go. However, walk-in diners are expected in most places. You may be placed on a waiting list and expected to return at the appointed time or wait in the adjacent bar, but you will usually be guaranteed a table within a fairly short time.

PRICES AND PAYING

Restaurant prices range from the very cheap to the very expensive in Washington. Prices vary according to location, cuisine, and décor. Most restaurants take major credit cards, although street vendors and fast food places may only accept cash. A 15 percent tip is expected for good service in

restaurants; some places even recommend 20 percent. The tip is seldom automatically added to the bill except in the case of large parties, which may incur an automatic 15 percent gratuity.

Unlike many European cities, the fixed price meal is uncommon in Washington. Items are usually listed à la carte unless specified in the menu. Diners should expect to spend between $20 and $30 for dinner and a drink, including tip, at a moderate restaurant. However Indian, Ethiopian, Chinese, and Vietnamese restaurants are often considerably less expensive. It is also worth knowing that you will generally be charged about 25 percent less for the same meal if you eat at lunchtime rather than in the evening, so visitors on a budget may choose to eat their main meal at lunchtime. Breakfasts are usually under $10 for bacon and eggs with coffee and juice, but many hotels include a free continental breakfast (rolls, coffee, and juice) in the cost of the room.

B. Smith's grand Beaux Arts style dining room at historic Union Station

Mural on the side of Madam's Organ bar in Adams-Morgan

OPENING HOURS

It is unusual for a restaurant to be open 24 hours, except for those in very large hotels. Restaurants also rarely serve food continuously throughout the day; they usually have a break of several hours between lunch and dinner. Most restaurants are open all year (except Christmas Day) but a few may be closed on Sunday or Monday. It is best to call in advance. Restaurants often open for dinner between 5pm and 6pm, with the busiest period usually between 7pm and 8pm. The last seating is often at 9pm, and the last customers usually leave by 11pm. Bars are open until 2am. Remember that Metrorail trains stop running at 2am on Friday and Saturday, and at midnight the rest of the week.

ALCOHOL

Restaurants are required by law to have a liquor license in order to sell alcohol so you will notice that some do not offer it. Others may serve wine only but not hard liquor or mixed drinks.

Bars rarely serve food other than perhaps some appetizers. Other restaurants may have a a separate bar as well as a dining section. Patrons are not permitted to bring their own drinks to a restaurant.

The drinking age in DC, in Maryland, and in Virginia is 21. Restaurateurs can and will ask for proof of age in the form of a driver's license or passport since the penalty for serving alcohol to underage drinkers is severe.

SMOKING

In the District of Columbia smoking is still permitted in restaurants but may be restricted to designated areas. Americans are very conscious of smoking, especially in eating establishments, and smoking in a nonsmoking area may mean a fine of several hundred dollars.

DRESS CODE

Dress varies from the very casual (shorts, t-shirt, and sneakers) to the very formal. In some restaurants men will not be admitted without a jacket and tie (the maitre d' may have spares). But as a general guide, the more expensive the restaurant, the more formal the dress code will be. Some bars also have a very strict dress code, and customers may not be admitted in very casual dress. Respectable but casual attire is acceptable in the majority of establishments.

WHAT TO EAT

Washington offers a vast range of types of food to the visitor, but like most American cities it has a high concentration of fast-food establishments. Chains like McDonalds, Burger King, and Wendy's serve the same food worldwide and can be a reliable and popular source of sustenance for a family on the move. The hot dog vendors along the Mall offer an alternative. Other than fast food, Washington's cuisine is immensely multicultural, and you will find French, Chinese, Ethiopian, and Vietnamese restaurants, among others.

CHILDREN

The best indication as to whether children are welcome in a restaurant is the presence of a children's menu or the availability of high chairs. When dining in more formal places with children, it is best to reserve the earliest seating when the restaurant will not be too busy.

Tony and Joe's bar on the side of Washington harbor

WHEELCHAIR ACCESS

Restaurants are not required to be wheelchair accessible. In general, restaurants in older neighborhoods like Dupont Circle and Adams-Morgan are less likely to accommodate wheelchairs than modern establishments on K Street. The Smithsonian Museum restaurants are all accessible for the disabled.

Street vendor selling hot dogs, pretzels, ice cream, and drinks

What to Eat in Washington, DC

Washington is a place where everyone has an opinion, and culinary preferences are no exception. For some it's a power dining town, where châteaubriand is the dish of choice and "two-martini lunches" are common. Others would point to nearby Chesapeake Bay, and its delectable seafood dishes that appear on many menus. Still others would see the city's vibrant ethnic communities as the key to current food trends. There's no disagreement, however, that DC's dining scene reflects the diversity of the city. As well as drawing on the bountiful harvest of the Atlantic, the city's chefs also make good use of seasonal, local produce from the farms of Maryland and Virginia.

Chef at work in Kinkead's restaurant *(see p189)*

POWER DINING

True to its reputation, the city boasts an impressive collection of "power dining" restaurants, where lobbyists, pundits, and lawyers gather for steaks and cocktails. Slip into a cozy booth at one of these reputed steakhouses and you're likely to spot at least a few members of the United States Congress.

GLOBAL FLAVOURS

As the capital of the United States, Washington has long served as a gathering place for leaders and dignitaries from across the country and around the world, who have brought their own recipes and culinary traditions to the city. Refugees from places such as El Salvador, Ethiopia, and Cambodia have settled in Washington, introducing its well-traveled, globally-minded citizens to unusual flavors and dishes. In such ethnically diverse neighborhoods as Adams Morgan or Mount Pleasant, it's not unusual to find African, Asian, and South American restaurants standing side by side.

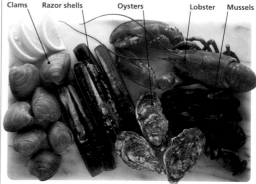

Clams   Razor shells   Oysters   Lobster   Mussels

Mouthwatering selection of Chesapeake Bay seafood

WASHINGTON'S SIGNATURE DISHES

Maryland crab cakes

The unique nature of the capital makes it difficult to pin down its specialty dishes. The *Washington Post* recently made a case for the "half-smoke," a mildly spicy hybrid of hot dog and smoked sausage, smothered in chili and cheese and often sold in sidewalk kiosks. Ben's Chili Bowl *(see p192)*, is the best known purveyor, and a favorite of comedian Bill Cosby. Maryland Blue Crabs are also popular, often appearing as succulent crab cakes or tangy She-Crab Soup. The federal side of the city could be summed up with Senate Navy Bean Soup which has been served every day in the Senate Dining Room for more than 100 years. It's a humble, unassuming dish, and yet it is eaten on a regular basis by the some of Washington's most influential residents.

Senate Navy Bean Soup
uses navy (haricot) beans and ham hock to make a delicious, simple yet hearty soup fit for Senators.

Choosing a Restaurant

The restaurants have been selected across a range of price categories for their exceptional food, good value, and interesting location. Restaurants are listed by area, and within these by price, both for central Washington, DC and the surrounding areas. Map references refer to the Street Finder, pages 224–229.

PRICE CATEGORIES
For a three-course meal for one, with a glass of wine, including cover, service, and tax:

$ Under $20
$$ $20–$30
$$$ $30–$45
$$$$ $45–$60
$$$$$ over $60

CAPITOL HILL

America
Union Station, 50 Massachusetts Ave, NE, 20002 **Tel** *682-9555*   **Map** *4 E3*

Located inside Union Station, with a great view of the Capitol, America features regional dishes. Death by Chocolate is a favorite dessert on the 200-item menu. An enormous restaurant with an enormous menu, the place is spread over three stories of Union Station.

Bread and Chocolate
666 Pennsylvania Ave, SE, 20003 **Tel** *547-2875*   **Map** *4 F5*

This large and spacious neighborhood restaurant offers good French fare, including French onion soup. There's also a selection of quiches and a wide variety of delicious pastries, and freshly-baked cakes and breads. A special Sunday brunch is also served. The service is friendly.

Capitol Hill Brewing Company
2 Massachusetts Ave, NE (near 1st St), 20002 **Tel** *842-2337*   **Map** *4 E3*

Situated above the National Postal Museum, this restaurant/bar offers good pub food and a large award-winning selection of beers. Free parking is available in the lot across the street in the evenings. Day parking can be in the Union Station lot or on the street.

Hawk and Dove
329 Pennsylvania Ave, SE, 20003 **Tel** *543-3300*   **Map** *4 F4*

The oldest Irish bar in town offers a typically American menu including good burgers and pasta. You'll find an interesting mixture of locals and politicians, as well as 11 TVs with satellite programming. The Hawk and Dove also provides a good children's menu.

Le Bon Café
210 2nd St SE, 20003 **Tel** *547-7200*   **Map** *4 F4*

This small, but extremely pleasant café near the Library of Congress offers delicious soups and sandwiches. There are plenty of options for vegetarians, including the best *portobello* sandwich in town. It is often crowded, but well worth the wait. Open through the week for breakfast and lunch. MasterCard and Visa accepted.

Library of Congress Café
Madison Building, 101 Independence Ave, SE, 20540 **Tel** *707-5000*   **Map** *4 E4*

Located on the sixth floor of the Madison Building, the Congress Café has a splendid panoramic view of Washington.This buffet-style restaurant offers a good selection of American fare – soups, salads, and sandwiches – at very reasonable prices. On weekdays it is open 12:30–2pm only.

Market Lunch
Eastern Market, 225 7th St, SE (at C St), 20003 **Tel** *547-8444*   **Map** *4 F4*

The menu features authentic regional food and extensive seafood delicacies, such as crab cakes, crab sandwiches, river fish, and flavorful salads. The cafeteria-style breakfast and lunch is as casual as it is delicious. Expect a long wait on Sunday mornings. Closed on Mondays.

Taverna the Greek Islands
305 Pennsylvania Ave, SE, 20003 **Tel** *547-8360*   **Map** *4 F4*

Athenian chicken, moussaka, lamb with artichokes, and kebabs are all favorites at Taverna the Greek Islands, a neighborhood restaurant with a Greek island decor. Lunch is casual. White tablecloths and candles make for a more formal dinner. Closed on Sundays.

Tortilla Coast
400 I St, SE, 20003 **Tel** *546-6768*   **Map** *4 F5*

Great food and a friendly atmosphere. The menu is mostly Tex-Mex, but includes some American dishes as well. Burritos are a big hit as are the margaritas. American Express, MasterCard, and Visa are accepted. Closed on Sundays. George W. Bush was a customer here before his election.

Key to Symbols *see back cover flap*

U.S. Supreme Court Cafeteria
1 1st St, NE, 20543 **Tel** *479-3000*
Map *4 E4*

Located on the ground floor of the Supreme Court building, this place is open to the public on weekdays for breakfast and lunch. The US Supreme Court cafeteria offers good food at reasonable prices. A convenient stopping point on a tour of Capitol Hill.

Bullfeathers
401 1st St, SE, 20003 **Tel** *543-5005*
Map *4 E5*

This Victorian-style pub and outdoor café, popular with Congressional staffers and neighborhood residents, is known for "the best burgers on the Hill." Those curious about the name are told that "Bullfeathers!" was flamboyant President Teddy Roosevelt's favorite exclamation.

Two Quail
320 Masachusetts Ave, NE, 20003 **Tel** *543-8030*
Map *4 F3*

This refreshing American bistro with an eclectic decor has been voted the most romantic in Washington. The Two Quail is the signature dish. Their lamb, salmon, and homemade desserts are also excellent. Open Monday to Friday for lunch and dinner every night.

B. Smith's
Union Station, 50 Massachusetts Ave, NE, 20002 **Tel** *289-6188*
Map *4 E3*

The ornate setting of the former Presidential Waiting Room of Union Station is now one of the best places for Southern cooking. The *swamp thang* (shrimp, crawfish and scallops in a cream sauce over a bed of collard greens) is a specialty of the house. A jazz trio plays on Friday and Saturday evening.

Bistro Bis
15 E St, NW, 20001 **Tel** *661-2700*
Map *4 D4*

French food with an American twist is served in a beautiful, cozy dining area. This chic modern restaurant located near the Senate attracts a fashionable clientele. The duck confit and salmon Provençal come highly recommended. Valet parking is available after 5:30pm.

The Monocle
107 D St, NE, 20002 **Tel** *546-4488*
Map *4 E3*

A Capitol Hill institution popular with Senators and their staffers, the Monocle has a history of fostering alliances and deals. Steaks and crab cakes are their specialty. Closest restaurant to the Senate side of the Capitol, so call ahead for reservations when Congress is in session. Valet parking is available.

Tunnicliff's
222 7th St, SE (opposite Eastern Market), 20003 **Tel** *544-5680*
Map *4 F4*

The restaurant attracts a casual and diverse crowd. The popular Sunday brunch at Tunnicliff's features Eggs Chesapeake (a crab cake with 2 poached eggs), as well as peanut butter and jelly pizza. All major credit cards except Discover are accepted here.

THE MALL

Cascade Café
National Gallery of Art, Concourse level, Constitution Ave, NW, 20565 **Tel** *216-5966*
Map *4 D4*

One of the better options for hungry museum-goers, this café offers fast and convenient buffet-style foods. The Cascade's "open-kitchens" allow you the added pleasure of watching food being freshly prepared. There is also a separate Espresso and Gelato Bar next to the café.

Mitsitam Café
National Museum of the American Indian, Independence Ave & 4th St, SW, 20560 **Tel** *633-6990*
Map *4 D4*

Mitsitam means "let's eat" in the language of the Piscataway. It features an interesting menu inspired by Native Americans from the Northwest Coast, the Great Plains, Northern Woodlands, and Central and South America. The buffet-style café also has a range of prices.

Pavilion Café
Sculpture Garden, adjacent to the National Gallery West Building at 7th St, NW, 20565 **Tel** *289-3360* **Map** *4 D4*

This outdoor café offers a splendid view of the Sculpture Garden and of the ice-skating rink in winter. Choices include gourmet pizzas, wraps, and hot chocolate. There is a children's menu. Open Monday to Saturday 10am–4:30pm and Sunday 11am–5pm. Extended hours until 9pm during the ice-skating season.

The Atrium Café
National Museum of Natural History, Constitution Ave &10th St, NW, 20560 **Tel** *633-1000*
Map *3 C4*

The atrium of Washington's National Museum of Natural History is six stories high.This large food court on the ground level of the museum offers a wide selection of food including, pizza, sandwiches, soups, hot entrées, salads, and mouth-watering desserts.

Key to Price Guide *see p185* **Key to Symbols** *see back cover flap*

The Wright Place

National Air and Space Museum, 601 Independence Ave, SW, 20560 **Tel** *633-1000*   **Map** *4 D4*

Located in the National Air and Space Museum, The Wright Place offers a wide variety to choose from. The chain restaurants Boston Market, McDonalds, and Donato's pizza have taken over the food service area. Upstairs, the Mezza Café features panini sandwiches and specialty coffees.

CityZen

Mandarin Oriental Hotel, 1330 Maryland Ave, SW, 20024 **Tel** *787-6006*   **Map** *3 C5*

This 70-seat restaurant of the new, posh Mandarin Oriental Hotel, offers an exquisite dining experience. Each dish is imaginatively prepared and beautifully presented. The talented chef, Eric Ziebold, spent eight years at the world-renowned French Laundry in Napa Valley.

OLD DOWNTOWN

Fadó Irish Pub

808 7th St, NW, 20001 **Tel** *789-0066*   **Map** *3 C3*

Fadó has the look of an authentic Irish pub, with furnishings shipped over from Ireland. Serves typical Irish fare and fusion dishes. Contemporary Irish rock performances on Thursday nights. Live sporting events shown regularly, including hurling and Gaelic football. Located next to the MCI Center.

Full Kee

509 H St, NW, 20001 **Tel** *371-2233*   **Map** *4 D3*

The Cantonese noodles, dumplings and soups are excellent at this rather sparsely decorated, Chinatown restaurant. Full Kee is certainly a great place to grab a cheap, as well as a quick meal before an MCI Center event. Alcoholic beverages are not served here.

Reeves Restaurant and Bakery

1306 G St, NW, 20005 **Tel** *628-6350*   **Map** *3 B3*

The menu features American "comfort food," such as open-faced turkey sandwiches with mashed potatoes and cranberry sauce. It also serves Reeves's famous strawberry pie and shortcake. Only MasterCard and Visa are accepted. Open Monday to Friday 7am–6pm and Saturday till 4pm only.

Sky Terrace

Hotel Washington, 515 15th St, NW, 20004 **Tel** *638-5900*   **Map** *3 C2*

The Sky Terrace on the roof of Hotel Washington offers some of the best views, especially of the city's monuments and the White House. Dine year-round inside or on the outside terrace where lighter fare is served from April to October.

Spy City Café

800 F St, NW, 20004 **Tel** *393-7798*   **Map** *3 C3*

This bright, cheerful café offers breakfast and lunch. A hearty "spy breakfast" consists of scrambled eggs with American cheese, roasted potatoes and bacon at a reasonable price. The menu also offers made-to-order salads, grilled paninis, and Spy City dogs (American hot dogs in disguise). American Express not accepted.

District Chophouse and Brewery

509 7th St, NW, 20004 **Tel** *347-3434*   **Map** *3 C3*

This upscale hangout echoes the style and ambience of the 1940s with a cigar bar, pool tables, and swing music. Huge portions of steak, burgers and pizza can be washed down by the beers, which are brewed on the premises. It caters to sports fans from the MCI Center.

Hard Rock Café

999 E St, NW (at 10th St), 20004 **Tel** *737-7625*   **Map** *3 C3*

All the American classics are available, including burgers, sandwiches and salads. Videos, music, and memorabilia make the two floors of this restaurant an exciting tourist experience, though it can get a little hectic. Stained-glass windows honor rock-and-roll greats in this worldwide chain.

Jaleo

480 7th St, NW, 20004 **Tel** *628-7949*   **Map** *3 C3*

Not far from the monuments, and a stone's throw from the MCI Center, this Spanish tapas restaurant is a refreshing alternative with its colorful menu and decor. Jaleo attracts rave reviews for its eggplant flan and sautéed shrimp. Flamenco dancers perform on Wednesdays 7:45–8:45pm.

Morrison-Clark Restaurant

1015 L St, NW, 20001 **Tel** *898-1200*   **Map** *3 C2*

The 1864 Morrison-Clark Inn serves modern American food with a Southern influence in a restored Victorian-style dining room. The menu at this restaurant is a new surprise every season. Service is impeccable, while the atmosphere is extremely relaxing.

Old Ebbitt Grill
675 15th St, NW, 20005 **Tel** *347-4801*

P 🏃 ♿   **$$**

Map 3 B3

Expect this upbeat American grill to be packed with both locals and tourists. It's a chance to sample the DC scene as well as savor quality seafood, pasta, steaks, an excellent raw bar and wine list. The crab cakes and trout parmesan are house favorites.

Zaytinya's
701 9th St, NW (at G St), 20001 **Tel** *638-0800*

P 🏃 ♿ 🍴   **$$**

Map 3 C3

This restaurant with a striking modern decor offers a superb variety of authentic Greek, Turkish, and Lebanese mezze with excellent vegetarian selections. The ambience is sophisticated, warm and inviting, making this a favorite choice for Washingtonians.

Zola
800 F St, NW, 20004 **Tel** *654-0999*

P 🏃 ♿   **$$**

Map 3 C2

Upscale American cuisine in a stylish atmosphere, with booths, befitting the Spy Museum to which, it is connected. A varied menu includes dishes such as smoked beer and cheddar fondue, red snapper with clams, and lamb *tabouleh*. It boasts a good wine list as well.

Poste
Hotel Monaco, 555 8th St, NW, 20004 **Tel** *783-6060*

P 🏃 ♿ 🍴   **$$$**

Map 3 C3

The Poste was once part of the Old General Post Office, the first all-marble building in Washington. The menu has a slight French influence (venison, rabbit, striped bass), but limited vegetarian choices. There's a friendly bar area, a quiet room in the back, and a patio open in good weather.

Red Sage
605 14th St, NW, 20005 **Tel** *638-4444*

P 🏃 ♿ 🎵   **$$$**

Map 3 B3

Upstairs is a Southwestern café, downstairs a formal dining room with Western-influenced modern American dishes, including buffalo fillet. Other specialties include lamb chops, veal, and tuna. No vegetarian entrées. Live music only on Friday and Saturday.

Tenpenh
1001 Pennsylvania Ave, NW (at 10th St), 20004 **Tel** *393-4500*

P 🏃 ♿   **$$$**

Map 3 C3

Tenpenh has an eclectic fusion-menu featuring American food with an Asian influence and sophisticated modern decor. Furnishings come from Vietnam and other Southeast Asian countries. Open for lunch and dinner from Monday to Friday. Dinner only on Saturdays. Closed on Sundays.

THE WHITE HOUSE AND FOGGY BOTTOM

Bread Line
1751 Pennsylvania Ave, NW, 20006 **Tel** *822-8900*

🏃 ♿ 🍴   **$**

Map 3 A3

Bread line is characterized by a lot of hustle and bustle. The main attractions here include terrific sandwiches and soups. Try the Poor Boy, a fried oyster sandwich, which is usually available on Thursdays. Open Monday–Friday 7:30am–3:30pm.

Café des Artistes
Corcoran Museum of Art, 500 17th St, NW, 20006 **Tel** *639-1786*

🏃 ♿ 🎵   **$**

Map 3 A3

A pleasant café on the ground floor of the Corcoran Museum, which serves only lunch to its customers. The Sunday Gospel Brunch is served 10:30am–2pm and also features live music ($23). Café des Artistes is closed on Mondays and Tuesdays.

Cosi Sandwich Bar
1700 Pennsylvania Ave, NW, 20006 **Tel** *638-7101*

🏃 ♿ 🍴   **$**

Map 3 A3

Cosi serves exotic sandwiches with interesting combinations, such as pesto chicken and sundried tomato. A wide selection of freshly-baked cookies and pies are available for dessert. This eatery makes a good choice for lunch or a late-night snack during the week. There are several branches across the city.

Cup'a Cup'a
600 New Hampshire Ave, NW, 20037 **Tel** *466-3677*

🏃 ♿ 🍴   **$**

Map 2 D4

Across the street from the Kennedy Center, Cup'a Cup'a is a good choice for grabbing a bite before a performance. Delicious food, including espressos, lattes, and a variety of sandwiches and salads, is served at reasonable prices. Parking is available at the Watergate or the Kennedy Center.

Luigi's
1132 19th St, NW, 20036 **Tel** *331-7574*

🏃 🍴   **$**

Map 2 E2

This attractive trattoria with its red and white checkered tablecloths is one of the oldest Italian restaurants in the city. Its extensive menu includes a wide range of pizzas with 40 different kinds of toppings, pastas, and a very good tiramisu.

Key to Price Guide *see p185* **Key to Symbols** *see back cover flap*

Teaism   ⑤

800 Connecticut Ave, NW (at H St), 20006 **Tel** *835-2233*   **Map** *3 B2*

One can enjoy an exquisite selection of teas, as well as a good choice of Asian-inspired dishes in the restaurant's cozy surroundings. The menu features curries, bento boxes, and salads. Go for a meal or just for tea. Open Monday to Friday 7:30am–5:30pm.

Aquarelle   ⑤⑤

Watergate Hotel, 2650 Virginia Ave, NW, 20037 **Tel** *298-4455*   **Map** *2 D3*

The infamous Watergate building houses this Continental restaurant with a Mediterranean influence. It is newly decorated and offers spectacular views across the Potomac River. A *prix fixe* menu is available and suitable for Kennedy Center theater-goers.

Aroma   ⑤⑤

1919 I St, NW, 20006 **Tel** *833-4700*   **Map** *2 E3*

This North Indian restaurant is one of the best-kept secrets in Washington. It is casual yet elegant, and the food is excellent. Aroma offers an all-you-can-eat lunchtime buffet for a very reasonable price on Saturdays. The restaurant is closed on Sundays.

Asia Nora   ⑤⑤

2213 M St, NW, 20037 **Tel** *833-4700*   **Map** *2 E2*

A creative selection of Asian fusion cuisine using organic ingredients. Although the menu changes seasonally, the signature appetizer remains the tuna tartare. The setting is intimate and serene, with carvings from Bali and Malaysia decorating the walls.

Georgia Brown's   ⑤⑤

950 15th St, NW 20005 **Tel** *393-4499*   **Map** *3 B3*

Anyone who craves Carolina shrimp, grits (fried, coarse grain), gumbo, or fried green tomatoes should come here. Low-country Southern cooking with style is served in an inviting, but hectic atmosphere. A jazz trio performs during the Sunday brunch.

Kinkead's   ⑤⑤

Red lion Row, 2000 Pennsylvania Ave, NW, 20006 **Tel** *296-7700*   **Map** *2 E3*

You won't be disappointed at this Americal brasserie with an excellent seafood menu, one of the finest in town. Bob Kinkead's creations, such as the pepita-crusted salmon, are wonderfully complemented by the extensive wine list. Live jazz is performed on every weeknight.

Vidalia   ⑤⑤

1990 M St, NW 20036 **Tel** *659-1990*   **Map** *3 A2*

There's a distinctive cosmopolitan atmosphere to Vidalia's – call it swanky. This 4-star restaurant offers superb American cuisine with a Southern accent. Lunch is served from Monday to Friday, and dinner nightly. Valet parking is available in the evenings.

Bombay Club   ⑤⑤⑤

815 Connecticut Ave, NW, 20006 **Tel** *659-3727*   **Map** *2 F3*

The attentive service and exclusive clientele provide a glimpse of upper-crust Washington. Specialties include tandoori salmon and green chili chicken. A classical pianist performs nightly. Open for lunch from Monday to Friday, brunch on Sunday, and for dinner every night.

Galileo   ⑤⑤⑤

1110 2 1st St, NW, 20036 **Tel** *293-7191*   **Map** *2 E3*

The most talked-about Italian restaurant in DC, this restaurant is known for its elaborate dishes. Chef Roberto Donna's fame rests on his innovative menu, which changes daily. Choose from Galileo's range of homemade pastas (*linguini* with lobster), risottos, and game dishes. There's also a fine selection of wines.

Occidental   ⑤⑤⑤

1475 Pennsylvania Ave, NW (at 14th St), 20004 **Tel** *783-1475*   **Map** *3 B3*

An elegant setting and a varied menu including an excellent selection of seafood. Only a few blocks from the White House, it's a place to see and be seen. Pictures of the power elite, past and present, line the walls. Music is played only during Sunday brunch in summer.

Olives   ⑤⑤⑤

1600 K St, NW, 20006 **Tel** *452-1866*   **Map** *3 B2*

Dark wood, velvet-covered banquettes, and dim lighting make for a warm and inviting atmosphere in this Mediterranean-style restaurant. The world-renowned chef, Todd English, adds a Tuscan touch to the imaginative, and beautifully presented dishes. Closed on Sundays.

Primi Piatti   ⑤⑤⑤

2013 I St, NW, 20006 **Tel** *223-3600*   **Map** *2 E3*

This lively Northern Italian restaurant has a menu offering pasta and meat dishes. The staff is friendly, the food and wine list are reliably good, and the atmosphere is both fun and sophisticated. Closed on Sunday and no lunch served on Saturday.

Renaissance Mayflower, Café Promenade   P 🕴 ♿ 🎵 $$$

1127 Connecticut Ave, NW (at DeSales St), 20036 **Tel** *347-3000*   **Map** *3 A2*

The Mediterranean-influenced Café Promenade offers a menu featuring a variety of dishes from Spain, Greece, France, and Italy. Specialties include crab cakes and red snapper. There's a seafood buffet on Fridays and brunch on Sundays. Reservations recommended.

Roof Terrace   P 🕴 ♿ 🎵 $$$

Kennedy Center, New Hampshire Ave & Rock Creek Pkwy, 20037 **Tel** *416-8555*   **Map** *2 D4*

Theater-goers can enjoy a contemporary American meal here, coupled with a fabulous view of the Virginia skyline. Dishes include salmon, crab cakes, and pecan tart. The Roof Terrace kitchen also serves delicious desserts, such as a crème brulée sampler and the Sunday brunch buffet is superb.

GEORGETOWN

Café Divan   🕴 ♿ $

1834 Wisconsin Ave, NW (north of S St), 20007 **Tel** *338-1747*   **Map** *1 C1*

The mezze platter makes a reasonable lunch. Café Divan has a small take-out area as well as a dining room with bay windows for a leisurely meal. Specialties include lamb, chicken, seafood, and *pides* (Turkish pizza with a thin crust and a choice of eight toppings).

Café la Ruche   🕴 🎵 🍴 $

1039 31st St, NW, 20007 **Tel** *965-2684*   **Map** *2 D3*

A typical Parisian bistro with a comfortable atmosphere that is great for chatting with friends. A wide range of dishes includes rainbow trout, mussels Niçoise, pastries, and an excellent brunch. A guitarist performs on Monday and Tuesday evenings.

Marvelous Market   P 🕴 ♿ $

3217 P St, NW (at Wisconsin Ave), 20007 **Tel** *333-2591*   **Map** *1 C2*

A great place for lunch or a snack, Marvelous Market serves a wide range of sandwiches, pizzas, and salads, as well as the breads and pastries that are reputed to be consistently excellent. The restaurant is open for breakfast, lunch, and dinner throughout the week.

Patisserie Poupon   🕴 🍴 $

1645 Wisconsin Ave, NW, 20007 **Tel** *342-3248*   **Map** *1 C2*

A bright, charming café with some of the best pastries in town and one of the few places to find marzipan. The soups, quiches, and salads attract a neighborhood crowd. There is a coffee bar in the back. Lunchtime is very busy. Closed on Mondays.

Pizzeria Paradiso   🕴 ♿ $

3282 M St, NW (near 33rd St), 20007 **Tel** *337-1245*   **Map** *1 C2*

The lively, friendly atmosphere makes this an excellent choice for a casual meal. Some consider their pizza to be the best in DC – thin crust Neapolitan style, baked in a wood-burning stove. Serves alcohol. There is a downstairs dining room for private parties. Accepts all major credit cards except American Express.

Zed's Ethiopian Cuisine   🕴 🍴 $

1201 28th St, NW, 20007 **Tel** *333-4710*   **Map** *1 C2*

An Ethiopian restaurant, popular with vegetarians, Zed's offers traditional *wats* (red pepper sauces), *alechas* (stews), and *injera* (bread). The atmosphere is quiet and romantic and the decor features Ethiopian textiles, paintings, and woodcarvings.

Bistro Français   🕴 ♿ $$

3128 M St, NW, 20007 **Tel** *338-3830*   **Map** *1 C2*

This attractive French bistro in the heart of Georgetown, serves traditional-style dishes. The menu includes Coquilles St-Jacques or sirloin steak with bone marrow in a cracked pepper sauce. The *prix fixe* menu ($19.95), served 5–7pm and 10:30pm–1am, includes a glass of house wine.

Blues Alley   🕴 🎵 $$

1073 Wisconsin Ave, NW, 20027 **Tel** *337-4141*   **Map** *1 C3*

This very popular jazz supper club has performances by a variety of artists seven nights a week. Dizzy Gillespie recorded a live album here, as more recently did Wynton Marsalis and Eva Cassidy. The menu features New Orleans-style cooking – Jambalaya is a specialty. Cover charge varies depending on the performer (usually $16–35).

Café Bonaparte   🕴 ♿ 🍴 $$

1522 Wisconsin Ave, NW, 20007 **Tel** *333-8830*   **Map** *1 C2*

Warm and cozy, with bright yellow walls and black-and-white photographs of Europe, Café Bonaparte looks out on Wisconsin. Students and locals flock here to enjoy a French meal comprising crêpes, soup, and salad, or to just while away the afternoon with a cappuccino at a table by the window.

Key to Price Guide *see p185*   **Key to Symbols** *see back cover flap*

Clyde's of Georgetown
3236 M St, NW, 20007 **Tel** *333-9180*
Map *1 C2*

A Washington institution, Clyde's of Georgetown has been highly popular since it first opened 40 years ago. Just as any causal American-style restaurant, it mainly serves hamburgers and rôtisserie chicken, while it could claim to have invented Sunday brunch. Gets loud and crowded, but the food is always very good.

Curry Club
1734 Wisconsin Ave, NW, 20007 **Tel** *625-9090*
Map *1 C1*

Inside an attractive, red rowhouse, you'll find a romantic setting with banquettes covered with silk cushions on two levels. The food is carefully prepared and beautifully presented. The *prix fixe* lunch is reasonably priced. Closed on Sundays. American Express, MasterCard and Visa accepted.

Martin's Tavern
1264 Wisconsin Ave, NW (at N St), 20007 **Tel** *333-7370*
Map *1 C2*

Established in 1933, this is the oldest family-owned restaurant in DC. It is also a charming location for pub food. The front room can get noisy, but the booths in the back provide a quiet respite.The menu offers a range of prices. On Saturdays the bar stays open until 2pm.

Old Glory All American Barbecue
3139 M St, NW, 20007 **Tel** *337-3406*
Map *1 C2*

This homely restaurant serves traditional American barbecue – spare ribs and hickory-smoked chicken. The menu also features wood-fried shrimp and desserts such as apple crisp and coconut cherry cobbler. There's a new rooftop deck with outdoor seating and views of Georgetown.

Paolo's
1303 Wisconsin Ave, NW (at N St), 20007 **Tel** *333-7353*
Map *1 C2*

This Italian- and Californian-style restaurant is as trendy and international as its Georgetown surroundings. A place to peoplewatch while enjoying a light salad, pasta dish, or a pizza. A Sunday brunch buffet is available 10:30am–3pm. Happy-hour appetizer specials 4–7pm on weekdays.

Sequoia
Washington Harbor, 3000 K St, NW (at 30th St), 20007 **Tel** *944 4200*
Map *2 D3*

A trendy restaurant combining American cuisine with fabulous views of the Potomac and Virginia skyline. The casual, large seating area outside is especially delightful. The brunch is excellent. Parking is in the building on the K St side. A jazz band performs every other Wednesday.

1789
1226 36th St, NW (at Prospect St), 20007 **Tel** *965-1789*
Map *1 B2*

Chef Ris Lacoste, one of Washington's premier chefs, makes a creative use of seasonal ingredients. Superb, modern American food is served in four separate dining areas of a Federal town house. The setting is intimate and comfortable, with a cozy country-inn feel. Open for dinner every night.

Café Milano
3251 Prospect St, NW (off Wisconsin Ave), 20007 **Tel** *333-6183*
Map *1 C2*

Overlooking a pretty garden, Café Milano is known for its lively atmosphere, excellent wine list, great food, and celebrity sightings. The menu includes traditional homemade pasta. There is a main dining room as well as smaller rooms which can be used for private parties.

Japan Inn
1715 Wisconsin Ave, NW (corner R St), 20007 **Tel** *337-3400*
Map *1 C1*

Authentic food and plenty of options give the choice of sitting at a communal table while the dinner is grilled, or ordering from a traditional menu. Lunch from Monday to Friday, and dinner from Monday to Saturday. American Express, MasterCard, and Visa accepted.

Tony & Joe's Seafood Place
Washington Harbor, 3000 K St, NW (at 30th St), 20007 **Tel** *944-4545*
Map *2 D3*

The outdoor setting overlooking the Potomac is a wonderful place to spend an afternoon or evening. The seafood is simply prepared, fresh, and delicious. A live jazz combo plays in the evening from Thursday to Saturday, and during Sunday brunch.

Bistrot Lepic and Wine Bar
1736 Wisconsin Ave, NW, 20007 **Tel** *333-0111*
Map *1 C1*

This bistro, two floors of a bright yellow brick townhouse, serves some of the town's best French food. The romantic, intimate setting is quite popular. A wine bar, rated among the top 10 in the US, offers smaller dishes at more reasonable prices. The service is friendly. Closed on Mondays.

Citronelle
Latham Hotel, 3000 M St, NW (at 30th St), 20007 **Tel** *625-2150*
Map *2 D2*

This award-winning restaurant serves sophisticated French dishes, such as pastry "cigars" stuffed with wild mushrooms, and potato-crusted halibut. *Prix fixe* for a three-course starts at $85. You can also splurge on a nine-course tasting menu for $150.

FARTHER AFIELD

ADAMS MORGAN Madam's Organ

2461 18th St, NW (near Columbia Rd), 20009 **Tel** *667-5370*

This popular, boisterous nightspot offers a combination soul food and a blues bar. The venue serves salads, burgers, fried chicken, as well as dishes such as black-eyed peas and candied yams. Bluegrass, R&B, and blues bands perform nightly.

ADAMS MORGAN Cashion's Eat Place

1819 Columbia Rd, NW, 20009 **Tel** *797-1819*

New American cuisine, with European influences, and an award-winning wine list are the main draws of Cashion's Eating Place. The atmosphere is romantic with dim lighting and the staff is friendly. Open for dinner and Sunday brunch. The restaurant is closed on Mondays.

DUPONT CIRCLE Fin

1200 19th St, NW, 20036 **Tel** *530-4430* **Map** *2 F2*

Fin offers high-quality seafood at a moderate price. The crab cakes are said to be the best in town. Specialties also include some non-fish dishes: veal meatloaf as well as pork tenderloins with five spices. The service is quick and friendly and the decor is modern and trendy. Complimentary valet parking available after 5pm.

DUPONT CIRCLE Iron Gate Inn

1734 N St, NW, 20036 **Tel** *737-1370* **Map** *3 A2*

It's hard to find a more romantic spot with such reasonable prices. The interior is warm and cozy with working fireplaces, and the garden is lovely. Food is imaginatively prepared and nicely presented. Lunch from Monday to Friday and dinner from Monday to Saturday.

DUPONT CIRCLE Pesce

2016 P St, NW, 20036 **Tel** *466-3474* **Map** *2 E2*

The French and Italian menu changes daily, but always includes delicious seafood and a fabulous wine list. The exposed brick walls, fish art, and cozy bar add to Pesce's appeal. Open for lunch from Monday to Friday, and for dinner every night.

DUPONT CIRCLE Tabard Inn

1739 N St, NW, 20036 **Tel** *331-8528*

The menu of this historic inn always offers a delicious surprise. The garden is lovely and the funky interior has several inviting nooks and crannies. Valet parking on Friday, Saturday evenings, and Sunday brunch. A jazz duo performs on Sundays 7:30–10:30pm.

DUPONT CIRCLE Nora's

2132 Florida Ave, NW (corner of R St), 20008 **Tel** *462-5143* **Map** *2 E1*

One of the stalwarts of Washington dining, featuring organic seasonal ingredients and a varied menu of contemporary American cuisine. The decor is warm and cozy with Amish and Mennonite quilts adorning the walls. Open for dinner only and closed on Sundays.

DUPONT CIRCLE Obelisk

2029 P St, NW, 20036 **Tel** *872-1180* **Map** *2 E2*

A five-course fixed-price menu is offered, featuring classic Italian cuisine, but with a contemporary twist. This top-notch, 12-table restaurant has an intimate feel and a menu that changes daily. Reservations are recommended. Dinner only from Tuesday to Thursday. Closed on Sunday and Monday. American Express not accepted.

U STREET/SHAW Ben's Chili bowl

1213 U St, NW, 20009 **Tel** *667-0909*

A timeless Washington institution, Ben's Chili Bowl is popular with anyone who loves a good, high-calorie meal. Bill Cosby is one such devoted fan. The chili dogs are known nationally and the milk shakes hit the spot. Best loved are its salmon cakes, grits, scrapple, and blueberry pancakes, offered during breakfast hours (6–11am).

U STREET/SHAW Coppi's Organic

1414 U St, NW, 20009 **Tel** *319-7773*

A small, intimate restaurant, Coppi's Organic serves pizza and pasta made from organic ingredients. Its daily-changing menu also features a selection of antipasti, meat and fish dishes, and desserts. Pictures of bicyclists, the owner's passion, line the walls. Open for dinner only.

WISCONSIN AVENUE 2 Amy's

3715 Macomb St, NW (just off Wisconsin Ave), 20016 **Tel** *885-5700*

The pizza here has DOC status – it is recognized by the Italian government as authentic Neapolitan pizza. There's an extensive choice of toppings and a good wine selection. Though crowded on weekends, it's worth the wait. Only MasterCard, and Visa accepted.

Key to Price Guide *see p185* **Key to Symbols** *see back cover flap*

WISCONSIN AVENUE Austin Grill

2404 Wisconsin Ave, NW, 20007 **Tel** *337-8080*

There's a fun atmosphere at Austin Grill, where the music is loud and the walls sport coyotes and cowboys. Considered Washington's most authentic Tex-Mex restaurant, the managers here visit Austin, Texas, several times a year for research purposes. American Express, MasterCard, and Visa accepted.

WISCONSIN AVENUE Busara

2340 Wisconsin Ave, NW (south of Calvert St), 20007 **Tel** *337-2340*

Busara has a sleek interior and a very pleasant garden, both comfortable surroundings for enjoying a good variety of Thai dishes. The menu includes green curries, grilled seafood, and vegetarian dishes. House favorites are the Thai Bouillabaisse in coconut milk and Pad Thai.

WISCONSIN AVENUE Cactus Cantina

3300 Wisconsin Ave, NW (at Macomb St), 20016 **Tel** *686-7222* **Fax** *362-5649*

Fun, but often crowded, Cacus Cantina is a Mexican restaurant serving great food at reasonable prices. It is popular with families, and the atmosphere is always noisy and festive. Known to use fresh ingredients, its menu also features entrées, such as mesquite chicken, quail, broiled shrimp, as well as combination platters.

WISCONSIN AVENUE Guapo's Restaurant

4515 Wisconsin Ave (at Tenleytown), 20016 **Tel** *686-3588* **Fax** *686-5490*

A popular Mexican restaurant, offering terrific food at reasonable prices, Guapo's is famed for its fajitas and margaritas. The staff is friendly and accommodating. It's conveniently located, next to the Tenleytown Metro. A Mexican band plays on Thursday evenings.

WISCONSIN AVENUE Krupin's

4620 Wisconsin Ave, 20016 **Tel** *686-1989*

New York deli food served at table in the bright, well-lit Krupin's just north of the Tenleytown metro. The Reuben sandwich, matzo ball soup, and blintzes are only some of its specialties. The restaurant accepts American Express, MasterCard, and Visa.

WISCONSIN AVENUE Rocklands

2418 Wisconsin Ave, NW (south of Calvert St), 20007 **Tel** *333-2558*

Barbecue cooked to perfection, a good selection of hot sauces, and traditional homemade sides make this an excellent choice for a quick All-American meal. Small space only allows for a counter. American Express, MasterCard, and Visa are accepted. Limited parking is available.

WISCONSIN AVENUE Café Deluxe

3228 Wisconsin Ave (near Macomb St), 20016 **Tel** *686-2233*

Count on Café Deluxe for a good meal, but you may have to wait. Large windows, wooden booths, and an attractive bar make it one of the more appealing restaurants in the neighborhood. Offers a weekend brunch. American Express, MasterCard, and Visa accepted.

WISCONSIN AVENUE Heritage India

2400 Wisconsin Ave, NW, 20007 **Tel** *333-3120*

An elegant Indian restaurant on the second story overlooking Wisconsin Avenue. Special platters with small samplings of a large variety of dishes, vegetarian as well as non-vegetarian come recommended. Fiery lamb *vindaloo* is the critics' favorite.

WISCONSIN AVENUE Matisse Café Restaurant

4934 Wisconsin Ave, NW (at Fessenden St), 20016 **Tel** *244-5222*

North on Wisconsin Avenue, the attractions of this restaurant are its visually arresting decor inspired by Matisse and the innovative French food. Sunday brunch is superb. Open for lunch and dinner from Tuesday to Friday, only dinner on Saturday. Closed on Mondays during winter.

WOODLEY PARK/CLEVELAND PARK Alero Restaurant

3500 Connecticut Ave, NW (at Ordway St), 20008 **Tel** *966-2530*

You'll find an appealing mix of great food, reasonable prices, and friendly staff at this neighborhood Mexican restaurant. The outdoor tables at Alero are pleasant and the interior has charm. All major credit cards, except Discover and Diners Club, are accepted.

WOODLEY PARK/CLEVELAND PARK Indique

3512 Connecticut Ave, NW, 20008 **Tel** *244-6600*

Visit Indique to sample a unique selection of excellent southern Indian dishes. This two-story restaurant, has stunning modern decor and a most welcoming atmosphere. The bar area is lively as well as attractive. Valet parking is available from Thursday to Sunday.

WOODLEY PARK/CLEVELAND PARK Ivy's Place

3520 Connecticut Ave. NW, 20008 **Tel** *363-7802*

Open since 1982, this was Washington's first Indonesian restaurant. You'll find mild and spicy dishes and friendly service in this simple, but cozy establishment. The menu also features *rijsttafel*, a lavish combination of multiple dishes for two or more.

WOODLEY PARK/CLEVELAND PARK Lebanese Taverna

2641 Connecticut Ave, NW, 20008 **Tel** *265-8681*

This lively, often crowded, restaurant has an attractive Middle-Eastern decor and offers an extensive menu. One of the most popular family-dining venues, Lebanese Taverna serves sumptuous platters, both vegetarian and non-vegetarian. It also has an interesting wine list.

WOODLEY PARK/CLEVELAND PARK Nam Viet

3419 Connecticut Ave, NW , 20008 **Tel** *237-1015*

Nam Viet is considered one of the best Vietnamese restaurants in the area. It offers an overwhelming number of choices including vegetarian dishes. Signature dishes include the specialty, Nam-Viet special seasoned shrimp, and the entrée, Nam-Viet grilled combo.

WOODLEY PARK/CLEVELAND PARK Ardeo

3311 Connecticut Ave, NW, 20008 **Tel** *244-6750*

This trendy and busy, modern American restaurant features an interesting and innovative menu. Specialties include Black Angus sirloin burger with applewood-smoked bacon served with Fontina cheese and French fries. Bardeo, an annex next door, is a wine bar offering small plates with tapas and panini, as well as wine tastings.

WOODLEY PARK/CLEVELAND PARK Lavandou

3321 Connecticut Ave, NW, 20008 **Tel** *966-3002*

Walk into this small and charming restaurant and you'll feel transported to southern France. The menu features dishes from Provence, with over 90 wines to complement the fresh grilled seafood and soups. Open for lunch from Monday to Friday, and every night for dinner.

WOODLEY PARK/CLEVELAND PARK Petits Plats

2653 Connecticut Ave, NW, 20008 **Tel** *518-0018*

This charming restaurant, located in a Woodley Park townhouse, has several small dining rooms with five working fireplaces. It makes for a comfortable casual lunch or a candlelit dinner. The reasonably priced bistro fare includes shrimp and mussels dishes, prepared in the Provençal style.

WOODLEY PARK/CLEVELAND PARK Spice's

3333 Connecticut Ave, NW, 20008 **Tel** *686-3833*

Spice's offers a great selection of Asian dishes from several countries. The sushi bar is very popular, with almost half the menu devoted to sushi dishes. The restaurant attracts a young crowd who are looking for great food at reasonable prices. Spicy ginger chicken and the tasty tangerine-peel beef are real treats.

BEYOND WASHINGTON, DC

ALEXANDRIA, VA Gadsby's Tavern

138 N. Royal St, 22314 **Tel** *703-548-1288*

This establishment dates back to 1792 and is connected to the Gadsby's Tavern museum. The waiters are in Colonial costume, and the decor in the style of the 1700s. The menu includes duck, prime rib, seafood, and pies. Live music on Friday and Saturday evenings.

ALEXANDRIA, VA Le Refuge

127 N. Washington St, 22314 **Tel** *703-548-4661*

Across the street from historic Christ Church, this small French restaurant has great charm and wonderful French country food. *Bouillabaisse* and soft shelled crabs (in season) are specialties of the house. Closed on Sundays. All major credit cards, except Discover, are accepted.

ANNAPOLIS, MD Middleton Tavern Oyster Bar & Restaurant

2 Market Space, 21401 **Tel** *410-263-3323*

Established in 1750, the historic Middleton Tavern Oyster Bar & Restaurant is located across the street from the harbor. This is an indoor/outdoor spot, perfect to soak up the view. The oyster shooters come with beer. Also on the menu are crab cakes, seafood, and pasta dishes.

BALTIMORE, MD Obrycki's Crab House

1727 East Pratt St, 21231 **Tel** *410-732-6399*

A seasonal restaurant offering superb seafood dining. Obrycki's Crab House is located in Fells Point, the historic district of downtown Baltimore. A favorite of the house is the hard-shell steamed crabs. Closed from November 20 to March 15.

BETHESDA, MD Mon Ami Gabi

7239 Woodmont Ave (at Bethesda Ave), 20814 **Tel** *301-654-1234*

Located in Bethesda's restaurant row, Mon Ami Gabi is a good choice for traditional French food in a casual atmosphere. While it has the authentic *steak frites*, *bouillabaisse*, crêpes, and quiches to choose from, the emphasis is on rustic simplicity. Live jazz performance on Tuesday and Thursday evenings. Valet parking is available at night.

BETHESDA, MD Persimmon

7003 Wisconsin Ave, 20815 **Tel** *301-654-9860*

Considered one of the best restaurants in Bethesda, Persimmon is an American bistro with a cozy, romantic atmosphere. Parking is available on the street and in the municipal lot behind the building. Open for lunch from Monday to Friday and for dinner daily.

CHARLOTTESVILLE, VA Michie Tavern

683 Thomas Jefferson Parkway, 22902 **Tel** *434-977-1234*

Casual dining (buffet style) with a Colonial touch – the staff dresses in period costume, and the decor is rustic. Take a tour of the 200-year-old inn and outbuildings. The homemade Southern fare, based on 18th century recipes, is hearty – try the outstanding Southern fried chicken. Only lunch is served here.

GETTYSBURG, VA Farnsworth House B & B

401 Baltimore St, 17325 **Tel** *717-334-8838*

The tavern and dining room have a Civil War theme. Waiters dress in period clothes and the menu features Civil War dishes. Favorites are the game pie, spoonbread, sweet potato pudding, and pumpkin fritters. The dining room is not wheelchair accessible. Live music only occasionally.

MIDDLEBURG, VA The Coach Stop

9 East Washington Street (Rte 50), 22117 **Tel** *540-687-5515*

Located on the main street of Middleburg, The Coach Stop is a casual restaurant with a relaxed atmosphere. Popular with the locals, its extensive menu includes hamburgers, crab cakes, onion rings, and milk shakes. Open for breakfast, lunch, and dinner.

MIDDLEBURG, VA Red Fox Inn

2 East Washington St, 22117 **Tel** *540-687-6301*

Built in 1728, this inn has tried to retain the look of an 18th century tavern. The atmosphere is cozy with pine tables, Windsor chairs and working stone fireplaces. Elegant dining and a wine list, featuring wines from local vineyards. Live music on Tuesday evenings during summer.

PARIS, VA The Ashby Inn

692 Federal St, 20130 **Tel** *540-592-3900*

Widely considered the region's best restaurant, the inn looks out on the Blue Ridge Mountains. The menu is limited, but each dish is well prepared. Built in 1829, it's located in a small town an hour from Washington. Only MasterCard and Visa are accepted.

POTOMAC, MD Old Angler's Inn

10801 MacArthur Blvd (near Great Falls), 20854 **Tel** *301-365-2425*

This quaint English pub-style restaurant is a short trip from the city. Next to the C&O Canal, it is a cozy place to enjoy a meal by the fire. The outdoor seating is equally romantic. The sophisticated kitchen serves new American cuisine with flair. If the weather is pleasant, you could dine on the stone terrace.

SHEPHERDSTOWN, WV Yellow Brick Bank

201 German St, 25443 **Tel** *304-876-2208*

Housed in what was once a bank, this charming restaurant offers a sophisticated menu. Every dish is specially prepared. A jazz pianist performs on Friday and Saturday evenings at 9 pm. It's about an hour and a half away from Washington.

ST. MICHAELS, MD The Crab Claw

304 Mill St at Navy Point (Rte 33 West), 21663 **Tel** *410-745-2900*

A seasonal seafood restaurant, The Crab Claw is located on the harbor, with up-close views of the boats. Maryland blue crabs are a house specialty, so are its several other dishes based on shrimps, lobsters, and clams. Closed from December to February.

WASHINGTON, VA Inn at Little Washington

389 Main Street, 22747 **Tel** *540-675-3800*

This five-star and five-diamond restaurant, one of the most celebrated in the world, offers regional, and eclectic American cuisine. The kitchen was inspired by the dairy room at Windsor Castle, no detail has been overlooked. A 90-minute drive from Washington. MasterCard and Visa accepted.

WILLIAMSBURG, VA Christiana Campbell's Tavern

Waller St (near the Capitol), 23187 **Tel** *757-229-2141*

Run by Colonial Williamsburg, this historic tavern offers seafood specialties. The menu includes sherried crab stew, crab cakes, and "sea pye" (made with crab, shrimp, lobster, and cream), all served with spoonbread or sweet potato muffins.

WILLIAMSBURG, VA The Trellis

403 Duke of Gloucester St, 23187 **Tel** *757-229-8610*

Located near the historic district, this restaurant features contemporary American cuisine with an emphasis on fresh food – the menu changes every season. It also offers an extensive wine list with more than 20 wines from Virginia. Parking is available at Merchant Square lots.

SHOPPING IN WASHINGTON, DC

Washington's vast selection of stores makes shopping in the capital a pleasurable experience. Souvenirs can be found anywhere from fashion boutiques and specialist food stores to museum and gallery gift shops. The many museums on the Mall and around the city sell a wide variety of unusual gifts, reproduction prints, and replica artifacts selected from all over the world.

US Capitol in straw-work

Although the many smart shopping malls and department stores in the DC area can provide hours of shopping, Georgetown offers visitors a far more lively and authentic environment in which to browse. It is a neighborhood packed with fashionable clothing boutiques and endless interesting shops that sell everything from antiques to hair dye, from one-dollar bargains to priceless works of art.

East Hall of the Union Station shopping mall

OPENING HOURS

Most department stores, shopping malls, and other centers are open from 10am until 8 or 9pm, Monday through Saturday, and from noon until 6pm on Sunday. Smaller shops and boutiques are generally open from noon until 6pm on Sundays, and from 10 until 6 or 7pm on all other days. Convenience stores such as supermarkets and local grocery stores may open for longer hours. Drugstores (pharmacies) are also often open for extended hours.

HOW TO PAY

Goods may be paid for in cash, in traveler's checks (in US dollars), or by credit card. VISA and MasterCard are the most popular credit cards in the United States, while American Express is often, but not always, accepted. A tax of 5.75% is added to all purchases at the cash register.

SALES

Department stores, such as **Hecht's** in the Old Downtown area and **Nordstrom** farther out in Arlington, often hold sales during holiday weekends, including Memorial Day, the 4th of July, Labor Day, and Columbus Day. Check the newspapers for advertisements to find good prices on electronics, jewelry, kitchenwares, shoes, and clothing. White sales (towels and bedlinen) occur in January.

MUSEUM SHOPS

All the museums on the Mall have an incredibly wide selection of products on sale in their museum shops. The **National Gallery of Art** shop sells artwork reproductions, books, art-related games and children's toys, and the **Museum of African Art** shop offers a range of African textiles, ceramics, basketry, musical instruments, and books.

The **National Museum of American History** shop is the largest of the Smithsonian museum shops and carries a range of souvenirs, including American crafts, reproductions, and T-shirts, as well as a range of books on American history. The museum's music shop sells recordings from the 1940s to the 1970s, including Doo Wop, Motown, and Disco, from the Smithsonian Recordings and Smithsonian Folkways labels.

Also well worth a visit are two museum shops near the White House. **The Renwick Gallery** museum shop sells contemporary crafts made from glass, wood, fiber, metal, and ceramic, as well as silk scarves and tapestry purses. The shop at the **Decatur House Museum**, home of Stephen Decatur, a naval hero from the War of 1812, has a collection of items for sale related to Washington's history, art, and architecture.

For a selection of interesting books on architecture, contemporary design, and historic preservation, as well as a range of toys, ties, frames, and gifts, pay a visit to the **National Building Museum** shop at Judiciary Square.

Stalls selling an eclectic range of goods at Eastern Market

Entrance to Hecht's Department Store on G Street, NW

MALLS AND DEPARTMENT STORES

There are a few small-scale shopping malls in central Washington, such as Georgetown Park and Union Station. **Georgetown Park** combines modern retail shops with a Victorian-style interior. It is situated at the intersection of Wisconsin Avenue and M Street, right in the heart of Georgetown. **Union Station**, the beautifully renovated train station in the Capitol Hill area *(see p55)*, houses 130 shops and restaurants on three levels, in a very pleasant environment. There are name-brand stores as well as an extensive collection of specialty shops that sell clothing, gifts, souvenirs, crafts, jewelry, and more.

Two small shopping malls are located on upper Wisconsin Avenue in the Friendship Heights neighborhood – **Mazza Gallerie** and **Chevy Chase Pavilion**. The metro is very convenient, but there is also plenty of parking for cars. Visitors can shop at Hecht's, one of several department stores, or the specialty boutiques and name-brand stores.

The larger malls are located in the Maryland and Virginia suburbs. The **Fashion Center at Pentagon City** is easily reached by metro. Discount-hunters should head for the 230 outlets at **Potomac Mills**, situated 30 miles (48 km) south of the city on I-95.

GALLERIES, ARTS, AND CRAFTS

Visitors will discover a cornucopia of art galleries and crafts shops in three of Washington's neighborhoods – Georgetown, Dupont Circle, and Adams-Morgan. Here visitors can spend a few hours feasting their eyes on the delightful objects on display.

Work by several local artists is on sale in the **Addison/Ripley Fine Arts**, located in Dupont Circle and Georgetown. Some of the best pottery can be found in the **Appalachian Spring** shops in Georgetown and at Union Station. **Eastern Market** in Capitol Hill offers a vibrant mix of stalls from antiques to ethnic artifacts, and is best at weekends.

Art lovers should browse along 7th Street, NW, between D Street and the MCI Center. Among the highlights are pieces of sculpture and contemporary art at **Zenith Gallery** for sale from $50 to $50,000. Out of town, in Alexandria, the **Torpedo Factory Art Center** is excellent for lovers of all kinds of arts and crafts.

Torpedo Factory Art Center logo

SOUVENIRS

Collectors' items and DC memorabilia are abundant at Political Americana and Made in America, two shops in **Union Station**. The **Old Post Office Pavilion** near Metro Center is also worth a visit for DC souvenirs. The gift shops in the **Kennedy Center** sell gifts and books about the performing arts and Washington in general. People looking for religious items or unusual souvenirs should try the **Washington National Cathedral** museum and book shop in the basement of the cathedral or the Herb Cottage, a renovated octagonal baptistry in the Cathedral grounds.

CLOTHES

Wisconsin Avenue and M Street in Georgetown are home to a wide range of clothing stores. National high-street chains include **The Gap**, while those seeking something a little out of the ordinary should visit **Urban Outfitters**. **Eddie Bauer** has relocated to Pentagon City Mall in Arlington, VA.

Betsey Johnson specializes in sleek city fashions. Unique designs in ladieswear can be purchased at **Gazelle** in Chevy Chase Pavilion as well as at **Relish** on Wisconsin Avenue. **H & M**, the international discount store, has clothing for men, women, and kids. There is also a great variety of clothes shops at Friendship Heights.

FOOD AND WINE

For something unusual, tasty, or exotic in the culinary field, there are several delicatessens worth visiting in Washington. In particular, try **Dean & Deluca** in Georgetown, or alternatively visit **Sutton Place Gourmet** at American University Park, near Massachusetts Avenue. Both have an excellent selection of gourmet foods and offer a fine range of American and European wines. While there, it is possible to sample the food and drinks available in their pleasant on-site cafés.

The Old Post Office Pavilion

One of many antique centers in Frederick

ANTIQUES

There are some wonderful hidden treasures to be discovered in the many antique stores scattered throughout Washington. Along Wisconsin Avenue, between P and S streets and also along M and O streets, there are around 20 antique shops. Some specialize in expensive antiques, others in prints, lamps, silverware, perfume bottles, or just interesting knick-knacks.

Adams-Morgan and Dupont Circle are also good neighborhoods for antique hunting. **Brass Knob Architectural Antiques**, on 18th Street, is worth visiting for their range of salvaged curiosities, including clawfoot bathtubs and unusual antique light fixtures. Customers are bound to leave with just the perfect relic for their home, which could be anything from a chandelier to an iron gate.

There is also a number of centers for antiques outside central Washington. Kensington in Maryland and Old Town Alexandria in Virginia are areas rich in antiques. **Bird-in-the-Cage Antiques** in Alexandria sells all kinds of antiques, such as dolls, china, and silver, but specializes in books. In Frederick, Maryland, is the enormous **Emporium at Creekside Antiques**. This paradise for antiques lovers houses over 100 shops that sell everything from huge pieces of furniture through household wares to jewelry.

BOOKS AND MUSIC

Book lovers will enjoy spending time browsing in the myriad bookstores that can be found in Washington.

As well as the large chainstores, such as **Barnes and Noble**, there are several excellent independent and second-hand bookstores, especially in the Dupont Circle area, such as **Olsson's Books and Records**. In **Kramerbooks & Afterwords Café**, customers can sit with their new purchase and a coffee, and it is also a full-service restaurant. **Second Story Books** is DC's biggest second-hand store.

Farther north, on Connecticut Avenue, is the **Politics &** **Prose Bookstore**, a favorite among Washingtonians for its combination of books and coffee. Customers can chat with the knowledgeable staff, browse, or attend a reading. (The Sunday book review section of the *Washington Post* lists readings.)

The chainstore **Borders**, like Olsson's, sells both books and compact discs, which are competitively priced. Located near George Washington University is the music store **Tower Records**, which has the largest choice of compact discs in Washington, while **Melody Record Shop** sells music at discount prices.

MISCELLANEOUS

The many department stores in and around Washington, such as **Hecht's** and **Neiman-Marcus**, are well-stocked with good quality household wares from linens to cutlery and crockery. They are also prepared to order any out-of-stock items for their customers.

Wake Up Little Suzie sells unusual and unique gifts, such as handmade books, jewelry, and hanging mobiles. Similarly, **Chocolate Moose**, on L Street, is a treasure trove of the unusual and unconventional, including ceramics, chocolates, jewelry, ceramics, and children's toys, amongst other things. For visitors fascinated by maps and travel, a visit to the **ADC Map and Travel Center** is essential. This shop has over 5,000 maps from around the world, as well as globes, guidebooks, and language books.

Everything in contemporary products for the home, from kitchenware to furniture, can be found at **Crate & Barrel** in Spring Valley and in Georgetown's **Pottery Barn**. Also in Georgetown is **Restoration Hardware**, which offers everything from decorative door knobs through gardening supplies and lamps, to old-fashioned toys and the popular, heavy oak Mission furniture that originated in the Arts and Crafts Movement.

Shoppers browsing in the window of Olsson's bookstore

DIRECTORY

MALLS AND DEPARTMENT STORES

Chevy Chase Pavilion
5335 Wisconsin Ave, NW.
Tel 686-5335.

Fashion Center at Pentagon City
1100 South Hayes St,
Arlington, Virginia.
Tel (703) 415-2400.

Georgetown Park
3222 M St, NW.
Map 1B2. *Tel* 342-8190

Hecht's Department Store
12th & G St, NW.
Map 3C3.
Tel 628-6661

Mazza Gallerie Mall
5300 Wisconsin Ave, NW.
Tel 966-6114.

Neiman-Marcus
Mazza Gallerie.
Map 1B1.
Tel 966-9700

Nordstrom
Fashion Center at
Pentagon City.
Tel (703) 415-1121.

Potomac Mills
Dale City, VA.
Tel (800) 826-4557.

Union Station Shops
40 Massachusetts Ave, NE.
Map 4 E3. *Tel* 371-9441.

GALLERIES, ARTS, AND CRAFTS

Addison/Ripley Fine Arts
1670 Wisconsin Ave, NW.
Map 1 C2. *Tel* 338-5180.

Appalachian Spring
1415 Wisconsin Ave, NW.
Map 1C2. *Tel* 337-5780.

Eastern Market
225 7th St, SE.
Map 4 F4.
Tel 544-0083.

Torpedo Factory Art Center
105 N. Union Street
Alexandria, VA.
Tel (703) 838-4565.

Zenith Gallery
413 7th St, NW.
Map 3 C2.
Tel 783-2963.

ANTIQUES

Bird-in-the-Cage Antiques
110 King St,
Alexandria, VA.
Tel (703) 549-5114.

Emporium at Creekside Antiques
112 E. Patrick St,
Frederick, MD.
Tel (301) 662-7099.

Brass Knob Architectural Antiques
2311 18th St, NW.
Map 3 A1.
Tel 332-3370.

Georgetown Flea Market
Wisconsin Ave, between
S & T Sts, NW.
Map 1 C3.

SOUVENIRS

Kennedy Center
New Hampshire Ave &
Rock Creek Parkway, NW.
Map 2 D4.
Tel 416-8346.

Old Post Office Pavilion
Pennsylvania Ave
& 12th St, NW. Map 3C3.
Tel 289-4224.

Washington National Cathedral
Massachusetts &
Wisconsin Ave, NW.
Tel 537-6267.

BOOKS AND MUSIC

Barnes and Noble
3040 M St, NW.
Map 2 D2. *Tel* 965-9880.

Borders
1800 L St, NW.
Map 2 E3. *Tel* 466-4999.

Kramerbooks & Afterwords Café
1517 Connecticut Ave,
NW.
Map 2 E2.
Tel 387-1400.

Melody Record Shop
1623 Connecticut Ave,
NW.
Map 2 E2. *Tel* 232-4002.

Olsson's Books and Records
1307 19th St, NW.
Map 2 F2. *Tel* 785-1133.

Politics & Prose Bookstore
5015 Connecticut Ave,
NW.
Map 2 E2. *Tel* 364-1919.

Second Story Books
2000 P Street, NW.
Map 1B1. *Tel* 659-8884.

Tower Records
2000 Pennsylvania Ave,
NW. Map 2 E3.
Tel 331-2400.

MUSEUM SHOPS

Decatur House Museum
1610 H St, NW.
Map 3 A3.
Tel 842-1856.

National Building Museum
401 F St, NW. Map 4 D3.
Tel 272-7706.

National Gallery of Art
Constitution Ave at
6th St, NW. Map 4 D4.
Tel 842-6475.

National Museum of African Art
950 Independence Ave,
SW. Map 3 C4.
Tel 786-2147.

National Museum of American History
The Mall between
12th and 14th Sts, NW.
Map 3 B4.
Tel 357-1528.

Renwick Gallery
17th & Pennsylvania
Ave, NW.
Map 3 A3.
Tel 357-1445.

CLOTHES

Betsey Johnson
1319 Wisconsin Ave, NW.
Map 1 C2. *Tel* 338-4090.

Eddie Bauer
Pentagon City Mall,
Arlington, VA.
Tel (703) 418-6112.

The Gap
1258 Wisconsin Ave, NW.
Map 1 B1.
Tel 333-2657.

Gazelle Ltd.
Chevy Chase Pavilion,
5335 Wisconsin Ave, NW.
Tel 686-5656.

H & M
Georgetown Park
(Wisconsin Ave and
M St, NW).
Map 1 C2.
Tel 298-6792.

Relish
5454 Wisconsin Ave,
Chevy Chase, Md.
Tel (301) 654-9899.

Urban Outfitters
3111 M St, NW. Map1 C2.
Tel 342-1012.

FOOD AND WINE

Balducci's
3201 New Mexico Ave,
NW. *Tel* 363-5800.

Dean & Deluca
3276 M St, NW.
Map 1 C2. *Tel* 342-2500.

MISCELLANEOUS

ADC Map and Travel Center
1636 I (Eye) St, NW.
Map 2 F3. *Tel* 628-2608.

Chocolate Moose
1743 L St, NW.
Map 2 F2. *Tel* 463-0992.

Crate & Barrel
4820 Massachusetts Ave,
NW. *Tel* 364-6500.

Pottery Barn
3077 M St, NW.
Map 1 C2. *Tel* 337-8900.

Restoration Hardware
1222 Wisconsin Ave, NW.
Map 1 C2. *Tel* 625-2771.

Wake-Up Little Suzie
3409 Connecticut Ave,
NW.
Tel 244-0700.

ENTERTAINMENT IN WASHINGTON, DC

Baseball player

Visitors to Washington will never be at a loss for entertainment, from flying a kite in the grounds of the Washington Monument to attending a concert at the Kennedy Center. The city's diverse, international community offers a rich array of choices. If you are looking for swing dancing you will find it; you will also hear different beats around town, including salsa, jazz, and rhythm and blues. Outdoor enthusiasts can choose from cycling on the Rock Creek bike path to canoeing on the Potomac River. If you are looking for something less active, take in a film at the Smithsonian. Theatergoers have a wide range of choices, from Shakespeare through highly respected repertory companies to Broadway musicals. No matter what your budget is, you will find something to do. There are more free activities in DC than in any other American city.

Façade of the John F. Kennedy Center for the Performing Arts

INFORMATION SOURCES

The best place to find information is in the Weekend section of Friday's edition of the *Washington Post*. This lists concerts, plays, movies, children's activities, outdoor recreation, and fairs and festivals. Internet users can check out *Style Live*, the entertainment guide on the *Washington Post* website.

The "Where & When" section in the monthly *Washingtonian* magazine also lists events.

BOOKING TICKETS

Tickets may be bought in advance at box offices, or by phone, fax, and, in many cases, the Internet. Tickets for all events at the **Kennedy Center** can be obtained by phone through **Instant Charge**. Tickets for the MCI Center, the Nissan Pavilion, and the Warner Theater can be bought by phone through **Ticketmaster**. For Arena, Lisner Auditorium, Ford's Theatre, Merriweather Post Pavilion, and Woolly Mammoth tickets, contact **www.tickets.com**.

DISCOUNT TICKETS

Most theaters give group discounts, and several offer student and senior discounts for same-day

Façade of the Shakespeare Theatre on 7th Street

performances. Half-price tickets for seats on the day of the performance may be obtained in person at **Ticketplace**, situated inside the Old Post Office Pavilion.

In addition, theaters offer their own special discounts: The Arena sells a limited number of "Hottix," half-price seats, 30 to 90 minutes before the show. The Shakespeare Theatre offers 20 percent off for senior citizens Sunday through Thursday, 50 percent one hour before curtain rise for students, and discounts for all previews. The Kennedy Center has a limited number of half-price tickets available to students, senior citizens, and anyone with permanent disabilities. These go on sale at noon on the day of the performance (some are available before the first performance). Standing-room tickets may be available if a show is sold out.

FREE EVENTS

The daily newspapers provide up-to-date listings of free lectures, concerts, gallery talks, films, book signings, poetry readings, and shows.

Local artists offer free performances on the Millennium Stage at the Kennedy Center every evening at 6pm.

The **National Symphony Orchestra** gives a free outdoor concert on the West Lawn of the Capitol on Labor Day and Memorial Day weekends, and on the Fourth of July.

Courtyard concert in the National Gallery of Art

In summer, various military bands such as the **United States Marine Band**, the Navy, Air Force or the **US Army Band** give free concerts (contact them direct for details).

From October to June, the **National Gallery of Art** sponsors Sunday evening concerts at 7pm in the West Garden Court, and also summer jazz concerts on Friday evenings in the Sculpture Garden. Free lectures and gallery talks are held at the **Library of Congress** and at the National Gallery of Art.

OPEN-AIR ENTERTAINMENT

During the summer months at **Wolf Trap Farm Park for the Performing Arts** world famous performers can be seen on any night. Check their calendar of events and find your favorite form of entertainment – opera, jazz, Broadway musical, ballet, folk, or country music. You can bring a picnic to enjoy on the lawn.

On Thursday evenings in summer, the **National Zoo** hosts concerts on Lion Tiger Hill. They start at 6:30pm.

If you are in Washington in June try to catch the **Shakespeare Theatre Free for All** held at Carter Barron Amphitheater in Rock Creek Park.

The *Washington Post* lists the local fairs and festivals, held every weekend in warm weather. On the first weekend in May, the **Washington National Cathedral** sponsors the Flowermart, a festival featuring an old-fashioned carousel, children's games, crafts, and good food. The **Smithsonian Folklife Festival**, a two-week extravaganza held on the Mall at the end of June and early July, brings together folk artists from around the world. For details of other annual events in the city, *see* Washington, DC Through The Year *(pp36–9)*.

FACILITIES FOR THE DISABLED

All the major theaters in Washington are wheelchair accessible. For information on the Kennedy Center's accessibility services, check its website.

Many theaters, including the Kennedy Center, Ford's Theatre, the Shakespeare Theatre, and Arena Stage, have audio enhancement devices, as well as a limited number of signed performances. For the hearing impaired, TTY phone numbers are listed in the Weekend section of the *Washington Post*.

The National Gallery of Art provides assisted listening devices for lectures. Sign-language interpretation is available with three weeks' notice, and a telecommunications device for the deaf (TDD) can be found near the Concourse Sales Shop. For those with limited sight, the theater Arena Stage offers audio description, touch tours of the set, and program books in large print and Braille.

DIRECTORY

INFORMATION SOURCES

Washington Post
www.washingtonpost.com

BOOKING TICKETS

John F. Kennedy Center for the Performing Arts
New Hampshire Ave at Rock Creek Parkway, NW.
Map 2 D4.
Tickets booked via Instant Charge
Tel 467-4600
or (800) 444-1324.
www.kennedy-center.org

Ticketmaster
Tel 432-7328.
Tickets may be obtained at Hecht's Department Store, 12th & G Sts, NW.
www.ticketmaster.com

Tickets.com
Tel (800) 955-5566.
www.tickets.com

DISCOUNT TICKETS

Ticketplace
Old Post Office Pavilion, 1100 Pennsylvania Ave, NW.
Map 3 C3.
Tel 842-5387.

FREE EVENTS

US Army Band
Tel (703) 696-3399.
www.usarmyband.com

Library of Congress
1st St & Independence Ave, SE.
Map 4 F4.
Tel 707-2905.
www.loc.gov

National Gallery of Art
Constitution Ave at 6th St, NW.
Map 4 D4.
Tel 737-4215.
www.nga.gov

National Symphony Orchestra
Tel 467-4600.

US Marine Band
Tel 433-4011.
www.marineband.usmc.mil

OPEN-AIR ENTERTAINMENT

National Zoo
3001 Connecticut Ave, NW.
Tel 673-4800.
www.si.edu/natzoo

Shakespeare Theatre Free for All
Carter Barron Amphitheater, 16th St & Colorado Ave, NW.
Tel 334-4790.
www.shakespearetheatre.org

Smithsonian Folklife Festival
Tel 357-2700.

Washington National Cathedral
Massachusetts and Wisconsin Aves, NW.
Tel 537-6200.
www.nationalcathedral.org

Wolf Trap Farm Park for the Performing Arts
1551 Trap Rd, Vienna, VA.
Tel (703) 255-1868 (info).
Tel (703) 218-6500 (tickets)
www.wolftrap.org

Cultural Events

For an evening out, Washington has much to offer. A seafood dinner on the waterfront followed by a play at Arena Stage, Washington's oldest repertory company; dancing at one of the new clubs on U Street; jazz in Georgetown; a late-night coffee bar in Dupont Circle; or opening night at the opera at the Kennedy Center and a nightcap in the west end. Or if you are staying downtown and do not want to venture far from your hotel, see a show at the Warner or the National Theater, where the best of Broadway finds a home.

Dancing to live music at the Kennedy Center

Sign on the façade of the Warner Theatre on 13th Street

FILM AND THEATER

For daily screenings of movie classics, as well as film premieres, the **Film Theatre** at the **Kennedy Center** is the place to go. Museums such as **The National Gallery of Art** show films relating to current exhibitions. **The Library of Congress** offers a free film series of documentaries and films related to the exhibits in the museum, shown in the Mary Pickford Theater. The DC Film Festival is based at the Lincoln Theatre.

National touring theater companies bring shows to the **John F. Kennedy Center for the Performing Arts**, the **Warner Theatre**, and the **National Theatre**. For a more intimate setting, try **Ford's Theatre. Arena Stage** has a well-established repertory company. **The Studio, The Source,** and the **Woolly Mammoth Theatre** produce contemporary works.

The Shakespeare Theatre produces works in a modern, elegant setting. For plays performed in Spanish, seek out the **Gala Hispanic Theater**.

OPERA AND CLASSICAL MUSIC

Based at the Kennedy Center, the **Washington National Opera Company** is often considered one of the capital's crown jewels. Although many performances do sell out, standing room tickets are sometimes available. **The National Symphony Orchestra** performs classical and contemporary works.

A rich variety of chamber ensembles and choral groups perform regularly around the city. **The Washington Performing Arts Society** brings internationally renowned performers to DC.

DANCE

The Kennedy Center offers a magnificent ballet and dance season every year, with sell-out productions from the world's finest companies including the Bolshoi, the American Ballet Theater, the Royal Swedish Ballet, and the Dance Theater of Harlem.

Dance Place showcases its own professional modern dance companies, as well as international contemporary dance companies.

If you would prefer to take to the floor yourself, make your way to **Glen Echo Park** where people from ages 7 to 70 enjoy evenings of swing dancing, contra dancing (line dancing), Louisiana Cajun zdeco dancing, and waltzes. The Kennedy Center also occasionally has dancing to live bands.

ROCK, JAZZ, AND BLUES

To see the "biggest names and the hottest newcomers" in jazz, head for the KC Jazz Club at the Kennedy Center. Oscar Brown, Jr., Phil Woods, Ernie Watts, and many more are featured here. You can hear international jazz stars at **Blues Alley** in Georgetown, or visit **Madam's Organ** in Adams-Morgan, home to some of the best R&B in Washington.

If you want to hear really big name rock stars or jazz artists, join thousands of fans at the **Merriweather Post Pavilion** in Columbia, Maryland, or at the **Nissan Pavilion** in Manassas, Virginia.

Interior of the highly respected Shakespeare Theatre

CLUBS, BARS, AND CAFES

For late night dancing and clubbing, try the U Street neighborhood. Most highly recommended are **Club U** and the **930 Night Club**.

For salsa try the **Rumba Café** in Adams-Morgan. If you fancy a cigar and a martini, then check out **Ozio Martini and Cigar Lounge** downtown. If Irish music is more your thing, head to **Ireland's Four Provinces** in Cleveland Park. **Georgetown Billiards** and other billiard parlors are also popular, as are the city's many coffee bars. **Cosi Coffee and Bar** in Dupont Circle serves coffees and cocktails.

GAY CLUBS

Many of the gay bars in DC can be found in the Dupont Circle area. **JR's Bar and Grill** attracts young professionals. **The Fireplace** is popular and stays open late. For a good meal, visit **Annie's Paramount Steak House**.

Interior of Rumba Café

DIRECTORY

FILM AND THEATER

Arena Stage
1101 6th St, SW.
Map 4 D5. **Tel** 488-3300.
www.arenastage.org

Film Theatre at the Kennedy Center
New Hampshire Ave & Rock Creek Parkway, NW.
Map 2 D4. **Tel** 467-4600 or (800) 444-1324.
www.kennedy-center.org

Ford's Theatre
511 10th St, NW.
Map 3 C3. **Tel** 347-4833.
www.fordstheatre.org

Gala Hispanic Theater
2437 15th St, NW.
Tel 234-7174.

Library of Congress
Mary Pickford Theater,
Madison Building,
101 Independence Ave, SE.
Map 4 E4.
Tel 707-5677.
www.loc.gov

National Gallery of Art
Constitution Ave at 6th St,
NW. **Map** 4 D3. **Tel** 737-4215. www.nga.org

National Theatre
1321 Pennsylvania Ave,
NW. **Map** 3 B3.
Tel 628-6161.
www.nationaltheatre.org

Shakespeare Theatre
450 7th St, NW.
Map 3 C3.
Tel 547-1122.
www.shakespearetheatre.org

Source Theatre Company
1835 14th St,
NW.
Tel 462-1073.
www.sourcetheatre.com

The Studio Theatre
1333 P St, NW.
Map 3 B1.
Tel 332-3300.
www.studiotheatre.org

Warner Theatre
13th St
(between E and F Sts),
NW.
Map 3 C3.
Tel 783-4000.
www.warnertheatre.com

Woolly Mammoth Theatre
7th and D sts,
NW.
Map 3 C3.
Tel 393-3939.
www.woollymammoth.net

OPERA AND CLASSICAL MUSIC

National Symphony Orchestra
Tel 467-4600.

Washington Performing Arts Society
Tel 833-9800.

DANCE

Dance Place
3225 8th St, NE.
Tel 269-1600.

Glen Echo Park
Spanish Ballroom,
7300 MacArthur Blvd,
Glen Echo, MD.
Tel (301) 492-6229.

ROCK, JAZZ, AND BLUES

Blues Alley
1073 Wisconsin Ave,
NW.
Map 1 C3.
Tel 337-4141.

Madam's Organ
2461 18th St, NW.
Map 2 F1.
Tel 667-5370.

Merriweather Post Pavilion
Columbia, MD.
Tel (301) 455-SEAT.
(Tickets.com) or
(800) 955-5566.

Nissan Pavilion
7800 Cellar Door Drive,
Haymarket, VA.
Tel (703) 754-6400

CLUBS, BARS, AND CAFES

Club U
2000 14th St, NW.
Tel 328-8859.
www.club-u.com

Cosi Coffee and Bar
1647 20th St, NW.
Map 3 A1.
Tel 332-6364.

Georgetown Bar and Billiards
3251 Prospect St, NW.
Map 1 C2.
Tel 965-7665.

Ireland's Four Provinces
3412 Connecticut Ave,
NW.
Tel 244-0860.

930 Night Club
815 V St, NW.
Tel 393-0930.
www.930tickets.com

Ozio Martini and Cigar Lounge
1813 M St, NW.
Map 3 A1.
Tel 822-6000.

Rumba Café
2443 18th St, NW.
Tel 588-5501.

GAY CLUBS

Annie's Paramount Steak House
1609 17th St, NW.
Map 2 F2.
Tel 232-0395.

The Fireplace
2161 P St, NW.
Map 2 E2.
Tel 293-1293.

JR's Bar and Grill
1519 17th St, NW.
Map 2 F2.
Tel 328-0090.

Sports and Outdoor Activities

The people of Washington are known for putting in long hours – whether on the floor of the Senate, the office of a federal agency, or in a newsroom. They compensate, however, by taking their leisure hours very seriously by rooting for their favorite teams or spending as much time as possible outdoors. You can join in the fun at the MCI Center or the RFK Stadium, both of which attract hordes of fans. You can meet joggers, cyclists, and in-line skaters on the Mall and around the monuments.

Cyclists enjoying the fine weather outdoors in DC

SPECTATOR SPORTS

Fans of the NHL Capitals (National Hockey League), the NBA Wizards (National Basketball Association), and the WNBA Mystics (Women's National Basketball Association) should purchase tickets at the **MCI Center**, an impressive sports arena that opened in December 1997 and has helped revitalize the downtown area.

Depending on the season, you might also see Disney on Ice, the Harlem Globetrotters, or the Ringling Brothers Circus. Visit the MCI's National Sports Gallery, which houses sports memorabilia and interactive sports games. There is plenty to eat at the MCI Center, but you may prefer to slip out to one of the restaurants in Chinatown, which surrounds the MCI Center.

If you are not a season-pass holder, it is very difficult to get a ticket to a Washington Redskins game at the **FedEx Field** stadium, but you can always watch the game from one of Washington's popular sports bars. The DC United team plays soccer at the **RFK Stadium**. College sports are also very popular in DC – you will find Washingtonians cheering either for the **Georgetown Hoyas** or the **Maryland Terrapins**.

FISHING AND BOATING

If you want to spend an hour or perhaps an entire day by the Potomac River, the best place to start is **Fletcher's Boat House** at Canal and Reservoir Roads. You must obtain a permit if you are between 16 and 64, which lasts for a year but does not cost much. You can fish from the riverbank or rent a rowboat or canoe, which are available by the hour or the day.

Redskins team member

In Georgetown there are boats for rent at **Thompson's Boat Center** and **Jack's Boats**. Snacks can be bought at Fletcher's, or you may want to bring a picnic. If you go to Thompson's or Jack's there are cafés and restaurants along the waterfront.

CYCLING

Rock Creek Park is one of Washington's greatest treasures and offers amazing respite from busy city life. Closed to traffic on weekends, it is a great place for cycling. Another popular trail is the Capital Crescent, which starts on the C&O Canal towpath in Georgetown and runs to Maryland.

One of the more beautiful bike trails in the area will take you 16 miles (26 km) to Mount Vernon. Bikes can be rented at Fletcher's Boat House, Thompson's Boat Center, **Bike the Sites**, or **Big Wheels** in Georgetown. For maps or trail information call or write to the **Washington Area Bicyclist Association,** or consult one of the bike rental shops in the city.

TENNIS, GOLF, AND HORSEBACK RIDING

Several neighborhood parks have outdoor tennis courts, available on a first-come, first-served basis. Two public clubs in the city accept reservations: **East Potomac Tennis Center** at Hains Point, and the **Washington Tennis Center**. Each has outdoor and indoor courts.

If you want to take in views of the monuments while walking the golf fairways, go to the **East Potomac Golf Course & Driving Range**. (There is an 18-hole miniature golf course here as well.) Two other courses are open to the public: **Langston Golf Course** on the Anacostia River and

RFK Stadium, a major sports and entertainment venue

Rock Creek Golf Course, tucked into Rock Creek Park. You will also find **Rock Creek Park Horse Center**, where you can make reservations for a guided trail ride.

EXPLORING NATURE

For an amazing array of trees and plants, visit the **National Arboretum** *(see p144)*, which covers 444 acres in northeast Washington. There is something interesting to see all year round in the arboretum. Special displays, such as the National Bonsai Collection of miniature plants, can be enjoyed at any time of year. To catch the best of the flowering shrubs, the beautiful camellias and magnolias flower in late March through early April, and the stunning, rich colors of the azaleas, rhododendron, and dogwood appear from late April through early May There is a 1,600-ft (490-m) long "touch and see trail" at the garden for visually impaired visitors.

The beautiful and tranquil grounds of the National Arboretum

An alternative to the arboretum is **Kenilworth Aquatic Gardens**, which has 14 acres of ponds with more than 100,000 water lilies, lotuses, and other plants. It is a good idea to plan a trip early in the day when the blooms are open and before the sun gets too hot. Frogs and turtles can be seen regularly along the footpaths around the ponds. Park naturalists conduct nature walks around the gardens on summer weekends.

One of the most enjoyable ways to spend time outdoors is with a picnic in the park. Visit **Dumbarton Oaks Park** in Georgetown when the wildflowers are in bloom, or visit **Montrose Park**, right next door to Dumbarton Oaks, where you can enjoy the variety of birds and the boxwood maze.

DIRECTORY

SPECTATOR SPORTS

FedEx Field
Arena Drive,
Landover, MD.
Tel (301) 276-6000.
www.redskins.com

Georgetown Hoyas
Tel 687-4692
(for tickets).

Maryland Terrapins
Tel (800) 462-8377
(for tickets).

MCI Center
601 F St, NW.
Map 4 D3. **Tel** 628-3200.

RFK Stadium
2400 East Capitol St, SE.
Tel 547-9077.

FISHING AND BOATING

Fletcher's Boat House
4940 Canal Rd, NW.
Map 1 A2. **Tel** 244-0461.

Jack's Boats
3500 Water St, NW.
Map 2 D2.
Tel 337-9642.

Thompson Boat Center
Rock Creek Parkway
& Virginia Ave, NW.
Map 2 D3. **Tel** 333-9543.
www.thethompsonboat
center.com

CYCLING

Big Wheel Bikes
1034 33rd St, NW.
Map 1 C2.
Tel 337-0254.
www.bigwheelbikes.com

Bike the Sites
1100 Pennsylvania Ave, NW.
Map 3 C3.
Tel 842-BIKE (2453).
www.bikethesites.com

Washington Area Bicyclist Association
733 15th St, NW.
Map 3 B1. **Tel** 628-2500.
www.waba.org

TENNIS, GOLF, AND HORSEBACK RIDING

East Potomac Golf Course
972 Ohio Drive, SW at Hains
Point. **Map** 3 A5. **Tel** 554-
7660. **www**.golfdc.com

East Potomac Tennis Center
1090 Ohio Drive, SW at
Hains Point. **Map** 3 A5.
Tel 554-5962.
www.eastpotomactennis
.com

Langston Golf Course
26th St & Benning Rd, NE.
Tel 397-8638.

Rock Creek Golf Course
16th & Rittenhouse Sts,
NW. **Tel** 882-7332.

Rock Creek Park Horse Center
Military & Glover Rds, NW.
Tel 362-0118. **www**.
rockcreekhorsecenter.com

Rock Creek Tennis Center
16th & Kennedy Sts, NW.
Tel 722-5949.

EXPLORING NATURE

Dumbarton Oaks Park
Entrance on Lovers Lane,
off R & 31st Sts, NW.
Map 1 C1.

Kenilworth Park and Aquatic Gardens
1550 Anacostia Ave, NE.
Tel 426-6905.

Montrose Park
R & 31st Sts, NW.
Map 2 D1.

National Arboretum
New York Ave
& Bladensburg Rd, NE.
Tel 245-2726.
www.usna.usda.gov

Children's Washington, DC

Visiting the city's monuments can be one of the favorite and most memorable activities for children in DC. Call in advance to arrange a tour with a park ranger, during which you take a trip in the elevator to the top of the Washington Monument, then walk down the steps. Young children will like feeding the ducks at the Reflecting Pool or Constitution Gardens. You can view the Jefferson Memorial from a paddleboat on the Tidal Basin, and before you leave Washington be sure to see the monuments lit up against the night-time sky.

Children in front of the National Museum of Natural History

PRACTICAL ADVICE

One of the best sources of comprehensive information on specific events for children can be found in the "Saturday's Child" page which is in the Weekend section of Friday's *Washington Post*.

As you would expect in a major city, food is widely available in DC, whether it is hot dogs from a seller along the Mall or even strange space food (such as freeze-dried ice cream) from the **National Air and Space Museum** gift shop *(see pp62–65)*.

Sea lion at the National Zoo

of the **National Zoo** *(see pp138–9)* is a good place for a walk, and you can also enjoy watching elephant training and sea lion demonstrations.

For a break from the Mall museums, take a ride on the **Carousel on the Mall**, in front of the Arts and Industries Building. Also worth a visit is the carousel in **Glen Echo Park**, built in 1921. From December to March, ice skaters can head for the outdoor rink at the **National Gallery of Art Sculpture Garden**. Or try **Pershing Park Ice Rink**, located on Pennsylvania Avenue, across from the Willard Hotel. Skate rentals are available.

OUTDOOR FUN

For a trip into the past, take a ride on *The Georgetown*, a mule-drawn barge on the C&O Canal from April to mid-October (contact the **C&O Canal Visitor Center** for details). Park Service rangers dressed in 19th-century costumes add to the experience.

The beautiful wooded park

MUSEUMS

The Discovery Center, a vast educational complex with an IMAX® theater, is housed in the **National Museum of Natural History** *(see pp70–71)*.

If you want to experience outer space, then see "To Fly!" and the Albert Einstein Planetarium at the **National**

Air and Space Museum. A series of children's films and family programs are run by the **National Gallery of Art** *(see pp58–61)*. Children can discuss paintings and take part in a whole range of hands-on activities.

The **National Museum of the American Indian** *(see pp68–9)* has many events, films and demonstrations designed for the family.

Children are always fascinated by the **National Postal Museum** *(see p53)*, with its many intriguing hands-on activities.

CHILDREN'S THEATER

The Arts and Industries Building *(see p66)* houses the **Discovery Theater**, which stages puppet shows and plays. See a puppet show or fairytale production at the **Adventure Theater** in Glen Echo Park. The theater company **BAPA Imagination Stage**, located north of Washington in Bethesda, Maryland, presents lively theater productions for children.

The **Kennedy Center** *(see pp118–9)* and **Wolf Trap Farm Park for the PerformAlting Arts** also provide information on all sorts of children's events in the city.

A LITTLE BIT OF HISTORY

Children studying American history will be fascinated by a visit to Cedar Hill, once the home of Frederick Douglass, in Anacostia. The video in the

Children's tour in Cedar Hill, the historic home of Frederick Douglass

visitors' center helps to tell the amazing story of this American hero.

You can take a tour of **Ford's Theatre** *(see p96)* where President Lincoln was shot and the house across the street where he died.

On Saturdays the **Washington National Cathedral** *(see pp142–3)* runs a Medieval Workshop. This is a hands-on learning center where children can make their own stained-glass windows, create clay gargoyles, or make brass rubbings. The Gargoyle Tour of the Cathedral is particularly interesting; weather permitting.

SHOPPING

The **Discovery Channel Stores**, which are located in Union Station and Fashion Central, Pentagon City, sell a range of international merchandise, including science kits, fossils, books, and globes.

The **National Museum of Natural History** *(see pp70–71)* shops stock books, science kits, natural history toys, and games related to sea life, dinosaurs, and nature.

The **National Geographic**

Simulation of sea exploration in the National Geographic Society's Jason Project

Society *(see p134)* has special exhibitions which children find absorbing and fascinating, and the store stocks videos, books, and back issues of its famous magazine.

DIRECTORY

PRACTICAL ADVICE

National Air and Space Museum
6th St & Independence Ave, SW.
Map 4 D4.
Tel 357-2700.

National Museum of American History
Constitution Ave between 12th & 14th Sts, NW.
Map 3 B4
Tel 357-2700.

OUTDOOR FUN

C&O Canal Visitor Center
1057 Thomas Jefferson St, NW. **Map** 2 D3.
Tel 653-5190.

Carousel on the Mall
Arts and Industries Blg, 900 Jefferson Drive, SW.
Map 3 B4.
Tel 357-2700.

Glen Echo Park Carousel
7300 MacArthur Blvd, Glen Echo, MD.
Tel (301) 492-6229.
www.glenechopark.org

National Gallery of Art Sculpture Garden Rink
7th St & Constitution Ave, NW. **Map** 4 D4.
Tel 842-1310.

National Zoo
3001 Connecticut Ave.
Tel 673-4800.

Pershing Park Ice Rink
Pennsylvania Ave & 14th St, NW.
Map 3 B3.
Tel 737-6938.

MUSEUMS

National Air and Space Museum
6th St & Independence Ave, SW. **Map** 4 D4.
Tel 357-1686, (IMAX ® film schedule).

National Gallery of Art
Constitution Ave between 3rd & 7th Sts, NW.
Map 4 D3.
*Tel 789-4995
(children's film program).
Tel 789-3030
(family program).*

National Museum of American History
Constitution Ave between 12th & 14th Sts, NW. **Map** 3 B4.
Tel 357-2700.

National Museum of the American Indian
4th St & Independence Ave, SW. **Map** 4 D4.
Tel 633-1000. **www**.
americanindian.si.edu

National Museum of Natural History
10th St & Constitution Ave, NW.
Map 3 C4.
*Tel 357 2700 (general information).
Tel 633-7400 (IMAX ® film schedule).*

National Postal Museum
2 Massachusetts Ave, NE.
Map 4 E3.
Tel 357-2700.

CHILDREN'S THEATER

Adventure Theater
7300 MacArthur Blvd, Glen Echo Park, Md.
Tel (301) 320-5331.

BAPA Imagination Stage
4908 Auburn Ave, Bethesda, MD.
Tel (301) 961-6060.
www.imagination stage.org

Discovery Theater
900 Jefferson Drive, SW.
Map 3 C4.
Tel 357-1500.

Wolf Trap Farm Park for the Performing Arts
1551 Trap Rd, Vienna, VA.
Tel (703) 255-1900.
www.wolftrap.org

A LITTLE BIT OF HISTORY

Ford's Theatre
511 10th St, NW.
Map 3 C3.
Tel 347-4833.
www.fordstheatre.org

Frederick Douglass National Historic Site
1411 W St, SE.
Tel 426-5961.

Washington National Cathedral
Massachusetts & Wisconsin Aves, NW.
*Tel 537-2934
(Medieval workshop and Gargoyle tour).*
www.national cathedral.org

SHOPPING

Discovery Channel Store
Fashion Central, Pentagon City. *Tel (703) 413-3425.*
Union Station.
Tel 842-3700.

National Geographic Store
17th & M Sts, NW.
Map 3 B2. *Tel 857-7591.*

National Museum of Natural History Shops
Constitution Ave between 12th and 14th Sts, NW.
Map 3 C4. *Tel 357-1535.*

SURVIVAL
GUIDE

PRACTICAL INFORMATION 210–217

TRAVEL INFORMATION 218–223

WASHINGTON, DC
STREET FINDER 224–229

PRACTICAL INFORMATION

Washington, DC is the heart of the American political world. It is a visitor-friendly place, especially to children and the disabled, since wheelchair accessibility is required almost everywhere. The whole city shuts down on federal holidays as well as anytime the government

Tour operator sign

requires it to, which may be right in the middle of your vacation. With the President of the US and other world leaders often coming and going in the city, unexpected delays and closures can occur. Spring and fall are the best times to visit as the summer can get very hot and the winters very cold.

Visitor Information Center at the Ellipse, near the White House

FOREIGN VISITORS

Citizens of the UK, most western European countries, Australia, New Zealand, and Japan need a valid passport but are not required to have a visa to visit the US, as long as they stay for less than 90 days, hold a return ticket, and enter on an airline in the visa waiver program (which includes all the major carriers). Canadian citizens need only proof of residence. Citizens of all other countries require a valid passport and a tourist visa. Stricter security since September 2001 means that anyone entering the US on a visa must be photographed and have their fingerprints checked before being allowed entry.

TOURIST INFORMATION

The Washington area welcomes visitors. Visitor information desks at the airports will provide guides and maps, and staff will be able to answer questions. Major hotels usually have a knowledgeable and helpful guest services desk. There are also a number of other organizations it may be worth contacting before your visit, especially the **Washington, DC Convention and Visitors Association**.

OPENING HOURS

For the most part business hours in DC are from 9am to 5pm. Often malls or department stores will stay open later or have extended hours on a certain day of the week. Shopping on Sundays can be limited, though many gas stations and convenience stores stay open 24 hours. Federal holidays are taken seriously in DC, and many businesses close. Before making arrangements it is worth checking if any such days occur during your stay.

ETIQUETTE

Smoking is prohibited in many buildings, restaurants, and stores in the DC area. Check for no-smoking signs before lighting up, or simply smoke outside if you are not sure. Tipping is expected for most services: in restaurants tip 15-20 percent of the bill, give $1.00 per bag to airport and hotel porters, and $2.00 to valet parking attendants. Bartenders expect 50 cents to $1.00 per drink; if you visit a hair salon or barbershop, 10 percent of the bill should suffice.

TAX

In DC and the surrounding area taxes will be added to hotel and restaurant charges, theater tickets, some grocery and store sales, and for almost all other purchases. Be sure to ask whether the tax is included in the price. Sales tax is 5.75 percent, hotel tax is 14.5 percent, with 10 percent tax on food and beverages.

ALCOHOL AND CIGARETTES

The legal age for drinking alcohol in Washington is 21, and you may need photo identification (I.D.) as proof of your age in order to purchase alcohol and be allowed into bars. It is illegal to drink alcohol in public parks or to carry an open container of alcohol in your car, and penalties for driving under the influence of alcohol are severe. Cigarettes can be purchased by those over 18 years old; proof of age may be required.

ELECTRICITY

Standard US two-prong plug

Electricity flows at the standard US 110-120 volts, and a two-prong plug is required. For non-US appliances you will need a plug adapter and a voltage converter. Without a voltage converter you will find that powerful electrical appliances such as hairdryers will not only operate poorly but may also overload. You will find that many hotels will provide guests with such items as hairdryers and coffee machines. There are sockets for electrical shavers in most rooms.

International Student Identity Card, accepted as I.D. in America.

STUDENTS

Students from abroad should purchase an International Student I.D. before traveling to Washington, as many discounts are available in the city to students. The ISIC handbook lists places and services in the US that offer discounts to card holders, including accommodations, museums, and theaters. The **Student Advantage Card** is available to all American college undergraduates and offers a range of discounts.

CHILDREN

Washington is a very child-friendly city; it even boasts its own children's museum, the Capital Children's Museum (*see p53*). Many other museums offer exciting hands-on facilities or interesting exhibits for children, such as the collection of 18th- and 19th-century dolls at the Daughters of the American Revolution museum (*see p114*).

For further information on entertainment for children in Washington, see pp206–7.

Restaurants are becoming increasingly family-oriented, and many provide children's menus or small portions to suit a child's appetite.

SENIOR CITIZENS

Anyone over the age of 65 is eligible for discounts with the appropriate proof of age. Contact the **American Association of Retired Persons** for further information. Also the Smithsonian produces a free booklet called *Smithsonian Access* with valuable information on parking areas, wheelchair accessibility, and sign language interpreters available around the DC area.

DISABLED VISITORS

Washington is one of the most convenient cities for people with disabilities.

Disabled sign

Almost all public buildings, including most hotels and restaurants, are required to be wheelchair accessible. For more information contact the **Society for Accessible Travel and Hospitality** or the Washington, DC Convention and Visitors Association for a free fact sheet on accessibility around the city.

GUIDED TOURS

There are many city bus tours available in DC. **Tourmobile Sightseeing** has numerous signed pick-up points and extensive routes. But for something a bit different try the **DC Ducks**. Another entertaining option is the **Scandal Tour**, a bus ride around the city to the sites of various political scandals.

The **Old Town Trolley Tours** offer an excellent ride around the main sites in an old-fashioned trolley bus.

A restored 1942 amphibious vehicle used by DC Ducks to tour the city

Personal Security and Health

Park police badge

Although as in any major city there is crime, Washington has made great efforts in reducing problems and cleaning up its streets, and with great success. If you stick to the tourist areas and avoid straying into outlying areas, you should not run into any trouble. The main sights are located in safe areas where there are lots of people, and major crime is rare. When visiting sights off the beaten track, take a taxi to and from the destination. Most importantly, pay attention to your surroundings.

LAW ENFORCEMENT

There are nine different police forces in Washington, including the secret service, park rangers, S.W.A.T. (Special Weapons and Tactics) teams, and the more typical M.P.D.C. (Metropolitan Police, Washington, DC) police in blue uniforms.

Because the city is home to the President, whenever he travels, members of the law enforcement agencies follow. When foreign political leaders visit, the police are even more visible than usual: you will see them on horseback, on bicycles, in cars, and even on top of buildings.

As a visitor, should you encounter any trouble, approach any of the blue-uniformed M.P.D.C. officers that regularly patrol the city streets.

M.P.D.C. officer   **Park ranger**

GUIDELINES ON SAFETY

Serious crime is rarely witnessed in the main sightseeing areas of Washington. However, avoid wandering into areas that you have no reason to visit, either during the day or at night. Pickpockets do operate in the city and will target anyone who looks like a tourist. Police officers regularly patrol the tourist areas, but it is still advisable to prepare the day's itinerary in advance, use common sense, and stay alert. Try not to advertise that you are a tourist; study your map before you set off, avoid wearing expensive jewelry, and carry your camera or camcorder securely. Carry small amounts of cash; credit cards or traveler's checks are a more secure option. Keep these close to your body in a money belt or inside pocket. Before you leave home, make a photocopy of your important documents, including your passport and visa, and keep them with you, though separate from the originals. Also make a note of your credit card numbers, in case of theft or loss. Keep an eye on your belongings at all times, whether you are checking into or out

Hospital sign

of a hotel, standing in the airport, or sitting in a restaurant. Do not allow strangers into your hotel room or give them details of where you are staying. It is a good idea to put any valuables in the hotel safe – do not carry them around with you. Most hotels will not guarantee the security of any belongings that you leave in your room.

LOST PROPERTY

Although the chances of retrieving lost property are slim, you should report all stolen items to the police. Telephone the **Police Non-Emergency Line** for guidance. Make sure you keep a copy of the police report, which you will need when you make your insurance claim. In case of loss, it is useful to have a list of serial numbers or a photocopy of all documents; keep these separate as proof of possession. If you can remember to do so, it is useful to make a mental note of the taxi company or bus route you use; it might make it easier to retrieve lost items.

If your passport is lost or stolen, get in touch with your country's embassy or consulate immediately.

If you lose your credit cards, most card companies have toll-free numbers for reporting a loss or theft, as do Thomas Cook and American Express for lost traveler's checks (see p215).

TRAVEL INSURANCE

Travel insurance is not compulsory but strongly recommended when traveling to the United States. It is particularly important to have insurance for emergency medical and dental care, which can be very expensive in the States. Even with medical coverage you may have to pay for the services, then claim reimbursement from your insurance company. If you take medication, bring a back-up prescription with

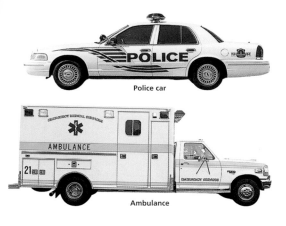
Police car

Ambulance

Fire engine

DIRECTORY

LOST PROPERTY

Police Non-Emergency Line
Tel 311 or 737-4404.

MEDICAL MATTERS

CVS 24-Hour Pharmacy
1199 Vermont Ave, NW.
Map 3 B2.
Tel 628-0720.

6 Dupont Circle, NW.
Map 2 F2.
Tel 785-1466.

EMERGENCIES

Police, Fire, Medical (all emergencies)
Tel Call 911, or dial 0 for the operator.

Medical Services
Medical Referrals
Tel 800 362-8677.

Dental Services
Dental Referrals
Tel 800 547-7615.

Area Hospitals
Tel Call 411 for directory assistance.

Crime Victims Line
Tel 232 6682.

EMBASSIES

Australia
1601 Massachusetts Ave, NW.
Map 2 F2.
Tel 797-3000.
www.austemb.org

Canada
501 Pennsylvania Ave, NW.
Map 4 D3.
Tel 682-1740.
www.canadianembassy.org

Ireland
2234 Massachusetts Ave, NW.
Map 3 A1.
Tel462-3939.
www.irelandemb.org

New Zealand
37 Observatory Circle, NW.
Tel 328-4800.
www.nzemb.org

United Kingdom
3100 Massachusetts Ave, NW.
Tel 462-1340.
www.britainusa.com

you. In addition, it is advisable to make sure your personal property is insured and obtain coverage for lost or stolen baggage and travel documents, as well as trip cancellation fees, legal advice, and accidental death or injury.

EMERGENCIES

If you are involved in a medical emergency, go to a hospital emergency room. Should you need an ambulance, call 911 and one will be sent. Also call 911 for police or fire assistance.

If you have your medical insurance properly arranged, you need not worry about medical costs. Depending on the limitations of your insurance, it is better to avoid the overcrowded city-owned hospitals listed in the phone book Blue Pages, and opt instead for one of the private hospitals listed in the Yellow Pages. Alternatively ask at your hotel desk or at the nearest convenience store for information. Or you can ask your hotel to call a doctor or dentist to visit you in your room.

PHARMACIES

If you need a prescription dispensed, there are plenty of pharmacies (drugstores) in and around the city, some staying open 24 hours. Ask your hotel for the nearest one.

LEGAL ASSISTANCE

Non-US citizens requiring legal assistance should telephone their embassy. The embassy will not lend you money but can help with advice on legal matters in emergencies. Should you be arrested for any reason, you have the right to remain silent. Do not offer the police money in the form of a bribe; this could land you in jail.

Fire Department logo

RESTROOMS

All visitor's centers, museums, and galleries have public restrooms, and invariably offer disabled and baby-changing facilities as well. All restaurants and hotels also have restrooms, but may only be available to paying customers.

Banking and Currency

Throughout Washington there are various places to access and exchange your money, from banks to cash machines to bureaux de change. The most important thing to remember is not to carry all your money and credit cards with you at once, and have enough cash to get you through Sunday when most banks and currency exchange offices are closed.

ATM for Chevy Chase Bank, one of the popular banks in DC

BANKING

Generally, most banks are open Monday through Friday from 9am to 2 or 3pm, although some may open earlier and close later. Most banks also open Saturday mornings from 9am to noon or 1pm. All banks are closed on Sundays and Federal holidays (see p39.)

Always ask if there are any special fees before you make your transaction. At most banks, traveler's checks in US dollars can be cashed with any photo identification, although passports are usually required to exchange foreign money. Foreign currency exchange is available at the main branches of large banks; they often have a separate area or teller window specifically for foreign exchange.

ATMS

Automated teller machines (ATMs) are found all over the Washington area, usually near the entrance to banks, or inside many convenience stores and supermarkets.

Widely accepted bank cards include Cirrus, Plus, NYCE, and some credit cards such as VISA or MasterCard. Note that a fee may be levied on your withdrawal, depending on the bank. Check with your bank which ATMs your card can access and the various fees charged. To minimize the risk of robbery, use ATMs in well-lit, populated areas only. Avoid withdrawing money at night or in isolated areas, and be aware of the people around you.

CREDIT CARDS

American Express, VISA, MasterCard, Diner's Club, and the Discover Card are accepted almost everywhere in Washington, from theaters and hotels to restaurants and shops. Besides being a safer alternative to carrying a lot of cash, many credit cards also offer additional benefits such as insurance on goods purchased and bonus air miles on certain airline carriers. They are required to reserve a hotel or rental car.

In emergencies, credit cards are very useful when cash may not be readily available.

American Express credit cards

FOREIGN EXCHANGE

Exchange offices are generally open weekdays from 9am to 5pm, but some, especially those in shopping districts, may have extended opening hours.

Among the best known are **American Express Travel Service** and **Thomas Cook/ Travelex Currency Services**, both of which have branches in DC and the surrounding areas. **Sun Trust Bank** also has a foreign exchange service. For more listings look in the Yellow Pages for the main branch location of any major bank. Most exchange offices charge a fee or commission, so it is worth looking around to get the best value rates. Hotels often charge a higher rate of exchange or commission than currency exchange offices or banks.

TRAVELER'S CHECKS

When buying traveler's checks, be sure to get them in US dollars rather than your own currency. It is often simpler to pay by US dollars traveler's checks, where possible, rather than cashing them in advance, and checks issued by American Express and Thomas Cook in US dollars are accepted as payment without a fee by most stores, restaurants, and hotels. However, traveler's checks in foreign currencies can be cashed at a bank or with a cashier at a major hotel. Exchange rates are listed in all daily newspapers and are posted at banks where currency exchange services are offered, and at all exchange offices. A fee or commission is always charged; ask about this before you exchange your money – it is a good idea to shop around for the best deal as commission rates can vary.

Personal checks issued by foreign banks are rarely accepted in the United States so cannot be relied upon as a means of obtaining cash.

Coins

American coins (actual size shown) come in 1-dollar, 50-, 25-, 10-, 5-, and 1-cent pieces. There are also goldtone $1 coins in circulation and State quarters, which feature an historical scene on one side. Each coin has a popular name: 25-cent pieces are called quarters, 10-cent pieces are called dimes, 5-cent pieces are called nickels, and 1-cent pieces called pennies.

**25-cent coin
(a quarter)**

**10-cent coin
(a dime)**

**5-cent coin
(a nickel)**

**1-cent coin
(a penny)**

**An American Eagle
on a $1 gold coin**

Bills (Bank Notes)

Units of currency in the United States are dollars and cents. There are 100 cents to a dollar. Bills come in $1, $5, $10, $20, $50 and $100s. All bills are the same color, so check the amount carefully. The new $5, $10, $20, $50, and $100 bills (below) are now in circulation; they have very large numbers.

DIRECTORY

BUREAUX DE CHANGE

American Express Travel Service
1150 Connecticut Ave, NW.
Tel 457-1300.
Map 2 F2.

Thomas Cook/Travelex Currency Services
Tel 872-1233
(for general information).
www.travelex.com

Branches at:

1800 K St, NW.
Map 3 A2.
Tel 872-1428.

Union Station,
50 Massachusetts Ave, NE.
Tel 371-9220.
Map 4 E3.

Sun Trust Bank
1445 New York Ave, NW.
Map 3 B3.
Tel 879-6000.
Tel (888) 786 8787.
www.suntrust.com

1- dollar bill ($1)

5- dollar bill ($5)

10- dollar bill ($50)

20- dollar bill ($20)

50- dollar bill ($50)

100- dollar bill ($100)

Communications

US Mail stamp

Coin- or card-operated public pay-phones are easy to find on many streets and in restaurants, theaters, bars, department stores, hotel lobbies, and gas stations. Since Washington, DC is the political capital of the United States, news is readily available from newspapers, magazines, television, and radio. For help with the correct postage when sending mail, ask at your hotel or go to one of the many post offices around the city.

PUBLIC TELEPHONES

Public telephones are found on street corners all over the DC area. The area code for Washington is 202. When dialing within the district, omit the code. When dialing outside the district from within DC, you will need to use the appropriate area code.

Credit card calls can be made by calling 1-800-CALL-ATT or by having ample change to put in the phone when the charge for using the card is announced. Directory Assistance is 411 and calls are charged as a local rate.

Sign for Western Union

TELEPHONE CHARGES

Local calls cost around 35 cents for three minutes from pay phones. Calls made from hotel rooms will cost much more, so it is a good idea to walk to the pay phone in the lobby of your hotel to make a call, rather than using the phone in your room. Operator assistance can be used for making calls, but

again, this will cost more. Phone cards of various values can be purchased from most supermarkets, 24-hour stores, newspaper stands, and some branches of **Western Union**.

FAXES

Fax machines can be found in Western Union and **UPS** offices; they charge per page to send or to receive. Many hotels provide a fax service too, but again charges may be incurred.

CYBERCAFÉS

Keeping in touch via the Internet is made easy by visiting any one of the Internet cafés in the city, such as the **Cyberstop Café**. For around $8 an hour you can surf the Net or send e-mails on one of their six computers.

USEFUL DIALING CODES

- To make a direct-dial call outside the local area code, but within the US and Canada, dial **1** before the area code. Useful area codes for DC and the surrounding area include: Baltimore **410**; MD **301**; Delaware *302*; Northern Virginia *703*; West Virginia **304**.
- For international direct-dial calls, dial **011** followed by the appropriate country code. Then dial the area code, omitting the first 0, and the local number.
- To make an international call via the operator, dial **01** and then follow the same procedure as detailed above.
- For international operator assistance, dial **01**.
- For local operator assistance, dial **0**.
- For international directory inquiries, dial **00**.
- For local directory inquiries, dial **411**.
- For emergency police, fire, or ambulance services, dial **911**.
- **1-800** and **888** indicate a toll-free number.

USING A COIN-OPERATED PHONE

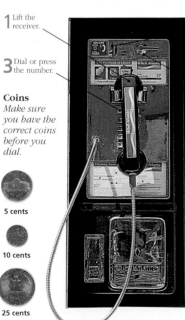

1 Lift the receiver.

3 Dial or press the number.

Coins
Make sure you have the correct coins before you dial.

5 cents

10 cents

25 cents

2 Insert the necessary coin or coins. The coin drops as soon as you insert it.

4 If you do not want to complete your call or it does not get through, retrieve the coin(s) by pressing the coin return.

5 If the call is answered and you talk longer than the allotted three minutes, the operator will interrupt and ask you to deposit more coins. Pay phones do not give change.

POSTAL SERVICE

Post offices are open from 9am to 5pm, Mondays through Fridays, and have limited Saturday service, usually 9am to noon. Post offices are closed Sundays and all Federal holidays.

If the correct postage is affixed, you can send a letter by putting it in one of the blue mailboxes found on street corners all over Washington. Times of mail pickup are written inside the mailbox's lid. There are usually several collections a day. Include a zip code to ensure faster delivery of letters within the United States.

Depending on how far the mail needs to travel in the US, it can take from one to five days to arrive at its destination. Send overseas mail via airmail; otherwise it will take weeks to arrive. Express and Priority mail are also available at the post office for a faster, though more expensive, service. If you are a visitor to the city and you wish to receive mail, you can have it sent to you by addressing it care of "General Delivery" at the Main Post Office or any other postal station. They will hold the mail for you to collect.

US Mailbox

TELEVISION AND RADIO

Televisions are everywhere in the United States, from bars and restaurants to hotels and stores. Most have cable hook-up, allowing access to more than 60 different channels. Some of the best to view are CBS (Channel 9), NBC (Channel 4), CNN (Channel 10), ABC (Channel 7), and Fox (Channel 5). For those interested in the political goings-on in the city, tune in to channels C-Span 1 and C-Span 2 to watch the proceedings in Congress as they are broadcast live. Radios can be found in most hotel rooms, as well as in rental cars, and offer a wide range of music, from country through classical and jazz to rock. Popular radio stations include National Public Radio (WAMU at 90.9 and 88.5), modern rock on WHFS (99.1), and soft rock on Easy 101 (101).

NEWSPAPERS

The most widely read newspaper in the DC area is the *Washington Post*, which is also one of the best newspapers published in the country. The local *Washington Times* is widely available as are *USA Today*, *The Wall Street Journal* and *The New York Times*. Newspapers can be bought in street dispensers (boxes on the sidewalk that dispense newspapers), newsstands, gas stations, convenience stores, hotel lobbies, and bookstores. Newsstands and some bookstores carry newspapers from most large US cities and many foreign countries.

Newspaper vendor

WASHINGTON TIME

Washington is on Eastern Standard Time. Daylight Saving Time begins on the last Sunday in April when clocks are set ahead one hour, and ends on the last Sunday in October when clocks go back one hour.

City and Country	Hours + or – EST	City and Country	Hours + or – EST
Chicago (US)	–1	Moscow (Russia)	+8
Dublin (Ireland)	+5	Paris (France)	+6
London (UK)	+5	Sydney (Australia)	+15
Los Angeles (US)	–3	Tokyo (Japan)	+14
Madrid (Spain)	+6	Vancouver (Canada)	–3

DIRECTORY

PHONE CARDS

Western Union
Branches all over the DC area.
For the nearest one call:
***Tel** (800) 325-6000.*
www.westernunion.com

FAX FACILITIES

UPS
4401 Connecticut Ave, NW.
***Tel** 244-7299.*
www.ups.com
American University,
4410 Massachusetts Ave, NW
***Tel** 686-2100.*

POST OFFICES

Farragut Station
1125 19th St, NW.
Map 2 F2.

Friendship Station
4005 Wisconsin Ave, NW.

Georgetown Station
3050 K St, NW.
Map 2 D2.

Martin Luther King Jr. Station
1400 L St, NW.
Map 2 F3.

National Capitol Station
2 Massachusetts Ave, NE.
Map 4 E3.

Temple Heights Station
1921 Florida Ave, NW.
Map 2 E1.
For the nearest branch call:
***Tel** (800) 275-8777.*

CYBERCAFES

Cyberstop Café
1513 17th St, NW.
Map 3 B2.
***Tel** 234-2470.*
www.cyberstopcafe.com
@ feedback@cyberstopcafe.com

GETTING TO WASHINGTON, DC

Washington is easy to get to via any mode of transportation. Three airports serve the DC area, which in turn are used by most major airlines for domestic and international flights. Two major bus lines also operate to the city,

United Airlines plane

as do the Amtrak trains that arrive at and depart from Union Station, right in the center of Washington. Visitors often tend to travel first to DC, base themselves in the city, and then arrange day or weekend trips into Maryland and Virginia.

Glass-walled interior of Reagan National Airport

ARRIVING BY AIR

There are three main airports in the Washington, DC area: **Dulles International Airport**, **Reagan National Airport** (known as "National" airport), and **Baltimore-Washington International Airport** (known as BWI). Most of the major carriers, including American Airlines, British Airways, Air France, and United Airlines, fly to at least one of these airports. The majority of international and overseas flights land at Dulles International, 26 miles (42 km) west of Washington in Virginia. There is a connecting shuttle service, the **Washington Flyer Coach Service**, to take

new arrivals to West Falls Church Metro. The **Super-Shuttle** bus service runs every hour, and a taxi is also an option from Dulles to downtown DC – but make sure the fare is negotiated before the journey.

Located about 5 miles (8 km) outside the city in Arlington County, Virginia, the Ronald Reagan Washington National Airport is the most convenient airport for central Washington. The city is easily accessible using the Metrorail's yellow and blue lines, or by taking the SuperShuttle (every 30 minutes), the Washington Flyer Express Bus, or a taxi.

Baltimore-Washington International Airport, situated 30 miles (48 km) northeast of DC, tends to be used by low-cost airlines. **The Maryland Rail Commuter Service (MARC)** is the cheapest way to get from the airport to the city, but it runs only on weekdays. **Amtrak** offers the next-best train service for just a few dollars more. The Super-Shuttle is also available from BWI, but it is more costly and takes longer than a trainride.

The taxi fare into central DC is rather expensive.

For security reasons, anyone arriving in the US on a visa is now photographed, and must have their fingerprints taken and checked, before being allowed into the country.

AIR FARES

The busiest season for travel to the US is March through June and September through early November. Christmas is also busy. Flights will be at their most expensive during these periods. Flights in June and July are usually the most expensive but there are many discounted accommodations available at this time. Weekend flights are usually less expensive than weekday flights, while Apex tickets are often the best deal but must be booked at least one week in advance, and your visit must include a Saturday night.

Cheap air fares can be obtained by shopping around, so it is worth checking with several airlines and travel agents before you book.

Consolidated tickets (those

The Washington Flyer runs from Dulles to West Falls Church Metro

AIRPORT	ℹ INFORMATION	DISTANCE/TIME TO WASHINGTON, DC	TAXI FARE	SHUTTLE EXPRESS
Dulles	(703) 572-2700	26 miles (42 km) 40 minutes	$60–75	$20–25
National	(703) 417-8000	10 miles (16 km) 15 minutes	$20–29	$10–15
BWI	(800) 435-9294	30 miles (48 km) 50 minutes	$60–64	$30–35

Lining up for tickets at an Amtrak desk

bought from a travel agent) are often considerably cheaper than those bought directly from airlines and can usually offer more flexibility. These can be obtained via the Internet by contacting **NOW Voyager** or in person from **Consolidators: Air Travel's Bargain Basement**.

PACKAGE DEALS

Fly-drive vacations offer a great deal of freedom once you reach your destination and are a popular choice for visitors from outside the US. Information about these and other package deals is available from travel agents. For "romance" and "weekend getaways," as well as family packages, vacations, and special events trips, it is worth contacting the Washington, DC Convention and Visitors Association *(see p211)*.

United Airlines, US Airways, Amtrak, and others also offer their own package deals.

ARRIVING BY TRAIN

Amtrak is one of the best ways to travel to the DC area. Trains from other cities arrive in Washington at Union Station. Trains are also available from Union Station to Baltimore, Philadelphia, Richmond, and Williamsburg. Amtrak offers a deluxe train service to and from New York City, called the Metroliner, which travels slightly faster and more comfortably than the regular train, but is also more expensive. The "Acela" train is a new high-speed service connecting DC with

New York and Boston. It is also more expensive. Another train service available is MARC, Maryland's commuter train, which departs on weekdays to Baltimore.

ARRIVING BY CAR

The center of Washington, DC is surrounded by Interstates I-95 and I-495, which together form the congested Capital Beltway. Interstate I-66 connects Washington to West Virginia, and Interstate I-50 heads east from DC to Annapolis, Maryland, and the surrounding areas. Beyond the Beltway, Interstate I-95 goes north toward Baltimore, Philadelphia, and New York. Interstate I-270 heads north to Frederick, Maryland.

Greyhound bus, an inexpensive way to see the whole country

ARRIVING BY BUS

Taking a bus is the slowest but usually the least expensive way to get to DC. **Greyhound Busline** and **Peter Pan Buslines** both offer routes from around the country, and provide discounts for children and senior citizens. The bus terminals are located in a rather remote part of town, at 1005 1st St, NE at L St. It is advisable to take a taxi from here at night.

DIRECTORY

AIRPORTS

Baltimore-Washington Airport (BWI)
Baltimore, MD.
Tel (800) I-FLY-BWI
Tel (410) 859-7387 (Lost & Found.)
www.bwiairport.com

Dulles International Airport
Chantilly, VA.
Tel (703) 572-2700
Tel (703) 572-2954 (Lost & Found.)
www.metwashairports.com

Reagan National Airport
Arlington County, VA.
Tel (703) 417-8000
Tel (703) 417-8560 (Lost & Found.)
www.metwashairports.com

AIR FARES

Consolidators: Air Travel's Bargain Basement
Intrepid Traveler, PO Box 531, Branford, CT 06405.
Tel (203) 488-5341.
www.intrepidtraveler.com

NOW Voyager
45 W. 21st St, New York, NY 10010. *Tel (212) 459-1616.*
www.nowvoyagertravel.com

PUBLIC TRANSPORT

Amtrak
Union Station,
50 Massachusetts Ave, NE.
Tel 484-7540.
Tel (800) USA-RAIL.
www.amtrak.com

Maryland Rail Commuter Service (MARC)
Tel (410) 906-3104.
Tel (800) 325 RAIL.
www.mtamaryland.com

SuperShuttle
Tel (800) BLUEVAN.
www.supershuttle.com

Washington Flyer Coach Service
Tel (888) WASH-FLY.
www.washfly.com

Greyhound Busline
1005 1st St, NE.
Tel (800) 231-2222.
Tel 289-5154.
www.greyhound.com

Peter Pan Trailways
Tel (800) 343-9999.
Tel 289-5160.
www.peterpanbus.com

Getting Around Washington, DC

Washington has a very comprehensive public transportation system. Visitors and locals alike find that it is easier to get around by public transportation than by car, especially as they do not have the aggravation of finding a much coveted parking space. All the major tourist attractions in the capital are accessible on foot, by Metrorail, by Metrobus, or by taxi.

Busy night-time traffic in central DC

PLANNING YOUR TRIP

The Washington DC, Maryland, and Virginia tourism departments are all helpful contact points, and hotels should also be able to help guests during their stay.

The **Smithsonian Dial-a-Museum** and **Dial-a-Park** lines are useful resources for finding out about local events. If you plan to visit in winter the weather can be unpredictable, so check with **Weather Update** to find out what the day has in store.

Tourists checking their routes at a tourist information kiosk

GETTING YOUR BEARINGS

Washington is a terrific city for walking, as long as you wear comfortable shoes and keep your wits about you. Many of the principal sights are clustered on or around the Mall. In other places, such as Georgetown, walking is undoubtedly the best way to soak up the atmosphere and see the sights.

It is important to know that, with the exception of Georgetown, the city is made up of four quadrants: northeast (NE), northwest (NW), southeast (SE), and southwest (SW), with the US Capitol at the central point. Every address in DC includes the quadrant code (NE, and so on) and, with building numbers running into the thousands on the same street in each quadrant, its use is necessary to distinguish the location.

A useful tip for when you are first trying to find your way around the city is to remember that most numbered streets run North and South, and most lettered streets run East and West. However, be aware that there is no "J," "X," "Y," or "Z" Street, and

that "I" Street is often written as "Eye" Street.

The northwest quadrant contains most of the tourist sights and neighborhoods, with other sights and places of interest located around the Capitol and south of the Mall, in the southwest quadrant.

METRORAIL

A map of the Metrorail is one of the most important pieces of information visitors will need when trying to get around DC (*see* back endpaper). The system takes some getting used to, and the instructions are in English only, so allow plenty of time when first using the Metrorail (or "Metro," as it is also called.)

The cost of the fare depends on the time and distance you wish to travel, and ranges from $1.35 to $3.90.

Tickets, or "farecards," for single or multiple trips can be bought from vending machines. Coins and bills (but no bills over $20) can be used to pay the exact fare; or add more money if you wish to use the farecard again.

Passengers swipe their farecards through the turnstile at the beginning and end of the trip, so don't discard your farecard after boarding a train. If there is any unused fare left at the final destination the ticket will be returned to you; if not, the ticket will be retained. You can top up tickets for further trips. A rail-to-bus transfer ticket can be bought if you wish to continue by bus. Metrorail passes range from one-day's duration ($5) to 28-days' duration ($100).

Five Metrorail lines operate in downtown DC, with frequent services: the Orange Line; Blue Line; Red Line; Yellow Line; and Green Line. Trains run from 5:30am to midnight Monday through Thursday, from 5:30am to 3am on Friday and 7am to 3am on Saturday, and from 7am to midnight on Sunday.

Metro sign

Washington, DC Metrobus

METROBUS

Like the Metrorail system, Metrobus is a fast and inexpensive way to get around the city. Metrobus stops are frequent – there are 15,800 of them scattered throughout the Metrobus network, which includes Virginia and Maryland.

The standard, off-peak fare on the bus costs around $1.20, with a 25 cent charge for a bus transfer. Discounts are available for disabled travelers and senior citizens. Up to two children under the age of five can travel for free with a fare-paying passenger. Fares can be paid to the driver either with the exact change or with a tourist pass.

Maps of all the bus routes are available in the Metrorail stations, and maps of specific Metrobus lines are posted at each Metrobus stop. Visitors can write to the **Metrobus** office in advance of their trip to request travel information and a bus map.

TAXIS

Finding a taxi in DC is not difficult. They can usually be hailed from the street corner, but if you need to be somewhere at a specific time it is advisable to call a taxi company. The **DC Taxi Cab Commission** will provide names of cab companies. Fares operate by zone rather than on a meter. Whatever the distance, rides within a single zone cost $5.50, but increase when zone boundaries are crossed. For example, a two-zone ride within the city will cost $7.60, and a three-zone ride will cost $9.50, and so on up to $17.00.

Each extra passenger costs $1.50. Bags, rush hour travel, and gas prices can all incur surcharges from 50 cents to $2.00. Always check with the driver to be sure he will take you across zones to your destination without charging. However, the zone system may be discontinued.

DRIVING AND PARKING IN THE CITY

Driving in DC need not be stressful as long as you avoid the rush hour (between 6:30 and 9:30 am, and 4 and 7 pm on weekdays.) During these times the direction of traffic flow can change, some roads become one way, and left turns may be forbidden to ease congestion. These changes are usually marked, but always pay close attention to the road. The city's layout is straightforward but drivers can be aggressive in heavy traffic.

Road sign

Curbside parking is hard to find at the more popular locations around the city, and during the rush hour curbside parking is illegal in many areas. It is important to keep within your time limit if you are parking at a meter; you could otherwise face a fine or risk being clamped. Parking restrictions on Sundays and public holidays are different from those on other days, so read the parking signs carefully to check where it is legal to park. Parking in a public garage can cost upward of $20 per day. Valet parking is available at some restaurants, hotels, and malls for a fee.

Almost every tourist sight is accessible via public transportation, and this is recommended over driving. If you do decide to drive to Washington, it is worth considering long-term parking in a garage and using the Metro or buses to get around the city. Try www.washington.org or www.downtowndc.org for more information.

DIRECTORY

USEFUL INFORMATION

Speaking Clock
Tel 844-1212.

Weather Update
Tel 936-1212.

Smithsonian's Dial-a-Museum
Tel 357-2020.

Dial-a-Park
Tel 619-7275.

METRORAIL AND METROBUS

Metrorail and Metrobus
600 5th St, NW,
Washington, DC 20001.
Tel 637-7000.
Tel 638-3780 TTY.
www.wmata.com

TAXIS

DC Taxi Cab Commission
2041 Martin Luther King Jr. Ave,
SE, Washington,
DC 20020.
Tel 645-6005.

Diamond Cab
Tel 332-6200.

Yellow Cab
Tel 544-1212.

DRIVING AND PARKING IN THE CITY

www.washington.org
www.downtowndc.org
under "Getting Here."

Typical Washington, DC taxi cab

Exploring Beyond Washington, DC

There is much to see beyond Washington's city limits, and traveling by car is easy with a good map. Many of the sights are reachable by public transportation, but it is generally easier and quicker to drive. Car rental is widely available but often expensive. Buses and trains are a cheaper alternative, but your choice of destinations may be more limited.

Inline skaters enjoying a clear road

RULES OF THE ROAD

The highway speed limit in the DC area is 55 miles per hour (mph) (88 kmph) – much lower than in many European countries. In residential areas the speed limit ranges from 20–35 mph (32–48 kmph), and near schools it can be as low as 15 mph (24 kmph). Roads are generally well-signed but it is still wise to plan your route ahead. It is important to obey the signs, especially "No U-turn" signs, or you risk getting a ticket. If you are pulled over by the police, be courteous or you may face an even greater fine. In addition, all drivers are required to carry a valid drivers' license and be able to produce registration documents for their vehicle.

Roadsign

CAR RENTAL

You must usually be at least 25 years old with a valid driving license to rent a car. All agencies require a major credit card. Damage and liability insurance is recom-

mended just in case something unexpected should happen. It is advisable always to return the car with a full tank of gas; otherwise you will be required to pay the inflated fuel prices charged by the rental agencies.

It is often less expensive to rent a vehicle at an airport, as car rental taxes are $2 a day more in the city. As rental rates and special deals vary from agency to agency, it is worth checking the offers of more than one company. Agencies with bureaus at the Washington airports include **Alamo**, **Avis**, **Budget**, and **Hertz**.

GASOLINE (PETROL)

Gas comes in three grades – regular, super, and premium. There is an extra charge if an attendant serves you, but patrons can fill their own tanks at self-service pumps without incurring an extra fee. Gas is generally cheap in the US, and payment can often be made by credit card or traveler's check, as well as in cash, which is often preferred.

BREAKDOWNS

In the unlucky event of a breakdown, the best course of action is to pull completely off the road and put on the hazard lights to alert other drivers that you are stationary. There are emergency phones along some of the major interstate highways, but in other situations breakdown services or even the police can be contacted from land or mobile phones. In case of breakdown, drivers of rental cars should contact the car rental company first.

Members of the American Automobile Association (AAA) can have their vehicle towed to the nearest service station to be fixed.

PARKING

Most of the major sights that lie beyond Washington have adequate parking for visitors, but there may be a charge to use the facility.

In general it is good practice to read all parking notices carefully to avoid fines, being clamped, or being towed away.

Parking sign

CYCLING

There are some great bicycle paths in the Greater Washington, DC area. Bike shops rent out bikes and will be able to suggest routes. They can

Cycling is a pleasant way to see the sights in Washington

Tourmobile bus, one of many sightseeing tour buses available in DC

TRAINS

Amtrak Trains travel from DC's central Union Station to New York City and most of the surrounding areas, including Williamsburg, Richmond, and Baltimore. The MARC, Maryland's commuter rail, also runs from DC to Baltimore on weekdays for a few dollars less.

DIRECTORY

usually provide route maps. **Better Bikes** will deliver a rental bike to you for a cost of $25–$50 per day. The company **Bike the Sites, Inc** offers a selection of tours in and around the city, including a one-hour Early Bird Fun Ride and a 10-mile (16-km) Capital Sites Ride. They provide riders with a 21-speed bike, helmet, water bottle, and a snack.

BUS TOURS

Several companies offer bus tours of DC *(see p211)* and its historic surroundings. **Gray Line** takes you on the Black Heritage tour, to Gettysburg, Colonial Williamsburg, or Monticello; **Tourmobile**'s destinations include Mount Vernon, the Frederick Douglass House, and Arlington Cemetery.

CAR RENTAL AGENCIES

Alamo
Tel (800) 327-9633.
www.goalamo.com

Avis
Tel (800) 331-1212.
www.avis.com

Budget
Tel (800) 527-0700.
www.budget.com

Hertz
Tel (800) 654-3131.
www.hertz.com

BREAKDOWN ASSISTANCE

American Automobile Association (AAA)
701–15th St, NW, Washington, DC 20005.
Tel 331-3000 *(Washington office).*
Tel (800) 222-4357 *(general breakdown assistance for members).*
www.aaa.com

BICYCLE RENTAL

Better Bikes
Tel 293-2080.
www.betterbikesinc.com

Bike The Sites, Inc
1100 Pennsylvania Ave, NW.
Tel 842-2453.
www.bikethesites.com

BUS TOURS

Gray Line
Union Station,
50 Massachusetts Ave.
Tel (800) 862-1400.
Tel 289-1995.
www.graylinedc.com

Tourmobile Sightseeing
1000 Ohio Drive, S.W.,
Washington, D.C. 20024
Tel 554-5100.
www.tourmobile.com

TIPS AND SAFETY FOR DRIVERS

- Traffic moves on the right-hand side of the road.
- Seat belts are compulsory in front seats and suggested in back; children under three must ride in a child seat in back.
- You can turn right at a red light as long as you first come to a complete stop, and if there are no signs that prohibit it.
- A flashing yellow light at an intersection means slow down, look for oncoming traffic, and proceed with caution.
- Passing (overtaking) is allowed on any multi-lane road, and you must pass on the left.
- Crossing a double-yellow line, either by U-turn or by passing the car in front, is illegal, and you will be charged a fine if caught.
- If a school bus stops, all traffic from both sides must stop completely and wait for the bus to drive off.
- Driving while intoxicated (DWI) is a punishable offense that incurs heavy fines or even a jail sentence. Do not drink if you plan to drive.
- Avoid driving at night if unfamiliar with the area. Washington's streets change from safe to dangerous in a single block, so it is better to take a taxi than your own car if you do not know where you are going.
- Single women should be especially careful driving in unfamiliar territory, day or night.
- Keep all doors locked when driving around. Do not stop in a rural area, or on an unlit block if someone tries to get your attention. If a fellow driver points at your car, suggesting something is wrong, drive to the nearest gas station and get help. Do not get out of your car.
- Avoid sleeping in your car.
- Avoid short cuts and stay on well-traveled roads.
- Avoid looking at a map in a dark, unpopulated place. Drive to the nearest open store or gas station before pulling over.

Street Finder Index

KEY TO THE STREET FINDER

■ Major sight	🅿 Main parking lot	✡ Synagogue	
■ Minor sight	ℹ Tourist information office	⊠ Post office	
□ Place of interest	✚ Hospital with emergency room	— Pedestrian street	
🚆 Railroad station	🚓 Police station	⛴ Ferry terminal	
Ⓜ Metrorail station	✝ Church		
🚌 Bus station	☪ Mosque		

0 meters   300
0 yards   300
1:19,100

KEY TO ABBREVIATIONS USED IN THE STREET FINDER

Ave	Avenue	**Dr**	Drive	**Pkwy**	Parkway	**St**	Street/Saint
DC	District	**NE**	Northeast	**Pl**	Place	**SW**	Southwest
	of Columbia	**NW**	Northwest	**SE**	Southeast	**VA**	Virginia

1st Street NE	**4E4**	14th Street NW	**3B3**	44th Street NW	**1A2**	**D**	
1st Street NW	**4E3**	14th Street SW	**3B5**	45th Street NW	**1A2**		
1st Street SE	**4E5**	15th Street NW	**3B3**			D Street NE	**4F3**
1st Street SW	**4E4**	15th Street SW	**3B4**			D Street NW	**4D3**
2nd Street NE	**4F4**	16th Road	**1B4**	**A**		D Street SE	**4F5**
2nd Street NW	**4D3**	16th Street North	**1A4**	A Street NE	**4F4**	D Street SW	**3B5**
2nd Street SE	**4F5**	16th Street NW	**2F3**	A Street SE	**4F4**	Daniel French Dr SW	**2E5**
2nd Street SW	**4D5**	17th Street North	**1A4**	Arlington Boulevard	**1A5**	Decatur Street NW	**2E1**
2nd Street SW	**4E4**	17th Street NW	**2F3**	Arlington Memorial		Delaware Avenue NE	**E4**
2nd Street SW	**4E5**	17th Street NW	**3B2**	Bridge SW	**2D5**	Dent Place NW	**1C2**
3rd Street NE	**4F4**	18th Street North	**1B4**	Arlington Ridge Road	**1C4**	Desales Street NW	**2F3**
3rd Street NW	**4D3**	18th Street NW	**2F4**	Avon Place NW	**2D1**	Duddington Pl SE	**4F5**
3rd Street SW	**4D5**	18th Street NW	**3A3**			Dumbarton Street NW	**2D2**
4th Street NE	**4F1**	19th Street NW	**2F4**			Dupont Circle	**2F2**
4th Street NW	**4D3**	19th Street NW	**3A3**	**B**			
4th Street SE	**4F5**	19th Street	**1B4**	Bancroft Street NW	**2E1**	**E**	
4th Street SW	**4D5**	20th Road	**1A4**	Bates Street NW	**4D1**		
5th Street NE	**4F1**	20th Street NW	**2E4**	Belmont Road NW	**2D1**	E Street NW	**2E4**
5th Street NW	**4D3**	20th Street NW	**3A3**	Brentwood NE	**4F2**	E Street SE	**4F5**
5th Street SE	**4F4**	21st Road	**1A3**			E Street SW	**4D5**
6th Street NE	**4F4**	21st Street North	**1A3**			East Basin Drive SW	**2F5**
6th Street NW	**4F4**	21st Street NW	**2E4**	**C**		East Basin Drive SW	**3B4**
6th Street SE	**4F5**	21st Street NW	**3A3**	C Street NE	**4E3**	East Capitol Street	**4E4**
6th Street SW	**4D5**	21st Street	**1A3**	C Street NW	**3A3**	East Place NW	**2D2**
7th Street NE	**4F4**	22nd Street NW	**2E4**	C Street SE	**4E5**	Eckington Place NE	**4E1**
7th Street NW	**3C3**	22nd Street	**1A3**	C Street SW	**3B5**	Ellipse Road NW	**2F4**
7th Street SE	**4F5**	23rd Street NW	**2E5**	California Street NW	**2D1**	Ellipse Road NW	**3B3**
7th Street SW	**3C5**	24th Street NW	**2E3**	Cambridge Place NW	**2D2**	Executive	
8th Street NE	**4F4**	25th Street NW	**2D3**	Canal Road NW	**1A2**	Avenue NW	**2F4**
8th Street NW	**3C3**	26th Street NW	**2D3**	Canal Street NW	**1C3**	Executive	
8th Street SE	**4F5**	27th Street NW	**2D3**	Cecil Place NW	**1C3**	Avenue NW	**3B3**
9th Street NW	**3C3**	28th Street NW	**2D2**	Church Street NW	**2F2**		
9th Street SW	**3C5**	29th Street NW	**2D2**	Church Street NW	**3A1**		
10th Street NW	**3C3**	30th Street NW	**2D2**	Colonial Terrace	**1B4**	**F**	
10th Street SW	**3C5**	31st Street NW	**1C1**	Columbia Road NW	**2E1**		
11th Street NW	**3C3**	31st Street NW	**2D2**	Columbia Street NW	**3C1**	F Street NE	**4F3**
12th Street North	**1B5**	32nd Street NW	**1C1**	Connecticut		F Street NW	**2E4**
12th Street NW	**3C2**	33rd Street NW	**1C2**	Avenue NW	**2E1**	F Street NW	**3A3**
12th Street SW	**3C5**	34th Street NW	**1C2**	Connecticut		F Street SE	**4E5**
13th Street SW	**3C5**	35th Street NW	**1C2**	Avenue NW	**3A1**	Fairfax Drive	**1A5**
13th Street NW	**3C3**	36th Street NW	**1B2**	Constitution		Farragut Square	**3A2**
13th Street	**1A5**	37th Street NW	**1B2**	Avenue NE	**4F4**	Florida Avenue NE	**4F1**
14th St Bridge SW	**3B5**	38th Street NW	**1B1**	Constitution		Florida Avenue NW	**2E1**
14th Street North	**1A5**	39th Street NW	**1B1**	Avenue NW	**2E4**	Florida Avenue NW	**4D1**
				Corcoran Street NW	**2F2**	Folger Square	**4F5**
				Custer Road	**1A5**	Fort Myer Drive	**1B4**

Foxhall Road NW	**1A2**		
Franics Scott			
Key Memorial			
Bridge NW	**1B3**		
Franklin Square	**3B2**		
Franklin Street NW	**4D1**		
Freedom Plaza	**3B3**		
French Street NW	**3C1**		

G

G Street NE	**4F3**
G Street NW	**2E3**
G Street NW	**3A3**
G Street SE	**4F5**
G Street SW	**4D5**
George Washington	
Memorial Parkway	**1A3**
Grace Street NW	**1C3**

H

H Place NE	**4E2**
H Street NE	**4F3**
H Street NW	**2E3**
H Street NW	**3A3**
Hanover Place NW	**4E1**
Henry Bacon Dr NW	**2E5**
Hoban Road NW	**1A1**

I

I (Eye) Street NE	**4E2**
I (Eye) Street NW	**2E3**
I (Eye) Street NW	**3A2**
I Street SW	**4E5**
I Street SW	**4F5**
Independence	
Avenue SE	**4F4**
Independence	
Avenue SW	**2E5**
Independence	
Avenue SW	**3A4**
Indiana Avenue NW	**4D3**

J

Jackson Avenue	**1B5**
Jefferson Davis	
Highway	**1C5**
Jefferson Drive SW	**3B4**

K

K Street NE	**4F2**
K Street NW	**2E3**
K Street NW	**3A2**
Kalorama Road NW	**2D1**
Key Boulevard	**1B4**
Kirby St NW	**4D2**
Kutz Memorial	
Bridge SW	**2F5**
Kutz Memorial	
Bridge SW	**3A4**

L

L Street NE	**4E2**
L Street NW	**2D3**
L Street NW	**3A2**
L'enfant Drive	**1B5**
Lafayette Square	**3B3**
Lee Highway	**1A4**
Logan Circle	**3C1**
Louisiana Avenue NW	**4E4**
Lovers Lane	
Walkway NW	**2D1**

M

M Street NE	**4F2**
M Street NW	**1C2**
M Street NW	**3A2**
MacArthur	
Boulevard NW	**1A2**
Madison Drive NW	**3C4**
Maine Avenue SW	**3C5**
Marion Street NW	**4D1**
Maryland Avenue SW	**4D4**
Massachusetts	
Avenue NW	**2D1**
Massachusetts	
Avenue NW	**3A1**
McPherson Square	**3B2**
Moore Street	**1B4**
Morgan Street NW	**4D2**
Mount Vernon Square	**3C2**

N

N Street NE	**4E2**
N Street NW	**1C2**
N Street NW	**3A2**
Nash Street	**1B4**
Neal Place NE	**4F1**
New Hampshire	
Avenue NW	**3A2**
New Hampshire	
Avenue NW	**2E3**
New Jersey	
Avenue NW	**4D1**
New Jersey	
Avenue SE	**4E5**
New York	
Avenue NW	**3B3**
Newport Place NW	**2E2**
North Capitol Street	**4E3**
North Key Boulevard	**1A4**
North Meade Street	**1B5**
North Nash Street	**1B4**
North Oak Street	**1B4**
North Rhodes Street	**1A4**
North Taft Street	**1A5**
North Troy Street	**1A5**
North Uhle Street	**1A3**
North Veitch Street	**1A4**
North Wayne Street	**1A5**
North Carolina Ave SE	**4E5**
North Kent Street	**1C4**

North Lynn Street	**1B4**
North Quinn Street	**1B4**
North Uhle Street	**1A4**
North Veitch Street	**1A5**

O

O Street NW	**1C2**
O Street NW	**3A1**
O Street SW	**3B1**
Ode Street	**1B4**
Ohio Drive SW	**2E5**
Ohio Drive SW	**3A5**
Olive Street NW	**2D2**
Ord and	
Weitzel Drive	**1B5**

P

P Street NE	**4E1**
P Street NW	**1A2**
P Street NW	**3A1**
Parker Street NE	**4F2**
Patterson Street NE	**4E2**
Penn Street NE	**4F1**
Pennsylvania	
Avenue NW	**2E3**
Pennsylvania	
Avenue NW	**3A2**
Pennsylvania	
Avenue SE	**4F4**
Phelps Place NW	**2E1**
Phelps Street NW	**2E1**
Pierce Street NW	**4D2**
Pierce Street NE	**4E2**
Pierce Street	**1B5**
Poplar Street NW	**2D2**
Potomac	
Parkway NW	**2D4**
Prospect Street NW	**1C2**

Q

Q Street NE	**4E1**
Q Street NW	**1C2**
Q Street NW	**3A1**
Queen Street	**1B5**
Quincy Place NE	**4E1**
Quinn Street	**1A3**

R

R Street NE	**4E1**
R Street NW	**1B1**
R Street NW	**3A1**
Randolph Place NW	**4D1**
Reservoir Road NW	**1A1**
Rhode Island	
Avenue NW	**3A2**
Ridge Place NW	**4D2**
Riggs Place NW	**2F1**
Riggs Place NW	**3A1**
Riggs Street NW	**2F1**
Rock Creek and	**2D3**
Rolfe Street	**1A3**

S

S Street NW	**1C1**
S Street NW	**3A1**
School Street SW	**4D5**
Scott Circle	**2F2**
Scott Circle	**3B1**
Scott Pl NW	**1C1**
Scott Street	**1A3**
Seward Square	**4F4**
Sheridan Circle	**2E1**
South Street NW	**1C3**
Stanton Square	**4F3**
Sth Capitol Street	**4E4**
Swann Street NW	**2F1**

T

T Street NW	**1B1**
Taft Street	**1A3**
Theodore Roosevelt	
Memorial Bridge NW	**1C4**
Thomas Circle	**3B2**
Thomas Jefferson	
Street NW	**2D3**
Tracy Place NW	**2D1**
Troy Street	**1A3**

U

U Street NW	**2F1**
Uhle Street	**1A4**

V

V Street NW	**2F1**
Vermont Avenue NW	**3B2**
Virginia Avenue NW	**2E4**
Virginia Avenue NW	**3A3**
Virginia Avenue SE	**4F5**
Virginia Avenue SW	**4D5**
Volta Place NW	**1A2**

W

Washington	
Avenue SW	**4D4**
Water Street SW	**3C5**
West Basin	
Drive SW	**2E5**
West Basin	
Drive SW	**3A5**
Whitehaven	
Parkway NW	**1B1**
Whitehaven	
Street NW	**1C1**
Whitehurst	
Freeway NW	**1C3**
Willard Street NW	**2F1**
Wilson Boulevard	**1A4**
Winfield Lane NW	**1B2**
Wisconsin	
Avenue NW	**1B1**
Wyoming	
Avenue NW	**2D1**

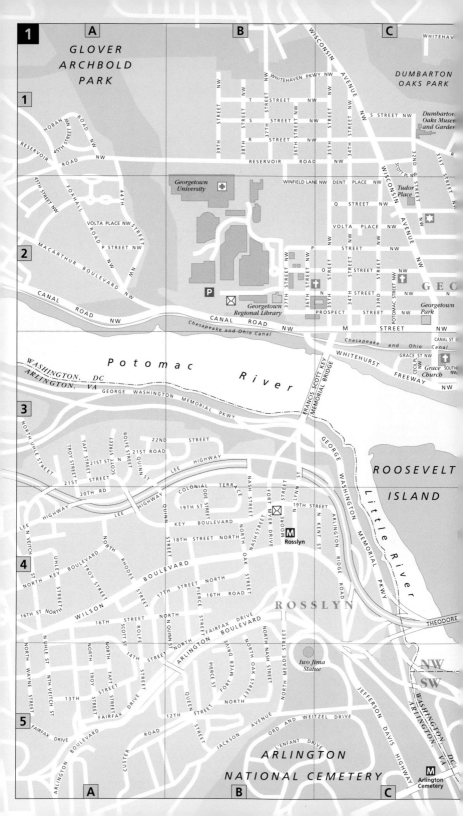

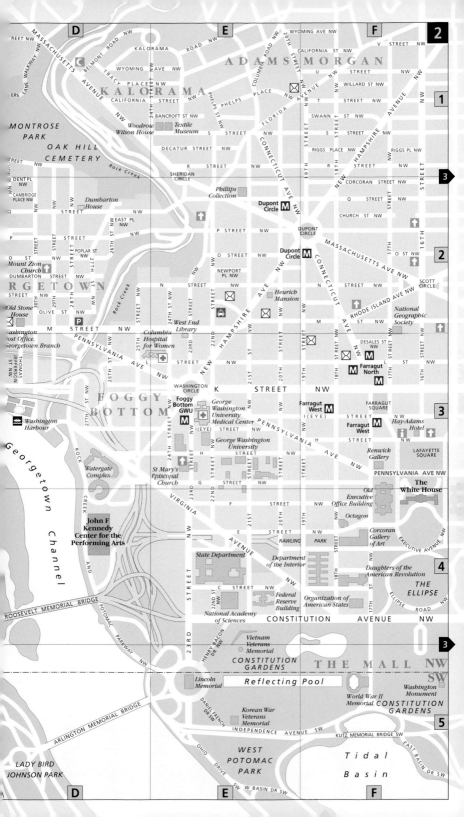

General Index

Page numbers in **bold** refer to main entries

A

Abraham Lincoln's Birthday 39
Achelous and Hercules (Benton) 98
Adams, Abigail 19
Adams, Henry 22, 112
Adams, John 26
    Union Tavern 124
    White House 19, 108, 110
Adams, John Quincy 20, 26
Adams-Morgan **137**
ADC Map and Travel Center 199
Addison/Ripley Fine Arts 199
Adventure Theater 207
African American Civil War Museum and Memorial 11, **133**
African American History Month 39
Air Force Memorial 133
Air travel **218–19**
    National Air and Space Museum **62–65**
Aitken, Robert 48
Alamo (car rental) 223
The Alba Madonna (Raphael) **58**, 60
Albright, Madeleine 28
Alcohol 183, 210
Alcott, Louisa May 21, 124
Aldrin, Buzz 62
Alexandria *see* Old Town Alexandria
Alexandria Academy 151
Alexandria Waterfront Festival 37
Alma-Tadema, Sir Lawrence 163
Alsop, Joseph 182
American Association for Retired Persons 211
American Automobile Association (AAA) 223
American Express Travel Agency 215
American Visionary Art Museum (Baltimore) 163
Amtrak 219
Anacostia Museum **145**
Anderson, Marian 23, 24, 55, 115
Annapolis **162**
Annie's Paramount Steak House 203
Annual Seafaring Celebration 38
Antietam National Battlefield **164**
Antiques shops **198**, 199
Appalachian Spring 199
Aquariums
    National Aquarium (Baltimore) **162**, 163
    National Aquarium (Washington) **95**
Arboretum *see* National Arboretum
Arena Stage 203
Arlington, VA
    hotels 180
Arlington County Fair 37
Arlington National Cemetery **130–31**
Armstrong, Neil 62
Army of the Potomac 21
Art Museum of the Americas 115
Arthur, Chester A. 26
Arthur M. Sackler Gallery **72–3**
    Street-by-Street map 56
Arts and crafts shops **197**, 199
Arts and Industries Building **66–7**
    Street-by-Street map 57

Assateague **167**
Athenaeum (Old Town Alexandria) 150
ATMs (automated teller machines) 214
Avis 223

B

BAPA Imagination Stage 207
Bach, J.S. 123
Bacon, Francis 66
Bacon, Henry 84–5
Balducci's 199
Baltimore **162–3**
    hotels 179–80
    restaurants 191
Baltimore, Lord 17
Baltimore Museum of Art (Baltimore) 163
Baltimore-Washington Airport (BWI) **218**, 219
Bankhead, Tallulah 101
Banking **214**
Banknotes 215
Banneker, Benjamin 19
Barnes & Noble 199
Barry, Marion 25
Bars 203
Bartholdi, Frédéric August 52
Bartholdi Park and Fountain **52**
Basilica of the National Shrine of the Immaculate Conception **144**
Baskin, Leonard 84
Bastille Day 37
Beall, Ninian 121, 127
Bearfence Mountain 156
    Skyline Drive 165
Bed-and-Breakfast 173
Bed-and-Breakfast Accommodations Ltd 173
Bellange, Pierre-Antoine 110
Belmont, Alva Vanderbilt 49
Benjamin Franklin Statue **94**
    Street-by-Street map 88
Ben's Chili Bowl 11
Benton, Thomas Hart
    Achelous and Hercules 98
Berks, Robert 116
    Bust of JFK 119
Berlin, MD
    hotels 180
Best Western 173
Bethune, Mary McLeod 140
Betsey Johnson 199
Better Bikes 223
Bicycles *see* Cycling
Big Meadows
    Skyline Drive 165
Big Wheel Bikes 205
Bike The Sites, Inc 205, 223
Bird-in-the-Cage Antiques 198, 199
Blacks
    civil rights movement 24
    Martin Luther King Jr. **97**
    slavery **20–21**
Bleifeld, Stanley 92
Bliss, Robert and Mildred Woods 127
Blue Ridge Mountains
    Skyline Drive **165**
Blues **202**, 203
Blues Alley 11, 203
Boating **204**, 205

Bodley, George 142
Bombay Club 188
Bonaparte, Jerome 124
Bonnard, Pierre 135
Bookshops **198**, 199
Booth, John Wilkes 21, 96
Borders Books & Music 199
Botanic Garden *see* US Botanic Garden
Botticelli, Sandro 60
Boucher, François 60
Bourgeois, Louise 61
Boyhood Home of Robert E. Lee (Old Town Alexandria) **158**
Bradlee, Benjamin 124
Brass Knob Architectural Antiques 199
Brass Knob's Back Doors 199
Brent, Robert 19
Brown, Denise Scott 94
Brown, John 164
Brumidi, Constantino 50, 51
Buchanan, James 26
Budget (car rental) 223
Bureau of Engraving and Printing **79**
Bureaux de Change **214**, 215
Burnham, Daniel 22–3
Burroughs, Helen 77
Buses 218, **219**
    tours 223
Bush, Barbara 27
Bush, George 27, 103

C

C & O Canal 149
Cady's Alley 149
Cafés 203
    cybercafés **216**, 217
Caitlin, George 100
    Old Bear, a Medicine Man 98
Calder, Alexander 59, 61, 163
Camp Hoover
    Skyline Drive 165
Camping 173
Canals
    Chesapeake and Ohio Canal **122–23**
Capitol *see* US Capitol
Capitol Hill **43–53**
    area map 43
    hotels 174
    Library of Congress **46–7**
    restaurants 186
    Street-by-Street map 44–5
    United States Capitol **50–51**
Capitol Hill Brewing Company 186
Capitol Reservations/Discounter 173
Captain's Row 150
Caribbean Summer in the Park 37
Carlyle, John 158
Carlyle House (Old Town Alexandria) 151, **158**
Carnegie Library Building **96**
Carousel on the Mall 207
Carroll, John 121, 126
Cars
    arriving in Washington **219**
    driving in Washington **221**
    exploring beyond Washington, DC **222–3**
    hotel parking 172

Cars (cont.)
  renting **222**, 223
  see also Tours by car
Carter, D. Jeffrey 117
Carter, Jimmy 27
Carter, Rosalynn 27, 76
Casey, Edward Pearce 114
"Casey" Stengel (Sherbell) 99
Cassatt, Mary
  Hirshhorn Museum 66
  National Gallery of Art 61
  National Museum of American Art 99, 100
  National Museum of Women in the Arts 96
Casselli, Henry C. Jr.
  Ronald Reagan 101
Castle, Wendell 113
Cathedrals
  National Cathedral **142–3**, 207
Cazenove, William E. 159
Cedar Hill 206
Cemeteries
  Arlington National Cemetery **130–31**
  Mount Zion Cemetery 126
  Oak Hill Cemetery **126–7**
Cézanne, Paul 61, 135
Chand, Nek 53
Chandor, Douglas 109
Charlottesville **166**
  hotels 180
  restaurants 191
Chase, William Merritt 100
Cherry trees
  Cherry Blossom Festival 36
  Tidal Basin 79
Chesapeake Bay 157, **167**
  restaurants 191
Chesapeake Bay Maritime Museum 167
Chesapeake and Ohio Canal 20, **122–3**, 207
Chevy Chase Pavilion 199
Children **206–7**, 211
  in hotels 173
  in restaurants 183
Chinatown 10, **97**
Chincoteague **167**
Chinese New Year 39
Chinn, Joseph 164
Chocolate Moose 199
Christ Church (Old Town Alexandria) **159**
Christ Cleansing the Temple (El Greco) 60
Christmas 39
Christy, Howard Chandler 110
Chrysalis Vineyard 164
Churches in Washington
  Basilica of the National Shrine of the Immaculate Conception **144**
  Ebenezer United Methodist Church **52**
  Grace Church **123**
  Mount Zion Church **126**
  St. John's 112
  St. Mary's Episcopal Church **117**
Churchill, Winston 127
  statue of 136, 137
Cinema *see* Film
City Bikes 205
City Hall (Old Town Alexandria) 151

City Segway Tours 211
Civil rights movement 24
  Martin Luther King Jr. **97**
Civil War 21
  Antietam National Battlefield **164**
  Fredericksburg 166
  Gettysburg National Military Park **163**
  Museum of the Confederacy (Richmond) 167
Clark, William 19, 74, 77
Clark, Senator William A. 113
Cleveland, Grover 26, 27, 141
Cleveland Park **141**
Cliffs of the Upper Colorado River (Moran) **98**, 100
Climate 36–9
Clinton, Bill 25, 27
  George Washington University 117
  Georgetown University 126
  portrait bust of 101
  White House 111
Clinton, Hillary 27
Clothes
  in restaurants 183
  shops **197**, 199
Club U 203
Clubs 203
Cocktails 185
Coins 215
Collins, Michael 62
Colonial National Historical Park 167
Colonial Williamsburg **168–9**
Columbus, Christopher 51
Columbus Day 38, 39
Columbus Memorial 53
Communications **216–17**
Composition No. III (Mondrian) 135
Consolidators: Air Travel's Bargain Basement 219
Constitution Day Commemoration 38
Constitution of the United States 18, 28, **91**
Continental Congress 18
Coolidge, Calvin 27
Coolidge, Mrs. Calvin 110
Cooper, James Fenimore 110
Copley, John Singleton
  Self-portrait 99
Corcoran, William Wilson 113, 126
Corcoran Gallery of Art 10, 32, **113**
  Street-by-Street map 106
Cornwallis, Lord 18
Corot, Jean-Baptiste Camille 113
Cosi Coffee and Bar 203
Cox's Row 149
Crafts shops **197**, 199
Craig, Dr. John 158
Crate & Barrel 199
Credit cards **214**
  in shops 196
  telephones 216
Cret, Paul P. 116
Crime 212
Crime Victims Line 213
Cronkite, Walter 133
Cultural events **202–3**
Cunningham, Merce 100
Currency **214–15**
Custis, George Washington Parke 158
CVS 24-Hour Pharmacy 213
Cybercafés **216**, 217
Cyberstop Café 217
Cycling **204**, 205, **222–23**

D

Dance **202**, 203
Dance Africa 37
Dance Place 203
Dangerfield Island 155
Danoff, Bill 125
DAR Building 106
  Street-by-Street map 106
Daughters of the American Revolution (DAR) 23, 106, **114**
Davidson, Bruce 101
DC Ducks 211
DC Open House 38
DC Taxi Cab Commission 221
de Kooning, Elaine 96
de Kooning, Willem 66, 106, 113
Dean & Deluca 149, 199
Decatur House Museum 199
Declaration of Independence (1776) 18
Degas, Edgar
  Baltimore Museum of Art (Baltimore) 163
  Hirshhorn Museum 66
  Mary Cassatt 99
  National Gallery of Art 61
  Phillips Collection 135
Dentists 2137
Department of the Interior Building **115**
Department stores **197**, 199
DeWeldon, Felix 132
Dewing, Thomas Wilmer 73
Dial-a-Park 221
Dialing codes 216
Diana and Endymion (Fragonard) 60
Dillinger, John 93
Disabled travelers 211
  entertainment 201
  in hotels 173
  in restaurants 183
Discovery Channel Destination Store 207
Discovery Theater 207
District Building 95
Doctors 213
Don Quixote Statue (Teno) 118
Dorsey, William 127
Douchez, Jacques 118
Douglas, William 122
Douglass, Frederick 22, 67, **145**
  Frederick Douglass House **145**
  Frederick Douglass National Historic Site 207
Downing, Andrew Jackson 67
Dulles International Airport **218**, 219
Dumbarton House 148
Dumbarton Oaks **127**, 149, 205
Dunbar, Paul 23
Dupont, Francis 134
Dupont Circle **134**

E

Earhart, Amelia 63
East Potomac Golf Course 205
East Potomac Tennis Center 205
Easter 39
Eastern Market **52**, 199
Easton, MD
  hotels 180
Ebenezer United Methodist Church **52**

Eddie Bauer 199
Einstein, Albert
  statue of 116
Eisenhower, Dwight D. 27, 118
Eisenhower Old Executive Office
  Building 105, **113**
  Street-by-Street map 106
Eisenhower Theater 118
Electricity 210
Eliot, T.S. 101
Ellicott, Andrew 19
Ellington, Duke 23, 140, 141
Embassy Row **136–7,** 147
Emergencies 213
Emmet, Robert 137
Emporium at Creekside Antiques
  199
Entertainment **200–7**
Estern, Neil 85
Etiquette 210
Evanti, Madame 23
Everett, Edward 163
Evermay (Georgetown) 148
Excursions **153–69**
  restaurants 191
  travel **222–3**

F

Fabergé, Peter Carl 163
Fall in Washington **38**
Farmers Market (Old Town
  Alexandria) **159**
Farragut Station post office 217
Farrand, Beatrix Jones 127
Fashion Center at Pentagon City
  199
Faxes **216**, 217
FBI Building **93**
  Street-by-Street map 88
Federal Courthouse 102
Federal government **28–9**
Federal holidays 39
Federal Reserve Building **116**
FedEx Field stadium 205
Fendall, Philip 159
Ferris, Keith 65
Festivals **36–9**
Fillmore, Millard 26
Film **202**, 203
Fin 190
Fire services 213
The Fireplace 203
First Division Monument
  105
First Lady **27**
Fishing **204**, 205
Fitzgerald, Ella 140
Fitzhugh, Mary Lee 158
Flagg, Ernest 113
Fletcher's Boat House 205
Flower Mart 36
Floyd, Pretty Boy 93
Foggy Bottom *see* The White House
  and Foggy Bottom
Folger, Henry Clay 48
Folger Shakespeare Library **48**
  Street-by-Street map 45
Food and drink
  shops **197**, 199
  What to Eat in Washington, DC
  184–5
  see also Restaurants
Ford, Gerald 27, 117
Ford, John T. 96
Ford's Theatre 10, **96**, 203, 207

Foreign exchange **214**, 215
Four Seasons Hotel 11
Fragonard, Jean-Honoré
  Diana and Endymion 60
Francis Scott Key Park 149
Frankfurter, Felix 84
Franklin, Benjamin
  Benjamin Franklin Statue 88,
  94
  Constitution of the United States
  91
  statue of 87
Franklin D. Roosevelt Memorial 33,
  84–5
Frederick **163**
Frederick Douglass House 10,
  145
Frederick Douglass National Historic
  Site 207
Fredericksburg **166**
  hotels 181
Free events 200–1
Freed, James Inigo 93
Freedmen's Bureau 22
Freedom Park 133
Freedom Plaza **94–5**
Freer, Charles Lang 73
Freer Gallery of Art **73**
  Street-by-Street map 56
French, Daniel Chester 85
Freud, Lucien 66
Friendship Firehouse 151
Friendship Station post office
  217
Frohman, Philip 142
Fuente, Larry
  Game Fish **99**, 113

G

Gadsby, John 158
Gadsby's Tavern Museum (Old Town
  Alexandria) 151, **158**
Gagarin, Yuri 65
Gala Hispanic Theater 203
Gallatin, Albert 49
Galleries *see* Museums and galleries
Game Fish (Fuente) **99**, 113
Gap, The 199
Gardener, Alexander 101
Gardens *see* Parks and gardens
Garfield, James A. 26, 66
Garland, Judy 74, 77, 101
Gasoline 222
Gay clubs 203
Gazelle Ltd. 199
George Washington (Teale) 16
George Washington University
  116–17
George Washington's Birthday
  Parade 39
Georgetown 11, **121–27**
  area map 121
  hotels 176–7
  90-minute Walk 148–9
  restaurants 189
Georgetown Billiards 203
Georgetown Flea Market 199
Georgetown Hoyas 205
Georgetown Park 149, 199
Georgetown Station post office
  217
Georgetown Theater Company
  123
Georgetown University **126,**
  149

Georgia Avenue Day 37
Gettysburg, PA
  hotels 180
  restaurants 191
Gettysburg Address **163**
Gettysburg National Military Park
  163
Giacometti, Alberto 66
Gilbert, Cass 45, 48
Ginevra de' Benci (Leonardo da
  Vinci) **58**, 60
Giotto
  Madonna and Child 60
Glen Echo Park 203
Glen Echo Park Carousel 207
Glenn, John 64, 133
Golf **204–5**
Goodhue, Bertram Grosvenor
  116
Government
  How the Federal Government
  Works **28–9**
Grace Church **123**
Grant, Ulysses S. 22, 26, 28
  Ulysses S. Grant Memorial 44,
  49
  White House 111
Gray Line 223
Great Falls Park **164**
  restaurants 191
Greater Washington
  map 15–15
El Greco 135
  Christ Cleansing the Temple 60
Greyhound Busline 219
Guided tours 211
Gunston Hall **162**

H

H & M 199
Halloween 38
Hamilton, Alexander 18–19
  statue of 106, 112
Hammond family 162
Hampton, James 100
Hardenbergh, Henry 95
Harding, Warren 27, 137
Harper, Robert 164
Harpers Ferry **164**
Harriman, Averill 124
Harriman, Pamela 124
Harrison, Benjamin 26
Harrison, William Henry 26, 92
Hart, Frederick 85, 142
Harwood family 162
Hassam, Childe 73, 100
  In the Garden 99
Hauge, Christian 137
Hawthorne, Nathaniel 95
Hay, John 22, 112
Hay-Adams Hotel **112**
  Street-by-Street map 107
Hayes, Helen 24
Hayes, Rutherford B. 26,
  111
Health care **213**
Healy, George Peter Alexander
  101, 108
  The Peacemakers 111
Hecht's Department Store 199
Hellmuth, Obata and Kassabaum
  62, 64
Henry, Joseph 72
Hertz 223
Heurich, Christian 133

Heurich Mansion **133**
Heye, George 68
Hiffernan, Joanna 59
Hillwood Museum **140**
Hilton 173
Hirshhorn, Joseph H. 66
Hirshhorn Museum **66**
  Street-by-Street map 57
Hispanic-Latino Festival 37
History **17–27**
Hoban, James 19, 108, 109
Hofman, Hans 100
Holiday, Billie 140
Holidays, federal 39
Holladay, Wilhelmina 96
Hollywood Cemetery (Richmond) 167
Holmes, Oliver Wendell 29
Holocaust Memorial Museum 32
Homer, Winslow 61, 100
Hoover, Herbert 27
  Camp Hoover 165
  Kalorama 137
Hoover, J. Edgar 93
Horseback riding 204–5
Hospitals 213
Hotels **172–81**
  Beyond Washington, DC 179–81
  Capitol Hill 174
  Farther Afield 177–9
  Georgetown 176–7
  The Mall 174
  Old Downtown 174–5
  taxes 210
  The White House and Foggy Bottom 175–6
Houdon, Jean Antoine 160, 167
House of Representatives 29
Howard, General Oliver Otis 22, 144
Howard Johnson 173
Howard University 22, **144**
Howe, Julia Ward 95
Hughes, Langston 23
Hull, Cordell 113
Hunter, Margaret 169
Hutchins, Stilson 94

I

Imagination Celebration 36
Impressionists 100, 135
In the Garden (Hassam) 99
Independence Day 37, 39
Inman, Henry 110
Instant Charge 201
Insurance 212–13
Inter-American Development Bank 25
International Children's Festival 38
International Monetary Fund 25
International Spy Museum **102**
Irving, Washington 124
Isabella, Queen of Spain 106
Iwo Jima Memorial 32, **132–3**

J

Jack's Boats 205
Jackson, Andrew 26
  statue of 107, 112
  The White House 111
James I, King of England 17
Jamestown 156, **167**
Jazz **202**, 203

Jazz (cont.)
  Memorial Day Jazz Festival 36
Jefferson, Thomas 18–19, 26, 167
  grave of 166
  Jefferson Memorial 33, **79**
  Library of Congress 45, 46
  Monticello (Charlottesville) 155, **166**
  Richmond State Capitol 167
  Thomas Jefferson's Birthday 36
  The White House 109, 110
Jews
  US Holocaust Memorial Museum 32, **80–81**
Joan of Arc 49
  statue of 45
John F. Kennedy Center for the Performing Arts *see* Kennedy Center
Johns, Jasper 100
Johnson, Andrew 26
  Treasury Building 112
  White House 111
Johnson, Claudia 110
Johnson, Linda 117
Johnson, Lyndon B. 25, 27
Johnson, Magic 102
Johnson, Philip 127
Jones, Chuck 53
JR's Bar and Grill 203

K

Kahlo, Frieda 96
Kalorama **137**
Kenilworth Park and Aquatic Gardens 205
Kenmore Plantation and Gardens (Fredericksburg) 166
Kennedy, Edward 29
Kennedy, Jackie 24, 27, 76
  Thomas Beall House 125
  White House 109, 110
Kennedy, John F. 27
  assassination 24
  grave of 131
  Kennedy Center 118, 119
  National Academy of Sciences 116
  Naval Heritage Center 92
  Pennsylvania Avenue 92
  portrait bust of 119
Kennedy Center 11, **118–19**, 199, 201, 203
  Holiday Festival 38
  Open House 38
Key, Francis Scott 74, 77, 124, 163
  Francis Scott Key Memorial Bridge 122, 149
  Francis Scott Key Memorial Park 149
King, Charles Bird 100
King, Dr. Martin Luther Jr. **97**, 101
  assassination 24, 141
  "I Have a Dream" speech 55, 85, 97
  "March on Washington" 24
  Martin Luther King Jr.'s Birthday 39
  Martin Luther King Memorial Library **97**
Kite Festival 36
Kline, Franz 100
Korean War Veterans Memorial 32, **84**

Kosciuszki, Thaddeus
  statue of 112
Kramerbooks and Afterwords Café 199

L

Labor Day 39
Labor Day Weekend Concert 38
Lafayette, Marquis de 107, 112
  statue of 112
Lafayette Square **112**
  Street-by-Street map 107
Laird, John 125
Laird-Dunlop House 124, 125
Langston Golf Course 205
Lannuier, Charles-Honoré 110
Latrobe, Benjamin 50, 112
Law enforcement 212
Layman, Christopher 124
LeCompte, Rowan 143
Lee, Harry "Light Horse" 159
Lee, General Robert E. 21
  Antietam National Battlefield 164
  Arlington House 130, 131
  Boyhood Home of Robert E. Lee (Old Town Alexandria) 151, **158**
  Christ Church (Old Town Alexandria) 159
  Museum of the Confederacy (Richmond) 167
  Robert E. Lee's Birthday 39
  Stabler-Leadbeater Apothecary Shop (Old Town Alexandria) 158
  statue of 167
Lee-Fendall House Museum (Old Town Alexandria) 151, **159**
Legal assistance 213
L'Enfant, Major Pierre Charles 19, **22**, 122
  Capitol Hill 43
  Freedom Plaza 94
  The Mall 55, 67
  National Building Museum 103
  Old Stone House 124
  Pennsylvania Avenue 88, 92
  tomb of 131
  Washington Circle 117
Leonardo da Vinci 61
  Ginevra de' Benci **58**, 60
Lewis, Meriwether 19, 74, 77
Lewis Mountain
  Skyline Drive 165
Leyland, Frederick 73
Libraries
  Folger Shakespeare Library 45, **48**
  Martin Luther King Memorial Library **97**
Library of Congress 45, **46–7**
  films 203
  free events 201
Lichtenstein, Roy 61
Lin, Maya Ying 25, 85
Lincoln, Abraham 26
  Abraham Lincoln's Birthday 39
  assassination 21, **96**
  Civil War 21, 22, 145
  Emancipation Proclamation 164
  Gettysburg Address **163**

Lincoln, Abraham (cont.)
Lincoln Memorial 10, 23, 32, **84–5**
The Mall 67
portrait of 101
statue of 144
The White House 108, 109, 111
Lincoln, Mary Todd 111
Lincoln, Robert 125
Lincoln Memorial 32, **84–5**
Lincoln Theatre 11, **140**
Lindbergh, Charles 63, 64, 66–7
Lindsay, Sir Ronald 137
Little, Henry 142
Lloyd House 151
Locke, Alain 23
Lost property **212**, 213
Louis XVI, King of France 71, 94
The Luncheon of the Boating Party
(Renoir) 135
Lundy, Victor A. 102
Luray, VA
hotels 181
Lutyens, Sir Edwin 137
Lyceum (Old Town Alexandria) 151

M

M Street **124–5**
McCall, Robert T. 65
McClellan, General George B. 21
McCullough, John 95
McKim, Charles F. 23
McKim, Mead and White
Dumbarton Oaks 127
White House 109, 110, 111
McKinley, William 27
McMillan, James 22
Madam's Organ 203
Madison, Dolley 19, 27, 114
Madison, James 26
Constitution of the United States
91
inaugural parade 92
Montpelier 166
Octagon 106, 114
War of 1812 19
Madonna and Child (Giotto) 60
Malcolm X 145
The Mall **55–85**
area map 55
Franklin D. Roosevelt Memorial
84–5
History of the Mall **67**
hotels 174
National Air and Space Museum
62–5
National Gallery of Art **58–61**
National Museum of American
History **74–7**
National Museum of Natural
History **70–71**
restaurants 186
Street-by-Street map 56–7
United States Holocaust Memorial
Museum **80–81**
Washington Monument **78**
Manet, Edouard 61
Maps
Capitol Hill 43, 44–5
Chesapeake and Ohio Canal
122–3
Colonial Williamsburg 168–9
Exploring beyond Washington, DC
156–7
Farther Afield 129
Georgetown 121

Maps (cont.)
Greater Washington 14–15
The Mall 55, 56–7
Monuments and Memorials in
Washington, DC 34–5
Museums and Galleries in
Washington, DC 32–3
National Zoological Park 138–9
Old Downtown 87, 88–9
Old Town Alexandria 159
Skyline Drive 165
United States 12–13
Washington, DC and environs
13
The White House and Foggy
Bottom 105, 106–7
Markets
Eastern Market **52**
Farmers Market (Old Town
Alexandria) 150, **159**
Marriott 173
Marshall, John 48, 49
Marshall, Thurgood 29
Martin Luther King Jr. Station post
office 217
Martin Luther King Jr.'s Birthday 39
Martin Luther King Memorial Library
97
Mary Cassatt (Degas) 99
Mary McLeod Bethune Celebration
37
Mary McLeod Bethune Council House
National Historic Site **140**
Maryland Rail Commuter Service
(MARC) 219
Maryland Science Center (Baltimore)
162–3
Maryland Terrapins 205
Mason, George 162
Matisse, Henri 66, 163
Mazza Gallerie Mall 199
MCI Center **102**, 205
Medical insurance 212
Medical Services 213
Medici, Lorenzo de' 57
Meeting Solutions 173
Meigs, Montgomery C. 66, 103
Mellon, Andrew 58, 60, 89
Mellon Fountain 89, **90**
Street-by-Street map 89
Melody Record Shop 199
Memin, Saint 115
Memorial Day 36, 39, 130
Memorial Day Jazz Festival 36
Memorial Day Weekend Concert
36
Memorials *see* Monuments
Merriwether Post Pavilion 203
Metrobus **221**
Metrorail **220**, 221
Meyhane 186
Michelangelo 103
Middleburg **164**
Mies van der Rohe, Ludwig 97
Millennium Stage 118
Miller, Don 97
Mills, Clark 107, 112, 117
Mills, Robert 20, 78, 112
Miró, Joan 61
Mrs. Adrian Iselin (Sargent) 61
Modernists 100
Mondrian, Piet
Composition No. III 135
Monet, Claude
Corcoran Gallery of Art 106, 113

Monet, Claude (cont.)
National Gallery of Art 61
Walters Art Gallery (Baltimore)
163
White House 110
Woman with a Parasol 59
Money **214–15**
Monroe, James 26
grave of 167
White House 108, 110, 111
Monroe, Marilyn 101
Monticello (Charlottesville) 155,
166
Montpelier 166
Montrose Park 148, 205
Monuments and memorials
Benjamin Franklin Statue 86, **94**
Columbus Memorial 53
First Division Monument 105
Francis Dupont Memorial Fountain
134
Franklin D. Roosevelt Memorial
33, **84–5**
Iwo Jima Memorial 32, **132–3**
Jefferson Memorial 33, **79**
Korean War Veterans Memorial
32, **83**
Lincoln Memorial 10, 32, **84–5**
Monuments and Memorials in
Washington, DC **34–5**
National Law Enforcement Officers
Memorial **103**
National WWII Memorial 10, **82**
Robert A. Taft Memorial 44, **49**
Ulysses S. Grant Memorial 44, **49**
US Navy Memorial **92**
Vietnam Veterans Memorial
32, **85**
Washington Monument 11, 33, 55,
78
Moore, Arthur Cotton 122
Moore, Henry 61, 66
Moran, Thomas 100
Cliffs of the Upper Colorado River
98, 100
Morisot, Berthe 96
Mosby, Colonel John S. 164
Mount Vernon 155, **160–61**
Mount Zion Cemetary 148
Mount Zion Church **126**, 148
Muir, Reverend 158
Mullet, Alfred B. 113
Museums and galleries (general)
children in **206**, 207
museum shops **196**, 199
Museums and galleries (individual)
American Visionary Art Museum
(Baltimore) 163
Anacostia Museum **145**
Arlington House 131
Art Museum of the Americas 115
Arthur M. Sackler Gallery
56, **72–3**
Arts and Industries Building **66–7**
Baltimore Museum of Art
(Baltimore) 163
Boyhood Home of Robert E. Lee
(Old Town Alexandria) **158**
Carlyle House (Old Town
Alexandria) **158**
Chesapeake Bay Maritime
Museum 167
Corcoran Gallery of Art 32, 106,
113
DAR Museum 114

Museums and galleries (cont.)
  Department of the Interior
    Museum 115
  Dumbarton Oaks 127
  FBI Building 93
  Frederick Douglass House **145**
  Freer Gallery of Art 56, **73**
  Gadsby's Tavern Museum (Old
    Town Alexandria) 151, **158**
  Gunston Hall **162**
  Heurich Mansion **133**
  Hirshhorn Museum 57, **66**
  International Spy Museum **102**
  Lee-Fendall House Museum
    (Old Town Alexandria) 150, **159**
    map 32–3
  Mary McLeod Bethune Council
    House National Historic Site
    10, **140**
  Maryland Science Center
    (Baltimore) 162–3
  Monticello 166
  Mount Vernon **160–61**
  Museum of the Confederacy
    (Richmond) 167
  National Air and Space Museum
    11, 33, 57, **62–5**, 207
  National Archives 10, 89, **90**
  National Building Museum **103**
  National Gallery of Art 11, 33, 57,
    58–61, 201, 203, 207
  National Geographic Society **134**
  National Museum of African Art
    56, **67**
  National Museum of American
    History 32, 56, **74–7**, 207
  National Museum of Natural
    History 33, 56, **70–71**, 206, 207
  National Museum of the American
    Indian **68–9**, 207
  National Museum of Women in the
    Arts **96**
  National Portrait Gallery 33,
    98–9, **101**
  National Postal Museum **53**, 207
  National Sports Gallery 102
  Naval Heritage Center 92
  Newseum **133**, 207
  Octagon 114
  Phillips Collection **135**
  Renwick Gallery 106, **113**
  Science Museum of Virginia 167
  Smithsonian American Art Museum
    33, **98–100**
  Smithsonian Castle 56, **72**
  Smithsonian Institution 20
  Stabler-Leadbeater Apothecary
    Shop (Old Town Alexandria)
    150, **158**
  Textile Museum **136**
  Torpedo Factory Art Center (Old
    Town Alexandria) 151, **159**
  US Holocaust Memorial Museum
    32, **80–81**
  US Naval Academy (Annapolis) 162
  Walters Art Gallery (Baltimore) 163
  Washington Doll House and Toy
    Museum 207
  Woodrow Wilson House **136**
Music
  dance **202**, 203
  Dance Africa 37
  John F. Kennedy Center for the
    Performing Arts Open House 38
  Labor Day Weekend Concert 38

Music (cont.)
  Memorial Day Jazz Festival 36
  Memorial Day Weekend Concert 36
  opera and classical music **202**, 203
  rock, jazz and blues **202**, 203
  shops **198**, 199
  Washington National Cathedral
    Summer Festival of Music 37
Myers, George Hewitt 136

N

N Street **124–5**, 148–9
Nahl, Christina 100
National Academy of Sciences **116**
National Air and Space Museum 11,
  33, **62–5**, 207
  floorplan 62–3
  Street-by-Street map 57
National Airport *see* Reagan National
  Airport
National Aquarium (Baltimore) **162**,
  163
National Aquarium (Washington) **95**
National Arboretum 129, **144**, 205
National Archives 10, **90**
National Building Museum **103**, 199
National Capitol Station post office
  217
National Cathedral *see* Washington
  National Cathedral
National Cherry Blossom Festival 36
National Christmas Tree Lighting 39
National Frisbee Festival 37
National Gallery of Art 33, **58–61**
  films 203
  floorplan 58–9
  free events 201
  Sculpture Garden 61, 207
  shop 199
  Street-by-Street map 57
  Visitors' Checklist 59
National Geographic Society **134**
National Geographic Store 207
National Japanese American
  Memorial **49**
National Law Enforcement Officers
  Memorial **103**
National Museum of African Art **67**
  shop 199
  Street-by-Street map 56
  Renwick Gallery 113
National Museum of American
  History 32, **74–7**, 199, 207
  floorplan 74–5
  Street-by-Street map 56
National Museum of Natural History
  33, **70–71**, 206, 207
  shops 207
  Street-by-Street map 56
National Museum of the American
  Indian **68–9**, 207
National Museum of Women
  in the Arts **96**
National Portrait Gallery 33, **98–9**, **101**
National Postal Museum **53**, 207
National Sports Gallery 102
National Symphony Orchestra 201, 203
National Theatre **95**, 203
National Women's Party 23, 45, 49
National WWII Memorial 10, **82**
National Zoological Park 11, **138–9**,
  201, 207
Naval Heritage Center 92
Nazis 81
Negro Alliance 23

Neiman-Marcus 199
Newspapers **217**
930 Night Club 203
Nissan Pavilion 203
Nixon, Richard 27
  resignation 24
  Watergate Scandal **117**
  White House 111
Noguchi, Isamu 61
Noland, Kenneth 100
Nordstrom 199
Norman, Jessye 135
North, Colonel Oliver 113
NOW Voyager 219

O

Oak Hill Cemetery **126–7**, 148
OAS Building
  Street-by-Street map 106
Octagon **114**, 115
  Street-by-Street map 106
Odiot, Jean-Baptist Claude 110
Ogle, Benjamin 115
O'Keeffe, Georgia 135
Old Bear, a Medicine Man (Caitlin)
  98
Old City Hall 102
Old Downtown 10, **86–103**
  area map 87
  hotels 174–5
  Old Downtown Renaissance
    102
  restaurants 187
  Street-by-Street map 88–9
Old Executive Office Building
  see Eisenhower Old Executive
  Office Building
Old Post Office 87, **94**
  Street-by-Street map 88
Old Post Office Pavilion 199
Old Presbyterian Meeting House
  (Old Town Alexandria) 150, **158**
Old Stone House **124**, 149
Old Town Alexandria **158–9**
  hotels 180
  map 159
  90-minute Walk 150–51
  restaurants 191
Old Town Trolley Tours 211
Olmstead, Frederick Law 138
Olsson's Books and Records 199
Open-air entertainment 201
Opening hours 210
  banks 214
  restaurants 183
  shops 196, 210
Opera **202**, 203
Opera House, Kennedy Center 119
Organization of the American States
  (OAS) 106, **115**
Ozio Martini and Cigar Lounge
  203

P

Paca, William 162
Page, Russell 144
Paris, VA
  hotels 181
Parking cars 222
Parks and gardens **205**
  Bartholdi Park and Fountain **52**
  Dumbarton Oaks 127, 205
  Kenilworth Aquatic Gardens 205
  Kenmore Plantation and Gardens
    (Fredericksburg) 166

Parks and Gardens (cont.)
  Monticello 166
  Montrose Park 205
  Mount Vernon **160–61**
  Rock Creek Park **141**
  US Botanic Garden 44, **52**
  US National Arboretum 129, **144**, 205
  The White House Fall Garden Tours 38
  The White House Spring Garden Tours 36
  William Paca House (Annapolis) 162
Passports 210
Patent Office building 100
Paul, Alice 23, 49
Payne, John Howard 127
The Peacemakers (Healy) 111
Peale, Rembrandt 110
  George Washington 16
Pei, I.M. 58
Pelz, Paul J. 46
Pennsylvania Avenue 30, **92–3**
  Street-by-Street map 88
Pentagon **132**
Pershing Park Ice Rink 207
Personal security **212–13**
Perugino, Pietro 60
Peter, Martha Custis 126
Peter Pan Trailways 219
Petersen House 96
Petersen, William 21
Petrol 222
Pharmacies 213
Philadelphia Brigade Monument (Gettysburg) 156
Phillips, Duncan and Marjorie 135
Phillips Collection **135**, 146
Phone cards 216, 217
Picasso, Pablo
  Baltimore Museum of Art (Baltimore) 163
  Corcoran Gallery of Art 106, 113
  Phillips Collection 135
Pickford, Mary 101
Piedmont Vineyards 164
Pierce, Franklin 26
Pierce Mill 141
Pinnacles Overlook
  Skyline Drive 165
Pocahontas 17, 101
Police **212**, 213
Politics & Prose Bookstore 199
Polk, James K. 26
Pollin, Abe 102
Pope, John Russell
  Jefferson Memorial 79
  National Gallery of Art 60
  Textile Museum 136
  US National Archives 90
Postal services **217**
  National Postal Museum **53**
Potomac Mills 199
Potomac River 21
  Great Falls Park **164**
  Mount Vernon 161
  Southwest Waterfront **132**
  Tidal Basin 79
Pottery Barn 199
Powell, Colin 117
Powhatan 17
Presidents **26–7**, 28
  Presidential Inaugural Parades **92**

President's Day 39
Prospect Street 149
ProTix 201
Public conveniences 213

R
Radio **217**
Railways *see* Trains
Rainfall 38
Ramsay House 150
Raphael
  The Alba Madonna **58**, 60
Rauschenberg, Robert
  Reservoir 100
Reagan, Nancy 27, 76
Reagan, Ronald 27, 92
  portrait of 101
  Ronald Reagan Building 88, **93**
Reagan National Airport **218**, 219
Relish 199
Rembrandt
  Corcoran Gallery of Art 106, 113
  National Gallery of Art 60–61
Remington, Frederick 100
Renoir, Auguste 61, 113
  The Luncheon of the Boating Party 135
Renting
  bicycles 223
  cars **222**, 223
Renwick, James 72
  Oak Hill Cemetery 126–7
  Renwick Gallery 113
  St. Mary's Episcopal Church 117
Renwick Gallery **113**, 199
  Street-by-Street map 106
Reservoir (Rauschenberg) 100
Restaurants **182–95**
  Capitol Hill 186
  choosing 186–91
  Excursions 191
  Farther Afield 190–91
  Georgetown 189
  The Mall 186
  Old Downtown 187
  tipping in 210
  What to Eat in Washington, DC **184–5**
  White House and Foggy Bottom 188–9
  see also Food and drink
Restoration Hardware 199
Restrooms, public 213
RFK Stadium 204, 205
Richardson, Henry Hobson 112
Richmond **167**
  hotels 181
  restaurants 191
Riding 204–5
Riggs National Bank 123
Ripley, S. Dillon 66
Robbins, Warren 67
Robert A. Taft Memorial **49**
  Street-by-Street map 44
Robert E. Lee's Birthday 39
Rochambeau, Comte de
  statue of 112
Rock Creek Golf Course 205
Rock Creek Park **141**
Rock Creek Park Horse Center 205
Rock Creek Park Nature Center 141
Rock Creek Tennis Center 205
Rock music **202**, 203

Rockefeller, John D. 127, 168
Rodin, Auguste 66, 163
Rogers, Cal 64
Rogers, Randolph 51
Rogers, Will 101
Rolfe, John 17
Ronald Reagan (Casselli) 101
Ronald Reagan Building **93**
  Street-by-Street map 88
Roosevelt, Alice 23
Roosevelt, Eleanor 23, 27, 55, 140
  statue of 84
  White House 109, 110
Roosevelt, Franklin D. 27, 92
  Franklin D. Roosevelt Memorial 33, **84–5**
  Kalorama 137
  and Mary McLeod Bethune 140
  "New Deal" 23
  Pentagon 132
  United Nations 127
  Washington Monument 78
  White House 108
Roosevelt, Theodore 27, 112
  Roosevelt Island 133
  statue of 133
  teddy bears 76
  White House 19, 108, 109, 110, 111
Roosevelt Island **133**
Rosenthal, Joe 132
Ross, Diana 101
Rothko, Mark 135
Rubens, Peter Paul 60, 61, 163
Rumba Café 203
Rundell, Philip 110
Ruth, Babe 101, 102
Ryder, Albert Pinkham 100

S
Sackler, Dr. Arthur M.
  Arthur M. Sackler Gallery 56, 72–3
Safety **212**
  driving 223
St. John's 112
St. John's Episcopal Church 149
St. Mary's Episcopal Church **117**
St. Patrick's Day 36
Sales 196
Sales tax 196, 210
Sargent, John Singer
  Corcoran Gallery of Art 113
  Freer Gallery of Art 73
  Hirshhorn Museum 66
  Mrs. Adrian Iselin 61
  National Museum of American Art 100
Scandal Tour 211
Science Museum of Virginia 167
Seaton, George 150
Second Story Books 197, 199
Security **212–13**
Segal, George 85
Senate 28, 29
Senior citizens 211
Servais, Adrien François 77
Seurat, Georges 61
Sewall, Robert 49
Sewall-Belmont House **49**
  Street-by-Street map 45
Shahan, Bishop Thomas 144
Shakespeare, William
  Folger Shakespeare Library 45, **48**
  Shakespeare's Birthday

Shakespeare, William (cont.)
  Celebration 36
  Shakespeare Free for All 37
  Shakespeare Theatre 201, 203
Shaw, Bernard 133
Shaw, Colonel Robert Gould 141
Shaw Neighborhood 10, **141**
Shenandoah National Park 156
  Skyline Drive **165**
Shenandoah River 164
Shepard, Alan 65, 162
Shepherd, Alexander "Boss" 22
Sherbell, Rhoda
  "Casey" Stengel 99
Shops **196–9**
  antiques **198**, 199
  books and music **198**, 199
  for children 207
  clothes **197**, 199
  food and wine **197**, 199
  galleries, arts and crafts **197**, 199
  how to pay 196
  malls and department stores
    197, 199
  museum shops **196**, 199
  opening hours 196, 210
  sales 196
  souvenirs **197**, 199
  taxes 196, 210
Shoumatoff, Elizabeth 110
Shrady, Henry Merwin 49
Siklcr, Aaron 110
Skyline Drive 155, **165**
  restaurants 191
Slavery **20–21**
  Frederick Douglass **145**
Smith, Captain John 17
Smithmeyer, John L. 46
Smith Row 149
Smithson, James 20, **72**
Smithsonian American Art Museum
  33, **98–100**
  Renwick Gallery **113**
Smithsonian Castle **72**
  Street-by-Street map 56
Smithsonian Folklife Festival 37,
  201
Smithsonian Institution 72
  National Zoological Park 138
  Smithsonian Dial-a-Museum 221
  Smithsonian Information 211
Smithsonian Kite Festival 36
Smoking 183, 210
Snow, Beverly 20
Snow Riot (1835) 20
Society for Accessible Travel and
  Hospitality 211
Source Theatre Company 203
Southwest Waterfront **132**
Souvenir shops **197**, 199
Speaking Clock 221
Spectator sports **204**, 205
Speed limits 222
Spencer family 126
Sports **204–5**
  National Sports Gallery 102
Spotswood, Alexander 168
Spring in Washington **36**
Stabler-Leadbeater Apothecary
  Shop (Old Town Alexandria) 150,
  158
Stanley, John Mix 100
State Department **116**
Stengel, Casey 99, 101
Steuben, Baron von statue of 112

Stone, Edward Durrell 118, 134
Storr, Paul 110
Stowe, Harriet Beecher 145
Stradivari, Antonio 77
Stuart, Gilbert 19, 101, 110
Stuart, General Jeb 164
Students 211
Studio Theater 203
Summer in Washington **37**
Sunshine 37
Sun Trust Bank 214, 215
SuperShuttle 219
Supreme Court *see* US Supreme
  Court
Supremes, The 101
Swedenburg Winery 164

T
Taft, Lorado 53
Taft, Robert A.
  Robert A. Taft Memorial 44, **49**
Taft, William Howard 27, 49
  Kalorama 137
  US Supreme Court 48
Taste of DC 38
Taxes
  in hotels 172, 210
  sales tax 196, 210
Taxis 218, **221**
Tayloe, Ann 115
Tayloe, Colonel John III 114, **115**
Tayloc family **115**
Taylor, Zachary 26
Telephones **216**, 217
Television 201
Temperatures 39
Temple Heights Station post office
  217
Tennis **204–05**
Teno, Aurelio
  Don Quixote Statue 118
Textile Museum **136**
Thanksgiving 39
Thaxter, Celia 99
Theater **202**, 203
  for children **206**, 207
  discount tickets 200
  Ford's Theatre **96**
  Lincoln Theatre **140**
  National Theatre **95**
Theft 212
Thomas, Helen 133
Thomas Beall House 125
Thomas Cook/Travelex Currency
  Services 215
Thomas Jefferson's Birthday 36
Thompson Boat Center 205
Thornton, William 20
Thornton, Dr. William
  M Street 124
  Octagon 114, 115
  Tudor Place 126
Ticketmaster 201
Ticketplace 201
Tickets
  for entertainments **200**, 201
Tidal Basin **79**
Tiffany, Louis Comfort 126
Tilghman Island, MD
  hotels 180
Time **217**
Tintoretto, Jacopo 60
Tipping 182, 210
Titian 60, 113
Toomer, Jean 23

Topaz 179
Torpedo Factory Art Center (Old
  Town Alexandria) 151, **159**, 199
Toulouse-Lautrec, Henri de 61
Tourist information **210**
Tourmobile Sightseeing 223
Tours 211
  bus 223
Tours by car
  Skyline Drive **165**
Tower Records 199
Trains 218, **219**, **223**
  Union Station **53**
Travel **218–23**
  air **218–19**
  buses 218, **219**
  Capitol Hill 43
  cars **219**
  Excursions Beyond Washington, DC
    157, **222–3**
  Georgetown 121
  insurance 212–13
  The Mall 55
  Metrobus **221**
  Metrorail **220**, 221
  Old Downtown 87
  taxis 218, **221**
  trains 218, **219**, **223**
  The White House and Foggy
    Bottom 105
Traveler's checks 196, **214**
Treasury Building **112**
  Street-by-Street map 107
Trevilians, VA
  hotels 181
Troop, Captain Robert 17
Truman, Harry S. 27
  White House 109, 111
Truman, Margaret 117
Trumball, John 110
Tudor Place **126**, 148
Twachtman, John Henry 100
Twilight Tattoo Military Pageant
  36
Tyler, John 26
  grave of 167

U
Udvar-Hazy Center, Steven F.
  165
Ulysses S. Grant Memorial **49**
  Street-by-Street map 44
Union Station **53**
Union Station Shops 199
Union Tavern 124
United Nations **127**
United States Marine Band 201
United States Tax Court 102
Universities
  George Washington University
    116–17
  Georgetown University **126**
  University of Virginia 166
Urban Outfitters 199
US Botanic Garden **52**
  Street-by-Street map 44
US Capitol 29, 30, **50–51**, 55
  Street-by-Street map 44
US Congress 29
  Library of Congress 46
US Holocaust Memorial Museum 32,
  80–81
  Street-by-Street map 89
US Naval Academy (Annapolis)
  162

US Navy Memorial **92**
Street-by-Street map 89
US Supreme Court 29, 43, **48–9**
Street-by-Street map 45

V

Van Buren, Angelica Singleton 110
Van Buren, Martin 26, 110
Van Dyck, Sir Anthony 60, 61
Van Gogh, Vincent
Baltimore Museum of Art (Baltimore) 163
National Gallery of Art 61
Phillips Collection 135
Vaughan, Henry 142
Vedder, Elihu 47
Venturi, Robert 94
Veteran's Day 38, 39
Vever, Henri 73
Victoria, Queen of England 111
Vietnam Veterans Memorial 10, 32, **83**
Visas 210

W

Wake-Up Little Suzie 199
Walking 220
Wallace, Henry A. 28
Walter, Thomas U. 50
Walters Art Museum (Baltimore) 163
War of 1812 19
War of Independence 18
Wardman, Harry 112
Warhol, Andy 100, 163
Warner Theater 95, 203
Warren, Earl 29
Washington, Augustine 160
Washington, George 16, 26
becomes president 18
builds Washington 19
Christ Church (Old Town Alexandria) 151, 159
Farmers Market (Old Town Alexandria) 150, 159
Gadsby's Tavern Museum (Old Town Alexandria) 151, 158
George Washington University **116–17**
George Washington's Birthday Parade 39
Harpers Ferry 164
The Mall 67
Mount Vernon 155, **160–61**
Old Presbyterian Meeting House (Old Town Alexandria) 150, 158
Old Stone House 124
portraits of 101
Stabler-Leadbeater Apothecary Shop (Old Town Alexandria) 150, 158
statues of 32, 117, 144, 167
and Tayloe family 115

Washington, George (cont.)
tomb of 161
Union Tavern 124
US Capitol 50
The White House 108, 109, 110
Wisconsin Avenue 123
Washington, Martha
Gadsby's Tavern Museum (Old Town Alexandria) 158
Mount Vernon 160
portrait of 101
Tudor Place 126
Washington, Walter E. 25
Washington, VA
hotels 181
Washington Abolition Society 20
Washington Area Bicyclist Association 205
Washington Circle **117**
Washington, DC Accommodations 173
Washington, DC Convention and Visitors Association 211
Washington Flyer Coach Service 219
Washington Harbor 11, **122**, 149
Washington Home and Garden Show 36
Washington Monument 11, 20, 33, 55, **78**
Washington National Cathedral **142–3**, 199, 207
Christmas Services 39
Flowermart 201
Summer Festival of Music 37
Washington Performing Arts Society 203
Washington Post 201
Washington Post Office
Georgetown Branch **125**
Waterfalls
Great Falls Park **164**
Waterfront *see* Southwest Waterfront
Watergate Complex **117**
Watergate Scandal **117**
Watterston, George 20
Wayne, John 101
Weather 36–9
Weather Update 221
Webster, Daniel 29
Weldon, Felix de 118
Western Union 217
Wheatley Row 124
Wheelchair access *see* Disabled travelers
Whistler, James McNeill 73
The White Girl **59**, 61
White, Edward H. 65
The White Girl (Whistler) **59**, 61
White House, The 10, 28, **108–11**
Candlelight Tours 39
Fall Garden Tours 38
floorplan 108–9
history 19
Visitor Center **111**
The White House Egg Roll 36,

White House and Foggy Bottom, The **105–119**
area map 105
hotels 175–6
Kennedy Center **118–19**
restaurants 188–9
Street-by-Street map 106–7
Whiteoak Canyon
Skyline Drive 165
Whitman, Walt 21, 94
Wildlife
Chincoteague and Assateague 167
Roosevelt Island **133**
see also Zoo
Willard, Henry 95
Willard Hotel **95**
Williams, Anthony 25
Williamsburg, VA
hotels 181
restaurants 191
see also Colonial Williamsburg
Wilson, Edith Galt 136
Wilson, Woodrow 23, 27
Freedom Plaza 94
Kalorama 137
tomb of 144
Woodrow Wilson House **136**
Wilson, Mrs. Woodrow 110
Wine shops **197**, 199
Winter in Washington **39**
Wisconsin Avenue **122–3**
Wolf Trap Farm Park for the Performing Arts 201, 207
Woman with a Parasol (Monet) 59
Wood, Waddy Butler 115, 136
Woodrow Wilson House **136**
Woolly Mammoth Theater 203
World Bank 24
World War I 23, 65
World War II 24
Iwo Jima Memorial 32, **132–3**
Memorial **82**
National Air and Space Museum 65
US Holocaust Memorial Museum 32, **80–81**
Wright Brothers 33
National Air and Space Museum 63, 64

Y

Yorktown **167**
Young, Ammi B. 125
A Young Man with His Tutor (de Largilliere) **58**
Youth hostels 173

Z

Zenith Gallery 199
Zoo
National Zoological Park 11, **138–9**, 201, 207